Japanese
Vocabulary

by

NOBUO AKIYAMA
Professorial Lecturer, Japanese Language
The Paul H. Nitze
School of Advanced International Studies
The Johns Hopkins University

and

CAROL AKIYAMA
Language Training Consultant
Washington, D.C.

BARRON'S

All inquiries should be addressed to:
Barron's Educational Series, Inc.
250 Wireless Boulevard
Hauppauge, New York 11788

Library of Congress Catalog Card No. 90-27642

International Standard Book No. 0-8120-4743-5

Library of Congress Cataloging-in-Publication Data

Akiyama, Nobuo.
   Japanese vocabulary / by Nobuo Akiyama and Carol Akiyama.
      p. cm.
   Includes index.
   ISBN 0-8120-4743-5
   1. Japanese language — Conversation and phrase books — English.
2. Japanese language — Glossaries, vocabularies, etc. I. Akiyama, Carol.
II. Title.
PL539.A654 1991
495.6'83421 — dc20   90-27642
                                                        CIP

PRINTED IN THE UNITED STATES OF AMERICA
1234 5500 987654321

CONTENTS

HOW TO USE THIS BOOK

THIS IS NOT JUST ANOTHER DICTIONARY!

Though called *Japanese Vocabulary*, this book offers you much more than its title implies. A dictionary lists words in alphabetical order. This book, on the other hand, organizes words by category — from basic numbers to the advanced high-tech language of the nineties.

OVERALL DESIGN

The book begins with an easy pronunciation guide. The main body consists of nine chapters, followed by an English-Japanese Wordfinder.

Each chapter is divided into parts that deal with a particular aspect or function of human experience. For example, the chapters on daily life (Sections 23 through 29) deal with seven themes: At Home, Eating and Drinking, Shopping and Errands, Banking and Commerce, Games and Sports, The Arts, Holidays and Going Out. This organization enables you to locate related terms about a particular topic without having to look up each alphabetically.

USING THIS BOOK FOR DIFFERENT LEARNING GOALS

Beginners or advanced students of Japanese alike can use this book successfully. If you are a beginner, you will find the text user friendly, an easy system for acquiring basic vocabulary. If you already know some Japanese, you will appreciate the convenient arrangement of the words into categories. It gives you instant access to the expressions you need for discussing or reporting on specific topics.

FEATURES

Within each category, the English word is on the left side of the page, the Japanese equivalent is in the middle column, and the pronunciation is in the column on the right. The English items are arranged in alphabetical order, unless the nature of the theme requires some other logical system of organization. Related items, concepts, or specific uses are indented under the main item.

Special *FOCUS* sections deal with specific parts of a category by providing more information about it. Idiomatic expressions and other useful material are boxed for easy reference.

The English-Japanese Wordfinder at the back of the book lists the reference section for each word, and also provides the Japanese characters for each entry.

Nobuo Akiyama
Carol Akiyama

ABBREVIATIONS

n	noun. Since nouns are the largest number of items, most nouns are *not* identified. This abbreviation is used only in certain cases for clarity.
v	verb
vi	intransitive verb
vt	transitive verb
adj	adjective, adjectival phrase
adv	adverb, adverbial phrase
conj	conjunction
inf	informal usage
~	denotes that something additional must be supplied, and where. For example:

    almost never hotondo ~nai   **every, each** dono ~ mo

                  hotondo <u>ikanai</u>   dono <u>hon</u> mo

                  go   book

           (almost never go)   (each book, every book)

PRONUNCIATION GUIDE

Japanese is not difficult to pronounce if you follow a few simple guidelines. Take the time to read this section, and try out each sound presented.

Let's start with the vowels. If you have studied Spanish, it may help you to know that Japanese vowels are more like those of Spanish than those of English.

VOWELS

The following vowels are short and pure, with <u>no glide</u> — that is, they are not diphthongs.

Japanese Vowel	English Equivalent	Example
a	as in f**a**ther	**akai** (*ah-kah-ee*) red
e	as in m**e**n	**ebi** (*eh-bee*) shrimp
i	as in s**ee**	**imi** (*ee-mee*) meaning
o	as in b**oa**t	**otoko** (*oh-toh-koh*) male
u	as in f**oo**d	**uma** (*oo-mah*) horse

The following vowels are like the ones above, but lengthened.

Japanese Vowel	English Equivalent	Example
ā	as in father, but lenghthened	batā (*bah-tāh*) butter
ei	as in men, but lenghthened	eigo (*ēh-goh*) English
ii	as in see, but lenghthened	iiharu (*ēe-hah-roo*) insist
ō	as in boat, but lenghthened	ōsama (*oh-sah-mah*) king
ū	as in food, but lenghthened	yūbin (*yōo-been*) mail

And keep in mind these points:

1. Long vowels are important. Pronouncing a long vowel incorrectly can result in a different word or even an unintelligible one.

   For example, obasan (*oh-bah-sahn*) means aunt

      obāsan   (*oh-bāh-sahn*) means grandmother

      ojisan   (*oh-jee-sahn*) means uncle
      ojiisan   (*oh-jēe-sahn*) means grandfather

      seki   (*seh-kee*) means seat
      seiki   (*sēh-kee*) means century

2. Sometimes the i and the u are not pronounced. This usually occurs between voiceless consonants (p, t, k, ch, f, h, s, sh), or at the end of a word following a voiceless consonant. Here's an example you may already know:

                   sukiyaki (*skee-yah-kee*)

   This word for a popular Japanese dish begins with **skee**, not **soo**. The u is not pronounced.

   One more example:

                   tabemashita (*tah-beh-mahsh-tah*) I ate

   The i is not pronounced.

CONSONANTS

With a few exceptions, Japanese consonants are similar to those of English. Note those that are different:

f The English **f** is pronounced with a passage of air between the upper teeth and the lower lip. To make the Japanese **f**, blow air lightly between your lips as if you were just beginning a whistle.

g Always pronounced as in **go**, never as in **age**. You may also hear it pronounced as the **ng** sound in **sing**, but not at the beginning of a word.

r This is different from the English **r**. To make the Japanese **r**, lightly touch the tip of your tongue to the bony ridge behind the upper teeth, almost in the English **d** position. It's more like the Spanish **r**, but it's not trilled.

s Always hissed, as in **so**, never voiced, as in **his** or **pleasure**.

And note the following points as well:

1. If you have trouble making these consonants the Japanese way, your English pronunciation will still be intelligible.

2. Some Japanese consonants are doubled. In English, this is just a feature of spelling and often does not affect pronunciation. In Japanese, the doubling is important and may change the meaning of a word. For example:

kite kudasai (*kee-teh koo-dah-sah-ee*) means
"Please put it (clothing) on."

kitte kudasai (*keet-teh koo-dah-sah-ee*) means
"Please cut it."

In a word with a doubled consonant, do not say the consonant twice — simply hold the sound longer.

CONVENTIONS

Macrons

A macron, or bar, above a vowel means it should be lengthened. For example:

butter   batā   *bah-tah*

In the above word, the macron above the second vowel means you should hold the sound twice as long as you normally would.

Capital Letters

Capital letters in the pronunciation indicate pitch. This is not stress, or loudness. Rather, it is a slight rise in the tone. For example:

Where do you live?   Doko ni osumai desu ka.   *DOH-koh nee oh soo-mah-ee*
                                                dehs kah.

The first syllable of the Japanese, *DOH*, should be voiced at a higher tone than the rest. It does not mean that the syllable is stressed, but that the pitch of the voice is slightly higher.

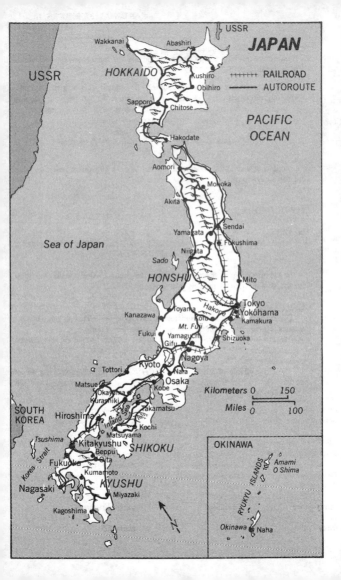

BASIC INFORMATION

---

1. ARITHMETIC

a. CARDINAL NUMBERS

zero	zero/rei	*zeh-roh/reh*
one	ichi	*ee-chee*
two	ni	*nee*
three	san	*sahn*
four	shi/yon	*shee/yohn*
five	go	*goh*
six	roku	*roh-koo*
seven	shichi/nana	*shee-chee/nah-nah*
eight	hachi	*hah-chee*
nine	ku/kyū	*koo/kyoo*
ten	jū	*joo*
eleven	jūichi	*joo-ee-chee*
twelve	jūni	*joo-nee*
thirteen	jūsan	*joo-sahn*
fourteen	jūshi/jūyon	*joo-shee/joo-yohn*
fifteen	jūgo	*joo-goh*
sixteen	jūroku	*joo-roh-koo*
seventeen	jūshichi	*joo-shee-chee*
	jūnana	*joo-nah-nah*
eighteen	jūhachi	*joo-hah-chee*
nineteen	jūku/jūkyū	*joo-koo/joo-kyoo*
twenty	nijū	*nee-joo*
twenty-one	nijūichi	*nee-joo-ee-chee*
twenty-two	nijūni	*nee-joo-nee*
twenty-three	nijūsan	*nee-joo-sahn*
twenty-four	nijūshi/nijūyon	*nee-joo-shee/nee-joo-yohn*
twenty-five	nijūgo	*nee-joo-goh*
twenty-six	nijūroku	*nee-joo-roh-koo*
twenty-seven	nijūshichi	*nee-joo-shee-chee*
	nijūnana	*nee-joo nah-nah*
twenty-eight	nijūhachi	*nee-joo-hah-chee*
twenty-nine	nijūku	*nee-joo-koo*
	nijūkyū	*nee-joo-kyoo*
thirty	sanjū	*sahn-joo*
thirty-one	sanjūichi	*sahn-joo-ee-chee*
thirty-two	sanjūni	*sahn-joo-nee*
thirty-three	sanjūsan	*sahn-joo-sahn*
...		
forty	yonjū	*yohn-joo*

forty-one	yonjūichi	*yohn-jōō-ee-chee*
forty-two	yonjūni	*yohn-jōō-nee*
forty-three	yonjūsan	*yohn-jōō-sahn*
...		
fifty	gojū	*goh-jōō*
fifty-one	gojūichi	*goh-jōō-ee-chee*
...		
sixty	rokujū	*roh-koo-jōō*
...		
seventy	nanajū	*nah-nah-jōō*
...		
eighty	hachijū	*hah-chee-jōō*
...		
ninety	kyūjū	*kyōō-jōō*
...		
one hundred	hyaku	*hyah-koo*
one hundred and one	hyakuichi	*hyah-koo-ee-chee*
one hundred and two	hyakuni	*hyah-koo-nee*
one hundred ten	hyakujū	*hyah-koo-jōō*
one hundred twenty	hyakunijū	*hyah-koo-nee-jōō*
...		
two hundred	nihyaku	*nee-hyah-koo*
two hundred and one	nihyakuichi	*nee-hyah-koo-ee-chee*
two hundred ten	nihyakujū	*nee-hyah-koo-jōō*
...		
three hundred	sanbyaku	*sahn-byah-koo*
...		
four hundred	yonhyaku	*yohn-hyah-koo*
...		
five hundred	gohyaku	*goh-hyah-koo*
...		
six hundred	roppyaku	*rohp-pyah-koo*
...		
seven hundred	nanahyaku	*nah-nah-hyah-koo*
...		
eight hundred	happyaku	*hahp-pyah-koo*
...		
nine hundred	kyūhyaku	*kyōō-hyah-koo*
...		
one thousand	sen	*sehn*
one thousand and one	sen-ichi	*sehn-ee-chee*
one thousand ten	senjū	*sehn-jōō*
one thousand three hundred	sensanbyaku	*sehn-sahn-byah-koo*
two thousand	nisen	*nee-sehn*

two thousand and one	nisen-ichi	*nee-sehn-ee-chee*
two thousand four hundred	nisen-yonhyaku	*nee-sehn-yohn-hyah-koo*
three thousand	sanzen	*sahn-zehn*
...		
four thousand	yonsen	*yohn-sehn*
...		
five thousand	gosen	*goh-sehn*
...		
six thousand	rokusen	*roh-koo-sehn*
...		
seven thousand	nanasen	*nah-nah-sehn*
...		
eight thousand	hassen	*hahs-sehn*
...		
nine thousand	kyūsen	*kyōo-sehn*
...		
ten thousand	ichiman	*ee-chee-mahn*
ten thousand and one	ichiman-ichi	*ee-chee-mahn-ee-chee*
ten thousand ten	ichimanjū	*ee-chee-mahn-jōo*
ten thousand two hundred	ichiman-nihyaku	*ee-chee-mahn-nee-hyah-koo*
eleven thousand	ichimansen	*ee-chee-mahn-sehn*
...		
twelve thousand	ichimannisen	*ee-chee-mahn-nee-sehn*
thirteen thousand	ichimansanzen	*ee-chee-mahn-sahn-zehn*
fourteen thousand	ichiman-yonsen	*ee-chee-mahn-yohn-sehn*
fifteen thousand	ichimangosen	*ee-chee-mahn-goh-sehn*
sixteen thousand	ichimanrokusen	*ee-chee-mahn-roh-koo-sehn*
seventeen thousand	ichimannanasen	*ee-chee-mahn-nah-nah-sehn*
eighteen thousand	ichimanhassen	*ee-chee-mahn-hahs-sehn*
nineteen thousand	ichimankyūsen	*ee-chee-mahn-kyōo-sehn*
twenty thousand	niman	*nee-mahn*
thirty thousand	sanman	*sahn-mahn*
forty thousand	yonman	*yohn-mahn*
fifty thousand	goman	*goh-mahn*
sixty thousand	rokuman	*roh-koo-mahn*
seventy thousand	nanaman	*nah-nah-mahn*
eighty thousand	hachiman	*hah-chee-mahn*
ninety thousand	kyūman	*kyōo-mahn*
one hundred thousand	jūman	*jōo-mahn*
two hundred thousand	nijūman	*nee-jōo-mahn*
one million	hyakuman	*hyah-koo-mahn*
one million and one	hyakuman-ichi	*hyah-koo-mahn-ee-chee*

one million and two	hyakuman-ni	*hyah-koo-mahn-nee*
...		
two million	nihyakuman	*nee-hyah-koo-mahn*
...		
three million	sanbyakuman	*sahn-byah-koo-mahn*
ten million	senman	*sehn-mahn*
...		
one hundred million	ichioku	*ee-chee-oh-koo*
...		
one billion	jūoku	*jōō-oh-koo*
...		
two billion	nijūoku	*nee-jōō-oh-koo*
...		
ten billion	hyakuoku	*hyah-koo-oh-koo*
one hundred billion	sen-oku	*sehn-oh-koo*
...		
one trillion	itchō	*eet-chōh*
...		
two trillion	nichō	*nee-chōh*

Another system for cardinal numbers from one through ten is listed below. From eleven on, they are the same as the previous set of cardinal numbers.

---

one	hitotsu	*hee-TOH-tsoo*
two	futatsu	*foo-TAH-tsoo*
three	mittsu	*meet-TSOO*
four	yottsu	*yoht-TSOO*
five	itsutsu	*ee-TSOO-tsoo*
six	muttsu	*moot-TSOO*
seven	nanatsu	*nah-NAH-tsoo*
eight	yattsu	*yaht-TSOO*
nine	kokonotsu	*koh-KOH-noh-tsoo*
ten	tō	*tōh*

FOCUS: *Counting Different Kinds of Things*

---

people		
one (person)	hitori	*hee-toh-ree*
two (persons)	futari	*foo-tah-ree*
three (persons)	sannin	*sahn-neen*

long, thin objects (pencils, bottles, trees, etc.)

one	ippon	*eep-pohn*
two	nihon	*nee-hohn*
three	sanbon	*sahn-bohn*

bound objects (books, notebooks, magazines, etc.)

one	issatsu	*ees-sah-tsoo*
two	nisatsu	*nee-sah-tsoo*
three	sansatsu	*sahn-sah-tsoo*

thin, flat objects (paper, bills, cloth, tickets, dishes, etc.)

one	ichimai	*ee-chee-mah-ee*
two	nimai	*nee-mah-ee*
three	sanmai	*sahn-mah-ee*

liquid or dry measures (glasses or cups of water, coffee, tea, etc.)

one	ippai	*eep-pah-ee*
two	nihai	*nee-hah-ee*
three	sanbai	*sahn-bah-ee*

small objects not in the categories above

one	ikko/hitotsu	*eek-koh/hee-toh-tsoo*
two	niko/futatsu	*nee-koh/foo-tah-tsoo*
three	sanko/mittsu	*sahn-koh/meet-tsoo*

floors of buildings

one	ikkai	*eek-kah-ee*
two	nikai	*nee-kah-ee*
three	sangai	*sahn-gah-ee*

b. ORDINAL NUMBERS

One way of forming the ordinal numbers is by adding **-banme** to the end of the corresponding cardinal number.

first	ichibanme	*ee-chee-bahn-meh*
second	nibanme	*nee-bahn-meh*
third	sanbanme	*sahn-bahn-meh*
fourth	yobanme	*yoh-bahn-meh*
fifth	gobanme	*goh-bahn-meh*
sixth	rokubanme	*roh-koo-bahn-meh*

seventh	nanabanme	*nah-nah-bahn-meh*
eighth	hachibanme	*hah-chee-bahn-meh*
ninth	kyūbanme	*kyōō-bahn-meh*
tenth	jūbanme	*jōō-bahn-meh*
eleventh	jūichibanme	*jōō-ee-chee-bahn-meh*
twelfth	jūnibanme	*jōō-nee-bahn-meh*
thirteenth	jūsanbanme	*jōō-sahn-bahn-meh*
twenty-third	nijūsanbanme	*nee-jōō-sahn-bahn-meh*
hundredth	hyakubanme	*hyah-koo-bahn-meh*
thousandth	senbanme	*sehn-bahn-meh*
ten thousandth	ichimanbanme	*ee-chee-mahn-bahn-meh*
millionth	hyakumanbanme	*hyah-koo-mahn-bahn-meh*
billionth	jūokubanme	*jōō-oh-koo-bahn-meh*

Another way of forming the ordinal numbers is by attaching **dai-** to the front of the corresponding cardinal number.

---

first	daiichi	*dah-ee-ee-chee*
second	daini	*dah-ee-nee*
third	daisan	*dah-ee-sahn*
fourth	daiyon	*dah-ee-yohn*
fifth	daigo	*dah-ee-goh*
sixth	dairoku	*dah-ee-roh-koo*
seventh	dainana	*dah-ee-nah-nah*
eighth	daihachi	*dah-ee-hah-chee*
ninth	daiku	*dah-ee-koo*
tenth	daijū	*dah-ee-jōō*
eleventh	daijūichi	*dah-ee-jōō-ee-chee*
twelfth	daijūni	*dah-ee-jōō-nee*

For another system of cardinal numbers, the ordinal numbers through ninth are formed by adding **-me** to the end of the corresponding number. Tenth works with **-banme** or **dai-**.

---

first	hitotsume	*hee-toh-tsoo-meh*
second	futatsume	*foo-tah-tsoo-meh*
third	mittsume	*meet-tsoo-meh*
fourth	yottsume	*yoht-tsoo-meh*
fifth	itsutsume	*ee-tsoo-tsoo-meh*
sixth	muttsume	*moot-tsoo-meh*
seventh	nanatsume	*nah-nah-tsoo-meh*
eighth	yattsume	*yaht-tsoo-meh*

| ninth | kokonotsume | *koh-koh-noh-tsoo-meh* |
| tenth | jūbanme/daijū | *joo-bahn-meh/dah-ee-joo* |

c. FRACTIONS

one-half	nibun no ichi	*nee-boon noh ee-chee*
one-third	sanbun no ichi	*sahn-boon noh ee-chee*
one-fourth	yonbun no ichi	*yohn-boon noh ee-chee*
one-fifth	gobun no ichi	*goh-boon noh ee-chee*
two-thirds	sanbun no ni	*sahn-boon noh nee*
three-fourths	yonbun no san	*yohn-boon noh sahn*
four-ninths	kyūbun no yon	*kyoo-boon noh yohn*

d. TYPES OF NUMBERS

number	kazu/sūji	*kah-zoo/soo-jee*
• number	bangō o tsukeru (*v*)	*bahn-goh oh tsoo-keh-roo*
• numeral	sūji	*soo-jee*
• numerical	kazu no (*adj*)	*kah-zoo noh*
Arabic numeral	Arabia sūji	*ah-rah-bee-ah soo-jee*
cardinal number	kisū	*kee-soo*
complex number	fukusosū	*foo-koo-soh-soo*
digit	sūji	*soo-jee*
even number	gūsū	*goo-soo*
fraction	bunsū	*boon-soo*
• fractional	bunsū no (*adj*)	*boon-soo noh*
imaginary number	kyosū	*kyoh-soo*
integer	seisū	*seh-soo*
irrational number	murisū	*moo-ree-soo*
natural number	shizensū	*shee-zehn-soo*
negative number	fusū	*foo-soo*
odd number	kisū	*kee-soo*
ordinal number	josū	*joh-soo*
positive number	seisū	*seh-soo*
prime number	sosū	*soh-soo*
rational number	yūrisū	*yoo-ree-soo*
real number	jissū	*jees-soo*
reciprocal number	gyakusū	*gyah-koo-soo*
Roman numeral	Rōma sūji	*roh-mah soo-jee*

e. BASIC OPERATIONS

| arithmetical operations | enzan | *ehn-zahn* |
| add | kuwaeru (*v*)/tasu (*v*) | *koo-wah-eh-roo/tahs* |

• **addition**	tashizan	*tah-shee-zahn*
• **plus**	purasu kigō	*poo-rahs kee-goh*
• **two plus two equals four**	ni tasu ni wa yon	*nee tahs nee wah yohn*
subtract	hiku (*v*)	*hee-koo*
• **subtraction**	hikizan	*hee-kee-zahn*
• **minus**	mainasu kigō	*mah-ee-nahs kee-goh*
• **three minus two equals one**	san hiku ni wa ichi	*sahn hee-koo nee wah ee-chee*
multiply	kakeru (*v*)	*kah-keh-roo*
• **multiplication**	kakezan	*kah-keh-zahn*
• **multiplication table**	kuku no hyō	*koo-koo noh hyoh*
• **multiplied by**	kaketa	*kah-keh-tah*
• **three times two equals six**	ni kakeru san wa roku	*nee kah-keh-roo sahn wah roh-koo*
divide	waru (*v*)	*wah-roo*
• **divided by**	watta	*waht-tah*
• **division**	warizan	*wah-ree-zahn*
• **six divided by three equals two**	roku waru san wa ni	*roh-koo wah-roo sahn wah nee*
raise to a power	ruijōsuru (*v*)	*roo-ee-joh-soo-roo*
• **to the power of**	ruijō	*roo-ee-joh*
• **squared**	nijō no	*nee-joh noh*
• **cubed**	sanjō no	*sahn-joh noh*
• **to the fourth power**	yonjō	*yohn-joh*
• **to the nth power**	enujō	*en-noo-joh*
• **two squared equals four**	ni no nijō wa yon	*nee no nee-joh wah yohn*
extract a root	kon o hiraku (*v*)	*kohn oh hee-rah-koo*
• **square root**	heihōkon	*heh-hoh-kohn*
• **cube root**	rippōkon	*reep-poh-kohn*
• **nth root**	enujokon	*eh-noo-joh-kohn*
• **(the) square root of nine is three**	kyū no heihōkon wa san	*kyoo noh heh-hoh-kohn wah sahn*
ratio	hirei	*hee-reh*
• **twelve is to four as nine is to three**	jūni tai yon wa kyū tai san	*joo-nee tah-ee yohn wah kyoo tah-ee sahn*

FOCUS: *Arithmetical Operations*

Addition — tashizan
$2 + 3 = 5$ two plus three equals five   ni tasu san wa go

Subtraction — hikizan
$9 - 3 = 6$ nine minus three equals six   kyū hiku san wa roku

---

Multiplication — kakezan
$4 \times 2 = 8$ four times two equals eight   yon kakeru ni wa hachi
$4 \cdot 2 = 8$

Division — warizan
$10 \div 2 = 5$ ten divided by two equals five   jū waru ni wa go

Raising to a power — ruijō
$3^2 = 9$ three squared (or to the   san no nijō wa kyū
                    second power) equals nine
$2^3 = 8$ two cubed (or to the third   ni no sanjō wa hachi
                    power) equals eight
$2^4 = 16$ two to the fourth power   ni no yonjō wa jūroku
                    equals sixteen
x^n x to the nth power   ekkusu no enujō

Extraction of root — kon no kaihō
$\sqrt[2]{4} = 2$ the square root of four is   yon no heihōkon wa ni
                    two
$\sqrt[3]{27} = 3$ the cube root of twenty-seven   nijūnana no rippōkon
                    is three   wa san
$\sqrt[n]{x}$ the nth root of x   ekkusu no enujōkon

Ratio — hirei
$12:4 = 9:3$ twelve is to four as nine   jūni tai yon wa kyū tai
                    is to three   san

f. ADDITIONAL MATHEMATICAL CONCEPTS

algebra	daisū	*dah-ee-soo*
• **algebraic**	daisū no (*adj*)	*dah-ee-soo noh*
arithmetic	sansū	*sahn-soo*
• **arithmetical**	sansū no (*adj*)	*sahn-soo noh*
average	heikin	*heh-keen*
calculate	keisansuru (*v*)	*keh-sahn-soo-roo*
• **calculation**	keisan	*keh-sahn*
constant	teisū	*teh-soo*
count	kazoeru (*v*)	*kah-zoh-eh-roo*
• **countable**	kazoerareru (*adj*)	*kah-zoh-eh-rah-reh-roo*
decimal	shōsū	*shoh-soo*
difference	sa	*sah*
equality	dōtō	*doh-toh*

• equals	hitoshii	*hee-toh-shee*
• does not equal	hitoshikunai	*hee-toh-shee-koo-nah-ee*
• is equivalent to	sōtōsuru	*soh-toh-soo-roo*
• is greater than	yori ōkii	*yoh-ree oh-kee*
• is less than	yori chiisai	*yoh-ree chee-sah-ee*
• is similar to	ruijishiteiru	*roo-ee-jee-shteh-ee-roo*
equation	hōteishiki	*hoh-teh-shkee*
factor	insū	*een-soo*
• factor	insū ni bunkaisuru (*v*)	*een-soo nee boon-kah-ee-soo-roo*
• factorization	insūbunkai	*een-soo-boon-kah-ee*
function	kansū	*kahn-soo*
logarithm	taisū	*tah-ee-soo*
• logarithmic	taisū no (*adj*)	*tah-ee-soo noh*
multiple	baisū no (*adj*)	*bah-ee-soo noh*
percent	pāsento	*pah-sehn-toh*
• percentage	ritsu	*ree-tsoo*
problem	mondai	*mohn-dah-ee*
• problem to solve	kaiketsusuru mondai	*kah-ee-keh-tsoo-soo-roo mohn-dah-ee*
product	seki	*seh-kee*
quotient	shō	*shoh*
set	shūgō	*shoo-goh*
solution	kaiketsuhō	*kah-ee-keh-tsoo-hoh*
• solve	kaiketsusuru (*v*)	*kah-ee-keh-tsoo-soo-roo*
statistics	tōkei	*toh-keh*
• statistical	tōkei no (*adj*)	*toh-keh noh*
sum	gōkei	*goh-keh*
• sum up	gōkeisuru (*v*)	*goh-keh-soo-roo*
symbol	kigō	*kee-goh*
variable	hensū	*hehn-soo*

2. GEOMETRY

a. FIGURES

<u>plane figures</u>	heimen zukei	*heh-mehn zoo-keh*
triangle	sankakukei	*sahn-kah-koo-keh*

a lovers' triangle (*lit*. triangle relation)	= sankaku kankei	*sahn-kah-koo kahn-keh*
to look daggers at someone (*lit*. make one's eyes triangular)	= me o sankaku ni suru	*meh oh sahn-kah-koo nee soo-roo*

• acute-angled	eikaku (*adj*)	*eh-kah-koo*
• equilateral	tōhen (*adj*)	*toh-hehn*
• isosceles	nitōhen (*adj*)	*nee-toh-hehn*
• obtuse-angled	donkaku (*adj*)	*dohn-kah-koo*
• right-angled	chokkaku (*adj*)	*chohk-kah-koo*
• scalene	futōhen/sha (*adj*)	*ftoh-hehn/shah*
four-sided figures	shihenkei	*shee-hehn-keh*
• parallelogram	heikōshihenkei	*heh-koh-shee-hehn-keh*
• rectangle	chōhōkei	*choh-hoh-keh*
• rhombus	hishigata	*hee-shee-gah-tah*
• square	seihōkei	*seh-hoh-keh*
• trapezium	daikei	*dah-ee-keh*
n-sided figures	enuhenkei	*eh-noo-hehn-keh*
• pentagon	gokakukei	*goh-kah-koo-keh*
• hexagon	rokkakukei	*rohk-kah-koo-keh*
• heptagon	nanakakukei	*nah-nah-kah-koo-keh*
• octagon	hakkakukei	*hahk-kah-koo-keh*
• decagon	jukkakukei	*jook-kah-koo-keh*
circle	en	*ehn*

| a happy home (*lit*. round and full home) | = enman na katei | *ehn-mahn nah kah-teh* |

• center	chūshin	*choo-sheen*
• circumference	enshū	*ehn-shoo*
• diameter	chokkei	*chohk-keh*
• radius	hankei	*hahn-keh*
• tangent	sessen	*sehs-sehn*
solid figures	rittai	*reet-tah-ee*
prism	kakuchū	*kahk-choo*
• right prism	chokkakuchū	*chohk-kahk-choo*
parallelepiped	heikōrokumentai	*heh-koh-roh-koo-mehn-tah-ee*
cube	seirokumentai	*seh-roh-koo-mehn-tah-ee*
pyramid	kakusui	*kahk-soo-ee*
polyhedron	tamentai	*tah-mehn-tah-ee*
• tetrahedron	shimentai	*shee-mehn-tah-ee*
• octahedron	hachimentai	*hah-chee-mehn-tah-ee*
• dodecahedron	jūnimentai	*joo-nee-mehn-tah-ee*
• icosahedron	nijūmentai	*nee-joo-mehn-tah-ee*
cylinder	enchū	*ehn-choo*
cone	ensuitai	*ehn-soo-ee-tah-ee*
sphere	kyūkei	*kyoo-keh*

FOCUS: *Geometrical Figures*

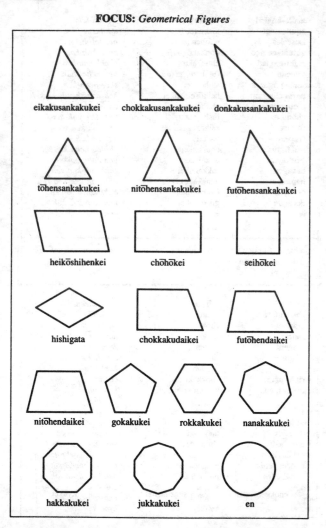

eikakusankakukei · chokkakusankakukei · donkakusankakukei

tōhensankakukei · nitōhensankakukei · futōhensankakukei

heikōshihenkei · chōhōkei · seihōkei

hishigata · chokkakudaikei · futōhendaikei

nitōhendaikei · gokakukei · rokkakukei · nanakakukei

hakkakukei · jukkakukei · en

FOCUS: *Geometrical Solids*

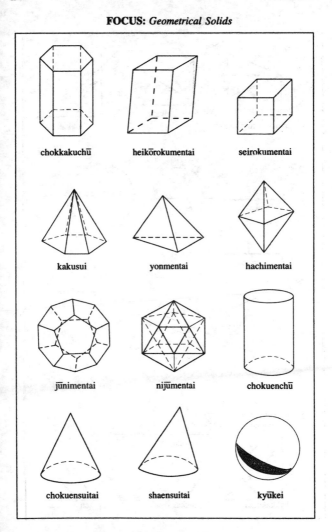

chokkakuchū

heikōrokumentai

seirokumentai

kakusui

yonmentai

hachimentai

jūnimentai

nijūmentai

chokuenchū

chokuensuitai

shaensuitai

kyūkei

FOCUS: *Angles*

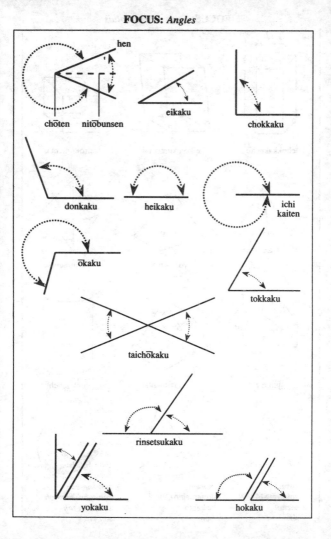

b. CONCEPTS

angle	kakudo	*kah-koo-doh*
• **acute angle**	eikaku	*ēh-kah-koo*
• **adjacent angle**	rinsetsukaku	*reen-seh-tsoo-kah-koo*
• **bisector**	nitōbunsen	*nee-tōh-boon-sehn*
• **complementary angle**	yokaku	*yoh-kah-koo*
• **concave angle**	ōkaku	*ōh-kah-koo*
• **convex angle**	tokkaku	*tohk-kah-koo*
• **obtuse angle**	donkaku	*dohn-kah-koo*
• **one turn (360°)**	ichi kaiten	*ee-chee kah-ee-tehn*
• **opposite angle**	taichōkaku	*tah-ee-chōh-kah-koo*
• **right angle**	chokkaku	*chohk-kah-koo*
• **side**	hen	*hehn*
• **straight angle**	heikaku	*hēh-kah-koo*
• **supplementary angle**	hokaku	*hoh-kah-koo*
• **vertex**	chōten	*chōh-tehn*
axis	jiku	*jee-koo*
coordinate	zahyō	*zah-hyōh*
degree	do	*doh*
draw	sen o hiku (*v*)	*sehn oh hee-koo*
drawing instruments	seizu kikai	*sēh-zoo kee-kah-ee*
• **compass**	konpasu	*kohn-pahs*
• **eraser**	keshigomu	*keh-shee-goh-moo*
• **pen**	pen	*pehn*
• **pencil**	enpitsu	*ehn-pee-tsoo*
• **protractor**	bundoki	*boon-doh-kee*
• **ruler**	jōgi	*jōh-gee*
• **template**	tenpurēto	*tehn-poo-rēh-toh*
geometry	kika	*kee-kah*
• **geometrical**	kika no (*adj*)	*kee-kah noh*
line	sen	*sehn*
• **broken line**	hasen	*hah-sehn*
• **curved line**	kyokusen	*kyohk-sehn*
• **parallel lines**	heikōsen	*hēh-kōh-sehn*
• **perpendicular line**	suisen	*soo-ee-sehn*
• **segment line**	senbun	*sehn-boon*
• **straight line**	chokusen	*chohk-sehn*
point	ten	*tehn*
space	kūkan	*kōō-kahn*
trigonometry	sankakuhō	*sahn-kah-koo-hōh*
• **trigonometric**	sankakuhō no (*adj*)	*sahn-kah-koo-hōh noh*
• **cosecant**	kosekanto	*koh-seh-kahn-toh*
• **cosine**	kosain	*koh-sah-een*
• **cotangent**	kotanjento	*koh-tahn-jehn-toh*
• **secant**	sekanto	*seh-kahn-toh*
• **sine**	sain	*sah-een*

FOCUS: *Lines*

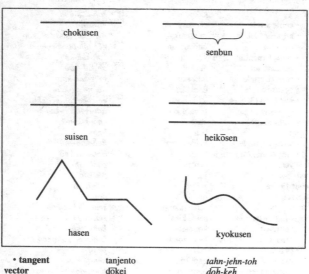

chokusen	senbun
suisen	heikōsen
hasen	kyokusen

| • tangent | tanjento | *tahn-jehn-toh* |
| vector | dōkei | *doh-keh* |

3. *QUANTITY AND SPACE*

a. WEIGHTS AND MEASURES

area	menseki	*mehn-seh-kee*
• **hectare**	hekutāru	*hehk-tah-roo*
• **square centimeter**	heihōsenchi	*heh-hoh-sehn-chee*
• **square kilometer**	heihōkiro	*heh-hoh-kee-roh*
• **square meter**	heihōmētoru	*heh-hoh-meh-toh-roo*
• **square millimeter**	heihōmiri	*heh-hoh-mee-ree*
length	nagasa	*nah-gah-sah*
• **centimeter**	senchi	*sehn-chee*
• **kilometer**	kiro	*kee-roh*
• **meter**	mētoru	*meh-toh-roo*
• **millimeter**	miri	*mee-ree*
speed	sokudo	*sohk-doh*
• **per hour**	jisoku	*jee-soh-koo*
• **per minute**	funsoku	*foon-soh-koo*
• **per second**	byōsoku	*byoh-soh-koo*

volume	taiseki/yōseki	*tah-ee-seh-kee/yoh-seh-kee*
• cubic centimeter	rippōsenchi	*reep-poh-sehn-chee*
• cubic kilometer	rippōkiro	*reep-poh-kee-roh*
• cubic meter	rippōmētoru	*reep-poh-meh-toh-roo*
• cubic millimeter	rippōmiri	*reep-poh-mee-ree*
• liter	rittoru	*reet-toh-roo*
• quart	kuōto	*koo-oh-toh*
weight	jūryō	*joo-ryoh*
• gram	guramu	*goo-rah-moo*
• hectogram	hekutoguramu	*hehk-toh-goo-rah-moo*
• kilogram	kiroguramu	*kee-roh-goo-rah-moo*

b. WEIGHING AND MEASURING

dense	mitsudo no takai (*adj*)	*mee-tsoo-doh noh tah-kah-ee*
• density	mitsudo/nōdo	*mee-tsoo-doh/noh-doh*
dimension	jigen	*jee-gehn*
extension	enchō	*ehn-choh*
heavy	omoi (*adj*)	*oh-moh-ee*
light	karui (*adj*)	*kah-roo-ee*
long	nagai (*adj*)	*nah-gah-ee*
• length	nagasa	*nah-gah-sah*
mass	ryō	*ryoh*
maximum	saidai	*sah-ee-dah-ee*
measure	hakaru (*v*)	*hah-kah-roo*
measuring tape	tēpumejā	*teh-poo-meh-jah*
medium	hōhō	*hoh-hoh*
	chūkan no (*adj*)	*choo-kahn noh*
minimum	saishō	*sah-ee-shoh*
narrow	semai (*adj*)	*seh-mah-ee*
short	mijikai (*adj*)	*mee-jee-kah-ee*
size	saizu	*sah-ee-zoo*
tall	takai (*adj*)	*tah-kah-ee*
thick	atsui (*adj*)	*ah-tsoo-ee*
thin	usui (*adj*)	*oo-soo-ee*
weigh	mekata o hakaru (*v*)	*meh-kah-tah oh hah-kah-roo*
wide	hiroi (*adj*)	*hee-roh-ee*
• width	hirosa	*hee-roh-sah*

c. CONCEPTS OF QUANTITY

a lot, much	takusan	*tahk-sahn*
all, everything	subete (*adv*)	*soo-beh-teh*
	zenbu	*zehn-boo*
• everyone	daremo	*dah-reh-mo*

almost, nearly	hotondo (*adv*)	hoh-tohn-doh
approximately	ōyoso	oh-yoh-soh
as much as	dake	dah-keh
big, large	ōkii (*adj*)	oh-kee-ee
• **become big**	ōkiku naru (*v*)	oh-kee-koo nah-roo
both	ryōhō	ryoh-hoh
capacity	yōryō/yōseki	yoh-ryoh/yoh-seh-kee
decrease	genshō	gehn-shoh
• **decrease**	genshōsuru (*vi*)	gehn-shoh-soo-roo
	genshōsaseru (*vt*)	gehn-shoh-sah-seh-roo
double	nibai no (*adj*)	nee-bah-ee noh
empty	kara no (*adj*)	kah-rah noh
• **empty**	kara ni suru (*v*)	kah-rah nee soo-roo
enough	jūbun na (*adj*)	joo-boon nah
	jūbun ni (*adv*)	joo-boon ni
entire	zentai no (*adj*)	zehn-tah-ee noh
every, each	dono ~ mo	doh-noh ~ moh
fill	mitasu (*v*)	mee-tah-soo
• **full**	ippai no (*adj*)	eep-pah-ee noh
grow	fueru (*vi*)	foo-eh-roo
	fuyasu (*vt*)	foo-yah-soo
• **growth**	zōdai	zoh-dah-ee
half	hanbun no (*adj*)	hahn-boon noh
how much	dono kurai	doh-noh koo-rah-ee
how much (*money*)	ikura	ee-koo-rah
increase	zōka	zoh-kah
• **increase**	zōkasuru (*vi*)	zoh-kah-soo-roo
	zōkasaseru (*vt*)	zoh-kah-sah-seh-roo
less	yori sukunai	yoh-ree skoo-nah-ee
little	chiisai (*adj*)	chee-sah-ee
• **a little**	sukoshi	skoh-shee
more	motto (*adv*)	moht-toh
no one	dare mo ~nai	dah-reh moh ~nah-ee
nothing	nani mo ~nai	nah-nee moh ~nah-ee
pair	kumi/tsui	koo-mee/tsoo-ee
part	bubun	boo-boon
piece	shōhen	shoh-hehn
portion	bubun	boo-boon
quantity	ryō	ryoh
several	ikutsuka no (*adj*)	ee-koots-kah noh
small	chiisai (*adj*)	chee-sah-ee
• **become small**	chiisakunaru (*v*)	chee-sah-koo-nah-roo
some	ikuraka no (*adj*)	ee-koo-rah-kah noh
sufficient	jūbun na (*adj*)	joo-boon nah
too much	ōsugi	oh-soo-gee
triple	sanbai no (*adj*)	sahn-bah-ee noh

d. CONCEPTS OF LOCATION

above	ue no (*adj*)	*oo-eh noh*
	ue ni (*adv*)	*oo-eh nee*
across	mukōgawa no (*adj*)	*moo-kōh-gah-wah noh*
ahead, forward	mukōgawa ni (*adv*)	*moo-kōh-gah-wah nee*
	saki no (*adj*)	*sah-kee noh*
among	naka ni (*adv*)	*nah-kah nee*
away	hedatatta (*adj*)	*heh-dah-taht-tah*
	hedatatte (*adv*)	*heh-dah-taht-teh*
back, backward	ushiro no (*adj*)	*oo-shee-roh noh*
	ushiro ni (*adv*)	*oo-shee-roh nee*
beside, next to	tonari no (*adj*)	*toh-nah-ree noh*
	tonari ni (*adv*)	*toh-nah-ree nee*
between	aida no (*adj*)	*ah-ee-dah noh*
	aida ni (*adv*)	*ah-ee-dah nee*
beyond	koeta (*adj*)	*koh-eh-tah*
	koete (*adv*)	*koh-eh-teh*
bottom	soko	*soh-koh*
• at the bottom	soko ni	*soh-koh nee*
compass	rashinban	*rah-sheen-bahn*
direction	hōkō	*hoh-koh*
distance	kyori	*kyoh-ree*
down	shita no (*adj*)	*shtah noh*
	shita ni (*adv*)	*shtah nee*
east	higashi	*hee-gah-shee*
• eastern	higashi no	*hee-gah-shee noh*
• to the east	higashi e	*hee-gah-shee eh*
edge	hashi	*hah-SHEE*
far	tōku no (*adj*)	*tōh-koo noh*
	tōku ni (*adv*)	*tōh-koo nee*
fast	hayai (*adj*)	*hah-yah-ee*
	hayaku (*adv*)	*hah-yah-koo*
from	kara	*kah-rah*
here	koko	*koh-koh*
horizon	suihei	*soo-ee-heh*
• horizontal	suihei no (*adj*)	*soo-ee-heh noh*
in	naka no (*adj*)	*nah-kah noh*
	naka ni (*adv*)	*nah-kah nee*
• inside	naka ni (*adv*)	*nah-kah nee*
in front of	mae no	*mah-eh noh*
in the middle of	naka no	*nah-kah noh*
left	hidari	*hee-dah-ree*
• to the left	hidari ni	*hee-dah-ree nee*
level	heimen	*heh-mehn*

near	chikai *(adj)*	*chee-kah-ee*
	chikaku ni *(adv)*	*chee-kah-koo nee*
north	kita	*kee-tah*
• **northern**	kita no	*kee-tah noh*
• **to the north**	kita ni	*kee-tah nee*
nowhere	dokonimo *(adv)*	*doh-koh-nee-moh*
on	ue no *(adj)*	*oo-eh noh*
	ue ni *(adv)*	*oo-eh nee*
outside	soto no *(adj)*	*soh-toh noh*
	soto ni *(adv)*	*soh-toh nee*
over there	asoko	*ah-soh-koh*
place	basho	*bah-shoh*
position	ichi	*ee-chee*
right	migi	*mee-gee*
• **to the right**	migi ni	*mee-gee nee*
somewhere	dokoka	*doh-koh-kah*
south	minami	*mee-nah-mee*
• **southern**	minami no *(adj)*	*mee-nah-mee noh*
• **to the south**	minami ni	*mee-nah-mee nee*
there	soko	*soh-koh*
through	tōshite *(adj)*	*toh-shteh*
to, at	ni/de	*nee/deh*
top	ichiban ue	*ee-chee-bahn oo-eh*
• **at the top**	ichiban ue de	*ee-chee-bahn oo-eh deh*
toward	ni taishite	*nee tah-ee-shteh*
under	shita no *(adj)*	*shtah noh*
	shita ni *(adv)*	*shtah nee*
up	ue no *(adj)*	*oo-eh noh*
	ue ni *(adv)*	*oo-eh nee*

FOCUS: *Compass Points*

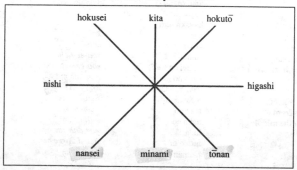

vertical	suichoku no (*adj*)	*soo-ee-choh-koo noh*
west	nishi	*nee-shee*
• **western**	nishi no (*adj*)	*nee-shee noh*
• **to the west**	nishi ni	*nee-shee nee*
where	doko ni (*adv*)	*doh-koh nee*

e. MOVEMENT

arrive	tsuku (*v*)	*tskoo*
come	kuru (*v*)	*koo-roo*
drive	untensuru (*v*)	*oon-tehn-soo-roo*
enter	hairu (*v*)	*hah-ee-roo*
fall	ochiru (*v*)	*oh-chee-roo*
follow	shitagau (*v*)	*shtah-gah-oo*
get up, rise	okiru (*v*)	*oo-kee-roo*
go	iku (*v*)	*ee-koo*
• **go away**	saru (*v*)	*sah-roo*
• **go down, descend**	sagaru (*vi*)	*sah-gah-roo*
	kudaru (*vt*)	*koo-dah-roo*
• **go on foot**	aruite iku (*v*)	*ah-roo-ee-teh ee-koo*
• **go out, exit**	deru (*v*)	*deh-roo*
• **go up, climb**	noboru (*vt*)	*noh-boh-roo*
leave, depart	shuppatsusuru (*v*)	*shoop-pah-tsoo-soo-roo*
lie down	yokotawaru (*v*)	*yoh-koh-tah-wah-roo*
lift	mochiageru (*v*)	*moh-chee-ah-geh-roo*
motion	ugoki	*oo-goh-kee*
move	ugoku (*vi*)	*oo-goh-koo*
	ugokasu (*vt*)	*oo-goh-kah-soo*
• **movement**	undō	*oon-doh*
pass by	tōrisugiru (*v*)	*toh-ree-soo-gee-roo*
pull	hipparu (*v*)	*heep-pah-roo*
put	oku (*v*)	*oh-koo*
• **put down**	oku (*v*)	*oh-koo*
quickly	hayaku (*adv*)	*hah-yah-koo*
return	kaeru (*vi*)	*kah-eh-roo*
	kaesu (*vt*)	*kah-eh-soo*
run	hashiru (*v*)	*hah-shee-roo*
send	okuru (*v*)	*oh-koo-roo*
sit down	suwaru (*v*)	*soo-wah-roo*
slow	osoi (*adj*)	*oh-soh-ee*
• **slowly**	osoku (*adv*)	*oh-soh-koo*
stop	tomaru (*vi*)	*toh-mah-roo*
	tomeru (*vt*)	*toh-meh-roo*
turn	magaru (*v*)	*mah-gah-roo*
walk	aruku (*v*)	*ah-roo-koo*
• **walk**	sanpo	*sahn-poh*

| • take a walk | sanpo ni iku (v) | *sahn-poh nee ee-koo* |

4. TIME

a. GENERAL EXPRESSIONS OF TIME

afternoon	gogo	*goh-goh*
• in the afternoon	gogo ni	*goh-goh nee*
• this afternoon	kyō no gogo	*kyoh noh goh-goh*
• tomorrow afternoon	ashita no gogo	*ahsh-tah noh goh-goh*
dawn	yoake	*yoh-ah-keh*
day	ichinichi	*ee-chee-nee-chee*
• all day	hi	*hee*
	ichinichijū	*ee-chee-nee-chee-jōō*
evening	yūgata	*yōō-gah-tah*
• in the evening	yūgata ni	*yōō-gah-tah nee*
• this evening	kyō no yūgata	*kyoh noh yōō-gah-tah*
• tomorrow evening	ashita no yūgata	*ahsh-tah noh yōō-gah-tah*
midnight	mayonaka	*mah-yoh-nah-kah*
• at midnight	mayonaka ni	*mah-yoh-nah-kah nee*
morning	asa	*ah-sah*
• in the morning	gozenchū ni	*goh-zehn-chōō nee*
• this morning	kesa	*keh-sah*
• tomorrow morning	ashita no asa	*ahsh-tah noh ah-sah*
night	yoru	*yoh-roo*
• at night	yoru ni	*yoh-roo nee*
• last night	yūbe	*yōō-beh*
• this night	konban	*kohn-bahn*
• tomorrow night	ashita no ban	*ahsh-tah noh bahn*
noon	hiruma	*hee-roo-mah*
• at noon	shōgo ni	*shoh-goh nee*
sunrise	hinode	*hee-noh-deh*
sunset	hinoiri	*hee-noh-ee-ree*
time (*in general*)	jikan	*jee-kahn*
• time (*hour*)	ji	*jee*
• time (*as in* every time)	toki	*toh-kee*

Time is money.	= Toki wa kane nari.	*toh-kee wah kah-neh nah-ree*
now and then	= tokidoki	*toh-kee-doh-kee*

today	kyō	*kyoh*
tomorrow	ashita	*ahsh-tah*
• day after tomorrow	asatte	*ah-saht-teh*
yesterday	kinō	*kee-noh*

• **day before yesterday**	ototoi	*oh-toh-toh-ee*
• **yesterday afternoon**	kinō no gogo	*kee-noh noh goh-goh*
• **yesterday morning**	kinō no asa	*kee-noh noh ah-sah*

b. TELLING TIME

What time is it?	Nanji desu ka.	*NAHN-jee dehs kah*
• **It's 1:00.**	Ichiji desu.	*ee-CHEE-jee dehs*
• **It's 2:00.**	Niji desu.	*nee-jee dehs*
• **It's 3:00.**	Sanji desu.	*SAHN-jee dehs*
• **It's exactly 3:00.**	Chōdo sanji desu.	*choh-doh SAHN-jee dehs*
• **It's 3:00 on the dot.**	Sanji kikkari desu.	*SAHN-jee keek-kah-ree dehs*
• **It's 1:10.**	Ichiji juppun desu.	*ee-CHEE-jee joop-poon dehs*
• **It's 4:25.**	Yoji nijūgofun desu.	*yoh-jee nee-jōō-goh-foon dehs*
• **It's 3:15.**	Sanji jūgofun desu.	*SAHN-jee jōō-goh-foon dehs*
• **It's 3:30.**	Sanji han desu.	*SAHN-jee hahn dehs*
• **It's 2:45.**	Niji yonjūgofun desu.	*nee-jee yohn-jōō-goh-foon dehs*
	Sanji jūgofun mae desu.	*SAHN-jee jōō-goh-foon mah-eh dehs*
• **It's 5:50.**	Rokuji juppun mae desu.	*roh-koo-jee joop-poon mah-eh dehs*
• **It's 5:00 AM.**	Gozen goji desu.	*goh-zehn goh-jee dehs*
• **It's 5:00 PM.**	Gogo goji desu.	*goh-goh goh-jee dehs*
• **It's 10:00 AM.**	Gozen jūji desu.	*goh-zehn jōō-jee dehs*
• **It's 10:00 PM.**	Gogo jūji desu.	*goh-goh jōō-jee dehs*
At what time?	Nanji ni.	*NAHN-jee nee*
• **At 1:00.**	Ichiji ni.	*ee-CHEE-jee nee*
• **At 2:00.**	Niji ni.	*nee-jee nee*
• **At 3:00.**	Sanji ni.	*SAHN-jee nee*

c. UNITS OF TIME

century	seiki	*seh-kee*
day	ichinichi	*ee-chee-nee-chee*
• **daily**	hi	*hee*
	mainichi no (*adj*)	*mah-ee-nee-chee noh*
decade	jūnenkan	*jōō-nehn-kahn*
hour	jikan	*jee-kahn*
• **hourly**	jikangoto no (*adj*)	*jee-kahn-goh-toh noh*
	jikangoto ni (*adv*)	*jee-kahn-goh-toh nee*
instant	shunji	*shoon-jee*

minute	fun	*foon*
moment	shunkan	*shoon-kahn*
month	tsuki	*tskee*
• monthly	maitsuki no (*adj*)	*mah-ee-tskee noh*
second	byō	*byoh*
week	shū	*shoo*
• weekly	maishū no (*adj*)	*mah-ee-shoo noh*
year	toshi	*toh-shee*
• yearly, annually	maitoshi no (*adj*)	*mah-ee-toh-shee noh*

d. TIMEPIECES

alarm clock	mezamashi	*meh-zah-mah-shee*
clock	okidokei	*oh-kee-doh-keh*
dial	mojiban	*moh-jee-bahn*
grandfather clock	hakogata ōdokei	*hah-koh-gah-tah oh-doh-keh*
hand of a clock	tokei no hari	*toh-keh noh hah-ree*
watch	tokei	*toh-keh*
• The watch is fast.	Tokei ga, susumigachi desu.	*toh-keh gah, soo-soo-mee-gah-chee dehs*
• The watch is slow.	Tokei ga, okuregachi desu.	*toh-keh gah, oh-koo-reh-gah-chee dehs*
watchband	tokei no bando	*toh-keh noh bahn-doh*
watch battery	tokei no denchi	*toh-keh no dehn-chee*
wind	neji o maku (*v*)	*neh-jee oh mah-koo*
wristwatch	udedokei	*oo-deh-doh-keh*

e. CONCEPTS OF TIME

after	ato de (*adv*)	*ah-toh deh*
again	mata (*adv*)	*mah-tah*
ago	mae ni (*adv*)	*mah-eh nee*
almost never	hotondo ~nai (*adv*)	*hoh-tohn-doh ~nah-ee*
already	sude ni (*adv*)/mō (*adv*)	*soo-deh nee/moh*
always	itsumo (*adv*)	*ee-tsoo-moh*
anterior	saki no (*adj*)	*SAH-kee noh*
	saki ni (*adv*)	*SAH-kee nee*
as soon as	sugu ni	*soo-goo nee*
at the same time	dōji ni	*doh-jee nee*
be about to, be on the point/verge of	~kaketeiru	*kah-keh-teh-ee-roo*
be on time	jikandōri ni	*jee-kahn-doh-ree nee*
become	~ni naru (*v*)	*~nee nah-roo*
before	mae ni (*adv*)	*mah-eh nee*

begin	hajimaru (*vi*)	*hah-jee-mah-roo*
	hajimeru (*vt*)	*hah-jee-meh-roo*
• **beginning**	hajimari	*hah-jee-mah-ree*
brief	kantan na (*adj*)	*kahn-tahn nah*
• **briefly**	kantan ni (*adv*)	*kahn-tahn nee*
change	kawaru (*vi*)	*kah-wah-roo*
	kaeru (*vt*)	*kah-eh-roo*
continue	tsuzuku (*vi*)	*tsoo-zoo-koo*
	tsuzukeru (*vt*)	*tsoo-zoo-keh-roo*
• **continually**	tsuzukete (*adv*)	*tsoo-zoo-keh-teh*
during	aida ni (*adv*)	*ah-ee-dah nee*
early	hayai (*adj*)	*hah-yah-ee*
	hayaku (*adv*)	*hah-yah-koo*
end, finish	owaru (*v*)	*oh-wah-roo*
• **end**	owari	*oh-wah-ree*
frequent	hinpan na (*adj*)	*heen-pahn nah*
• **frequently**	shibashiba	*shee-bah-shee-bah*
future	shōrai/mirai	*shoh-rah-ee/mee-rah-ee*
happen, occur	okoru (*vi*)	*oh-koh-roo*
in an hour's time	ichijikan nai ni	*ee-chee-jee-kahn nah-ee nee*
• **in two minutes' time**	nifunkan nai ni	*nee-foon-kahn nah-ee nee*
in the meanwhile	sono kan ni	*soh-noh kahn nee*
in time	maniatte	*mah-nee-aht-teh*
just now	tatta ima	*taht-tah ee-mah*
last	tsuzuku (*vi*)	*tsoo-zoo-koo*
	tsuzukeru (*vt*)	*tsoo-zoo-keh-roo*
• **last a long time**	nagai aida tsuzuku	*nah-gah-ee ah-ee-dah tsoo-zoo-koo*
• **last a short time**	tankikan tsuzuku	*tahn-kee-kahn tsoo-zoo-koo*
last	saigo no (*adj*)	*sah-ee-goh noh*
	mae no (*adj*)	*mah-eh noh*
• **last month**	sengetsu	*sehn-geh-tsoo*
• **last year**	kyonen	*kyoh-nehn*
late	osoi (*adj*)	*oh-soh-ee*
	osoku (*adv*)	*oh-soh-koo*
• **to be late**	osokunaru	*oh-soh-koo-nah-roo*

Better late than never.	= Shinai yori osoi hō ga mashi.	*shee-nah-ee yoh-ree oh-soh-ee hoh gah mah-shee*

long-term	chōkiteki na (*adj*)	*choh-kee-teh-kee nah*
look forward to	kitaisuru (*v*)	*kee-tah-ee-soo-roo*
never	kesshite ~nai (*adv*)	*kehs-shteh ~nah-ee*

• almost never	hotondo ~nai (*adv*)	hoh-tohn-doh ~nah-ee
now	ima/genzai	ee-mah/gehn-zah-ee
• for now	ima no tokoro	ee-mah noh toh-koh-roh
• from now on	korekara	koh-reh-kah-rah
nowadays	genzai dewa	gehn-zah-ee deh-wah
occasionally	tokidoki (*adv*)	toh-kee-doh-kee
often	yoku (*adv*)	yoh-koo
once	katsute (*adv*)	kah-tsoo-teh
• once in a while	tokidoki	toh-kee-doh-kee
• once upon a time	mukashimukashi	moo-kah-shee-moo-kah-shee
only	dake	dah-keh
past	kako	kah-koh
posterior	ato no (*adj*)	ah-toh noh
present	genzai	gehn-zah-ee
previous	mae no (*adj*)	mah-eh noh
• previously	mae ni (*adv*)	mah-eh nee
rare	mare na (*adj*)	mah-reh nah
• rarely	mare ni (*adv*)	mah-reh nee
recent	saikin no (*adj*)	sah-ee-keen noh
regular	kisokuteki na (*adj*)	kee-soh-koo-teh-kee nah
• regularly	kisokuteki ni (*adv*)	kee-soh-koo-teh-kee nee
right away	sugu ni (*adv*)	soo-goo nee
short-term	tanki no (*adj*)	tahn-kee noh
simultaneous	dōji no	dōh-jee noh
• simultaneously	dōji ni	dōh-jee nee
since	kara (*p*)	kah-rah
• since Monday	getsuyōbi kara	gehts-yōh-bee kah-rah
• since yesterday	kinō kara	kee-nōh kah-rah
slow	osoi (*adj*)	oh-soh-ee
• slowly	osoku (*adv*)	oh-soh-koo
soon	mōsugu (*adv*)	mōh-soo-goo
• as soon as	sugu ni	soo-goo nee
• sooner or later	sonouchi	soh-noh-oo-chee
spend (*time*)	sugosu (*v*)	soo-goh-soo
spend (*money*)	tsukau (*v*)	tsoo-kah-oo
sporadic	tokiori no (*adj*)	toh-kee-oh-ree noh
• sporadically	tokiori (*adv*)	toh-kee-oh-ree
still	mada (*adv*)	mah-dah
take place	okoru (*vi*)	oh-koh-roo
temporary	ichijiteki na (*adj*)	ee-chee-jee-teh-kee nah
• temporarily	ichijiteki ni (*adv*)	ee-chee-jee-teh-kee nee
then	sorekara (*conj*)	soh-reh-kah-rah
	sono toki	soh-noh toh-kee
timetable, schedule	yoteihyō	yoh-teh-hyōh
to this day	konnichi made	kohn-nee-chee mah-deh
until	made (*adv*)	mah-deh

usually	itsumo wa (*adv*)	*ee-tsoo-moh wah*
wait	matsu (*v*)	*mah-tsoo*
when	itsu (*adv*)	*ee-tsoo*
while	no aida ni	*noh ah-ee-dah nee*
within	inai ni	*ee-nah-ee nee*
yet	mada (*adv*)	*mah-dah*

5. DAYS, MONTHS, AND SEASONS

a. DAYS OF THE WEEK

day of the week	yōbi	*yōh-bee*
• **Monday**	getsuyōbi	*geh-tsoo-yōh-bee*
• **Tuesday**	kayōbi	*kah-yōh-bee*
• **Wednesday**	suiyōbi	*soo-ee-yōh-bee*
• **Thursday**	mokuyōbi	*moh-koo-yōh-bee*
• **Friday**	kinyōbi	*keen-yōh-bee*
• **Saturday**	doyōbi	*doh-yōh-bee*
• **Sunday**	nichiyōbi	*nee-chee-yōh-bee*
• **on Mondays**	getsuyōbi ni	*geh-tsoo-yōh-bee nee*
• **on Saturdays**	doyōbi ni	*doh-yōh-bee nee*
• **on Sundays**	nichiyōbi ni	*nee-chee-yōh-bee nee*
holiday	kyūjitsu	*kyōō-jee-tsoo*
weekend	shūmatsu	*shōō-mah-tsoo*

a weekend carpenter = nichiyō daiku	*nee-chee-yōh*
(*lit.* a Sunday	*dah-ee-koo*
carpenter)	

What day is it?	Kyō wa nani yōbi	*kyōh wah nah-nee yōh-*
	desu ka.	*bee dehs kah*
workday	heijitsu	*heh-jee-tsoo*

b. MONTHS OF THE YEAR

month of the year	ichinen no tsuki	*ee-chee-nehn noh tskee*
• **January**	ichigatsu	*ee-chee-gah-tsoo*
• **February**	nigatsu	*nee-gah-tsoo*
• **March**	sangatsu	*sahn-gah-tsoo*
• **April**	shigatsu	*shee-gah-tsoo*
• **May**	gogatsu	*goh-gah-tsoo*
• **June**	rokugatsu	*roh-koo-gah-tsoo*
• **July**	shichigatsu	*shee-chee-gah-tsoo*
• **August**	hachigatsu	*hah-chee-gah-tsoo*

• September	kugatsu	*koo-gah-tsoo*
• October	jūgatsu	*jōō-gah-tsoo*
• November	jūichigatsu	*jōō-ee-chee-gah-tsoo*
• December	jūnigatsu	*jōō-nee-gah-tsoo*
calendar	karendā	*kah-rehn-dāh*
leap year	uruudoshi	*oo-roo-oo-doh-shee*
month	tsuki	*tskee*
• monthly	maitsuki no (adj)	*mah-ee-tskee noh*
school year	gakunen	*gah-koo-nehn*
What month is it?	Nangatsu desu ka.	*NAHN-gah-tsoo dehs kah*

c. SEASONS

season	kisetsu	*kee-seh-tsoo*
• spring	haru	*hah-roo*
• summer	natsu	*nah-tsoo*
• fall	aki	*ah-kee*
• winter	fuyu	*foo-yoo*
equinox	bunten	*boon-tehn*
• autumnal equinox	shūbun	*shōō-boon*
• vernal equinox	shunbun	*shoon-boon*
moon	tsuki	*tskee*

FOCUS: *The Seasons*

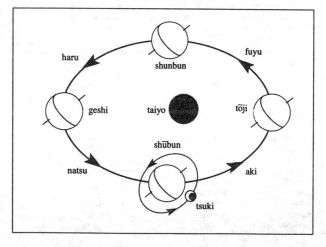

to be as different as chalk from cheese (*lit.* the moon and a terrapin)	= tsuki to suppon	*tskee toh soop-pohn*

solstice	shiten	*shee-tehn*
• summer solstice	geshi	*geh-shee*
• winter solstice	tōji	*toh-jee*
sun	taiyō	*tah-ee-yoh*

d. THE ZODIAC

horoscope	hoshiuranai	*hoh-shee-oo-rah-nah-ee*
zodiac	jūnikyūzu	*joo-nee-kyoo-zoo*
• signs of the zodiac	jūnikyūzu no sain	*joo-nee-kyoo-zoo noh sah-een*
• Aries	ohitsujiza	*oh-hee-tsoo-jee-zah*
• Taurus	oushiza	*oh-oo-shee-zah*
• Gemini	futagoza	*foo-tah-goh-zah*
• Cancer	kaniza	*kah-nee-zah*
• Leo	shishiza	*shee-shee-zah*
• Virgo	otomeza	*oh-toh-meh-zah*
• Libra	tenbinza	*tehn-been-zah*
• Scorpio	sasoriza	*sah-soh-ree-zah*
• Sagittarius	iteza	*ee-teh-zah*
• Capricorn	yagiza	*yah-gee-zah*
• Aquarius	mizugameza	*mee-zoo-gah-meh-zah*
• Pisces	uoza	*oo-oh-zah*

e. EXPRESSING THE DATE

What's today's date?	Kyō wa nannichi desu ka.	*kyoh wah NAHN-nee-chee dehs kah*
• It's October first.	Jūgatsu tsuitachi desu.	*joo-gah-tsoo tsoo-ee-tah-chee dehs*
• It's January second.	Ichigatsu futsuka desu.	*ee-chee-gah-tsoo foo-tsoo-kah dehs*
• It's May third.	Gogatsu mikka desu.	*goh-gah-tsoo meek-kah dehs*
What year is it?	Kotoshi wa nannen desu ka.	*koh-toh-shee wah NAHN-nehn dehs kah*
• It's 1991.	Sen kyūhyaku kyūjū ichi nen desu.	*sehn kyoo-hyahk kyoo-joo ee-chee nehn dehs*

| When were you born? | Itsu umaremashita ka. | *EE-tsoo oo-mah-reh-mahsh-tah kah* |
| I was born in 19... | Sen kyūhyaku ... nen ni umaremashita. | *sehn kyōo-hyahk ... nehn nee oo-mah-reh-mahsh-tah* |

f. IMPORTANT DATES

the New Year	shinnen	*sheen-nehn*
New Year's Day	ganjitsu	*gahn-jee-tsoo*
New Year's Eve	ōmisoka no ban	*oh-mee-soh-kah noh bahn*
National Foundation Day (February 11)	kenkoku kinenbi	*kehn-kohk kee-nehn-bee*
Constitution Day (May 3)	kenpō kinenbi	*kehn-pōh kee-nehn-bee*
Culture Day (November 3)	bunka no hi	*boon-kah noh hee*
Labor Thanksgiving Day (November 23)	kinrō kansha no hi	*keen-rōh kahn-shah noh hee*
Emperor's Birthday (December 23)	tennō tanjōbi	*tehn-nōh tahn-jōh-bee*

6. TALKING ABOUT THE WEATHER

a. GENERAL WEATHER VOCABULARY

air	kūki	*kōo-kee*
atmosphere	taiki	*tah-ee-kee*
• atmospheric conditions	kiatsu	*kee-ah-tsoo*
awful	hidoi (*adj*)	*hee-doh-ee*
• awful weather	hidoi tenki	*hee-doh-ee tehn-kee*
beautiful	subarashii (*adj*)	*soo-bah-rah-shēe*
• beautiful weather	subarashii tenki	*soo-bah-rah-shēe tehn-kee*
clear	harewatatta (*adj*)	*hah-reh-wah-taht-tah*
• The sky is clear.	Kaisei desu.	*kah-ee-sēh dehs*
climate	kikō	*kee-kōh*
• continental	tairikusei noh (*adj*)	*tah-ee-ree-koo-sēh noh*
• dry	kansōshita (*adj*)	*kahn-sōh-shtah*
• humid	shikke ga takai (*adj*)	*sheek-keh gah tah-kah-ee*
• Pacific	taiheiyō no (*adj*)	*tah-ee-heh-yōh noh*
• tropical	nettaisei no (*adj*)	*neht-tah-ee-sēh noh*
cloud	kumo	*koo-moh*

to sit on the fence (*lit.* watch the direction of the cloud moving)	= kumoyuki o miru	*koo-moh-yoo-kee oh mee-roo*

• cloudy	kumotta (*adj*)	*koo-moht-tah*
cold	samui (*adj*)	*sah-moo-ee*
• I am cold.	samui desu.	*sah-moo-ee dehs*
cool	suzushii (*adj*)	*soo-zoo-shee*
dark	kurai (*adj*)	*koo-rah-ee*
• It's dark already.	Mō kurai desu.	*moh koo-rah-ee dehs*
fine	ii (*adj*)	*ee*
• It's fine.	Ii tenki desu.	*ee tehn-kee dehs*
fog	kiri	*kee-ree*
• foggy	kiri noh (*adj*)	*kee-ree noh*
freeze	kōru (*vi*)	*koh-roo*
• frozen	kootta (*adj*)	*koh-oht-tah*
hail	arare	*ah-rah-reh*
• hail	arare ga furu (*vi*)	*ah-rah-reh gah foo-roo*
How's the weather?	Donna tenki desu ka.	*DOHN-nah tehn-kee dehs kah*
• It's a bit cold.	Chotto samui desu.	*choht-toh sah-moo-ee dehs*
• It's a bit hot.	Chotto atsui desu.	*choht-toh ah-tsoo-ee dehs*
• It's awful.	Hidoi tenki desu.	*hee-doh-ee tehn-kee dehs*
• It's beautiful.	Subarashii tenki desu.	*sbah-rah-shee tehn-kee dehs*
• It's cloudy.	Kumori desu.	*koo-moh-ree dehs*
• It's cold.	Samui desu.	*sah-moo-ee dehs*
• It's fine.	Ii tenki desu.	*ee tehn-kee dehs*
• It's foul.	Warui tenki desu.	*wah-roo-ee tehn-kee dehs*
• It's hot.	Atsui desu.	*ah-tsoo-ee dehs*
• It's humid.	Shikke ga takai desu.	*sheek-keh gah tah-kah-ee dehs*
• It's mild.	Atatakai desu.	*ah-tah-tah-kah-ee dehs*
• It's muggy.	Mushiatsui desu.	*moo-shee-ah-tsoo-ee dehs*
• It's pleasant.	Kaiteki desu.	*kah-ee-teh-kee dehs*
• It's raining.	Ame ga futte imasu.	*ah-meh gah foot-teh ee-mahs*
• It's snowing.	Yuki ga futte imasu.	*yoo-kee gah foot-teh ee-mahs*
• It's sunny.	Hi ga tette imasu.	*hee gah teht-teh ee-mahs*
• It's thundering.	Kaminari ga natte imasu.	*kah-mee-nah-ree gah naht-teh ee-mahs*

• It's very cold.	Totemo samui desu.	*toht-teh-moh sah-moo-ee dehs*
• It's very hot.	Totemo atsui desu.	*toht-teh-moh ah-tsoo-ee dehs*
• It's windy.	Kaze ga tsuyoi desu.	*kah-zeh gah tsoo-yoh-ee dehs*
• There's lightning.	Inazuma ga hikatte imasu.	*ee-nah-zoo-mah gah hee-kaht-teh ee-mahs*
humidity	shikke	*sheek-keh*
hurricane	harikēn	*hah-ree-kehn*
ice	kōri	*koh-ree*
light	akari	*ah-kah-ree*
lightning	inazuma	*ee-nah-zoo-mah*
• flash/bolt of lightning	inazuma no hikari	*ee-nah-zoo-mah noh hee-kah-ree*
mild	atatakai (*adj*)	*ah-tah-tah-kah-ee*
moon	tsuki	*tskee*
muggy	mushiatsui (*adj*)	*moo-shee-ah-tsoo-ee*
rain	ame	*ah-meh*
• rain	ame ga furu (*v*)	*ah-meh gah foo-roo*
• It's rainy.	Ame ga futte imasu.	*ah-meh gah foot-teh ee-mahs*
sea	umi	*oo-mee*
shadow/shade	kage	*kah-geh*
sky	sora	*soh-rah*
snow	yuki	*yoo-kee*
• snow	yuki ga furu (*v*)	*yoo-kee gah foo-roo*
star	hoshi	*hoh-shee*
storm	bōfuu	*boo-foo-oo*
sun	taiyō	*tah-ee-yoh*
thunder	kaminari	*kah-mee-nah-ree*
• clap of thunder	raimei	*rah-ee-meh*
• thunder	kaminari ga naru (*v*)	*kah-mee-nah-ree gah nah-roo*

to scold someone severely (*lit*. drop thunder on someone)	= kaminari o otosu	*kah-mee-nah-ree oh oh-toh-soo*

tornado	tatsumaki	*tah-tsoo-mah-kee*
typhoon	taifū	*tah-ee-foo*
weather	tenki	*tehn-kee*
• The weather is beautiful.	Subarashii tenki desu.	*soo-bah-rah-shee tehn-kee dehs*

a fickle person (*lit.* a weather-like person)	= otenkiya	*oh-tehn-kee-yah*
weather permitting (*lit.* if the weather is good)	= tenki ga yokereba	*tehn-kee gah yoh-keh-reh-bah*

wind	kaze	*kah-zeh*
• **be windy**	kaze ga tsuyoi	*kah-zeh gah tsoo-yoh-ee*

b. REACTING TO THE WEATHER

cold	samui (*adj*)	*sah-moo-ee*
• **I am cold.**	Samui desu.	*sah-moo-ee dehs*
have chills	samuke ga suru	*sah-moo-keh gah soo-roo*
• **I have chills.**	Samuke ga shimasu.	*sah-moo-keh gah shee-mahs*
hot	atsui (*adj*)	*ah-tsoo-ee*
• **I am hot.**	Atsui desu.	*ah-tsoo-ee dehs*
I can't stand the cold.	Samusa ni yowai desu.	*sah-moo-sah nee yoh-wah-ee dehs*
I can't stand the heat.	Atsusa ni yowai desu.	*AH-tsoo-sah nee yoh-wah-ee dehs*
I love the cold.	Samui no ga suki desu.	*sah-moo-ee noh gah skee dehs*
I love the heat.	Atsui no ga suki desu.	*ah-tsoo-ee noh gah skee dehs*
perspire	ase o kaku (*v*)	*ah-seh oh kah-koo*
warm up	atatakakunaru (*v*)	*ah-tah-tah-kah-koo-nah-roo*

c. WEATHER-MEASURING INSTRUMENTS AND ACTIVITIES

barometer	kiatsukei	*kee-ahts-keh*
• **barometric pressure**	kiatsu	*kee-ahts*
Celsius	sesshi	*sehs-shee*
centigrade	sesshi	*sehs-shee*
degree	do	*doh*
Fahrenheit	kashi	*kah-shee*
mercury	suigin	*soo-ee-geen*
minus	mainasu	*mah-ee-nahs*
plus	purasu	*poo-rahs*
temperature	kion	*kee-ohn*
• **high**	takai (*adj*)	*tah-kah-ee*
• **low**	hikui (*adj*)	*hee-koo-ee*

• maximum	saiko (no) (*adj*)	*sah-ee-koh (noh)*
• minimum	saitei (no) (*adj*)	*sah-ee-teh (noh)*
thermometer	ondokei	*ohn-doh-keh*
• boiling point	futtōten	*foot-toh-tehn*
• freezing point	hyōten	*hyoh-tehn*
• melting point	yūten	*yoo-tehn*
thermostat	jidō chōon sōchi	*jee-doh choh-ohn soh-chee*
weather forecast	tenki yohō	*tehn-kee yoh-hoh*
weatherman	tenki yohō gakari	*tehn-kee yoh-hoh gah-kah-ree*
zero	reido/hyōten	*reh-doh/hyoh-tehn*
• above zero	reido ijō no	*reh-doh ee-joh noh*
• below zero	hyotenka	*hyoh-tehn-kah*

7. COLORS

a. BASIC COLORS

What color is it?	Nani iro desu ka.	*nah-nee ee-roh dehs kah*
• black	kuro	*koo-roh*
	kuroi (*adj*)	*koo-roh-ee*
• blue	ao	*ah-oh*
	aoi (*adj*)	*ah-oh-ee*
• dark blue	kon	*kohn*
• light blue	akarui ao	*ah-kah-roo-ee ah-oh*
• brown	chairo	*chah-ee-roh*
	chairoi (*adj*)	*chah-ee-roh-ee*
• gold	kin-iro	*keen-ee-roh*
• gray	haiiro/gurē	*hah-ee-ee-roh/goo-reh*
• green	midori iro	*mee-doh-ree ee-roh*
• orange	orenji iro	*oh-rehn-jee ee-roh*
• pink	momoiro/pinku	*moh-moh-ee-roh/peen-koo*
• purple	murasaki iro	*moo-rah-sah-kee ee-roh*
• red	aka	*ah-kah*
	akai (*adj*)	*ah-kah-ee*
• silver	gin-iro	*geen-ee-roh*
• white	shiro	*shee-roh*
	shiroi (*adj*)	*shee-roh-ee*
• yellow	kiiro	*kee-roh*
	kiiroi (*adj*)	*kee-roh-ee*

in the black	= kuroji	*koo-roh-jee*
(*lit.* a black letter)		
in the red	= akaji	*ah-kah-jee*
(*lit.* a red letter)		
an utter stranger	= aka no tanin	*ah-kah noh tah-neen*
(*lit.* a red stranger)		
to be disgraced in public	= akahaji o kaku	*ah-kah-hah-jee oh*
(*lit.* to be put to red		*kah-koo*
shame)		

b. DESCRIBING COLORS

bright	hanayaka na (*adj*)	*hah-nah-yah-kah nah*
dark	koi (*adj*)	*koh-ee*
dull	nibui (*adj*)/shizunda (*adj*)	*nee-boo-ee/shee-zoon-dah*
light	akarui (*adj*)	*ah-kah-roo-ee*
lively	ikiikishita (*adj*)	*ee-kee-ee-kee-shtah*
opaque	futōmei na (*adj*)	*foo-toh-meh nah*
	kusunda (*adj*)	*ksoon-dah*
pale	usui (*adj*)	*oo-soo-ee*
pure	majirike no nai (*adj*)	*mah-jee-ree-keh noh nah-ee*
transparent	tōmei na (*adj*)	*toh-meh nah*
vivid	azayaka na (*adj*)	*ah-zah-yah-kah nah*

c. ADDITIONAL VOCABULARY: COLORS

color	iro	*ee-roh*
• **color**	iro o nuru (*v*)	*ee-roh oh noo-roo*
• **colored**	iro o nutta (*adj*)	*ee-roh oh noot-tah*
• **coloring**	saishoku	*sah-ee-shoh-koo*
• **food coloring**	shokumotsu no	*shoh-koo-moh-tsoo noh*
	chakushokuzai	*chahk-shoh-koo-zah-ee*
crayon	kureyon	*koo-reh-yohn*
felt pen	majikku pen	*mah-jeek-koo pehn*
paint (*art*)	egaku (*v*)	*eh-gah-koo*
paint (*house*)	penki o nuru (*v*)	*pehn-kee oh noo-roo*
painter (*art*)	gaka	*gah-kah*
painter (*house*)	penkiya	*pehn-kee-yah*
pen	pen	*pehn*
tint	iroai	*ee-roh-ah-ee*
• **tint**	iroai o tsukeru (*v*)	*ee-roh-ah-ee oh tskeh-roo*

8. BASIC GRAMMAR

a. GRAMMATICAL TERMS

adjective	keiyōshi	*keh-yoh-shee*
• demonstrative	shiji (*adj*)	*shee-jee*
• descriptive	kijutsu (*adj*)	*kee-joo-tsoo*
• indefinite	futei (*adj*)	*foo-teh*
• interrogative	gimon (*adj*)	*gee-mohn*
• possessive	shoyū (*adj*)	*shoh-yoo*
adverb	fukushi	*fook-shee*
alphabet	arufabetto	*ah-roo-fah-beht-toh*
• accent	akusento	*ahk-sehn-toh*
• consonant	shion	*shee-ohn*
• letter	moji	*moh-jee*
• phonetics	onpyōmoji	*ohn-pyoh-moh-jee*
• pronunciation	hatsuon	*hah-tsoo-ohn*
• vowel	boin	*boh-een*
article	kanshi	*kahn-shee*
• definite	tei (*adj*)	*teh*
• indefinite	futei (*adj*)	*fteh*
case	kaku	*kah-koo*
character	moji	*moh-jee*
• Chinese character	kanji	*kahn-jee*
• Japanese character	kana	*kah-nah*
• phonetic character in words of Japanese origin	hiragana	*hee-rah-gah-nah*
• phonetic character in words of foreign origin	katakana	*kah-tah-kah-nah*
clause	setsu	*seh-tsoo*
• main	shu (*adj*)	*shoo*
• relative	kankei (*adj*)	*kahn-keh*
• subordinate	jūzoku (*adj*)	*joo-zoh-koo*
comparison	hikaku	*hee-kah-koo*
conjunction	setsuzokushi	*sehts-zohk-shee*
counter	mono o kazoeru kotoba	*moh-noh oh kah-zoh-eh-roo koh-toh-bah*
discourse	wahō	*wah-hoh*
• direct	chokusetsu (*adj*)	*chohk-seh-tsoo*
• indirect	kansetsu (*adj*)	*kahn-seh-tsoo*
gender	sei	*seh*
• masculine	dansei	*dahn-seh*
• feminine	josei	*joh-seh*
• neuter	chūsei	*choo-seh*
grammar	bunpō	*boon-poh*

interrogative	gimonshi	*gee-mohn-shee*
mood	dōshi no hō	*dōh-shee noh hoh*
• **conditional mood**	jōkenhō	*joh-kehn-hoh*
• **imperative mood**	meireihō	*meh-reh-hoh*
• **indicative mood**	chokusetsuhō	*chohk-sehts-hoh*
• **subjunctive mood**	kateihō	*kah-teh-hoh*
noun	meishi	*meh-shee*
number	kazu	*kah-zoo*
• **plural number**	fukusū	*fkoo-soo*
• **singular number**	tansū	*tahn-soo*
object	mokutekigo	*mohk-teh-kee-goh*
• **direct**	chokusetsu (*adj*)	*chohk-seh-tsoo*
• **indirect**	kansetsu (*adj*)	*kahn-seh-tsoo*
participle	bunshi	*boon-shee*
• **past**	kako (*adj*)	*kah-koh*
• **present**	genzai (*adj*)	*gehn-zah-ee*
particle	joshi	*joh-shee*
person	ninshō	*neen-shoh*
• **first person**	ichininshō	*ee-chee-neen-shoh*
• **second person**	nininshō	*nee-neen-shoh*
• **third person**	sanninshō	*sahn-neen-shoh*
predicate	jutsubu	*joo-tsoo-boo*
preposition	zenchishi	*zehn-chee-shee*
pronoun	daimeishi	*dah-ee-meh-shee*
• **demonstrative**	shiji (*adj*)	*shee-jee*
• **indefinite**	futei (*adj*)	*foo-teh*
• **interrogative**	gimon (*adj*)	*gee-mohn*
• **personal**	ninshō (*adj*)	*neen-shoh*
• **possessive**	shoyū (*adj*)	*shoh-yoo*
• **reflexive**	saiki (*adj*)	*sah-ee-kee*
• **relative**	kankei (*adj*)	*kahn-keh*
sentence	bun	*boon*
• **affirmative**	kōtei (*adj*)	*koh-teh*
• **declarative**	heijo (*adj*)	*heh-joh*
• **interrogative**	gimon (*adj*)	*gee-mohn*
• **negative**	hitei (*adj*)	*hee-teh*
subject	shugo	*shoo-goh*
tense	jisei	*jee-seh*
• **future**	miraikei	*mee-rah-ee-keh*
• **past**	kakokei	*kah-koh-keh*
• **past perfect**	kakokanryōkei	*kah-koh-kahn-ryoh-keh*
• **past progressive**	kakoshinkōkei	*kah-koh-sheen-koh-keh*
• **present**	genzaikei	*gehn-zah-ee-keh*
• **present perfect**	genzaikanryōkei	*gehn-zah-ee-kahn-ryoh-keh*
• **present progressive**	genzaishinkōkei	*gehn-zah-ee-sheen-koh-keh*
verb	dōshi	*dōh-shee*

• active	nōdōtai no (*adj*)	*noh-doh-tah-ee noh*
• conjugation	dōshi no katsuyō	*doh-shee noh kah-tsoo-yoh*
• gerund	dōmeishi	*doh-meh-shee*
• infinitive	futeishi	*fteh-shee*
• intransitive verb	jidōshi	*jee-doh-shee*
• irregular verb	fukisokudōshi	*fkee-sohk-doh-shee*
• modal	johō no (*adj*)	*joh-hoh noh*
• passive	ukemi no (*adj*)	*oo-keh-mee noh*
• reflexive verb	saikidōshi	*sah-ee-kee-doh-shee*
• regular verb	kisokudōshi	*kee-soh-koo-doh-shee*
• transitive verb	tadōshi	*tah-doh-shee*

b. DEMONSTRATIVE ADJECTIVES

this	kono	*koh-noh*
these	korera no	*koh-reh-rah noh*
that	sono	*soh-noh*
those	sorera no	*soh-reh-rah noh*
that (*over there*)	ano	*ah-noh*
those (*over there*)	arera no	*ah-reh-rah noh*

c. PERSONAL PRONOUNS: SUBJECT

I	watakushi ga/wa	*wah-tahk-shee gah/wah*
you	anata ga/wa	*ah-nah-tah gah/wah*
he	kare ga/wa	*kah-reh gah/wah*
she	kanojo ga/wa	*kah-noh-joh gah/wah*
we	watakushitachi ga/wa	*wah-tahk-shee-tah-chee gah/wah*
you	anatatachi ga/wa	*ah-nah-tah-tah-chee gah/wah*
they (*all male, or male and female*)	karera ga/wa	*kah-reh-rah gah/wah*
they (*all female*)	kanojotachi ga/wa	*kah-noh-joh-tah-chee gah/wah*

d. PERSONAL PRONOUNS: POSSESSIVE

my, mine	watakushi no	*wah-tahk-shee noh*
your, yours	anata no	*ah-nah-tah noh*
his	kare no	*kah-reh noh*
her, hers	kanojo no	*kah-noh-joh noh*
our, ours	watakushitachi no	*wah-tahk-shee-tah-chee noh*
your, yours	anatatachi no	*ah-nah-tah-tah-chee noh*

| **their, theirs** (*all male,* *or male and female*) | karera no | *kah-reh-rah noh* |
| **their, theirs** (*all female*) | kanojotachi no | *kah-noh-joh-tah-chee noh* |

e. PERSONAL PRONOUNS: DIRECT OBJECT

me	watakushi o	*wah-tahk-shee oh*
you	anata o	*ah-nah-tah oh*
him	kare o	*kah-reh oh*
her	kanojo o	*kah-noh-joh oh*
us	watakushitachi o	*wah-tahk-shee-tah-chee oh*
you	anatatachi o	*ah-nah-tah-tah-chee oh*
them (*all male, or male and female*)	karera o	*kah-reh-rah oh*
them (*all female*)	kanojotachi o	*kah-noh-joh-tah-chee oh*

f. PERSONAL PRONOUNS: INDIRECT OBJECT

to me	watakushi ni	*wah-tahk-shee nee*
to you	anata ni	*ah-nah-tah nee*
to him	kare ni	*kah-reh nee*
to her	kanojo ni	*kah-noh-joh nee*
to us	watakushitachi ni	*wah-tahk-shee-tah-chee nee*
to you	anatatachi ni	*ah-nah-tah-tah-chee nee*
to them (*all male, or male and female*)	karera ni	*kah-reh-rah nee*
to them (*all female*)	kanojotachi ni	*kah-noh-joh-tah-chee nee*

g. REFLEXIVE PRONOUNS

myself	watakushi jishin	*wah-tahk-shee jee-sheen*
yourself	anata jishin	*ah-nah-tah jee-sheen*
himself	kare jishin	*kah-reh jee-sheen*
herself	kanojo jishin	*kah-noh-joh jee-sheen*
ourselves	watakushitachi jishin	*wah-tahk-shee-tah-chee jee-sheen*
yourselves	anatatachi jishin	*ah-nah-tah-tah-chee jee-sheen*
themselves (*all male, or male and female*)	karera jishin	*kah-reh-rah jee-sheen*
themselves (*all female*)	kanojotachi jishin	*kah-noh-joh-tah-chee jee-sheen*

The Japanese expression **jibun de** can be considered an all-purpose reflexive pronoun:

one's self	jibun	*jee-boon*
by one's self	jibun de	*jee-boon deh*

Examples:

I'm going myself.	Wakatushi wa, jibun de ikimasu.
She's doing it herself.	Kanojo wa, jibun de shite imasu.
Can you do it yourself?	Jibun de dekimasu ka.

h. INTERROGATIVE PRONOUNS

who	dare ga	*dah-reh gah*
what	nani ga/no/ni	*nah-nee gah/noh/nee*
whom	dare o	*dah-reh oh*
to whom	dare ni	*dah-reh nee*
whose	dare no	*dah-reh noh*
which	dore ga/dono/dore o	*doh-reh gah/doh-noh/ doh-reh oh*

i. OTHER PRONOUNS

all	zenbu	*zehn-boo*
everyone	daremo	*dah-reh-moh*
everything	nandemo mina	*nahn-deh-moh mee-nah*
nobody	daremo ~nai	*dah-reh-moh ~nah-ee*
no one	daremo ~nai	*dah-reh-moh ~nah-ee*
none	daremo ~nai	*dah-reh-moh ~nah-ee*
nothing	nanimo ~nai	*nah-nee-moh ~nah-ee*
one	hito	*hee-toh*
others	hoka no hito	*hoh-kah noh hee-toh*
some (*people*)	aru hito	*ah-roo hee-toh*
someone	dareka	*dah-reh-kah*
something	nanika	*nah-nee-kah*

j. PARTICLES

Japanese contains many particles — short words which are often called postpositions because they come after other words. These particles help to identify the relationship of the words they follow to other important parts of the sentence.

Some particles (such as the following) function as *markers* to identify grammatical elements, while others convey meaning.

wa/ga Subject markers. They occur with words that translate the English subject. More accurately, **wa** is a topic marker, and **ga** is the grammatical subject marker. Sometimes a sentence can have both.

o Direct object marker. Sometimes, for emphasis, **ga** has this function.

ni Indirect object marker

no Possessive marker

ka Question marker

and (*between nouns*)	to	*toh*
at	ni/de	*nee/deh*
by	de	*deh*
by means of	de	*deh*
(direct object marker)	o	*oh*
from	kara	*kah-rah*
in	ni/de	*nee/deh*
(indirect object marker)	ni	*nee*
of, ~'s	no	*noh*
on	ni/de	*nee/deh*
(possessive marker)	no	*noh*
(question marker)	ka	*kah*
(subject marker)	ga/wa	*gah/wah*
(topic marker)	wa	*wah*
to	e/ni/made	*eh/nee/mah-deh*
until	made	*mah-deh*
with	to/de	*toh/deh*

k. CONJUNCTIONS

and (*at the beginning of a sentence*)	soshite	*sohsh-teh*
because	nazenara	*nah-zeh-nah-rah*

but	keredomo	*keh-reh-doh-moh*
	shikashi	*shkah-shee*
furthermore	sonoue	*soh-noh-oo-eh*
however	keredomo	*keh-reh-doh-moh*
	shikashi	*shkah-shee*
or	matawa	*mah-tah-wah*
so, therefore	sorede	*soh-reh-deh*
then	sorekara	*soh-reh-kah-rah*

9. REQUESTING INFORMATION

answer	kotae	*koh-tah-eh*
• answer	kotaeru (*v*)	*koh-tah-eh-roo*
ask someone	dareka ni kiku	*dah-reh-kah nee kee-koo*
ask for	tanomu (*v*)	*tah-noh-moo*
• ask for something	nanika o tanomu	*nah-nee-kah oh tah-noh-moo*
Can you tell me ...?	...o, oshiete moraemasu ka.	*... oh, oh-shee-eh-teh moh-raheh-mahs kah*
How?	Dō yatte. (*inf*)	*doh yaht-teh*
How come?	Naze.	*nah-zeh*
How do you say that in Japanese?	Nihongo de, sore o nan to iimasu ka.	*nee-hohn-goh deh, soh-reh oh NAHN toh ee-mahs kah*
How much?	Dono kurai desu ka.	*doh-noh koo-rah-ee dehs kah*
How much? (*money*)	Ikura desu ka.	*EE-koo-rah dehs kah*
I don't understand.	Wakarimasen.	*wah-kah-ree-mah-sehn*
So?	Sorede.	*soh-reh-DEH*
What?	Nani. (*inf*)	*NAH-nee*
What does it mean?	Sore wa, donna imi desu ka.	*soh-reh wah, DOHN-nah ee-mee dehs kah*
When?	Itsu. (*inf*)	*EE-tsoo*
Where?	Doko. (*inf*)	*DOH-koh*
Which (*one*)?	Dore. (*inf*)	*DOH-reh*
Who?	Dare. (*inf*)	*DAH-reh*
Why?	Naze. (*inf*)	*NAH-zeh*

PEOPLE

---

10. FAMILY AND FRIENDS

a. FAMILY MEMBERS

> Japanese has two sets of words for family members.
>
> One set is used as follows:
>   • talking *about* members of your own family *to* someone outside the family
>
> Another set is used as follows:
>   • talking to members of your own family
>   • talking *about* members of someone else's family
>
> The two sets are given below.

Talking About One's Own Family to Others

aunt	oba	*oh-bah*
brothers	kyōdai	*kyoh-dah-ee*
brothers and sisters (*pl*)	kyōdai to shimai	*kyoh-dah-ee toh shee-mah-ee*
• **brother-in-law** (*spouse's elder brother, or elder sister's husband*)	gikei	*gee-keh*
• **brother-in-law** (*spouse's younger brother, or younger sister's husband*)	gitei	*gee-teh*
• **elder brother**	ani	*AH-nee*
• **younger brother**	otōto	*oh-toh-toh*
cousin	itoko	*ee-toh-koh*
daughter	musume	*moo-soo-meh*
• **daughter-in-law**	musuko no yome	*moos-koh noh yoh-meh*
family	kazoku	*kah-zoh-koo*
• **family relationship**	kazoku kankei	*kah-zoh-koo kahn-keh*
father	chichi	*chee-chee*
• **father-in-law**	gifu	*GEE-foo*
grandchildren	mago	*mah-goh*

grandfather	sofu	*SOH-foo*
grandmother	sobo	*SOH-boh*
husband	otto	*oht-toh*
mother	haha	*hah-hah*
• mother-in-law	gibo	*GEE-boh*
nephew	oi	*oh-ee*
niece	mei	*meh-ee*
parent	oya	*oh-yah*
parents	ryōshin	*ryoh-sheen*
relatives	shinseki	*sheen-seh-kee*
sisters	shimai	*shee-mah-ee*
• sister-in-law (*spouse's* elder sister, or elder brother's wife)	giri no ane	*gee-ree noh ah-neh*
• sister-in-law (*spouse's* younger sister, or younger brother's wife)	giri no imōto	*gee-ree noh ee-moh-toh*
• elder sister	ane	*ah-neh*
• younger sister	imōto	*ee-moh-toh*
son	musuko	*moos-koh*
• son-in-law	musume no otto	*moo-soo-meh noh oht-toh*
twin	futago	*ftah-goh*
uncle	oji	*oh-jee*
wife	tsuma	*tsoo-mah*

Talking to One's Own Family or About Someone Else's Family

aunt	obasan	*oh-bah-sahn*
brothers	gokyōdai	*goh-kyoh-dah-ee*
brothers and sisters (*pl*)	gokyōdai to goshimai	*goh-kyoh-dah-ee toh goh-shee-mah-ee*
• brother-in-law (*spouse's elder brother, or elder sister's husband*)	giri no oniisan	*gee-ree noh oh-nee-sahn*
• brother-in-law (*spouse's younger brother, or younger sister's husband*)	giri no otōtosan	*gee-ree noh oh-toh-toh-sahn*
• elder brother	oniisan	*oh-nee-sahn*
• younger brother	otōtosan	*oh-toh-toh-sahn*
cousin	itokosan	*ee-toh-koh-sahn*
daughter	ojōsan	*oh-joh-sahn*
• daughter-in-law	musukosan no oyomesan	*moos-koh-sahn noh oh-yoh-meh-sahn*
family	gokazoku	*goh-kah-zoh-koo*

• family relationship	gokazoku kankei	goh-kah-zoh-koo kahn-keh
father	otōsan	oh-toh-sahn
• father-in-law	giri no otōsan	gee-ree noh oh-toh-sahn
grandchildren	omagosan	oh-mah-goh-sahn
grandfather	ojiisan	oh-jee-sahn
grandmother	obāsan	oh-bah-sahn
husband	goshujin	goh-shoo-jeen
mother	okāsan	oh-kah-sahn
• mother-in-law	giri no okāsan	gee-ree noh oh-kah-sahn
nephew	oigosan	oh-ee-goh-sahn
niece	meigosan	meh-ee-goh-sahn
parents	goryōshin	goh-ryoh-sheen
relatives	goshinseki	goh-sheen-seh-kee
sisters	goshimai	goh-shee-mah-ee
• sister-in-law (*spouse's elder sister, or elder brother's wife*)	giri no onēsan	gee-ree noh oh-neh-sahn
• sister-in-law (*spouse's younger sister, or younger brother's wife*)	giri no imōtosan	gee-ree noh ee-moh-toh-sahn
• elder sister	onēsan	oh-neh-sahn
• younger sister	imōtosan	ee-moh-toh-sahn
son	musukosan	moos-koh-sahn
• son-in-law	ojōsan no goshujin	oh-joh-sahn noh goh-shoo-jeen
twin	futago	ftah-goh
uncle	ojisan	oh-jee-sahn
wife	okusan	ohk-sahn

b. FRIENDS

acquaintance	chijin	chee-jeen
boyfriend	otoko tomodachi	oh-toh-koh toh-moh-dah-chee
	bōi furendo	boh-ee foo-rehn-doh
chum	nakayoshi	nah-kah-yoh-shee
colleague	dōryō	doh-ryoh
enemy	teki	teh-kee
fiancé	konyakusha	kohn-yahk-shah
fiancée	konyakusha	kohn-yahk-shah
friend	tomodachi	toh-moh-dah-chee
• become friends	tomodachi ni naru (*v*)	toh-moh-dah-chee nee nah-roo
• between friends	tomodachi no aida no/ni/de	toh-moh-dah-chee noh ah-ee-dah noh/nee/deh

• **break off a friendship**	zekkōsuru (v)	*zehk-koh soo-roo*
• **close friend**	shinyū	*sheen-yoo*
• **dear friend**	shinyū	*sheen-yoo*
• **family friend**	kazoku no tomodachi	*kah-zoh-koo noh toh-moh-dah-chee*
• **friendship**	yūkō	*yoo-koh*
girlfriend	onna tomodachi	*ohn-nah toh-moh-dah-chee*
	gāru furendo	*gah-roo foo-rehn-doh*
lover	koibito	*koh-ee-bee-toh*
• **love affair**	renai	*rehn-ah-ee*

11. DESCRIBING PEOPLE

a. GENDER AND APPEARANCE

attractive	miryokuteki na (*adj*)	*mee-ryohk-teh-kee nah*
beautiful	utsukushii (*adj*)	*oots-koo-shee*
• **beauty**	bijin	*bee-jeen*
big	ōkii (*adj*)	*oh-kee*
• **become big**	ōkikunaru (v)	*oh-kee-koo-nah-roo*
• **bigness**	ōkisa	*oh-kee-sah*
blond	kinpatsu no (*adj*)	*keen-pahts noh*
• **blond**	kinpatsu no hito	*keen-pahts noh hee-toh*
body	karada	*kah-rah-dah*
• **bodily physique**	taikaku	*tah-ee-kah-koo*
boy	otoko no ko	*oh-toh-koh noh koh*
clean	kirei na (*adj*)	*kee-reh nah*
	seiketsu na (*adj*)	*seh-kehts nah*
curly-haired	chijirege no (*adj*)	*chee-jee-reh-geh noh*
dark-haired	kuroi kaminoke no (*adj*)	*koo-roh-ee kah-mee-noh-keh noh*
dirty	kitanai (*adj*)	*kee-tah-nah-ee*
elegance	yūga/jōhin	*yoo-gah/joh-heen*
• **elegant**	yūga na/jōhin na (*adj*)	*yoo-gah nah/joh-heen nah*
fat	futotta (*adj*)	*ftoht-tah*
• **become fat**	futoru (v)	*ftoh-roo*
• **obesity**	himan	*hee-mahn*
female	josei	*joh-seh*
• **feminine**	josei no (*adj*)	*joh-seh noh*
• **feminine (womanly)**	joseiteki na (*adj*)	*joh-seh-teh-kee nah*
gentleman	shinshi	*sheen-shee*
girl	onna no ko	*ohn-nah noh koh*
handsome (*masculine*)	hansamu na (*adj*)	*hahn-sah-moo nah*
health	kenkō	*kehn-koh*
• **healthy**	kenkōteki na (*adj*)	*kehn-koh-teh-kee nah*

height	se no takasa	*seh noh tah-kah-sah*
• **How tall are you?**	Anato no se no takasa wa, dono kurai desu ka.	*Ah-nah-tah noh SEH noh tah-kah-sah wah, doh-noh koo-rah-ee dehs kah*
• **I am … tall.**	Watakushi no se no takasa wa, … desu.	*Wah-tahk-shee noh SEH no tah-kah-sah wah, … dehs*
• **medium (average) height**	chūgurai no se no takasa	*choo-goo-rah-ee noh seh noh tah-kah-sah*
• **short**	se ga hikui	*seh gah hee-koo-ee*
• **tall**	se ga takai	*seh gah tah-kah-ee*
lady	fujin	*foo-jeen*
large	ōkii (*adj*)	*oh-kee*
male	dansei	*dahn-seh*
• **masculine**	dansei no (*adj*)	*dahn-seh noh*
• **virile**	danseiteki na (*adj*)	*dahn-seh-teh-kee nah*
man	dansei	*dahn-seh*
• **young man**	wakamono	*wah-kah-moh-noh*
red-haired	akai kaminoke no (*adj*)	*ah-kah-ee kah-mee-noh-keh noh*
sex	sei	*seh*
sick	byōki no (*adj*)	*byoh-kee noh*
• **become sick**	byōki ni naru (*v*)	*byoh-kee nee nah-roo*
• **sickness**	byōki	*byoh-kee*
small, little	chiisai (*adj*)	*chee-sah-ee*
strength	chikara/tsuyosa	*chee-kah-rah/tsyoh-sah*
• **strong**	tsuyoi (*adj*)	*tsyoh-ee*
weak	yowayowashii (*adj*)	*yoh-wah-yoh-wah-shee*
• **weakness**	yowayowashisa	*yoh-wah-yoh-wah-shsah*
• **become weak**	yowakunaru (*v*)	*yoh-wah-koo-nah-roo*
weight	omosa	*oh-moh-sah*
• **heavy**	omoi (*adj*)	*oh-moh-ee*
• **How much do you weigh?**	Anata no taijū wa, dono kurai desu ka.	*ah-nah-tah noh tah-ee-joo wah, doh-noh koo-rah-ee dehs kah*
• **I weigh …**	Watakushi no mekata wa, … desu.	*wah-tahk-shee noh meh-kah-tah wah, … dehs*
• **light**	karui (*adj*)	*kah-roo-ee*
• **lose weight**	yaseru (*v*)	*yah-seh-roo*
• **skinny, thin**	yaseta (*adj*)	*yah-seh-tah*
• **slim, slender**	hossorishita (*adj*)	*hohs-soh-ree-shtah*
• **weigh oneself**	jibun no taijū o hakaru	*jee-boon noh tah-ee-joo oh hah-kah-roo*
woman	josei	*joh-seh*

b. CONCEPTS OF AGE

adolescence	shishunki	*shee-shoon-kee*
• adolescent	shishunki no (*adj*)	*shee-shoon-kee noh*
• teenager	tīnējā	*teen-eh-jah*
adult	otona	*oh-toh-nah*
age	toshi/nenrei	*toh-shee/nehn-reh*
• age	toshitoru (*v*)	*tohsh-toh-roo*
baby	akachan	*ah-kah-chahn*
child	kodomo	*koh-doh-moh*
elderly person	nenpai no hito	*nehn-pah-ee noh hee-toh*
• have white hair	shiraga ga aru	*shee-rah-gah gah ah-roo*
grow up	sodatsu (*vi*)	*soh-dah-tsoo*
old	toshitotta (*adj*)	*tohsh-toht-tah*
• become old	toshitoru (*v*)	*tohsh-toh-roo*
• old age	rōgo	*roh-goh*
• older	toshiue no (*adj*)	*toh-shee-oo-eh noh*
• older brother	ani	*AH-nee*
• older sister	ane	*ah-neh*
• How old are you?	Toshi wa, ikutsu desu ka.	*toh-shee wah, EE-koots dehs kah*
• I am … old.	… sai desu.	*… sah-ee dehs*
young	wakai (*adj*)	*wah-kah-ee*
• younger	toshishita no (*adj*)	*toh-shee-shtah noh*
• younger brother	otōto	*oh-toh-toh*
• younger sister	imōto	*ee-moh-toh*
• youth	seinen jidai	*seh-nehn jee-dah-ee*
• youthful	wakawakashii (*adj*)	*wah-kah-wah-kah-shee*

c. MARRIAGE AND THE HUMAN LIFE CYCLE

anniversary	kekkon kinenbi	*kehk-kohn kee-nehn-bee*
• diamond anniversary	kekkon nanajūgoshūnen kinenbi	*kehk-kohn nah-nah-joo-goh-shoo-nehn kee-nehn-bee*
• golden anniversary	kekkon gojusshūnen kinenbi	*kehk-kohn goh-joos-shoo-nehn kee-nehn-bee*
• silver anniversary	kekkon nijūgoshūnen kinenbi	*kehk-kohn nee-joo-goh-shoo-nehn kee-nehn-bee*
bachelor	dokushin	*dohk-sheen*
birth	tanjō	*tahn-joh*
• birthday	tanjōbi	*tahn-joh-bee*
• celebrate one's birthday	tanjōbi o iwau	*tahn-joh-bee oh ee-wah-oo*
• Happy birthday!	Tanjōbi omedetō.	*tahn-joh-bee oh-meh-deh-toh*

• be born	umareru (*v*)	*oo-mah-reh-roo*
• I was born on ...	Watakushi wa, ... ni umaremashita.	*wah-tahk-shee wah, ... nee oo-mah-reh-mahsh-tah*
bride	hanayome	*hah-nah-yoh-meh*
death	shi	*shee*
	shibō	*shee-boh*
• die	shinu (*v*)	*shee-noo*
• die	nakunaru (*v, pol*)	*nah-koo-nah-roo*
divorce	rikon	*ree-kohn*
• divorce	rikonsuru (*v*)	*ree-kohn-soo-roo*
• divorced	rikonshita (*adj*)	*ree-kohn-shtah*
engagement	konyaku	*kohn-yah-koo*
• become engaged	konyakusuru (*v*)	*kohn-yahk-soo-roo*
• engaged	konyakushita (*adj*)	*kohn-yahk-shtah*
fiancé	konyakusha	*kohn-yahk-shah*
fiancée	konyakusha	*kohn-yahk-shah*
get used to	nareru (*v*)	*nah-reh-roo*
gift	okurimono	*oh-koo-ree-moh-noh*
• give a gift	okurimono o ageru	*oh-koo-ree-moh-noh oh ah-geh-roo*
go to school	gakkō ni iku	*gahk-koh nee ee-koo*
groom (bridegroom)	hanamuko	*hah-nah-moo-koh*
heredity	iden	*ee-dehn*
• inherit	iden de uketsugu (*v*)	*ee-dehn deh oo-keh-tsoo-goo*
honeymoon	shinkonryokō	*sheen-kohn-ryoh-koh*
husband	otto	*oht-toh*
kiss	seppun, kisu	*sehp-poon, kees*
• kiss	kisusuru (*v*)	*kees-soo-roo*
	seppunsuru (*v*)	*sehp-poon-soo-roo*
life	jinsei	*jeen-seh*
• live	sumu (*v*)	*soo-moo*
love	ai	*ah-ee*
• love	aisuru (*v*)	*ah-ee-soo-roo*
• fall in love	sukininaru (*v*)	*skee-nee-nah-roo*
• in love	renai chū	*rehn-ah-ee choh*
marital status	kekkon shikaku	*kehk-kohn shee-kah-koo*
marriage, matrimony	kekkon	*kehk-kohn*
• get married	kekkonsuru (*v*)	*kehk-kohn-soo-roo*
• married	kikon no (*adj*)	*kee-kohn noh*
• (to) marry (*someone*)	to kekkonsuru (*v*)	*toh kehk-kohn soo-roo*
• unmarried	mikon no (*adj*)	*mee-kohn noh*
newlyweds	shinkon fusai	*sheen-kohn fsah-ee*
pregnancy	ninshin	*neen-sheen*
• be pregnant	ninshin chū desu	*neen-sheen choh dehs*
• give birth	umu (*v*)	*oo-moo*

• **have a baby**	kodomo ga umareru	*koh-doh-moh gah oo-mah-reh-roo*
raise (*someone*)	sodateru (*v*)	*soh-dah-teh-roo*
reception (wedding)	hiröen	*hee-roh-ehn*
separation	bekkyo	*behk-kyoh*
• **separate**	bekkyosuru (*v*)	*behk-kyoh-soo-roo*
• **separated**	bekkyoshita (*adj*)	*behk-kyoh-shtah*
spouse	haigūsha	*hah-ee-gōo-shah*
wedding	kekkonshiki	*kehk-kohn-shkee*
• **wedding invitation**	kekkonshiki e no shōtai	*kehk-kohn-shkee eh noh shoh-tah-ee*
• **wedding ring**	kekkon yubiwa	*kehk-khon yoo-bee-wah*
widow	mibōjin	*mee-bōh-jeen*
widower	yamome	*yah-moh-meh*
wife	tsuma	*tsmah*

d. RELIGION AND RACE

agnosticism	fukachiron	*foo-kah-chee-rohn*
• **agnostic**	fukachiron no (*adj*)	*foo-kah-chee-rohn noh*
Arab	Arabiajin	*ah-rah-bee-ah-jeen*
archbishop	daishikyō	*dah-ee-shkyoh*
atheism	mushinron	*moo-sheen-rohn*
• **atheist**	mushinronsha	*moo-sheen-rohn-shah*
baptism	senrei	*sehn-rēh*
belief	shinnen	*sheen-nehn*
• **believe**	shinjiru (*v*)	*sheen-jee-roo*
• **believe in**	shinjiru (*v*)	*sheen-jee-roo*
• **believer**	shinja	*sheen-jah*
bishop	shikyo	*shee-kyoh*
black	kokujin	*koh-koo-jeen*
Buddhism	bukkyō	*book-kyoh*
• **Buddhist**	bukkyō no shinja	*book-kyōh noh sheen-jah*
• **Buddhist**	bukkyō no (*adj*)	*book-kyoh noh*
• **Buddhist priest**	obōsan	*oh-bōh-sahn*
• **Bhuddist temple**	otera	*oh-teh-rah*
catechism	kōkyōyori	*koh-kyoh-yoh-ree*
Catholic	katorikkukyōto	*kah-toh-reek-koo-kyōh-toh*
	katorikkukyō no (*adj*)	*kah-toh-reek-koo-kyōh noh*
• **Catholicism**	katorikkukyō shinkō	*kah-toh-reek-koo-kyōh sheen-kōh*
Christian	kirisutokyōto	*kee-rees-toh-kyōh-toh*
• **Christianity**	kirisutokyō	*kee-rees-toh-kyōh*
church	kyōkai	*kyōh-kah-ee*
confirmation	kenshinrei	*kehn-sheen-rēh*
Confucianism	jukyō	*joo-kyoh*

• Confucian	jusha	*joo-shah*
faith	shinkō	*sheen-koh*
• faithful	shinkōshin ga atsui (*adj*)	*sheen-koh-sheen gah ah-tsoo-ee*
God	kamisama	*kah-mee-sah-mah*
Hebrew, Jewish	Yudayajin no (*adj*)	*yoo-dah-yah-jeen noh*
Hindu	Hinzūkyōto	*heen-zoo-kyoh-toh*
human	ningen no (*adj*)	*neen-gehn noh*
• human being	ningen	*neen-gehn*
• humanity	ningensei	*neen-gehn-seh*
Islam (*religion*)	kaikyō	*kah-ee-kyoh*
• Islamic	kaikyō no (*adj*)	*kah-ee-kyoh noh*
• Muslim (Moslem)	kaikyōto	*kah-ee-kyoh-toh*
Judaism	Yudayakyō	*yoo-dah-yah-kyoh*
• Jew	Yudayajin	*yoo-dah-yah-jeen*
• Jewish	Yudayajin no (*adj*)	*yoo-dah-yah-jeen noh*
lay person	hirashinto	*hee-rah-sheen-toh*
• laity	hirashinto	*hee-rah-sheen-toh*
Mass	misa	*mee-sah*
minister	bokushi	*bohk-shee*
monk	shūdōshi	*shoo-doh-shee*
mosque	mosuku	*mohs-koo*
myth	shinwa	*sheen-wah*
nun	nisō	*nee-soh*
Occidental	seiōjin	*seh-oh-jeen*
Oriental	Ajiajin	*ah-jee-ah-jeen*
Orthodox	Girishaseikyō no (*adj*)	*gee-ree-shah seh-kyoh noh*
pagan	ikyōto	*ee-kyoh-toh*
pray	oinorisuru (*v*)	*oh-ee-noh-ree-soo-roo*
• prayer	oinori	*oh-ee-noh-ree*
priest	seishokusha	*seh-shohk-shah*
Protestant	shinkyōto	*sheen-kyoh-toh*
• Protestantism	shinkyō	*sheen-kyoh*
rabbi	Yudayakyō no rippō hakase	*yoo-dah-yah-kyoh noh reep-poh-hah-kah-seh*
race	minzoku	*meen-zoh-koo*
religion	shūkyō	*shoo-kyoh*
• religious	shinkōbukai (*adj*)	*sheen-koh-boo-kah-ee*
ritual	gishiki	*geesh-kee*
Shintoism	shintō	*sheen-toh*
• Shintoist	shintō no shinja	*sheen-toh noh sheen-jah*
• Shinto priest	kannushi	*kahn-noo-shee*
• Shinto shrine	jinja	*jeen-jah*
soul	tamashii	*tah-mah-shee*
spirit	seishin	*seh-sheen*
• spiritual	seishinteki (*adj*)	*seh-sheen-teh-kee*
synagogue	Yudayakyō jiin	*yoo-dah-yah-kyoh jee-een*

temple	jiin	*jee-een*
western	seiō no (*adj*)	*seh-oh noh*
Zen Buddhism	zenshū	*zehn-shoo*

e. CHARACTERISTICS AND SOCIAL TRAITS

active	katsudōteki na (*adj*)	*kah-tsoo-doh-teh-kee nah*
• activity	katsudō	*kah-tsoo-doh*
adapt	tekigōsaseru (*vt*)	*teh-kee-goh-sah-seh-roo*
• adaptable	tekigōsei ga aru (*adj*)	*teh-kee-goh-seh gah ah-roo*
affection	aijō	*ah-ee-joh*
• affectionate	aijō no fukai (*adj*)	*ah-ee-joh noh fkah-ee*
aggressive	kōgekiteki na (*adj*)	*koh-geh-kee-teh-kee nah*
• aggressiveness	kōgekisei	*koh-geh-kee-seh*
altruism	aitashugi	*ah-ee-tah-shoo-gee*
• altruistic	aitateki na (*adj*)	*ah-ee-tah-teh-kee nah*
• altruist	aitashugisha	*ah-ee-tah-shoo-gee-shah*
ambition	taibō	*tah-ee-boh*
• ambitious	nozomi ga takai (*adj*)	*noh-zoh-mee gah tah-kah-ee*
anger	ikari	*ee-kah-ree*
• angry	okotta (*adj*)	*oh-koht-tah*
• become angry	okoru (*v*)	*oh-koh-roo*
anxious	shinpai na (*adj*)	*sheen-pah-ee nah*
• anxiety	fuankan	*foo-ahn-kahn*
arrogance	gōman	*goh-mahn*
• arrogant	gōman na (*adj*)	*goh-mahn nah*
artistic	geijutsuteki na (*adj*)	*geh-joo-tsoo-teh-kee nah*
astute	kibin na (*adj*)	*kee-been nah*
• astuteness	kibinsa	*kee-been-sah*
attractive	miryokuteki na (*adj*)	*mee-ryohk-teh-kee nah*
avarice, greed	donyoku	*dohn-yoh-koo*
• avaricious, greedy	yoku no fukai (*adj*)	*yoh-koo noh fkah-ee*
bad	warui (*adj*)	*wah-roo-ee*
brash	sekkachi na (*adj*)	*sehk-kah-chee nah*
brilliant	sainō ni michita (*adj*)	*sah-ee-noh nee mee-chee-tah*
calm	odayaka na (*adj*)	*oh-dah-yah-kah nah*
• calmness	odayakasa	*oh-dah-yah-kah-suh*
character	seikaku	*seh-kah-koo*
• characteristic	dokutoku na (*adj*)	*dohk-tohk nah*
• characterize	seikakuzukeru (*v*)	*seh-kah-koo-zoo-keh-roo*
clever	kenmei na (*adj*)	*kehn-meh nah*
conformist	junnōsha	*joon-noh-shah*
• nonconformist	hijunnōsha	*hee-joon-noh-shah*

conscience	ryōshin	ryoh-sheen
• conscientious	ryōshinteki na (adj)	ryoh-sheen-teh-kee nah
conservative	hoshuteki na (adj)	hoh-shoo-teh-kee nah
courage	yūki	yoo-kee
• courageous	yūki ga aru (adj)	yoo-kee gah ah-roo
courteous	reigi tadashii (adj)	reh-gee tah-dah-shee
• courtesy	reigi	reh-gee
• discourteous	shitsurei na (adj)	shtsoo-reh nah
creative	sōzōteki na (adj)	soh-zoh-teh-kee nah
critical	hihanteki na (adj)	hee-hahn-teh-kee nah
cry	naku (v)	nah-koo
cultured	kyōyō no aru (adj)	kyoh-yoh noh ah-roo
curiosity	kōkishin	koh-kee-sheen
• curious	kōkishin no tsuyoi (adj)	koh-kee-sheen noh tsoo-yoh-ee
delicate	sensai na (adj)	sehn-sah-ee nah
diligence	kinben	keen-behn
• diligent, hard-working	kinben na (adj)	keen-behn nah
diplomatic	gaikōteki na (adj)	gah-ee-koh-teh-kee nah
dishonest	fushōjiki na (adj)	fshoh-jee-kee nah
• dishonesty	fushōjiki	fshoh-jee-kee
dynamic	seiryokuteki na (adj)	seh-ryohk-teh-kee nah
eccentric	fūgawari na (adj)	foo-gah-wah-ree nah
egoism	rikoshugi	ree-koh-shoo-gee
• egoist	rikoshugisha	ree-koh-shoo-gee-shah
• egoistic	rikoteki na (adj)	ree-koh-teh-kee nah
eloquence	yūben	yoo-behn
• eloquent	yūben na (adj)	yoo-behn nah
energetic	enerugisshu na (adj)	eh-neh-roo-gees-shoo nah
• energy	enerugī	eh-neh-roo-gee
envious	urayamashii (adj)	oo-rah-yah-mah-shee
• envy	urayamu (v)	oo-rah-yah-moo
faithful	chūjitsu na (adj)	choo-jee-tsoo nah
fascinate	miwakusuru (vt)	mee-wahk-soo-roo
• fascinating	miwakuteki na (adj)	mee-wahk-teh-kee nah
• fascination	miwaku	mee-wah-koo
fool	bakamono	bah-kah-moh-noh
• foolish, silly	bakageta (adj)	bah-kah-geh-tah
friendly	shitashige na (adj)	shtah-shee-geh nah
funny	omoshiroi (adj)	oh-moh-shee-roh-ee
fussy	kourusai (adj)	koh-oo-roo-sah-ee
generosity	kandaisa	kahn-dah-ee-sah
• generous	kandai na (adj)	kahn-dah-ee nah
gentle	yasashii (adj)	yah-sah-shee
good	ii (adj)	ee
• goodness	zenryōsa	zehn-ryoh-sah
good at (something)	jōzu na (adj)	joh-zoo nah

graceful	yūga na (*adj*)	*yōo-gah nah*
habit	shūkan	*shōo-kahn*
happiness	shiawase	*shee-ah-wah-seh*
• happy	shiawase na (*adj*)	*shee-ah-wah-seh nah*
hate	ken-o	*kehn-oh*
• hate	totemo kirau (*v*)	*toh-teh-moh kee-rah-oo*
• hateful	iya na (*adj*)	*ee-yah nah*
honest	shōjiki na (*adj*)	*shoh-jee-kee nah*
• honesty	shōjikisa	*shoh-jee-kee-sah*
humanitarian	jindōshugi no (*adj*)	*jeen-dōh-shoo-gee noh*
humble	hikaeme na (*adj*)	*hee-kah-eh-meh nah*
• humility	kenson	*kehn-sohn*
humor	yūmoa	*yōo-moh-ah*
• humorous	kokkei na (*adj*)	*kohk-keh nah*
• sense of humor	yūmoa no kankaku	*yōo-moh-ah noh kahn-kah-koo*
idealism	risōshugi	*ree-sōh-shoo-gee*
• idealist	risōshugisha	*ree-sōh-shoo-gee-shah*
• idealistic	risōshugiteki na (*adj*)	*ree-sōh-shoo-gee-teh-kee nah*
imagination	sōzōryoku	*soh-zōh-ryoh-koo*
• imaginative	sōzōryoku ni tonda (*adj*)	*soh-zōh-ryoh-koo nee tohn-dah*
impudence	atsukamashisa	*ahts-kah-mah-shsah*
• impudent	atsukamashii (*adj*)	*ahts-kah-mah-shēe*
impulse	shōdō	*shoh-dōh*
• impulsive	shōdōteki na (*adj*)	*shoh-dōh-teh-kee nah*
independent	jishuteki na (*adj*)	*jee-shoo-teh-kee nah*
individualist	kojinshugisha	*koh-jeen-shoo-gee-shah*
ingenious	dokusōteki na (*adj*)	*dohk-sōh-teh-kee nah*
• ingenuity	dokusōsei	*dohk-sōh-seh*
innocence	mujaki	*moo-jah-kee*
• innocent	mujaki na (*adj*)	*moo-jah-kee nah*
insolence	ōhei	*ōh-heh*
• insolent	ōhei na (*adj*)	*ōh-heh nah*
intellectual	chishikijin	*chee-shee-kee-jeen*
	chiteki na (*adj*)	*chee-teh-kee nah*
intelligence	chisei	*chee-seh*
• intelligent	chiseiteki na (*adj*)	*chee-seh-teh-kee nah*
irascible	okorippoi (*adj*)	*oh-koh-reep-poh-ee*
irony	hiniku	*hee-nee-koo*
• ironical	hiniku na (*adj*)	*hee-nee-koo nah*
irritable	tanki na (*adj*)	*tahn-kee nah*
jealous	shittobukai (*adj*)	*sheet-toh-boo-kah-ee*
• jealousy	shitto	*sheet-toh*
kind	shinsetsu na (*adj*)	*sheen-seh-tsoo nah*
• kindness	shinsetsu	*sheen-seh-tsoo*

laugh	warau (v)	wah-rah-oo
• laughter	waraigoe	wah-rah-ee-goh-eh
laziness	bushō	boo-shōh
• lazy	bushō na (adj)	boo-shōh nah
liberal	kakushinshugisha	kahk-sheen-shoo-gee-shah
	kakushinteki na (adj)	kahk-sheen-teh-kee nah
lively	ikiikishita (adj)	ee-kee-ee-kee-shtah
	ikiikito (adv)	ee-kee-ee-kee-toh
love	ai	ah-ee
• love	aisuru (v)	ah-ee-soo-roo
• lovable	airashii (adj)	ah-ee-rah-shēe
madness	kyōki	kyōh-kee
• crazy, mad	kichigaijimita (adj)	kee-chee-gah-ee-jee-mee-tah
malicious	akui ni michita (adj)	ah-koo-ee nee mee-chee-tah
mischievous	itazurazuki na (adj)	ee-tah-zoo-rah-zoo-kee nah
mood	kigen	kee-gehn
• be in a good mood	kigen ga ii	kee-gehn gah ēe
• be in a bad mood	kigen ga warui	kee-gehn gah wah-roo-ee
neat	sapparishaita (adj)	sahp-pah-ree-shtah
nice	ii (adj)	ēe
not nice, odious	iya na (adj)	ee-yah nah
obstinate	gōjō na (adj)	goh-jōh nah
optimism	rakutenshugi	rahk-tehn-shoo-gee
• optimist	rakutenshugisha	rahk-tehn-shoo-gee-shah
• optimistic	rakutenteki na (adj)	rahk-tehn-teh-kee nah
original	sōsakuteki na (adj)	soh-sahk-teh-kee nah
patience	nintai	neen-tah-ee
• patient	nintaizuyoi (adj)	neen-tah-ee-zoo-yoh-ee
• impatient	kimijika na (adj)	kee-mee-jee-kah nah
perfection	kanzen	kahn-zehn
• perfectionist	kanzenshugisha	kahn-zehn-shoo-gee-shah
personality	seikaku	sēh-kah-koo
pessimism	hikanshugi	hee-kahn-shoo-gee
• pessimist	hikanshugisha	hee-kahn-shoo-gee-shah
• pessimistic	hikanteki na (adj)	hee-kahn-teh-kee nah
picky	kuchiyakamashii (adj)	koo-chee-yah-kah-mah-shēe
pleasant, likeable	tanoshii (adj)	tah-noh-shēe
• like	konomu (v)	koh-noh-moo
poor	misuborashii (adj)	mee-soo-boh-rah-shēe
possessive	shoyūyoku ga tsuyoi (adj)	shoh-yōo-yoh-koo gah tsoo-yoh-ee
presumptuous	buenryo na (adj)	boo-ehn-ryoh nah
pretentious	mie o hatta (adj)	mee-eh oh haht-tah
proud	hokori no takai (adj)	hoh-koh-ree noh tah-kah-ee

prudent	shinchō na (*adj*)	*sheen-chōh nah*
rebellious	hankōteki na (*adj*)	*hahn-kōh-teh-kee nah*
refined	jōhin na (*adj*)	*jōh-heen nah*
reserved	uchiki na (*adj*)	*oo-chee-kee nah*
restless	ochitsukanai (*adj*)	*oh-chee-tskah-nah-ee*
rich	yūfuku na (*adj*)	*yōō-fkoo nah*
romantic	romanchikku na (*adj*)	*roh-mahn-cheek-koo nah*
rough	soya na (*adj*)	*soh-yah nah*
rude	burei na (*adj*)	*boo-rēh nah*
sad	kanashige na (*adj*)	*kah-nah-shee-geh nah*
• sadness	kanashimi	*kah-nah-shee-mee*
sarcasm	hiniku	*hee-nee-koo*
• sarcastic	hiniku na (*adj*)	*hee-nee-koo nah*
seduction	yūwaku	*yōō-wah-koo*
• seductive	miwakuteki na (*adj*)	*mee-wahk-teh-kee nah*
self-sufficient	jiritsu shiteiru (*adj*)	*jee-ree-tsoo shteh-ee-roo*
sensitive	binkan na (*adj*)	*been-kahn nah*
sentimental	kanshōteki na (*adj*)	*kahn-shōh-teh-kee nah*
serious	majime na (*adj*)	*mah-jee-meh nah*
shrewd	nukemenonai (*adj*)	*noo-keh-meh-noh-nah-ee*
• shrewdness	nukemenasa	*noo-keh-meh-nah-sah*
shy	uchiki na (*adj*)	*oo-chee-kee nah*
simple	tanjun na (*adj*)	*tahn-joon nah*
sincere	seijitsu na (*adj*)	*sēh-jee-tsoo nah*
• sincerity	seijitsusa	*sēh-jee-tsoo-sah*
sloppy, disorganized	darashinai (*adj*)	*dah-rah-shee-nah-ee*
smart	rikō na (*adj*)	*ree-kōh nah*
smile	hohoemi	*hoh-hoh-eh-mee*
• smile	hohoemu (*v*)	*hoh-hoh-eh-moo*
snobbish	kidotta (*adj*)	*kee-doht-tah*
stingy	kechi na (*adj*)	*keh-chee nah*
strong	takumashii (*adj*)	*tahk-mah-shēē*
stubborn	ganko na (*adj*)	*gahn-koh nah*
stupid	oroka na (*adj*)	*oh-roh-kah nah*
superstitious	meishinbukai (*adj*)	*mēh-sheen-boo-kah-ee*
sweet	yasashii (*adj*)	*yah-sah-shēē*
traditional	dentōteki na (*adj*)	*dehn-tōh-teh-kee nah*
tricky	zurugashikoi (*adj*)	*zoo-roo-gah-shee-koh-ee*
troublemaker	monchaku o okosu hito	*mohn-chah-koo oh oh-kohs hee-toh*
vain	mieppari no (*adj*)	*mee-ehp-pah-ree noh*
versatile	tagei na (*adj*)	*tah-gēh nah*
vulnerable	kizutsukiyasui (*adj*)	*kee-zoo-tskee-yah-soo-ee*
weak	yowayowashii (*adj*)	*yoh-wah-yoh-wah-shēē*
well-mannered	reigitadashii (*adj*)	*rēh-gee-tah-dah-shēē*
willingly	kokoroyoku (*adv*)	*koh-koh-roh-yoh-koo*
wisdom	kenmei	*kehn-mēh*

| • wise | kenmei na *(adj)* | *kehn-meh nah* |

f. BASIC PERSONAL INFORMATION

> For jobs and professions see Section 38.

address	jūsho	*joo-shoh*
• avenue	gai	*gah-ee*
• city	shi	*shee*
• country	kuni	*koo-nee*
• Metropolis	to	*toh*
• prefecture	ken	*kehn*
• square	hiroba	*hee-roh-bah*
• state	shū	*shoo*
• street	tōri	*toh-ree*
• town	machi	*mah-chee*
• ward	ku	*koo*
• live	sumu *(v)*	*soo-moo*
• Where do you live?	Doko ni osumai desu ka.	*DOH-koh nee oh-soo-mah-ee dehs kah*
• I live ...	... ni sunde imasu	*... nee soon-deh ee-mahs*
be from ...	... kara kimashita	*... kah-rah kee-mah-shtah*
career	keireki	*keh-reh-kee*
date of birth	seinengappi	*seh-nehn-gahp-pee*
education	kyōiku	*kyoh-ee-koo*
• go to school	gakkō ni iku	*gahk-koh nee ee-koo*
• finish school	gakkō o oeru	*gahk-koh oh oh-eh-roo*
• elementary school	shōgakkō	*shoh-gahk-koh*
• junior high school	chūgaku	*choo-gah-koo*
• high school	kōkō	*koh-koh*
• junior college	tandai	*tahn-dah-ee*
• university	daigaku	*dah-ee-gah-koo*
• graduate school	daigakuin	*dah-ee-gah-koo-een*
• university degree	gakushigō	*gahk-shee-goh*
• diploma	sotsugyōshōsho	*soh-tsoo-gyoh-shoh-shoh*
• graduate	sotsugyōsei	*soh-tsoo-gyoh-seh*
• graduate	sotsugyōsuru *(v)*	*soh-tsoo-gyoh-soo-roo*
employment	koyō	*koh-yoh*
• employer	koyōsha	*koh-yoh-shah*
• employee	jūgyōin	*joo-gyoh-een*
fax number	fakkusu bangō	*fahk-koos bahn-goh*
identification	mibunshōmei	*mee-boon-shoh-meh*
job	shigoto	*shee-goh-toh*

married	kikon no (*adj*)	*kee-kohn noh*
name	namae	*nah-mah-eh*
• first name	namae	*nah-mah-eh*
• family name	myōji	*myōh-jee*
• surname	myōji	*myōh-jee*
• be called	yobareru (*v*)	*yoh-bah-reh-roo*
• How do you write your name?	Onamae wa, dō kakimasu ka.	*oh-nah-mah-eh wah, DŌH kah-kee-mahs kah*
• Print your name.	Onamae o, kaisho de kaite kudasai.	*oh-nah-mah-eh oh, kah-ee-shoh deh kah-ee-teh koo-dah-sah-ee*
• What's your name?	Onamae wa, nan desu ka.	*oh-nah-mah-eh wah NAHN dehs kah*
• My name is ...	Watakushi no namae wa, ... desu.	*wah-tahk-shee noh nah-mah-eh wah, ... dehs*
• sign	shomeisuru (*v*)	*shoh-meh-soo-roo*
• signature	shomei	*shoh-meh*

FOCUS: *Names and Titles*

Japanese use family names first, first names last.
Yamada Taro is Mr. Yamada. Taro is his first name. When Japanese introduce themselves to each other, they say the family name first.

Japanese prefer family names, not first names.
Japanese adults rarely use first names. Even among close friends, family names are the rule, first names the exception.

Japanese use titles with names.
When speaking to someone or when referring to another person, Japanese use **san** after the family name. It's like the English Mr., Mrs., Ms., or Miss. Even when using a friend's first name, they add **san**. For example, if they were using Yamada san's first name, people would say "Taro san," not "Taro." **San** is never used to refer to oneself.

Japanese use young children's first names followed by **chan**, older children's names followed by **san**.

Japanese use the word "teacher" for people other than teachers.
Teachers are called **sensei**, a term of respect. It's also used for people with profound knowledge, exceptional skill, or a certain social status. For example, doctors, dentists, artists, congressmen, and celebrities are also addressed as **sensei**.

nationality	kokuseki	*kohk-seh-kee*
place of birth	shusseichi	*shoos-seh-chee*
place of employment	koyōsaki	*koh-yoh-sah-kee*
profession	shokugyō	*shoh-koo-gyoh*
• **professional**	senmonteki na (*adj*)	*sehn-mohn-teh-kee nah*
residence	jūsho	*joo-shoh*
single	mikon no (*adj*)	*mee-kohn noh*
telephone number	denwabangō	*dehn-wah-bahn-goh*
title	shōgō	*shoh-goh*
• **Dr. (Ph.D.)**	hakase	*hah-kah-seh*
• **Miss, Ms.**	san	*sahn*
• **Mr.**	san	*sahn*
• **Mrs., Ms.**	san	*sahn*
• **Prof.**	kyōju	*kyoh-joo*
• **teacher**	sensei	*sehn-seh*
work	shigoto	*shee-goh-toh*
• **work**	hataraku (*v*)	*hah-tah-rah-koo*

12. THE BODY

a. PARTS OF THE BODY

> See also Section 40.

abdomen	fukubu	*foo-koo-boo*
ankle	ashikubi	*ah-shee-koo-bee*
arm	ude	*oo-deh*

> **capable** (*lit.* with an arm) | = ude no aru | *oo-deh noh ah-roo*

back	senaka	*seh-nah-kah*
beard	agohige	*ah-goh-hee-geh*
belly	onaka	*oh-nah-kah*
blood	chi/ketsueki	*chee/keh-tsoo-eh-kee*
body	karada	*kah-rah-dah*
bone	hone	*hoh-neh*
brain	nō	*noh*
breast	chibusa	*chee-boo-sah*
buttock	oshiri	*oh-shee-ree*
cheek	hoo	*hoh-oh*

| chest | mune | *moo-neh* |
| chin | ago | *ah-goh* |

> to order a person about = ago de tsukau   *ah-goh deh tskah-oo*
> (*lit.* to give orders by
> pointing with one's
> chin)

ear	mimi	*mee-mee*
elbow	hiji	*hee-jee*
eye	me	*meh*
eyebrow	mayuge	*mah-yoo-geh*
eyelash	matsuge	*mah-tsoo-geh*
eyelid	mabuta	*mah-boo-tah*
face	kao	*kah-oh*
finger	yubi	*yoo-bee*
• fingernail	tsume	*tsoo-meh*
• index finger	hitosashiyubi	*hee-toh-sah-shee-yoo-bee*
• little finger	koyubi	*koh-yoo-bee*
• middle finger	nakayubi	*nah-kah-yoo-bee*
• ring finger	kusuri yubi	*koo-soo-ree yoo-bee*
foot	ashi	*ah-shee*
forehead	hitai	*hee-tah-ee*
genitals	gaiinbu	*gah-ee-een-boo*
gland	sen	*sehn*
hair	kaminoke	*kah-mee-noh-keh*
hand	te	*teh*
head	atama	*ah-tah-mah*
heart	shinzō	*sheen-zōh*

> to be brazen (*lit.* the   shinzō ga tsuyoi   *sheen-zōh gah*
> heart is strong)   *tsoo-yoh-ee*

heel	kakato	*kah-kah-toh*
hip	oshiri	*oh-shee-ree*
intestines	chō	*chōh*
jaw	ago	*ah-goh*
kidney	jinzō	*jeen-zōh*
knee	hiza	*hee-zah*
knuckles	kobushi	*koh-boo-shee*
leg	ashi	*ah-shee*
lip	kuchibiru	*koo-chee-bee-roo*
liver	kanzō	*kahn-zōh*
lung	hai	*hah-ee*
moustache	kuchihige	*koo-chee-hee-geh*

mouth	kuchi	*koo-chee*
muscle	kinniku	*keen-nee-koo*
neck	kubi	*koo-bee*
nose	hana	*hah-nah*
nostril	bikō	*bee-koh*
organ	naizō	*nah-ee-zoh*
pancreas	suizō	*soo-ee-zoh*
penis	penisu	*peh-nees*
shoulder	kata	*kah-tah*
skin	hifu	*hee-foo*
spine, backbone	sebone	*seh-boh-neh*
stomach	i	*ee*
thigh	futomomo	*ftoh-moh-moh*
throat	nodo	*noh-doh*

FOCUS: *Parts of the Body*

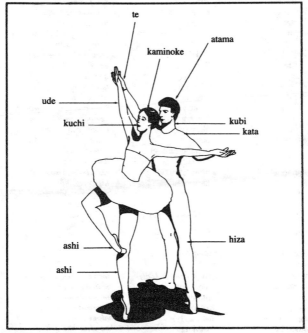

thumb	oyayubi	*oh-yah-yoo-bee*
toe	ashiyubi	*ah-shee-yoo-bee*
tongue	shita	*shtah*
tooth	ha	*hah*
vagina	chitsu	*chee-tsoo*
waist	koshi	*koh-shee*
wrist	tekubi	*teh-koo-bee*

b. PHYSICAL STATES AND ACTIVITIES

be cold	samui (desu)	*sah-moo-ee (dehs)*
be hot	atsui (desu)	*ah-tsoo-ee (dehs)*
be hungry	onaka ga suite imasu	*oh-nah-kah gah soo-ee-teh ee-mahs*
• **hunger**	kūfuku	*kōo-foo-koo*
be sleepy	nemui (desu)	*neh-moo-ee (dehs)*
• **sleep**	nemuru (v)	*neh-moo-roo*
be thirsty	nodo ga kawaite imasu	*noh-doh gah kah-wah-ee-teh ee-mahs*
be tired	tsukarete imasu	*tskah-reh-teh ee-mahs*
breathe	ikizuku (v)	*ee-kee-zoo-koo*
drink	nomu (v)	*noh-moo*
eat	taberu (v)	*tah-beh-roo*
fall asleep	nekomu (v)	*neh-koh-moo*
feel bad	kibun ga warui	*kee-boon gah wah-roo-ee*
feel well	kibun ga ii	*kee-boon gah ēe*
get up	okiru (v)	*oh-kee-roo*
go to bed	neru (v)	*neh-roo*
jog	jogingu suru (v)	*joh-geen-goo soo-roo*
nap	hirune	*hee-roo-neh*
• **nap**	hirunesuru (v)	*hee-roo-neh-soo-roo*
relax	kutsurogu (v)	*ktsoo-roh-goo*
rest	yasumu (v)	*yah-soo-moo*
run	hashiru (v)	*hah-shee-roo*
wake up	me o samasu (v)	*meh oh sah-mahs*
walk	aruku (v)	*ah-roo-koo*

c. SENSORY PERCEPTION

blind	me no mienai (adj)	*meh noh mee-eh-nah-ee*
• **blindness**	mōmoku	*mōh-moh-koo __*
deaf	mimi no tōi (adj)	*mee-mee noh tōh-ee*
flavor	aji	*ah-jee*
• **taste**	ajiwau (v)	*ah-jee-wah-oo*
hear	kiku (v)	*kee-koo*

• hearing	chōryoku	choh-ryoh-koo
listen to	kiku (v)	kee-koo
look	nagameru (v)	nah-gah-meh-roo
mute	gengoshōgai no (adj)	gehn-goh-shoh-gah-ee noh
noise	sōon	soh-ohn
• noisy	yakamashii (adj)	yah-kah-mah-shee
perceive	chikakusuru (v)	chee-kah-koo-soo-roo
• perception	chikakuryoku	chee-kah-koo-ryoh-koo
see	miru (v)	mee-roo
• sight	shikaku	shee-kah-koo
sense, feel	kanjiru (v)	kahn-jee-roo
• sense	kankaku	kahn-kah-koo
smell	nioi	nee-oh-ee
• smell	niou (vi)	nee-oh-oo
sound	oto	oh-toh
touch	shokkan	shohk-kahn
• touch	fureru (v)	foo-reh-roo

d. PERSONAL CARE

barber	rihatsushi	ree-hah-tsoo-shee
• barber shop	tokoya	toh-koh-yah
bath	ofuro	oh-foo-roh
• take a bath	ofuro ni hairu (v)	oh-foo-roh nee hah-ee-roo
beautician	biyōshi	bee-yoh-shee
brush	burashi	boo-rah-shee
• brush oneself	burashi o kakeru (v)	boo-rah-shee oh kah-keh-roo
clean	seiketsu na (adj)	seh-keh-tsoo nah
comb	kushi	koo-shee
• comb	kushi de tokasu (v)	koo-shee deh toh-kah-soo
curls	kāru	kah-roo
• curlers	kārā	kah-rah
cut one's hair	kaminoke o kiru (v)	kah-mee-noh-keh oh kee-roo
dirty	kitanai (adj)	kee-tah-nah-ee
dry	kawakasu (v)	kah-wah-kah-soo
facial	biganjutsu	bee-gahn-joo-tsoo
grooming	midashinami	mee-dah-shee-nah-mee
hairdresser	biyōshi	bee-yoh-shee
hair dryer	heā doraiyā	heh-ah doh-rah-ee-yah
hairspray	heā supurē	heh-ah spoo-reh
hygiene	eisei	eh-seh
• hygienic	eiseiteki na (adj)	eh-seh-teh-kee nah
makeup	keshō	keh-shoh
• put on makeup	okeshōsuru (v)	oh-keh-shoh-soo-roo

manicure	manikyua	*mah-nee-kyoo-ah*
mascara	masukara	*mahs-kah-rah*
massage	massāji	*mahs-sāh-jee*
nail polish	manikyuaeki	*mah-nee-kyoo-ah-eh-kee*
perfume	kōsui	*koh-soo-ee*
• put on perfume	kōsui o tsukeru (v)	*koh-soo-ee oh tskeh-roo*
permanent wave	pāmanento	*pāh-mah-nehn-toh*
razor	kamisori	*kah-mee-soh-ree*
• electric razor	denki kamisori	*dehn-kee kah-mee-soh-ree*
• razor blade	kamisori no ha	*kah-mee-soh-ree noh hah*
scissors	hasami	*hah-sah-mee*
shampoo	shanpū	*shahn-poo*
shave	hige o soru (v)	*hee-geh oh soh-roo*
shower	shawā	*shah-wāh*
• shower	shawā o abiru (v)	*shah-wāh oh ah-bee-roo*
soap	sekken	*sehk-kehn*
toothbrush	haburashi	*hah-boo-rah-shee*
toothpaste	nerihamigaki	*neh-ree-hah-mee-gah-kee*
towel	taoru	*tah-oh-roo*
wash	arau (v)	*ah-rah-oo*

THE PHYSICAL, PLANT, AND ANIMAL WORLDS

13. THE PHYSICAL WORLD

> For Signs of the Zodiac, see Section 5.

a. THE UNIVERSE

astronomy	tenmongaku	*tehn-mohn-gah-koo*
comet	suisei	*soo-ee-seh*
cosmos	uchū	*oo-choo*
eclipse	shoku	*shoh-koo*
• lunar eclipse	gesshoku	*gehs-shoh-koo*
• solar eclipse	nisshoku	*nees-shoh-koo*
galaxy	ginga	*geen-gah*
gravitation	inryoku	*een-ryoh-koo*
• gravity	inryoku	*een-ryoh-koo*
light	hikari/kōsen	*hee-kah-ree/koh-sehn*
• infrared light	sekigaisen	*seh-kee-gah-ee-sehn*
• light year	kōnen	*koh-nehn*
• ultraviolet light	shigaisen	*shee-gah-ee-sehn*
meteor	ryūsei	*ryoo-seh*
moon	tsuki	*tskee*
• full moon	mangetsu	*mahn-geh-tsoo*
• moonbeam, ray	gekkō	*gehk-koh*
• new moon	shingetsu	*sheen-geh-tsoo*
orbit	kidō	*kee-doh*
• orbit	kidō ni noru (*vi*)	*kee-doh nee noh-roo*
• orbit	kidō ni noseru (*vt*)	*kee-doh nee noh-seh-roo*
planet	wakusei	*wahk-seh*
• Earth	chikyū	*chee-kyoo*
• Jupiter	mokusei	*mohk-seh*
• Mars	kasei	*kah-seh*
• Mercury	suisei	*soo-ee-seh*
• Neptune	kaiōsei	*kah-ee-oh-seh*
• Pluto	meiōsei	*meh-oh-seh*
• Saturn	dosei	*doh-seh*
• Uranus	tennōsei	*tehn-noh-seh*
• Venus	kinsei	*keen-seh*
satellite	eisei	*eh-seh*
space	kūkan	*koo-kahn*

• **three-dimensional space**	sanjigenteki kūkan	*sahn-jee-gehn-teh-kee kōo-kahn*
star	kōsei	*kōh-seh*
sun	taiyō	*tah-ee-yōh*
• **sunlight**	nikkō	*neek-kōh*
• **sunray**	taiyō kōsen	*tah-ee-yōh kōh-sehn*
• **solar system**	taiyōkei	*tah-ee-yōh-kēh*
universe	uchū	*oo-chōo*
world	sekai	*seh-kah-ee*

b. THE ENVIRONMENT

See also Section 44.

air	kūki	*kōo-kee*
archipelago	guntō	*goon-tōh*
atmosphere	taiki	*tah-ee-kee*
• **atmospheric**	taiki no (*adj*)	*tah-ee-kee noh*
basin	bonchi	*bohn-chee*
bay	wan	*wahn*
beach	hama	*hah-mah*
channel	suiro	*soo-ee-roh*
cloud	kumo	*koo-moh*
coast	engan	*ehn-gahn*
• **coastal**	engan no (*adj*)	*ehn-gahn noh*
continent	tairiku	*tah-ee-ree-koo*
• **continental**	tairiku no (*adj*)	*tah-ee-ree-koo noh*
desert	sabaku	*sah-bah-koo*
dune	sakyū	*sah-kyōo*
earthquake	jishin	*jee-sheen*
environment	kankyō	*kahn-kyōh*
farmland	nōchi	*nōh-chee*
field	kōya	*kōh-yah*
forest	shinrin	*sheen-reen*
glacier	hyōga	*hyōh-gah*
grass	sōgen	*soh-gehn*
gulf	wan	*wahn*
hill	oka	*oh-kah*
ice	kōri	*kōh-ree*
island	shima	*shee-mah*
jungle	mitsurin	*mee-tsoo-reen*
lake	mizuumi	*mee-zoo-oo-mee*
land	rikuchi	*ree-koo-chee*

landscape	keshiki	*keh-shee-kee*
meadow	sōgen	*soh-gehn*
mountain	yama	*yah-mah*

---

to take a chance (*lit.* to bet a mountain)	= yama o kakeru	*yah-mah oh kah-keh-roo*

• **mountain chain**	sanmyaku	*sahn-myah-koo*
• **mountainous**	yama no ōi (*adj*)	*yah-mah noh oh-ee*
• **peak**	chōjō	*choh-joh*
nature	shizen	*shee-zehn*
• **natural**	shizen no (*adj*)	*shee-zehn noh*
ocean	taiyō	*tah-ee-yoh*
• **Antarctic Ocean**	nanpyōyō	*nahn-pyoh-yoh*
• **Arctic Ocean**	hoppyōyō	*hohp-pyoh-yoh*
• **Atlantic Ocean**	taiseiyō	*tah-ee-seh-yoh*
• **Pacific Ocean**	taiheiyo	*tah-ee-heh-yoh*
peninsula	hantō	*hahn-toh*
plain	heiya	*heh-yah*
plateau	kōgen	*koh-gehn*
rain forest	urin	*oo-reen*
river	kawa	*kah-wah*
• **flow**	nagareru (*v*)	*nah-gah-reh-roo*
rock	iwa	*ee-wah*
sand	suna	*snah*
sea	umi	*oo-mee*
sky	sora	*soh-rah*
soil	dojō	*doh-joh*
stone	ishi	*ee-shee*
swamp	shitchi	*sheet-chee*
tide	chōryū	*choh-ryoo*
• **high tide**	manchō	*mahn-choh*
• **low tide**	kanchō	*kahn-choh*
tropical	nettai no (*adj*)	*neht-tah-ee noh*
valley	tani	*tah-nee*
vegetation	kusaki	*ksah-kee*
volcano	kazan	*kah-zahn*
• **eruption**	funka	*foon-kah*
• **lava**	yōgan	*yoh-gahn*
water	mizu	*mee-zoo*
wave	nami	*nah-mee*
woods	mori	*moh-ree*

c. MATTER AND THE ENVIRONMENT

See also Section 42.

acid	san	*sahn*
• acid rain	sanseiu	*sahn-seh-oo*
air	kūki	*koo-kee*
ammonia	anmonia	*ahn-moh-nee-ah*
atom	genshi	*gehn-shee*
• charge	genshikaku no yōdenka	*gehn-shee-kah-koo noh yoh-dehn-kah*
• electron	denshi	*dehn-shee*
• neutron	chūseishi	*choo-seh-shee*
• nucleus	genshikaku	*gehn-shee-kah-koo*
• proton	yōshi	*yoh-shee*
bronze	seidō	*seh-doh*
carbon	tanso	*tahn-soh*
chemical	kagaku no (*adj*)	*kah-gah-koo noh*
• chemistry	kagaku	*kah-gah-koo*
chlorine	enso	*ehn-soh*
coal	sekitan	*seh-kee-tahn*
• coal mine	tankō	*tahn-koh*
• coal mining	tankō	*tahn-koh*
compound	kagōbutsu	*kah-goh-boo-tsoo*
copper	dō	*doh*
cotton	men	*mehn*
electrical	denki no (*adj*)	*dehn-kee noh*
• electricity	denki	*dehn-kee*
electronic	denshi no (*adj*)	*dehn-shee noh*
• electron	denshi	*dehn-shee*
element	genso	*gehn-soh*
energy	enerugī	*eh-neh-roo-gee*
• fossil fuel	saikutsunenryō	*sah-ee-koo-tsoo-nehn-ryoh*
• nuclear energy	kaku enerugī	*kah-koo eh-neh-roo-gee*
• radioactive waste	hōshasei haikibutsu	*hoh-shah-seh hah-ee-kee-boo-tsoo*
• solar energy	taiyō enerugī	*tah-ee-yoh eh-neh-roo-gee*
fiber	sen-i	*sehn-ee*
fuel	nenryō	*nehn-ryoh*
gas	gasu	*gah-soo*
• natural gas	tennen gasu	*tehn-nehn gah-soo*
gasoline	gasorin	*gah-soh-reen*
gold	kin	*keen*
heat	netsu	*neh-tsoo*
hydrogen	suiso	*soo-ee-soh*

industrial	kōgyō no (*adj*)	*koh-gyoh noh*
• industry	kōgyō	*koh-gyoh*
iodine	yōso	*yoh-soh*
iron	tetsu	*teh-tsoo*
laboratory	jikkenshitsu	*jeek-kehn-shee-tsoo*
lead	namari	*nah-mah-ree*
leather	kawa	*kah-wah*
liquid	ekitai	*eh-kee-tah-ee*
material	genryō	*gehn-ryoh*
matter	busshitsu	*boos-shee-tsoo*
mercury	suigin	*soo-ee-geen*
metal	kinzoku	*keen-zoh-koo*
methane	metan	*meh-tahn*
microscope	kenbikyō	*kehn-bee-kyoh*
mineral	kōbutsu	*koh-boo-tsoo*
molecular	bunshi no (*adj*)	*boon-shee noh*
• molecular model	bunshi kōzō mokei	*boon-shee koh-zoh moh-keh*
• molecular formula	bunshishiki	*boon-shee-shee-kee*
• molecular structure	bunshi kōzō	*boon-shee koh-zoh*
molecule	bunshi	*boon-shee*
natural resources	tennenshigen	*tehn-nehn-shee-gehn*
nitrogen	chisso	*chees-soh*
oil	sekiyu	*seh-kee-yoo*
organic	yūki no (*adj*)	*yoo-kee noh*
• inorganic	muki no (*adj*)	*moo-kee noh*
oxygen	sanso	*sahn-soh*
particle	bibunshi	*bee-boon-shee*
petroleum	sekiyu	*seh-kee-yoo*
physical	butsuri no (*adj*)	*boo-tsoo-ree noh*
• physics	butsuri	*boo-tsoo-ree*
plastic	purasuchikku	*poo-rahs-cheek-koo*
platinum	purachina	*poo-rah-chee-nah*
pollution	osen	*oh-sehn*
salt	shio	*shee-oh*
silk	kinu	*kee-noo*
silver	gin	*geen*
smoke	kemuri	*keh-moo-ree*
sodium	natoriumu	*nah-toh-ree-oo-moo*
solid	kotai no (*adj*)	*koh-tah-ee noh*
steel	tekkō	*tehk-koh*
• stainless steel	sutenresu suchīru	*stehn-rehs schee-roo*
stuff	shizai	*shee-zah-ee*
substance	busshitsu	*boos-shee-tsoo*
sulphur	iō	*ee-oh*
• sulphuric acid	ryūsan	*ryoo-sahn*
textile	orimono	*oh-ree-moh-noh*

vapor	kitai	*kee-tah-ee*
water	mizu	*mee-zoo*
wool	ūru	*oo-roo*

d. CHARACTERISTICS OF MATTER

artificial	jinzō no (*adj*)	*jeen-zoh noh*
authentic	honmono no (*adj*)	*hohn-moh-noh noh*
elastic	danryokusei no aru (*adj*)	*dahn-ryohk-seh noh ah-roo*
fake	nise no (*adj*)	*nee-seh noh*
hard	katai (*adj*)	*kah-tah-ee*
heavy	omoi (*adj*)	*oh-moh-ee*
light	karui (*adj*)	*kah-roo-ee*
malleable	katansei no aru (*adj*)	*kah-tahn-seh noh ah-roo*
opaque	futōmei na (*adj*)	*foo-toh-meh nah*
pure	junsui no (*adj*)	*joon-soo-ee noh*
resistant	teikōsei no aru (*adj*)	*teh-koh-seh noh ah-roo*
robust	ganjō na (*adj*)	*gahn-joh nah*
smooth	nameraka na (*adj*)	*nah-meh-rah-kah nah*
soft	yawarakai (*adj*)	*yah-wah-rah-kah-ee*
soluble	yōkaisei no aru (*adj*)	*yoh-kah-ee-seh noh ah-roo*
stable	anteishita (*adj*)	*ahn-teh-shtah*
strong	tsuyoi (*adj*)	*tsoo-yoh-ee*
synthetic	gōsei no (*adj*)	*goh-seh noh*
transparent	tōmei na (*adj*)	*toh-meh nah*
weak	yowai (*adj*)	*yoh-wah-ee*

e. GEOGRAPHY

> For names of countries, cities, etc. see Section 30.

Antarctic Circle	nankyokuken	*nahn-kyoh-koo-kehn*
Arctic Circle	hokkyokuken	*hohk-kyoh-koo-kehn*
border	kyōkai	*kyoh-kah-ee*
• border	sakaisuru (*v*)	*sah-kah-ee-soo-roo*
city	shi	*shee*
• capital	shuto	*shoo-toh*
continent	tairiku	*tah-ee-ree-koo*
• continental	tairiku no (*adj*)	*tah-ee-ree-koo noh*
country	kuni	*koo-nee*
equator	sekidō	*seh-kee-doh*
geographical	chirijō no (*adj*)	*chee-ree-joh noh*

• geography	chiri	*chee-ree*
globe	chikyū	*chee-kyoo*
hemisphere	hankyū	*hahn-kyoo*
• hemispheric	hankyūjō no (*adj*)	*hahn-kyoo-joh noh*
latitude	ido	*ee-doh*
location	ichi	*ee-chee*
• locate	ichisuru (*v*)	*ee-chee-soo-roo*
longitude	keido	*keh-doh*
map	chizu	*chee-zoo*
meridian	shigosen	*shee-goh-sehn*
• prime meridian	honsho shigosen	*hohn-shoh shee-goh-sehn*
nation	kokka	*kohk-kah*
• national	kokka no (*adj*)	*kohk-kah noh*
pole	kyoku	*kyoh-koo*
• North Pole	hokkyoku	*hohk-kyoh-koo*
• South Pole	nankyoku	*nahn-kyoh-koo*
province	shō	*shoh*
region	chihō	*chee-hoh*
state	shū	*shoo*
territory	ryōdo	*ryoh-doh*
tropic	kaikisen	*kah-ee-kee-sehn*
• Tropic of Cancer	kitakaikisen	*kee-tah-kah-ee-kee-sehn*
• Tropic of Capricorn	minamikaikisen	*mee-nah-mee-kah-ee-kee-sehn*
• tropical zone	nettaichitai	*neht-tah-ee-chee-tah-ee*

14. PLANTS

a. GENERAL VOCABULARY

agriculture	nōgyō	*noh-gyoh*
bloom	hana ga saku (*v*)	*hah-nah gah sah-koo*
blossom	hana	*hah-nah*
botanical	shokubutsu no (*adj*)	*shoh-koo-boo-tsoo noh*
• botany	shokubutsugaku	*shoh-koo-boo-tsoo-gah-koo*
branch	eda	*eh-dah*
bud	tsubomi	*tsoo-boh-mee*
• bud	tsubomi o motsu (*v*)	*tsoo-boh-mee oh moh-tsoo*
bulb	kyūkon	*kyoo-kohn*
cell	saibō	*sah-ee-boh*
• membrane	genkeishitsumaku	*gehn-keh-shee-tsoo-mah-koo*
• nucleus	kaku	*kah-koo*
chlorophyll	yōryokuso	*yoh-ryohk-soh*
cultivate	saibaisuru (*v*)	*sah-ee-bah-ee-soo-roo*

• **cultivation**	saibai	*sah-ee-bah-ee*
dig	horu (*v*)	*hoh-roo*
fertilize	hiryō o yaru (*v*)	*hee-ryōh oh yah-roo*
• **fertilizer**	hiryō	*hee-ryoh*
flower	hana	*hah-nah*
foliage	ha no shigeri	*hah noh shee-geh-ree*
gather, reap	shūkakusuru (*v*)	*shōō-kahk-soo-roo*
grain	kokurui	*koh-koo-roo-ee*
greenhouse	onshitsu	*ohn-shee-tsoo*
hedge	ikegaki	*ee-keh-gah-kee*
horticulture	engei	*ehn-geh*
insecticide	satchūzai	*saht-chōō-zah-ee*
leaf	ha	*hah*
organism	yūkibutsu	*yōō-kee-boo-tsoo*
photosynthesis	kōgōsei	*koh-gōh-seh*
pinch	tsumitoru (*v*)	*tsoo-mee-toh-roo*
plant	shokubutsu	*shoh-koo-boo-tsoo*
• **plant**	ueru (*v*)	*oo-eh-roo*
pollen	kafun	*kah-foon*
prune	senteisuru (*v*)	*sehn-tēh-soo-roo*
• **pruning**	sentei	*sehn-tēh*
reproduce	saiseisuru (*v*)	*sah-ee-sēh-soo-roo*
• **reproduction**	saisei	*sah-ee-seh*
ripe	jukushita (*adj*)	*joo-koo-shtah*
• **ripen**	jukusu (*v*)	*joo-koo-soo*
root	ne	*neh*
rotten	kusatta (*adj*)	*ksaht-tah*
seed	tane	*tah-neh*
• **seed**	tane o maku (*v*)	*tah-neh oh mah-koo*
species	hinshu	*heen-shoo*
stem	kuki	*koo-kee*
transplant	ishoku	*ee-shoh-koo*
• **transplant**	ishokusuru (*v*)	*ee-shoh-koo-soo-roo*
trim	karikomu (*v*)	*kah-ree-koh-moo*
trunk	miki	*mee-kee*
water	mizu	*mee-zoo*

b. FLOWERS

azalea	tsutsuji	*tsoo-tsoo-jee*
camellia	tsubaki	*TSOO-bah-kee*
carnation	kānēshon	*kah-nēh-shohn*
cherry blossom	sakura no hana	*sah-koo-rah noh hah-nah*

> **Bread is better than the** = Hana yori dango.   *hah-nah yoh-ree*
> **song of birds.** (*lit*. A   *dahn-goh*
> **dumpling is better**
> **than a cherry**
> **blossom.**)

chrysanthemum	kiku	*kee-koo*
cyclamen	shikuramen	*shee-koo-rah-mehn*
daffodil	suisen	*soo-ee-sehn*
dahlia	daria	*dah-ree-ah*
daisy	dējī	*deh-jee*
flower	hana	*hah-nah*
• bouquet of flowers	hanataba	*hah-nah-tah-bah*
• cut flower	kiribana	*kee-ree-bah-nah*
• dead flowers	kareta hana	*kah-reh-tah hah-nah*
• flower arrangement	ikebana	*ee-keh-bah-nah*
• flower bed	kadan	*kah-dahn*
• wildflower	nobana	*noh-bah-nah*
• wilted flower	shioreta hana	*shee-oh-reh-tah hah-nah*
geranium	jeranyūmu	*jeh-rah-nyoo-moo*
gladiolus	gurajiorasu	*goo-rah-jee-oh-rahs*
hydrangea	ajisai	*ah-jee-sah-ee*
iris	ayame	*ah-yah-meh*
lily	yuri	*yoo-ree*
morning glory	asagao	*ah-sah-gah-oh*
orchid	ran	*rahn*
petal	hanabira	*hah-nah-bee-rah*
petunia	pechunia	*peh-choo-nee-ah*
(to) pick flowers	hana o tsumu (*v*)	*hah-nah oh tsoo-moo*
poppy	keshi	*keh-shee*
rose	bara	*bah-rah*
sunflower	himawari	*hee-mah-wah-ree*
thorn	toge	*toh-geh*
tulip	chūrippu	*choo-reep-poo*
violet	sumire	*soo-mee-reh*
zinnia	hyakunichisō	*hyah-koo-nee-chee-soh*

c. TREES

beech tree	buna	*boo-nah*
birch	shirakaba	*shee-rah-kah-bah*
chestnut tree	kuri no ki	*koo-ree noh kee*
cypress tree	itosugi	*ee-toh-soo-gee*
dogwood	hanamizuki	*hah-nah-mee-zoo-kee*

fir	momi	*moh-mee*
fruit tree	kaju	*kah-joo*
• apple tree	ringo no ki	*reen-goh noh kee*
• cherry tree	sakura	*sah-koo-rah*
• fig tree	ichijiku no ki	*ee-chee-jee-koo noh kee*
• mandarin orange tree	mikan no ki	*mee-kahn noh kee*
• orange tree	orenji no ki	*oh-rehn-jee noh kee*
• peach tree	momo no ki	*moh-moh noh kee*
• pear tree	nashi no ki	*nah-shee noh kee*
• pomegranate tree	zakuro no ki	*zah-koo-roh noh kee*
• walnut tree	kurumi no ki	*koo-roo-mee noh kee*
ginko tree	ichō	*ee-chōh*
Japanese cedar	sugi	*soo-gee*
Japanese cypress	hinoki	*hee-noh-kee*
magnolia	mokuren	*moh-koo-rehn*
maple tree	kaede	*kah-eh-deh*
oak tree	kashi	*kah-shee*
palm tree	yashi no ki	*yah-shee noh kee*
pine tree	matsu	*mah-tsoo*
poplar tree	popura	*poh-poo-rah*
tree	ki	*kee*
willow	yanagi	*yah-nah-gee*

d. FRUITS

apple	ringo	*reen-goh*
apricot	anzu	*ahn-zoo*
banana	banana	*bah-nah-nah*
blueberry	burūberī	*boo-rōō-beh-rēē*
cherry	sakuranbo	*sah-koo-rahn-boh*
chestnut	kuri	*koo-ree*
citrus	kankitsurui	*kahn-kee-tsoo-roo-ee*
• citric	kankitsurui no (*adj*)	*kahn-kee-tsoo-roo-ee noh*
date	natsume	*nah-tsoo-meh*
fig	ichijiku	*ee-chee-jee-koo*
fruit	kudamono	*koo-dah-moh-noh*
grapefruit	gurēpufurūtsu	*goo-rēh-poo-foo-rōō-tsoo*
grapes	budō	*boo-doh*
lemon	remon	*reh-mohn*
loquat	biwa	*bee-wah*
mandarin orange	mikan	*mee-kahn*
mango	mangō	*mahn-gōh*
melon	meron	*meh-rohn*
nectarine	nekutarin	*nehk-tah-reen*
olive	orību	*oh-rēē-boo*
orange	orenji	*oh-rehn-jee*

papaya	papaiya	*pah-pah-ee-yah*
peach	momo	*moh-moh*
pear (Japanese)	nashi	*nah-shee*
pear (western)	yōnashi	*yoh-nah-shee*
persimmon	kaki	*kah-kee*
pineapple	painappuru	*pah-ee-nahp-poo-roo*
plum	sumomo	*soo-moh-moh*
pomegranate	zakuro	*zah-koo-roh*
prune	hoshisumomo	*hoh-shee-soo-moh-moh*
raisin	hoshibudō	*hoh-shee-boo-dōh*
raspberry	kiichigo	*kee-ee-chee-goh*
strawberry	ichigo	*ee-chee-goh*
walnut	kurumi	*koo-roo-mee*
watermelon	suika	*soo-ee-kah*

e. VEGETABLES AND HERBS

artichoke	ātichōku	*āh-tee-chōh-koo*
asparagus	asuparagasu	*ahs-pah-rah-gah-soo*
bamboo shoot	takenoko	*tah-keh-noh-koh*
basil	bajiru	*bah-jee-roo*
bean	mame	*mah-meh*
bean sprout	moyashi	*moh-yah-shee*
beet	satōdaikon	*sah-tōh-dah-ee-kohn*
broccoli	burokkori	*boo-rohk-koh-ree*
burdock	gobō	*goh-bōh*
cabbage	kyabetsu	*kyah-beh-tsoo*
carrot	ninjin	*neen-jeen*
cauliflower	karifurawā	*kah-ree-foo-rah-wāh*
celery	serori	*seh-roh-ree*
corn	tōmorokoshi	*tōh-moh-roh-koh-shee*
cucumber	kyūri	*kyōō-ree*
eggplant	nasu	*nah-soo*
garden	niwa	*nee-wah*
• **vegetable garden**	saien	*sah-ee-ehn*
garlic	ninniku	*neen-nee-koo*
green pepper	pīman	*pēē-mahn*
herb	hābu	*hāh-boo*
leek	naganegi	*nah-gah-neh-gee*
lentil	renzumame	*rehn-zoo-mah-meh*
lettuce	retasu	*reh-tahs*
lima bean	rimamame	*ree-mah-mah-meh*
lotus root	renkon	*rehn-kohn*
mint	minto	*meen-toh*
mushroom	kinoko	*kee-noh-koh*
onion	tamanegi	*tah-mah-neh-gee*

parsley	paseri	*pah-seh-ree*
pea	endōmame	*ehn-dōh-mah-meh*
potato	jagaimo	*jah-gah-ee-moh*
pumpkin	kabocha	*kah-boh-chah*
radish (Japanese)	daikon	*dah-ee-kohn*
rosemary	rōzumarī	*roh-zoo-mah-rēe*
spinach	hōrensō	*hoh-rehn-sōh*
spring onion	hosonegi	*hoh-soh-neh-gee*
string bean	sayaingen	*sah-yah-een-gehn*
sweet potato	satsumaimo	*sah-tsoo-mah-ee-moh*
taro	satoimo	*sah-toh-ee-moh*
tomato	tomato	*toh-mah-toh*
turnip	kabu	*kah-boo*
vegetable	yasai	*yah-sah-ee*
zucchini	zukkīni	*zook-kēe-nee*

15. THE ANIMAL WORLD

a. ANIMALS

animal	dōbutsu	*dōh-boo-tsoo*
bat	kōmori	*kōh-moh-ree*
bear	kuma	*koo-mah*
beast	kemono	*keh-moh-noh*
buffalo	baffarō	*bahf-fah-rōh*
bull	oushi	*oh-oo-shee*
camel	rakuda	*rah-koo-dah*
cat	neko	*neh-koh*
chimpanzee	chinpanjī	*cheen-pahn-jēe*
cow	meushi	*meh-oo-shee*
deer	shika	*shee-kah*
dog	inu	*ee-noo*
• bark	hoeru (*v*)	*hoh-eh-roo*
donkey	roba	*roh-bah*
elephant	zō	*zōh*
farm	nōjō	*noh-joh*
• barn	naya	*nah-yah*
• farmer	nōfu	*nōh-foo*
• fence	kakoi	*kah-koh-ee*
fox	kitsune	*kee-tsoo-neh*
giraffe	kirin	*kee-reen*
goat	yagi	*yah-gee*
gorilla	gorira	*goh-ree-rah*
hare	nousagi	*noh-oo-sah-gee*
hippopotamus	kaba	*kah-bah*
horse	uma	*oo-mah*

a prodigy (*lit*. **a giraffe child**)	= kirinji	*kee-reen-jee*
Even an expert makes mistakes. (*lit*. **Even a monkey falls from the tree.**)	= Saru mo ki kara ochiru.	*sah-roo moh kee kah-rah oh-chee-roo*
a miniscule amount (*lit*. **a sparrow's tear**)	= suzume no namida	*soo-zoo-meh noh nah-mee-dah*

• neigh	inanaku (*v*)	*ee-nah-nah-koo*
human	hito no (*adj*)	*hee-toh noh*
human being	ningen	*neen-gehn*
hunter	hantā	*hahn-tah*
• hunting	shuryō	*shoo-ryoh*
hyena	haiena	*hah-ee-eh-nah*
lamb	kohitsuji	*koh-hee-tsoo-jee*
leopard	hyō	*hyoh*
lion	raion	*rah-ee-ohn*
• roar	hoeru (*v*)	*hoh-eh-roo*
mammal	honyūrui	*hoh-nyoo-roo-ee*
mole	mogura	*moh-goo-rah*
monkey	saru	*sah-roo*
mouse	nezumi	*neh-zoo-mee*
mule	raba	*rah-bah*
ox	oushi	*oh-oo-shee*
panda	panda	*pahn-dah*
paw	ashi	*ah-shee*
pet	petto	*peht-toh*
pig	buta	*boo-tah*
pony	kouma	*koh-oo-mah*
primate	reichōrui	*reh-choh-roo-ee*
rabbit	usagi	*oo-sah-gee*
raccoon	araiguma	*ah-rah-ee-goo-mah*
rat	nezumi	*neh-zoo-mee*
rhinoceros	sai	*sah-ee*
sheep	hitsuji	*hee-tsoo-jee*
• bleat	mēmē naku (*v*)	*meh-meh nah-koo*
skunk	sukanku	*skahn-koo*
squirrel	risu	*ree-soo*
tail	shippo	*sheep-poh*
tiger	tora	*toh-rah*
vertebrate	sekitsui dōbutsu	*seh-kee-tsoo-ee doh-boo-tsoo*

• invertebrate	musekitsui dōbutsu	*moo-seh-kee-tsoo-ee*
		dōh-boo-tsoo
wild animal	yajū	*yah-jōo*
wolf	ōkami	*oh-kah-mee*
• howl	hoeru (*v*)	*hoh-eh-roo*
zebra	shimauma	*shee-mah-oo-mah*
zoo	dōbutsuen	*dōh-boo-tsoo-ehn*
• zoological	dōbutsugaku no (*adj*)	*dōh-boo-tsoo-gah-koo noh*
• zoology	dōbutsugaku	*dōh-boo-tsoo-gah-koo*

b. BIRDS AND FOWL

albatross	ahōdori	*ah-hōh-doh-ree*
beak	kuchibashi	*koo-chee-bah-shee*
bird	tori	*toh-ree*
bluejay	aokakesu	*ah-oh-kah-keh-soo*
canary	kanaria	*kah-nah-ree-ah*
chick	hina	*hee-nah*
chicken	niwatori	*nee-wah-toh-ree*
crane	tsuru	*tsoo-roo*
crow	karasu	*kah-rah-soo*
dove	kijibato	*kee-jee-bah-toh*
duck	ahiru	*ah-hee-roo*
eagle	washi	*wah-shee*
egg	tamago	*tah-mah-goh*
falcon	hayabusa	*hah-yah-boo-sah*
feather	hane	*hah-neh*
flamingo	furamingo	*foo-rah-meen-goh*
goose	gachō	*gah-chōh*
hawk	taka	*tah-kah*
hen	mendori	*mehn-doh-ree*
heron	sagi	*sah-gee*
jay	kakesu	*kah-keh-soo*
kingfisher	kawasemi	*kah-wah-seh-mee*
lark	hibari	*hee-bah-ree*
nest	su	*soo*
nightingale	naichingēru	*nah-ee-cheen-gēh-roo*
ostrich	dachō	*dah-chōh*
owl	fukurō	*foo-koo-rōh*
parakeet	sekiseiinko	*seh-kee-seh-een-koh*
parrot	ōmu	*oh-moo*
peacock	kujaku	*koo-jah-koo*
pelican	perikan	*peh-ree-kahn*
penguin	pengin	*pehn-geen*
pheasant	kiji	*kee-jee*
pigeon	hato	*hah-toh*

robin	komadori	*koh-mah-doh-ree*
rooster	ondori	*ohn-doh-ree*
seagull	kamome	*kah-moh-meh*
sparrow	suzume	*soo-zoo-meh*
stork	kōnotori	*kōh-noh-toh-ree*
swallow	tsubame	*tsoo-bah-meh*
swan	hakuchō	*hahk-chōh*
turkey	shichimenchō	*shee-chee-mehn-chōh*
wing	tsubasa	*tsoo-bah-sah*
woodpecker	kitsutsuki	*kee-tsoo-tsoo-kee*

c. FISH, REPTILES, AMPHIBIANS, AND MARINE ANIMALS

alligator	arigētā	*ah-ree-gēh-tāh*
amphibian	ryoseirui	*ryōh-sēh-roo-ee*
carp	koi	*koh-ee*
catfish	namazu	*nah-mah-zoo*
clam	hamaguri	*hah-mah-goo-ree*

---

clam up (*lit*. keep one's mouth shut like a clam)	= Hamaguri no yō ni, kuchi o tsumugu.	*hah-mah-goo-ree noh yōh nee, koo-chee oh tsoo-moo-goo*
Like father, like son. (*lit*. A frog's child is a frog.)	= Kaeru no ko wa kaeru.	*kah-eh-roo noh koh wah kah-eh-roo*

---

codfish	tara	*tah-rah*
crab	kani	*kah-nee*
crocodile	kurokodairu	*koo-roh-koh-dah-ee-roo*
dolphin	iruka	*ee-roo-kah*
eel	unagi	*oo-nah-gee*
fish	sakana	*sah-kah-nah*
• **fin**	hire	*hee-reh*
• **fish**	sakana o tsuru (*v*)	*sah-kah-nah oh tsoo-roo*
• **fisherman**	ryōshi	*ryōh-shee*
• **fishing**	tsuri	*tsoo-ree*
• **fishing rod**	tsurizao	*tsoo-ree-zah-oh*
• **hook**	tsuribari	*tsoo-ree-bah-ree*
flounder	hirame	*hee-rah-meh*
frog	kaeru	*kah-eh-roo*
herring	nishin	*nee-sheen*
goldfish	kingyo	*keen-gyoh*

jellyfish	kurage	*koo-rah-geh*
lizard	tokage	*toh-kah-geh*
lobster	robusutā	*roh-boo-stah*
marine animal	kaisei dōbutsu	*kah-ee-seh doh-boo-tsoo*
mackerel	saba	*sah-bah*
marlin	kajiki	*kah-jee-kee*
mussel	mūrugai	*moo-roo-gah-ee*
octopus	tako	*tah-koh*
otter	rakko	*rahk-koh*
oyster	kaki	*KAH-kee*
porgy	tai	*tah-ee*
reptile	hachūrui	*hah-choo-roo-ee*
salamander	sanshōuo	*sahn-shoh-oo-oh*
sardine	iwashi	*ee-wah-shee*
scallop	kaibashira	*kah-ee-bah-shee-rah*
sea bass	suzuki	*soo-zoo-kee*
seal	azarashi	*ah-zah-rah-shee*
sea urchin	uni	*oo-nee*
shark	same	*sah-meh*
shrimp	ebi	*eh-bee*
snake	hebi	*heh-bee*
sole	shitabirame	*shee-tah-bee-rah-meh*
squid	ika	*ee-kah*
swordfish	kajiki	*kah-jee-kee*
toad	hikigaeru	*hee-kee-gah-eh-roo*
trout	masu	*mah-soo*
tuna	maguro	*mah-goo-roh*
turtle	kame	*kah-meh*
walrus	seiuchi	*seh-oo-chee*
whale	kujira	*koo-jee-rah*

d. INSECTS AND OTHER INVERTEBRATES

ant	ari	*ah-ree*
bedbug	nankinmushi	*nahn-keen-moo-shee*
bee	hachi	*hah-chee*
beetle	kōchū	*koh-choo*
bug	mushi	*moo-shee*
butterfly	chōchō	*choh-choh*
caterpillar	kemushi	*keh-moo-shee*
cicada	semi	*seh-mee*
centipede	mukade	*moo-kah-deh*
cockroach	gokiburi	*goh-kee-boo-ree*

a no-good husband (*lit.* a cockroach husband)	= gokiburi teishu	goh-kee-boo-ree teh-shoo

cricket	kōrogi	koh-roh-gee
dragonfly	tonbo	tohn-boh
grasshopper	batta	baht-tah
firefly	hotaru	hoh-tah-roo
flea	nomi	noh-mee
fly	hae	hah-eh
insect	konchū	kohn-choo
invertebrate	musekitsui dōbutsu	moo-seh-kee-tsoo-ee doh-boo-tsoo
ladybug	tentōmushi	tehn-toh-moo-shee
louse (lice)	shirami	shee-rah-mee
maggot	uji	oo-jee
metamorphosis	hentai	hehn-tah-ee
microbe	biseibutsu	bee-seh-boo-tsoo
mosquito	ka	kah
moth	ga	gah
organism	yūkitai	yoo-kee-tah-ee
praying mantis	kamakiri	kah-mah-kee-ree
scorpion	sasori	sah-soh-ree
shellfish	kōkakurui	koh-kah-koo-roo-ee
silkworm	kaiko	kah-ee-koh
slug	namekuji	nah-meh-koo-jee
snail	katatsumuri	kah-tah-tsoo-moo-ree
spider	kumo	koo-moh
termite	shiroari	shee-roh-ah-ree
tick	dani	dah-nee
wasp	suzumebachi	soo-zoo-meh-bah-chee
worm	mushi	moo-shee

COMMUNICATING, FEELING, AND THINKING

16. BASIC SOCIAL EXPRESSIONS

a. GREETINGS AND FAREWELLS

Farewell!	Gokigenyō.	*goh-kee-gehn-yōh*
Good afternoon! (Hello!)	Konnichiwa.	*kohn-nee-chee-wah*
Good evening! (Hello!)	Konbanwa.	*kohn-bahn-wah*
Good morning! (Hello!)	Ohayō gozaimasu.	*oh-hah-yōh goh-zah-ee-mahs*
Good night!	Oyasuminasai.	*oh-yah-soo-mee-nah-sah-ee*
Good-bye!	Sayōnara.	*sah-yōh-nah-rah*
greet	aisatsusuru (*v*)	*ah-ee-sah-tsoo-soo-roo*
• **greeting**	aisatsu	*ah-ee-sah-tsoo*
Hi!	Yā (*inf*)	*yāh*
How have you been?	Ogenki desu ka.	*oh-gehn-kee dehs kah*
How's it going?	Ikaga desu ka.	*ee-kah-gah dehs kah*
• **Badly.**	Anmari yoku arimasen.	*ahn-mah-ree yoh-koo ah-ree- mah-sehn*
• **Fine!**	Junchō desu.	*joon-chōh dehs*
• **Not bad!**	Waruku arimasen.	*wah-roo-koo ah-ree- mah-sehn*
• **Quite well!**	Umaku itte imasu.	*oo-mah-koo eet-teh ee-mahs*
• **So, so!**	Māmā desu.	*māh-māh dehs*
• **Very well!**	Umaku itte imasu.	*oo-mah-koo eet-teh ee-mahs*
Please give my regards/ greetings to ...	... san ni yoroshiku otsutae kudasai.	*... sahn nee yoh-roh-shee- koo oh-tsoo-tah-ee koo-dah-sah-ee*
See you!	Soredewa, mata.	*soh-reh-deh-wah, mah-tah*
• **See you later!**	Soredewa, nochihodo.	*soh-reh-deh-wah, noh-chee-hoh-doh*
• **See you soon!**	Soredewa, chikaiuchi ni.	*soh-reh-deh-wah, chee-kah-ee-oo-chee nee*
• **See you Sunday!**	Soredewa, nichiyōbi ni.	*soh-reh-deh-wah, nee-chee-yōh-bee nee*
shake hands	akushusuru (*v*)	*ahk-shoo-soo-roo*
• **handshake**	akushu	*ahk-shoo*

b. FORMS OF ADDRESS AND INTRODUCTIONS

A pleasure!	Yorokonde.	*yoh-roh-kohn-deh*

• The pleasure is mine!	Kochirakoso.	*koh-chee-rah-koh-soh*
acquaintance	chijin	*chee-jeen*
Allow me to introduce myself.	Jikoshōkai sasete itadakimasu.	*jee-koh-shoh-kah-ee sah-seh-teh ee-tah-dah-kee-mahs*
Allow me to introduce you to ...	... san ni, goshō kai itashimasu.	*... sahn nee, goh-shoh-kah-ee ee-tah-shee-mahs*
be seated	koshikakeru (v)	*kohsh-kah-keh-roo*
• Be seated, please!	Dōzo okake kudasai.	*doh-zoh oh-kah-keh koo-dah-sah-ee*
calling card	meishi	*meh-shee*
Come in!	Ohairi kudasai.	*oh-hah-ee-ree koo-dah-sah-ee*
• enter	hairu (v)	*hah-ee-roo*
Delighted!	Ureshii desu.	*oo-reh-shee dehs*
Happy to make your acquaintance!	Shiriau koto ga dekite ureshii desu.	*shee-ree-ah-oo koh-toh gah deh-kee-tee oo-reh-shee dehs*
introduce	shōkaisuru (v)	*shoh-kah-ee-soo-roo*
• introduction	shōkai	*shoh-kah-ee*
know (someone)	shitteiru (v)	*sheet-teh-ee-roo*
Let me introduce you to ...	... san ni shōkai sasete kudasai.	*... sahn nee shoh-kah-ee sah-seh-teh koo-dah-sah-ee*
meet	au (v)	*ah-oo*
run into (someone)	deau (v)	*deh-ah-oo*
title	shōgō	*shoh-goh*
• doctor	igaku hakase	*ee-gah-koo hah-kah-seh*
• doctor (*direct address*)	sensei	*sehn-seh*
• Dr. (*Ph.D. degree*)	hakase	*hah-kah-seh*
• Miss	san	*sahn*
• Ms.	san	*sahn*
• Mr.	san	*sahn*
• Mrs.	san	*sahn*
What's your name?	Onamae wa, nan desu ka.	*oh-nah-mah-eh wah, NAHN dehs kah*
• My name is ...	Watakushi no namae wa, ... desu.	*wah-tahk-shee noh nah-mah-ee wah, ... dehs*
• I'm ...	Watakushi wa, ... desu.	*wah-tahk-shee wah, ... dehs*

c. COURTESY

Best wishes!	Gokōun o.	*goh-koh-oon oh*
Cheers!	Kanpai.	*kahn-pah-ee*
Congratulations!	Omedetō gozaimasu.	*oh-meh-deh-toh goh-zah-ee-mahs*

Don't mention it!	Iie, dō itashimashite.	$\overline{ee}$-eh, DŌH ee-tah-shee-mah-shteh
Excuse me!	Sumimasen.	soo-mee-mah-sehn
Good luck!	Goseikō o.	goh-sēh-koh oh
Happy birthday!	Tanjōbi omedetō.	tahn-jōh-bee oh-meh-deh-toh
Happy New Year!	Shinnen omedetō.	sheen-nehn oh-meh-deh-tōh
Have a good holiday!	Oyasumi o, otanoshimi kudasai.	oh-yah-soo-mee oh, oh-tah-noh-shee-mee koo-dah-sah-ee
Have a good time!	Tanoshii toki o, osugoshi kudasai.	tah-noh-shēe toh-kee oh, oh-soo-goh-shee koo-dah-sah-ee
Have a good trip!	Ryokō o, otanoshimi kudasai.	ryoh-kōh oh, oh-tah-noh-shee-mee koo-dah-sah-ee
Many thanks!	Kansha shimasu.	KAHN-shah shee-mahs
May I come in?	Haittemo yoroshii desu ka.	hah-eet-teh-moh yoh-roh-shēe dehs kah
May I help you?	Otetsudai shimashō ka.	oh-teh-tsoo-dah-ee shee-mah-shōh kah
Merry Christmas!	Kurisumasu omedetō.	koo-ree-soo-mahs oh-meh-deh-tōh
No.	Iie.	$\overline{ee}$-eh
No!	Dame desu.	dah-meh dehs
OK!	Ii desu yo.	$\overline{ee}$ dehs yoh
Please! (go ahead)	Dōzo.	doh-zoh
Please! (request)	Onegai shimasu.	oh-neh-gah-ee shee-mahs
Thank you!	Arigatō gozaimasu.	ah-ree-gah-tōh goh-zah-ee-mahs
Yes!	Hai.	hah-ee
You're welcome!	Iie, dō itashimashite.	$\overline{ee}$-eh, DŌH ee-tah-shee-mah-shteh

17. SPEAKING AND TALKING

a. SPEECH ACTIVITIES AND TYPES

accuse	hinansuru (v)	hee-nahn-soo-roo
• **accusation**	hinan	hee-nahn
advice	jogen	joh-gehn
• **advise**	jogensuru (v)	joh-gehn-soo-roo
allude	honomekasu (v)	hoh-noh-meh-kah-soo
analogy	ruihi	roo-ee-hee
announce	shiraseru (v)	shee-rah-seh-roo
• **announcement**	happyō	hahp-pyōh
answer	kotae	koh-tah-eh

• answer	kotaeru (v)	koh-tah-eh-roo
argue	gironsuru (v)	gee-rohn-soo-roo
• argument	giron	gee-rohn
articulate	hakkiri hyōgensuru (v)	hahk-kee-reż hyōh-gehn-soo-roo
ask	kiku (v)	kee-koo
beg	kongansuru (v)	kohn-gahn-soo-roo
blame	togameru (v)	toh-gah-meh-roo
call	yobu (v)	yoh-boo
change subject	wadai o kaeru (v)	wah-dah-ee o kah-eh-roo
chat	zatsudansuru (v)	zah-tsoo-dahn-soo-roo
communicate	tsutaeru (v)	tsoo-tah-eh-roo
• communication	dentatsu	dehn-tah-tsoo
compare	hikakusuru (v)	hee-kahk-soo-roo
• comparison	hikaku	hee-kah-koo
conclude	ketsuron o kudasu (v)	keh-tsoo-rohn oh koo-dah-soo
• conclusion	ketsuron	keh-tsoo-rohn
congratulate	iwau (v)	ee-wah-oo
conversation	kaiwa	kah-ee-wah
debate	tōronsuru (v)	toh-rohn-soo-roo
• debate	toron	toh-rohn
declare	sengensuru (v)	sehn-gehn-soo-roo
deny	hiteisuru (v)	hee-teh-soo-roo
describe	noberu (v)	noh-beh-roo
• description	kijutsu	kee-joo-tsoo
dictate	kōjutsusuru (v)	kōh-joo-tsoo-soo-roo
digress	wakimichi ni soreru (v)	wah-kee-mee-chee nee soh-reh-roo
discuss	rongisuru (v)	rohn-gee-soo-roo
• discussion	rongi	rohn-gee
emphasis	kyōchō	kyoh-choh
• emphasize	kyōchōsuru (v)	kyoh-choh-soo-roo
excuse	iiwake	ee-wah-keh
• excuse oneself	iiwakesuru (v)	ee-wah-keh-soo-roo
explain	setsumeisuru (v)	seh-tsoo-meh-soo-roo
• explanation	setsumei	seh-tsoo-meh
express	noberu (v)	noh-beh-roo
• expression	hyōgen	hyōh-gehn
figure of speech	hiyuteki hyōgen	hee-yoo-teh-kee hyōh-gehn
• allegory	tatoebanashi	tah-toh-eh-bah-nah-shee
• literal	mojidōri no (adj)	moh-jee-dōh-ree noh
• metaphor	inyu	een-yoo
• symbol	shōchō	shoh-choh
gossip	uwasabanashi	oo-wah-sah-bah-nah-shee
• gossip	uwasabanashi o suru (v)	oo-wah-sah-bah-nah-shee oh soo-roo

hesitation	tamerai	*tah-meh-rah-ee*
• **hesitate**	tamerau (*v*)	*tah-meh-rah-oo*
identify	shikibetsusuru (*v*)	*shkee-behts-soo-roo*
indicate	shisasuru (*v*)	*shee-sah-soo-roo*
• **indication**	shisa	*shee-sah*
inform	tsugeru (*v*)	*tsoo-geh-roo*
interpret	tsūyakusuru (*v*)	*tsōō-yahk-soo-roo*
interpretation	tsūyaku	*tsōō-yah-koo*
interrupt	saegiru (*v*)	*sah-eh-gee-roo*
• **interruption**	chūdan	*chōo-dahn*
invite	maneku (*v*)	*mah-neh-koo*
jest	karakau (*v*)	*kah-rah-kah-oo*
joke	jōdan	*jōh-dahn*
• **tell a joke**	jōdan o iu (*v*)	*jōh-dahn oh ee-oo*
keep quiet	kuchi o hikaeru (*v*)	*koo-chee oh hee-kah-eh-roo*
lecture	kōgi	*kōh-gee*
• **lecture**	kōgisuru (*v*)	*kōh-gee-soo-roo*

Speak of the devil, and he will appear. (*lit.* When you gossip about someone, the person's shadow will appear.)	= Uwasa o sureba kage to yara.	*oo-wah-sah oh soo-reh-bah kah-geh toh yah-rah*
all sorts of lies (*lit.* eight hundred lies)	= uso happyaku	*oo-soh hahp-pyah-koo*
The end justifies the means. (*lit.* A lie is sometimes expedient.)	= Uso mo hōben.	*oo-soh moh hōh-behn*
Silence is golden.	= Chinmoku wa kin.	*cheen-moh-koo wah keen*

lie	uso	*oo-soh*
• **lie**	uso o tsuku (*v*)	*oo-soh oh tsoo-koo*
• **liar**	usotsuki	*oo-soh-tsoo-kee*
listen to	kiku (*v*)	*kee-koo*
malign, speak badly	chūshōsuru (*v*)	*chōo-shōh-soo-roo*
mean	imisuru (*v*)	*ee-mee-soo-roo*
• **meaning**	imi	*ee-mee*
mention	noberu (*v*)	*noh-beh-roo*
mumble	bosoboso iu (*v*)	*boh-soh-boh-soh ee-oo*
murmur	tsubuyaku (*v*)	*tsoo-boo-yah-koo*

nag	gamigami iu (v)	gah-mee-gah-mee ee-oo
offend	kanjō o kizutsukeru (v)	kahn-jōh oh kee-zoo-tskeh-roo
offer	mōshideru (v)	mōh-shee-deh-roo
oral	kōtō no (adj)	koh-toh noh
• orally	kōtō de (adv)	koh-toh deh
order	meirei	meh-reh
• order	meireisuru (v)	meh-reh-soo-roo
outspokenly	enryonaku (adv)	ehn-ryoh-nah-koo
praise	homeru (v)	hoh-meh-roo
pray	inoru (v)	ee-noh-roo
• prayer	oinori	oh-ee-noh-ree
preach	sekkyōsuru (v)	sehk-kyōh-soo-roo
• sermon	sekkyō	sehk-kyōh
point out	shitekisuru (v)	shteh-kee-soo-roo
promise	yakusokusuru (v)	yahk-sohk-soo-roo
• promise	yakusoku	yahk-soh-koo
pronounce	hatsuonsuru (v)	hah-tsoo-ohn-soo-roo
• pronunciation	hatsuon	hah-tsoo-ohn
propose	mōshikomu (v)	mōhsh-koh-moo
protest	kōgi	koh-gee
• protest	kōgisuru (v)	koh-gee-soo-roo
recommend	suisensuru (v)	soo-ee-sehn-soo-roo
relate	kanrenzukeru (v)	kahn-rehn-zoo-keh-roo
repeat	kurikaesu (v)	koo-ree-kah-eh-soo
• repetition	kurikaeshi	koo-ree-kah-eh-shee
report	hōkoku	hōh-koh-koo
• report	hōkokusuru (v)	hōh-koh-koo-soo-roo
reproach	shikaru (v)	shee-kah-roo
request	tanomi	tah-noh-mee
• request	tanomu (v)	tah-noh-moo
rhetoric	shūji	shōo-jee
• rhetorical	shūjiteki na (adj)	shōo-jee-teh-kee nah
• rhetorical question	hango	hahn-goh
rumor	uwasa	oo-wah-sah
say, tell	iu (v)	ee-oo
shout, yell	sakebu (v)	sah-keh-boo
shut up	damaru (vi)	dah-mah-roo
• Shut up!	Damare!	dah-mah-reh
silence	chinmoku	cheen-moh-koo
• silent (person)	mukuchi na (adj)	mook-chee nah
speak, talk	hanasu (v)	hah-nah-soo
• speech, talk	hanashi	hah-nah-shee
state	noberu (v)	noh-beh-roo
• statement	seimei	seh-meh
story	monogatari	moh-noh-gah-tah-ree
• tell a story	itsuwa o hanasu (v)	ee-tsoo-wah oh hah-nah-soo

suggest	teiansuru (v)	*teh-ahn-soo-roo*
summarize	yōyakusuru (v)	*yoh-yahk-soo-roo*
• summary	yōyaku	*yoh-yah-koo*
swear (*in court*)	chikau (v)	*chee-kah-oo*
swear (*profanity*)	kitanai kotobazukai o suru (v)	*kee-tah-nah-ee koh-toh-bah-zoo-kah-ee oh soo-roo*
thank	kanshasuru (v)	*kahn-shah-soo-roo*
threat	odokashi	*oh-doh-kah-shee*
• threaten	odokasu (v)	*oh-doh-kah-soo*
toast	kanpai	*kahn-pah-ee*
• toast	kanpaisuru (v)	*kahn-pah-ee-soo-roo*
translate	honyakusuru (v)	*hohn-yahk-soo-roo*
• translation	honyaku	*hohn-yah-koo*
utter	tsubuyaku (v)	*tsoo-boo-yah-koo*
vocabulary	goi	*goh-ee*
warn	keikokusuru (v)	*keh-kohk-soo-roo*
• warning	keikoku	*keh-koh-koo*
whisper	sasayaku (v)	*sah-sah-yah-koo*
word	kotoba	*koh-toh-bah*
yawn	akubi	*ah-koo-bee*
• yawn	akubisuru (v)	*ah-koo-bee-soo-roo*

b. USEFUL EXPRESSIONS

Actually ...	Jitsu wa, ...	*jee-tsoo wah, ...*
As a matter of fact ...	Jissai, ...	*jees-sah-ee, ...*
Briefly, ...	Kantan ni nobereba, ...	*kahn-tahn nee noh-beh-reh-bah, ...*
By the way ...	Tokoro de, ...	*toh-koh-roh deh, ...*
Go ahead!	Dōzo.	*DŌH-zoh*
How do you say ... in Japanese?	... wa, nihongo de dō iimasu ka.	*... wah, nee-hohn-goh deh DŌH ee-mahs kah*
I didn't understand.	Wakarimasen deshita.	*wah-kah-ree-mah-sehn deh-shtah*
I don't understand.	Wakarimasen.	*wah-kah-ree-mah-sehn*
I'm sure that ...	Tashika ni, ... to omoimasu.	*TAH-shee-kah nee,... toh oh-moh-ee-mahs*
Isn't it so?	Sō dewanai desu ka.	*SŌH deh-wah-nah-ee dehs KAH*
It seems that ...	... mitai desu.	*... mee-tah-ee dehs*
It's necessary that ...	... ga, hitsuyō desu.	*... gah, hee-tsoo-yōh dehs*
It's not true!	Sore wa, hontō dewa arimasen.	*soh-reh wah, hohn-tōh deh-wah ah-ree-mah-sehn*
It's obvious that ...	... koto wa, akiraka desu.	*... koh-toh wah, ah-KEE-rah-kah dehs*
It's true!	Sore wa, hontō desu.	*soh-reh wah, hohn-tōh dehs*

Listen ...	... o, kiite kudasai.	... oh, kēē-teh koo-dah-sah-ee
Now ...	Ima, ...	ee-mah, ...
To sum up ...	... o yōyakusureba,	... oh yōh-yahk-soo-reh-bah,
What was I talking about?	Watakushi wa, nani o hanashite imashita ka.	wah-tahk-shee wah, NAH-nee oh hah-nah-shteh ee-mah-shtah kah
Who knows?	Dare mo, shirimasen yo.	dah-reh moh, shee-ree-mah-sehn yoh

18. THE TELEPHONE

a. TELEPHONES AND ACCESSORIES

answering machine	rusuban denwa	roo-soo-bahn dehn-wah
cable	kēburu	kēh-boo-roo
car telephone	jidōsha denwa	jee-dōh-shah dehn-wah
fax machine	fakkusu	fahk-koo-soo
intercom	tsūwa sōchi	tsōō-wah sōh-chee
pay phone	kōshū denwa	kōh-shōō dehn-wah
phone book	denwachō	dehn-wah-chōh
phone booth	denwa bokkusu	dehn-wah bohk-koo-soo
phone outlet	denwa no sashikomi-guchi	dehn-wah noh sahsh-koh-mee-goo-chee
plug	sashikomi	sahsh-koh-mee
portable phone	keitai denwa	kēh-tah-ee dehn-wuh
receiver	juwaki	joo-wah-kee
• earphone	iyahōn	ee-yah-hōhn
telecommunication	enkyori tsūshin	ehn-kyoh-ree tsōō-sheen
• telecommunications satellite	tsūshin eisei	tsōō-sheen ēh-sēh
telephone	denwa	dehn-wah
telephone credit card	terefon kādo	teh-reh-fohn kāh-doh
telex machine	terekkusu	teh-rehk-koo-soo
yellow pages	shokugyōbetsu denwa chō	shoh-koo-gyōh-beh-tsoo dehn-wah chōh

b. USING THE TELEPHONE

answer	denwa ni deru (v)	dehn-wah nee deh-roo
• pick up (the phone)	juwaki o toriageru (v)	joo-wah-kee oh toh-ree-ah-geh-roo
area code	shigaikyokuban	shee-gah-ee-kyoh-koo-bahn
busy	hanashichū	hah-nah-shee-chōō

collect call	jushinninbarai no denwa	*joo-sheen-neen-bah-rah-ee noh dehn-wah*
cut off	kiru (v)	*kee-roo*
dial	daiaru	*dah-ee-ah-roo*
• dial	daiaru o mawasu (v)	*dah-ee-ah-roo oh mah-wah-soo*
• direct dialing	daiaru chokutsū	*dah-ee-ah-roo chohk-tsoo*
fax	fakkusu	*fahk-koo-soo*
hang up	kiru (v)	*kee-roo*
information	jōhō	*joh-hoh*
local call	shinai denwa	*shee-nah-ee dehn-wah*
long-distance call	chōkyori denwa	*choh-kyoh-ree dehn-wah*
make a call	denwa o kakeru (v)	*dehn-wah oh kah-keh-roo*
• Hello!	Moshi moshi.	*MOH-shee moh-shee*
• Is ... in?	... wa, irasshaimasu ka.	*... wah, ee-rahs-shah-ee-mahs kah*
• This is ...	Watakushi wa, ... desu ga.	*wah-tahk-shee wah, ... dehs gah*
• Who's speaking?	Donata sama desu ka.	*DOH-nah-tah sah-mah dehs kah*
• Wrong number!	Machigai denwa desu.	*mah-chee-gah-ee dehn-wah dehs*
message	dengon	*dehn-gohn*
• Can I leave a message?	Dengon o nokoshitemo ii desu ka.	*dehn-gohn oh noh-koh-shteh-moh ee dehs kah*
• Can I take a message?	Nanika, dengon ga arimasu ka.	*NAH-nee-kah, dehn-gohn gah ah-ree-mahs kah*
operator	kōkanshu	*koh-kahn-shoo*
person-to-person call	pāsonaru kōru	*pah-soh-nah-roo koh-roo*
switchboard	kōkandai	*koh-kahn-dah-ee*
telephone	denwa	*dehn-wah*
telephone bill	denwa ryōkin no seikyūsho	*dehn-wah ryoh-keen noh seh-kyoo-shoh*
telephone call	denwa	*dehn-wah*
telephone line	kaisen	*kah-ee-sehn*
• Hold the line!	Kiranaide kudasai.	*kee-rah-nah-ee-deh koo-dah-sah-ee*
• This line is busy.	Hanashichū desu.	*hah-nah-shee-choo dehs*
telephone number	denwa bangō	*dehn-wah bahn-goh*
ring (phone)	naru (vi)	*nah-roo*

19. LETTER WRITING

a. FORMAL SALUTATIONS/CLOSINGS

Dear Sir	haikei	*hah-ee-keh*

Dear Madam	haikei	*hah-ee-keh*
To Whom it May Concern	kankeisha kakui dono	*kahn-keh-shah kah-koo-ee doh-noh*
Gentlemen	haikei	*hah-ee-keh*
Yours truly	keigu	*keh-goo*
Yours sincerely	keigu	*keh-goo*

b. FAMILIAR SALUTATIONS/CLOSINGS

Dear ...	... sama	*... sah-mah*
Dearest ...	shinai naru ... sama	*sheen-ah-ee nah-roo ... sah-mah*
Affectionately	kokoro o komete	*koh-koh-roh oh koh-meh-teh*
Give my regards to ...	... san ni yoroshiku	*... sahn nee yoh-roh-shkoo*

c. PARTS OF A LETTER/PUNCTUATION

body	honbun	*hohn-boon*
closing	musubi no kotoba	*moo-soo-bee noh koh-toh-bah*
date	hizuke	*hee-zoo-keh*
heading	midashi	*mee-dah-shee*
punctuation	kutōten	*ktoh-tehn*
• accent	akusento	*ahk-sehn-toh*
• apostrophe	aposutorofi	*ah-pohs-toh-roh-fee*
• asterisk	hoshijirushi	*hoh-shee-jee-roo-shee*
• bracket, parenthesis	kakko	*kahk-koh*
• capital letter	ōmoji	*oh-moh-jee*
• colon	koron	*koh-rohn*
• comma	konma	*kohn-mah*
• exclamation mark	kantanfu	*kahn-tahn-foo*
• hyphen	haifun	*hah-ee-foon*
• italics	itarikkutai	*ee-tah-reek-koo-tah-ee*
• period	shūshiten	*shoo-shtehn*
• question mark	gimonfu	*gee-mohn-foo*
• quotation mark	inyōfu	*een-yoh-foo*
• semicolon	semikoron	*seh-mee-koh-rohn*
• small letter	komoji	*koh-moh-jee*
• square bracket	kaku kakko	*kah-koo kahk-koh*
• underlining	andārain	*ahn-dah-rah-een*
salutation	aisatsu no kotoba	*ah-ee-sah-tsoo noh koh-toh-bah*
sentence	bun	*boon*
signature	shomei	*shoh-meh*

• **sign**	shomeisuru (v)	*shoh-meh-soo-roo*
spelling	tsuzuri	*tsoo-zoo-ree*
text	honbun	*hohn-boon*
• **abbreviation**	shōryakukei	*shoh-ryahk-keh*
• **clause**	setsu	*seh-tsoo*
• **letter** (*of the alphabet*)	arufabetto no moji	*ah-roo-fah-beht-toh noh moh-jee*
• **line**	gyō	*gyoh*
• **margin**	yohaku	*yoh-hah-koo*
• **P.S.**	tsuishin	*tsoo-ee-sheen*
• **paragraph**	danraku	*dahn-rah-koo*
• **phrase**	ku	*koo*
word	kotoba	*koh-toh-bah*

d. WRITING MATERIALS AND ACCESSORIES

brush	fude	*foo-deh*
clip	kurippu	*koo-reep-poo*
envelope	fūtō	*foo-toh*
eraser	keshigomu	*keh-shee-goh-moo*
glue	setchakuzai	*seht-chah-koo-zah-ee*
ink	inku	*een-koo*
ink stick (*calligraphy*)	sumi	*soo-mee*
inkstone (*calligraphy*)	suzuri	*soo-zoo-ree*
letter	tegami	*teh-gah-mee*
letterhead	binsen tōbu no jōhō insatsu	*been-sehn toh-boo noh joh-hoh een-sah-tsoo*
marker	majikku mākā	*mah-jeek-koo mah-kah*
pad	hagitorishiki hikkiyōshi	*hah-gee-toh-ree-shee-kee heek-kee-yoh-shee*
page	pēji	*peh-jee*
paper	kami	*kah-mee*
pen	pen	*pehn*
• **ballpoint pen**	bōru pen	*boh-roo pehn*
• **felt-tip pen**	feruto pen	*feh-roo-toh pehn*
• **fountain pen**	mannenhitsu	*mahn-nehn-hee-tsoo*
pencil	enpitsu	*ehn-pee-tsoo*
• **mechanical pencil**	shāpu penshiru	*shah-poo pehn-shee-roo*
ruler	jōgi	*joh-gee*
scissors	hasami	*hah-sah-mee*
Scotch tape	serotēpu	*seh-roh-teh-poo*
staple	hotchikisu no hari	*hoht-chee-kees noh hah-ree*
• **stapler**	hotchikisu	*hoht-chee-kees*
string	himo	*hee-moh*
typewriter	taipuraitā	*tah-ee-poo-rah-ee-tah*

carriage	kyareji	*kyah-reh-jee*
• keyboard	kībōdo	*kee-boh-doh*
• ribbon	ribon	*ree-bohn*
• space bar	supēsubā	*speh-soo bah*
• tab	tabu	*tah-boo*
• type	taipusuru (v)	*tah-ee-poo-soo-roo*
word processor	wāpuro	*wah-poo-roh*

e. AT THE POST OFFICE

abroad	gaikoku	*gah-ee-koh-koo*
address	jūsho	*joo-shoh*
• return address	sashidashinin jūsho	*sah-shee-dah-shee-neen joo-shoh*
addressee	naatenin	*nah-ah-teh-neen*
airmail	kōkūbin	*koh-koo-been*
business letter	bijinesu retā	*bee-jee-nehs reh-tah*
clerk	kyokuin	*kyoh-koo-een*
clerk's window	madoguchi	*mah-doh-goo-chee*
correspondence	tsūshin	*tsoo-sheen*
courier	haitatsunin	*hah-ee-tah-tsoo-neen*
envelope	fūtō	*foo-toh*
letter carrier, mailman	yūbin haitatsu	*yoo-been hah-ee-tah-tsoo*
mail	yūbin	*yoo-been*
• mail (letters)	dasu (v)	*dasu*
• mail (packages)	okuru (v)	*oh-koo-roo*
mail delivery	yūbin haitatsu	*yoo-been hah-ee-tah-tsoo*
mailbox	posuto	*pohs-toh*
money order	yūbin kawase	*yoo-been kah-wah-seh*
note	mijikai tegami	*mee-jee-kah-ee teh-gah-mee*
package	kozutsumi	*koh-zoo-tsoo-mee*
postage	yūbin ryōkin	*yoo-been ryoh-keen*
postal rate	yūbin ryōkin	*yoo-been ryoh-keen*
postcard	hagaki	*hah-gah-kee*
post office	yūbinkyoku	*yoo-been-kyoh-koo*
printed matter	insatsubutsu	*een-sah-tsoo-boo-tsoo*
registered letter	kakitome yūbin	*kah-kee-toh-meh yoo-been*
receive	uketoru (v)	*oo-keh-toh-roo*
reply	henji	*hehn-jee*
• reply	henji o dasu (v)	*hehn-jee oh dahs*
send	okuru (v)	*oh-koo-roo*
sender	sashidashinin	*sah-shee-dah-shee-neen*
special delivery	sokutatsu	*sohk-tah-tsoo*
stamp	kitte	*keet-teh*
surface mail	funabin	*foo-nah-been*

wait for	matsu (*v*)	*mah-tsoo*
write	kaku (*v*)	*kah-koo*
zip code	yūbin bangō	*yoo-been bahn-goh*

20. THE MEDIA

a. PRINT MEDIA

advertising	kōkoku	*koh-koh-koo*
appendix	furoku	*foo-roh-koo*
atlas	chizuchō	*chee-zoo-choh*
author	chosha	*choh-shah*
book	hon	*hohn*
comics	manga	*mahn-gah*
cover	hyōshi	*hyoh-shee*
critic	hyōronka	*hyoh-rohn-kah*
essay	essei	*ehs-seh*
fiction	shōsetsu	*shoh-seh-tsoo*
• nonfiction	nonfikushon	*nohn-feek-shohn*
• science fiction	saiensu fikushon	*sah-ee-ehn-soo feek-shohn*
index	sakuin	*sah-koo-een*
magazine	zasshi	*zahs-shee*
• weekly magazine	shūkanshi	*shoo-kahn-shee*
• monthly magazine	gekkanshi	*gehk-kahn-shee*
newspaper	shinbun	*sheen-boon*
• article	kiji	*kee-jee*
• criticism	hihyō	*hee-hyoh*
• daily newspaper	nikkanshi	*neek-kahn-shee*
• editor	henshūsha	*hehn-shoo-shah*
• editorial	shasetsu	*shah-seh-tsoo*
• evening paper	yūkan	*yoo-kahn*
• front page	ichimen	*ee-chee-mehn*
• headline	midashi	*mee-dah-shee*
• illustration	irasuto	*ee-rah-stoh*
• interview	intabyū	*een-tah-byoo*
• journalist	jānarisuto	*jah-nah-ree-stoh*
• news	nyūsu	*nyoo-soo*
• obituary	shibōkiji	*shee-boh-kee-jee*
• photo	shashin	*shah-sheen*
• reader	dokusha	*dohk-shah*
• reporter	repōtā	*reh-poh-tah*
• review	hyōron	*hyoh-rohn*
• weekly periodical	shūkanshi	*shoo-kahn-shee*
note	chūshaku	*choo-shah-koo*
• footnote	kyakuchū	*kyahk-choo*

novel	shōsetsu	shoh-seh-tsoo
• adventure	bōken	boh-kehn
• best-seller	besutoserā	beh-stoh-seh-rah
• mystery	misuterī	mee-steh-ree
• plot	suji	soo-jee
• romance	renai	rehn-ah-ee
page	pēji	peh-jee
pamphlet, brochure	panfuretto	pahn-foo-reht-toh
play	geki	geh-kee
• comedy	kigeki	kee-geh-kee
• drama	dorama	doh-rah-mah
• tragedy	higeki	hee-geh-kee
pocket book	bunkohon	boon-koh-hohn
poem	shi	shee
poetry	shi	shee
print medium	insatsu baitai	een-sah-tsoo-bah-ee-tah-ee
• print	insatsusuru (v)	een-sah-tsoo-soo-roo
• printing, typography	insatsujutsu	een-sah-tsoo-joo-tsoo
publish	shuppansuru (v)	shoop-pahn-soo-roo
• publisher	shuppansha	shoop-pahn-shah
read	yomu (v)	yoh-moo
reference book	sankōsho	sahn-koh-shoh
• definition	gogi	goh-gee
• dictionary	jisho	jee-shoh
• encyclopedia	hyakkajiten	hyuhk-kah-jee-tehn
science fiction	saiensu fikushon	sah-ee-ehn-soo feek-shohn
short story	tanpen shōsetsu	tahn-pehn shoh-seh-tsoo
text	honbun	hohn-boon
title	daimei	dah-ee-meh
turn pages, leaf through	pēji o mekuru (v)	peh-jee oh meh-koo-roo
write	kaku (v)	kah-koo

b. ELECTRONIC MEDIA

antenna	antena	ahn-teh-nah
audio equipment	ōdio sōchi	oh-dee-oh soh-chee
• amplifier	anpu	ahn-poo
• cassette deck	kasetto dekki	kah-seht-toh dehk-kee
• cassette tape	kasetto tēpu	kah-seht-toh teh-poo
• compact disc	konpakuto disuku	kohn-pahk-toh dee-skoo
	shīdī	shee-dee
• compact disc player	shīdī purēyā	shee-dee poo-reh-yah
• earphone	iyahōn	ee-yah-hohn
• headphones	heddohōn	hehd-doh-hohn

• loudspeaker	raudosupīkā	*rah-oo-doh-spee-kah*
• microphone	maikurohon	*mah-ee-koo-roh-hohn*
• play (*a record*)	kakeru (*v*)	*kah-keh-roo*
• receiver	reshībā	*reh-shee-bah*
• record	rekōdo	*reh-koh-doh*
• record	rokuonsuru (*v*)	*roh-koo-ohn-soo-roo*
• record player	rekōdo purēyā	*reh-koh-doh-poo-reh-yah*
• speaker	supīkā	*spee-kah*
• stereo	suterco	*steh-reh-oh*
• tape recorder	tēpu rekōdā	*teh-poo reh-koh-dah*
• tuner	chūnā	*choo-nah*
• turntable	tānteburu	*tahn-teh-boo-roo*
program	puroguramu	*poo-roh-goo-rah-moo*
projector	eishaki	*eh-shah-kee*
• slide projector	suraido purojekutā	*soo-rah-ee-doh poo-roh-jehk-tah*
radio	rajio	*rah-jee-oh*
• car radio	kārajio	*kah-rah-jee-oh*
• listen to	kiku (*v*)	*kee-koo*
• newscast	nyūsu hōsō	*nyoo-soo hoh-soh*
• news report	nyūsu bangumi	*nyoo-soo bahn-goo-mee*
• pocket radio	poketto rajio	*poh-keht-toh rah-jee-oh*
• portable radio	pōtaburu rajio	*poh-tah-boo-roo rah-jee-oh*
• radio-cassette player	rajikase	*rah-jee-kah-seh*
• station	hōsōkyoku	*hoh-soh-kyoh-koo*
show	shō bangumi	*shoh bahn-goo-mee*
television	terebi	*teh-reh-bee*
• channel	channeru	*chahn-neh-roo*
• closed circuit	kurōzudo sākitto	*koo-roh-zoo-doh sah-keet-toh*
• commercial	komāsharu	*koh-mah-shah-roo*
• documentary	dokyumentarī	*doh-kyoo-mehn-tah-ree*
• interview	intabyū	*een-tah-byoo*
• look at, watch	miru (*v*)	*mee-roo*
• network	hōsōmō	*hoh-soh-moh*
• news report	nyūsu bangumi	*nyoo-soo bahn-goo-mee*
• on the air	hōsōchū	*hoh-soh-choo*
• remote control	rimokon	*ree-moh-kohn*
• series	renzoku bangumi	*rehn-zoh-koo bahn-goo-mee*
• television set	terebi	*teh-reh-bee*
• transmission	sōshin	*soh-sheen*
• VCR	bideo	*bee-deh-oh*
• video game	bideo gēmu	*bee-deh-oh geh-moo*
• videocassette	bideo kasetto	*bee-deh-oh kah-seht-toh*
• videorock	bideo rokku	*bee-deh-oh rohk-koo*

• videotape	bideo kasetto	*bee-deh-oh kah-seht-toh*
turn off	kesu (*v*)	*keh-soo*
turn on	tsukeru (*v*)	*tskeh-roo*
walkie-talkie	toranshībā	*toh-rahn-shēē-bah*

21. FEELINGS

a. MOODS/ATTITUDES/EMOTIONS

active	kappatsu na (*adj*)	*kahp-pah-tsoo nah*
affection	aijō	*ah-ee-jōh*
• affectionate	aijō no fukai (*adj*)	*ah-ee-jōh noh fkah-ee*
agree	sanseisuru (*v*)	*sahn-seh-soo-roo*
• agreeable	kokoroyoi (*adj*)	*koh-koh-roh-yoh-ee*
aggressive	kōgekiteki na (*adj*)	*kōh-geh-kee-teh-kee nah*
anger	ikari	*ee-kah-ree*
• angry	okotta (*adj*)	*oh-koht-tah*
anxiety, anxiousness	fuan	*foo-ahn*
• anxious	fuan na (*adj*)	*foo-ahn nah*
assure	ukeau (*v*)	*oo-keh-ah-oo*
attitude	taido	*tah-ee-doh*
be down	ki ga meitte iru	*kee gah meh-eet-teh ee-roo*
be up	ki ga takamatte iru	*kee gah tah-kah-maht-teh ee-roo*
bold	daitan na (*adj*)	*dah-ee-tahn nah*
bore	unzarisaseru (*vt*)	*oon-zah-ree-sah-seh-roo*
• become bored	taikutsusuru (*vi*)	*tah-ee-ktsoo-soo-roo*
• bored	taikutsushita (*adj*)	*tah-ee-ktsoo-shtah*
• boredom	taikutsu	*tah-ee-ktsoo*
cheerful	yōki na (*adj*)	*yōh-kee nah*
complain	kujō o noberu (*v*)	*koo-jōō oh noh-beh-roo*
• complaint	kujō	*koo-jōh*
cruel	zankoku na (*adj*)	*zahn-koh-koo nah*
cry	naku (*v*)	*nah-koo*
• tears	namida	*nah-mee-dah*
depressed	yūutsu na (*adj*)	*yōō-oo-tsoo nah*
• depression	yūutsu	*yōō-oo-tsoo*
desperate	hisshi no (*adj*)	*hees-shee noh*
disagree	sansei shinai	*sahn-seh shee-nah-ee*
• disagreement	fusansei	*foo-sahn-seh*
• be against	hantaisuru (*v*)	*hahn-tah-ee-soo-roo*
disappoint	shitsubōsaseru (*vt*)	*shee-tsoo-bōh-sah-seh-roo*
• disappointed	gakkarishita (*adj*)	*gahk-kah-ree-shtah*
• disappointment	shitsubō	*shtsoo-bōh*
dissatisfaction	fuman	*foo-mahn*
• dissatisfied	fuman no aru (*adj*)	*foo-mahn noh ah-roo*

emotion	kanjō	*kahn-jōh*
• emotional	kanjōteki na (*adj*)	*kahn-jōh-teh-kee nah*
encourage	hagemasu (*v*)	*hah-geh-mahs*
• encouragement	gekirei	*geh-kee-rēh*
enthusiastic	nesshin na (*adj*)	*nehs-sheen nah*
faith, trust	shinrai	*sheen-rah-ee*
• trust	shinraisuru (*v*)	*sheen-rah-ee-soo-roo*
fear	osore	*oh-soh-reh*
• be afraid	osoreru (*v*)	*oh-soh-reh-roo*
feel	kanjiru (*v*)	*kahn-jee-roo*
• feeling	kanji	*kahn-jee*
flatter	oseji o iu (*v*)	*oh-seh-jee oh ee-oo*
• flattery	oseji	*oh-seh-jee*
fun, enjoyment	tanoshimi	*tah-noh-shee-mee*
• have fun, enjoy oneself	tanoshimu (*v*)	*tah-noh-shee-moo*
gentle	yasashii (*adj*)	*yah-sah-shēe*
gloomy	inki na (*adj*)	*een-kee nah*
happiness	shiawase	*shee-ah-wah-seh*
• happy	shiawase na (*adj*)	*shee-ah-wah-seh nah*
hope	nozomi	*noh-zoh-mee*
• hope	nozomu (*v*)	*noh-zoh-moo*
humble	hikaeme na (*adj*)	*hee-kah-eh-meh nah*
indifference	mukanshin	*moo-kahn-sheen*
• indifferent	mukanshin na (*adj*)	*moo-kahn-sheen nah*
joy	yorokobi	*yoh-roh-koh-bee*
kind	shinsetsu na (*adj*)	*sheen-seh-tsoo nah*
laugh	warau (*v*)	*wah-rah-oo*
• laughter	warai	*wah-rah-ee*
mood	kibun	*kee-boon*
• bad mood	warui kibun	*wah-roo-ee kee-boon*
• good mood	ii kibun	*ēe kee-boon*
need	hitsuyō	*hee-tsoo-yōh*
• need	iru (*v*)	*ee-roo*
negative	hiteiteki na (*adj*)	*hee-tēh-teh-kee nah*
oppose	hantaisuru (*v*)	*hahn-tah-ee-soo-roo*
passive	shōkyokuteki na (*adj*)	*shōh-kyoh-koo-teh-kee nah*
patience	nintai	*neen-tah-ee*
• patient	nintaizuyoi (*adj*)	*neen-tah-ee-zoo-yoh-ee*
positive	sekkyokuteki na (*adj*)	*sehk-kyoh-koo-teh-kee nah*
relief	anshin	*ahn-sheen*
• sigh of relief	ando no tameiki	*ahn-doh noh tah-meh-ee-kee*
sad	kanashii (*adj*)	*kah-nah-shēe*
• sadness	kanashimi	*kah-nah-shee-mee*
satisfaction	manzoku	*mahn-zoh-koo*
• satisfied	manzokushita (*adj*)	*mahn-zoh-koo-shtah*

shame	haji	*hah-jee*
• be ashamed	hajiru (*v*)	*hah-jee-roo*
smile	hohoemi	*hoh-hoh-eh-mee*
• smile	hohoemu (*v*)	*hoh-hoh-eh-moo*
sorrow	kanashimi	*kah-nah-shee-mee*
surprise	odoroki	*oh-doh-roh-kee*
• surprise	odorokasu (*vt*)	*oh-doh-roh-kah-soo*
sympathy	dōjō	*doh-joh*
• sympathetic	dōjōteki na (*adj*)	*doh-joh-teh-kee nah*
tense	kinchōshita (*adj*)	*keen-choh-shtah*
thankfulness	kansha	*kahn-shah*
• thankful	kansha no (*adj*)	*kahn-shah noh*
• thank	kanshasuru (*v*)	*kahn-shah-soo-roo*
timid	okubyo na (*adj*)	*oh-koo-byoh nah*
tolerance	kanyō	*kahn-yoh*
• tolerant	kanyō na (*adj*)	*kahn-yoh nah*
weep	naku (*v*)	*nah-koo*
wonderful	subarashii (*adj*)	*soo-bah-rah-shee*

b. LIKES AND DISLIKES

accept	ukeireru (*v*)	*oo-keh-ee-reh-roo*
• acceptable	ukeirerareru (*adj*)	*oo-keh-ee-reh-rah-reh-roo*
• unacceptable	ukeiregatai (*adj*)	*oo-keh-ee-reh-gah-tah-ee*
approval	zenin	*zeh-neen*
• approve	mitomeru (*v*)	*mee-toh-meh-roo*
be fond of, like	konomu (*v*)	*koh-noh-moo*
detest	kirau (*v*)	*kee-rah-oo*
disgust	mukamukasaseru (*v*)	*moo-kah-moo-kah-sah-seh-roo*
disgusted	unzarishita (*adj*)	*oon-zah-ree-shtah*
hate	nikumu (*v*)	*nee-koo-moo*
• hatred	ken-o	*kehn-oh*
kiss	kisu	*kee-soo*
• kiss	kisusuru (*v*)	*kee-soo-soo-roo*
like	konomu (*v*)	*koh-noh-moo*
• liking	konomi	*KOH-noh-mee*
• dislike	kirau (*v*)	*kee-rah-oo*
love	ai	*ah-ee*
• love	aisuru (*v*)	*ah-ee-soo-roo*
pleasant	tanoshii (*adj*)	*tah-noh-shee*
• unpleasant	fuyukai na (*adj*)	*foo-yoo-kah-ee nah*
prefer	konomu (*v*)	*koh-noh-moo*
• preference	konomi	*KOH-noh-mee*
reject	kyozetsusuru (*v*)	*kyoh-zeh-tsoo-soo-roo*
• rejection	kyozetsu	*kyoh-zeh-tsoo*

c. EXPRESSING EMOTIONS

Are you joking?	Jōdan desho.	*joh-dahn deh-shoh*
Be careful!	Ki o tsukete.	*kee oh tskeh-teh*
Enough! (No more!)	Mō yoshinasai.	*moh yoh-shee-nah-sah-ee*
Fortunately!	Un yoku.	*oon yoh-koo*
Good heavens!/Oh my!	Oya.	*oh-YAH*
I don't believe it!	Shinjiraremasen.	*sheen-jee-rah-reh-mah-sehn*
I don't feel like …	… ki ni naremasen.	*… kee nee nah-reh-mah-sehn*
I wish!	Sō da to iindesu ga.	*SOH dah toh een-dehs gah*
I'm serious!	Honki desu yo.	*hohn-kee dehs yoh*
I'm sorry!	Sumimasen.	*soo-mee-mah-sehn*
Impossible!	Muri desu yo.	*moo-ree dehs yoh*
It doesn't matter!	Kamaimasen.	*kah-mah-ee-mah-sehn*
My God!	Komatta. (*inf*)	*koh-maht-tah*
Poor man!	Kawaisō ni.	*kah-wah-ee-soh nee*
Poor woman!	Kawaisō ni.	*kah-wah-ee-soh nee*
Quiet!	Shizuka ni. (*inf*)	*shee-zoo-kah nee*
Really?	Hontō. (*inf*)	*hohn-TOH*
Shut up!	Damare. (*inf*)	*dah-mah-reh*
Thank goodness!	Arigatai. (*inf*)	*ah-ree-gah-tah-ee*
Too bad!	Zannen.	*zahn-nehn*
Unbelievable!	Shinjirarenai. (*inf*)	*sheen-jee-rah-reh-nah-ee*
Unfortunately!	Un waruku.	*oon wah-roo-koo*

22. THINKING

a. DESCRIBING THOUGHT

complicated	fukuzatsu na (*adj*)	*fkoo-zah-tsoo nah*
concept	gainen	*gah-ee-nehn*
conscience	ryōshin	*ryoh-sheen*
conscientious	ryōshinteki na (*adj*)	*ryoh-sheen-teh-kee nah*
difficult	muzukashii (*adj*)	*moo-zoo-kah-shee*
doubt	utagai	*oo-tah-gah-ee*
easy	yasashii (*adj*)	*yah-sah-shee*
existence	sonzai	*sohn-zah-ee*
hypothesis	kasetsu	*kah-seh-tsoo*
idea	aidia	*ah-ee-dee-ah*
ignorant	muchi no (*adj*)	*moo-chee noh*
imagination	sōzōryoku	*soh-zoh-ryoh-koo*
interesting	omoshiroi (*adj*)	*oh-moh-shee-roh-ee*
judgment	handan	*hahn-dahn*
justice	seigi	*seh-gee*

knowledge	chishiki	*chee-shee-kee*
knowledgeable	yoku shitteiru (*adj*)	*yoh-koo sheet-teh-ee-roo*
mind	kokoro	*koh-koh-roh*
opinion	iken	*ee-kehn*
• in my opinion	watakushi no iken dewa	*wah-tahk-shee noh ee-kehn deh-wah*
problem	mondai	*mohn-dah-ee*
• No problem!	Mondai arimasen.	*mohn-dah-ee ah-ree-mah-sehn*
reason	riyū	*ree-yoo*
simple	tanjun na (*adj*)	*tahn-joon nah*
thought	kangae	*kahn-gah-eh*
wisdom	chie	*chee-eh*

b. BASIC THOUGHT PROCESSES

agree	sanseisuru (*v*)	*sahn-seh-soo-roo*
be interested in	kyōmi ga aru (*v*)	*kyoh-mee gah ah-roo*
be right	tadashii (desu)	*tah-dah-shee (dehs)*
be wrong	machigai (desu)	*mah-chee-gah-ee (dehs)*
believe	shinjiru (*v*)	*sheen-jee-roo*
convince	nattokusaseru (*v*)	*naht-tohk-sah-seh-roo*
demonstrate	hyōmeisuru (*v*)	*hyoh-meh-soo-roo*
doubt	utagau (*v*)	*oo-tah-gah-oo*
forget	wasureru (*v*)	*wah-soo-reh-roo*
imagine	sōzōsuru (*v*)	*soh-zoh-soo-roo*
know	shiru (*v*)	*shee-roo*
learn	narau (*v*)	*nah-rah-oo*
persuade	settokusuru (*v*)	*seht-tohk-soo-roo*
reason	ronshōsuru (*v*)	*rohn-shoh-soo-roo*
reflect	shiansuru (*v*)	*SHEE-ahn-soo-roo*
remember	omoidasu (*v*)	*oh-moh-ee-dahs*
study	manabu (*v*)	*mah-nah-boo*
think	kangaeru (*v*)	*kahn-gah-eh-roo*
understand	rikaisuru (*v*)	*ree-kah-ee-soo-roo*

DAILY LIFE

23. AT HOME

a. PARTS OF THE HOUSE

attic	yaneurabeya	*yah-neh-oo-rah-beh-yah*
basement	chikashitsu	*chee-kah-shtsoo*
bathtub	yokusō	*yohk-soh*
ceiling	tenjō	*tehn-joh*
chimney	entotsu	*ehn-toh-tsoo*
corridor	rōka	*roh-kah*
door	to	*toh*
doorbell	yobirin	*yoh-bee-reen*
entrance	iriguchi	*ee-ree-goo-chee*
faucet	jaguchi	*jah-goo-chee*
fireplace	danro	*dahn-roh*
floor	yuka	*yoo-kah*
floor (*level*)	kai	*kah-ee*
garage	shako	*shah-koh*
garden	niwa	*nee-wah*
gate	mon	*mohn*
ground floor	ikkai	*eek-kah-ee*
house	ie	*ee-eh*
kitchen sink	nagashi	*nah-gah-shee*
mailbox	yūbinuke	*yoo-been-oo-keh*
porch	beranda	*beh-rahn-dah*
roof	yane	*yah-neh*
shelf	tana	*tah-nah*
shower	shawā	*shah-wah*
sink	senmendai	*sehn-mehn-dah-ee*
stairs	kaidan	*kah-ee-dahn*
switch	suitchi	*soo-eet-chee*
terrace	terasu	*teh-rah-soo*
toilet	otearai	*oh-teh-ah-rah-ee*
wall	kabe	*kah-beh*

The walls have ears.	= Kabe ni mimi ari.	*kah-beh nee mee-mee ah-ree*

window	mado	*mah-doh*
window sill	madowaku	*mah-doh-wah-koo*

b. ROOMS

FOCUS: *Features Unique to the Japanese House*

entrance hall (where shoes are removed and kept)	genkan	*gehn- kahn*
woven reed mat floor in a Japanese-style room	tatami	*tah-tah-mee*

The most important Japanese-style room in a house often has an alcove with a scroll and a flower arrangement.

alcove	tokonoma	*toh-koh-noh-mah*

In a Japanese house, the toilet and the bathroom are usually separate.

toilet	otearai	*oh-teh-ah-rah-ee*
bathroom	furoba	*foo-roh-bah*

alcove	tokonoma	*toh-koh-noh-mah*
bathroom (*western style*)	basurūmu	*bah-soo-roō-moo*
bathroom (*Japanese style*)	furoba	*foo-roh-bah*
bedroom	shinshitsu	*sheen-shee-tsoo*
closet	oshiire	*oh-shee-ee-reh*
dining room	shokudō	*shoh-koo-doh*
entrance hall	genkan	*gehn-kahn*
kitchen	daidokoro	*dah-ee-doh-koh-roh*
living room	ima	*ee-mah*
room	heya	*heh-yah*
• **Japanese-style room**	washitsu	*wah-shee-tsoo*
• **western-style room**	yōma	*yoh-mah*

c. FURNITURE AND DECORATION

Japanese rooms may have two kinds of sliding partitions:

screen made of paper and a wooden grid	shōji	*shoh-jee*
heavier screen made of paper or fabric	fusuma	*foo-soo-mah*

Many Japanese homes have a household Buddhist altar, a household Shinto shrine, or both.

household Buddhist altar	butsudan	*boo-tsoo-dahn*
household Shinto shrine	kamidana	*kah-mee-dah-nah*

armchair	hijikakeisu	*hee-jee-kah-keh-ee-soo*
bed	beddo	*behd-doh*
bedding (*Japanese mattress for the floor*)	futon	*ftohn*
bedside table	saidotēburu	*sah-ee-doh-teh-boo-roo*
bookcase	hondana	*hohn-dah-nah*
carpet, rug	jūtan	*joo-tahn*
chair	isu	*ee-soo*
chest of drawers (*Japanese style*)	tansu	*tahn-soo*
chest of drawers (*western style*)	yōdansu	*yoh-dahn-soo*
curtains	kāten	*kah-tehn*
drawer	hikidashi	*hee-kee-dah-shee*
furniture	kagu	*KAH-goo*
household Buddhist altar	butsudan	*boo-tsoo-dahn*
household Shinto shrine	kamidana	*kah-mee-dah-nah*
lamp	ranpu	*rahn-poo*
mirror	kagami	*kah-gah-mee*
painting	e	*eh*
screen with paper and wooden grid	shōji	*shoh-jee*
• heavier screen with paper or fabric	fusuma	*fsoo-mah*
sofa	sofā	*soh-fah*
table	tēburu	*teh-boo-roo*
writing desk	desuku	*dehs-koo*

d. APPLIANCES AND COMMON HOUSEHOLD ITEMS

bag	fukuro	*fkoo-roh*
• shopping bag	kaimonobukuro	*kah-ee-moh-noh-boo-koo-roh*
barrel	taru	*tah-roo*
basket	kago	*kah-goh*
bedspread	beddokabā	*behd-doh-kah-bah*
blanket	mōfu	*moh-foo*
bottle	bin	*been*
box	hako	*hah-koh*
broom	hōki	*hoh-kee*
case	kēsu	*keh-soo*
chopstick	hashi	*hah-shee*
• chopstick rest	hashioki	*hah-shee-oh-kee*
clothes hanger	hangā	*hahn-gah*
coffee machine	kōhīmēkā	*koh-hee-meh-kah*

coffee pot	kōhīpotto	_koh-hee-poht-toh_
cup	kōhījawan	_koh-hee-jah-wahn_
• tea cup (_Japanese_)	yunomijawan	_yoo-noh-mee-jah-wahn_
dishwasher	shokkiaraiki	_shohk-kee-ah-rah-ee-kee_
dryer	kansōki	_kahn-soh-kee_
fork	fōku	_foh-koo_
freezer	reitōko	_reh-toh-koh_
glass (_drinking_)	koppu	_kohp-poo_
kettle	yakan	_yah-kahn_
key	kagi	_kah-gee_
knife	hōchō	_hoh-choh_
• blade	ha	_hah_
• handle	totte	_toht-teh_
ladle	hishaku	_hee-shah-koo_
lid	futa	_foo-tah_
microwave oven	denshirenji	_dehn-shee-rehn-jee_
napkin	napukin	_nah-poo-keen_
pail	teoke	_teh-oh-keh_
pan	hiranabe	_hee-rah-nah-beh_
pillow	makura	_mah-koo-rah_
pillowcase	makurakabā	_mah-koo-rah-kah-bah_
plate	sara	_sah-rah_
pot	fukanabe	_fkah-nah-beh_
radio	rajio	_rah-jee-oh_
rice bowl (_Japanese_)	gohanjawan	_goh-hahn-jah-wahn_
refrigerator	reizōko	_reh-zoh-koh_
saucer	ukezara	_oo-keh-zah-rah_
sewing machine	mishin	_mee-sheen_
sheet (_bed_)	shītsu	_shee-tsoo_
soup bowl (_Japanese_)	owan	_oh-wahn_
spoon	supūn	_soo-poon_
• teaspoon	kosaji	_koh-sah-jee_
stove	renji	_rehn-jee_
tablecloth	tēburukurosu	_teh-boo-roo-koo-roh-soo_
tableware	shokutakuyō shokkigu	_shohk-tah-koo-yoh shohk-kee-goo_
teapot	tīpotto	_tee-poht-toh_
• small teapot (_Japanese_)	kyūsu	_kyoo-soo_
• large teapot (_Japanese_)	dobin	_doh-been_
television set	terebi	_teh-reh-bee_
toaster	tōsutā	_toh-stah_
tools	daikudōgu	_dah-ee-koo-doh-goo_
tray	obon	_oh-bohn_
vacuum cleaner	sōjiki	_soh-jee-kee_
washing machine	sentakuki	_sehn-tahk-kee_

e. SERVICES

air conditioning	reibō	*reh-boh*
• air conditioner	eakon	*eh-ah-kohn*
electricity	denki	*dehn-kee*
furnace	danbōro	*dahn-boh-roh*
gas	gasu	*gah-soo*
heating	danbō	*dahn-boh*
light	akari	*ah-kah-ree*
telephone	denwa	*dehn-wah*
water	suidō	*soo-ee-doh*

f. ADDITIONAL HOUSEHOLD VOCABULARY

at home	uchi de	*oo-chee-deh*
build	tateru (*v*)	*tah-teh-roo*
buy	kau (*v*)	*kah-oo*
clean	sōjisuru (*v*)	*soh-jee-soo-roo*
clear the table	atokatazukesuru (*v*)	*ah-toh-kah-tah-zoo-keh-soo-roo*
live in	sumikomu (*v*)	*soo-mee-koh-moo*
make the bed	beddo o totonoeru (*v*)	*behd-doh oh toh-toh-noh-eh-roo*
move	hikkosu (*v*)	*heek-koh-soo*
paint	penki o nuru (*v*)	*pehn-kee oh noo-roo*
put a room in order	heya o katazukeru (*v*)	*heh-yah oh kah-tah-zoo-keh-roo*
restore	shūfukusuru (*v*)	*shoo-foo-koo-soo-roo*
set the table	tēburu o totonoeru (*v*)	*teh-boo-roo oh toh-toh-noh-eh-roo*
wash	arau (*v*)	*ah-rah-oo*
• wash the clothes	sentakusuru (*v*)	*sehn-tahk-soo-roo*
• wash the dishes	sara o arau (*v*)	*sah-rah oh ah-rah-oo*

g. LIVING IN AN APARTMENT

In Japan, an inexpensive, small, and not-so-modern apartment is called **apāto** (apartment). In contrast with **apāto**, a modern, larger, and upscale apartment is distinguished by the name **manshon** (mansion).

apartment (*an inexpensive one*)	apāto	*ah-pah-toh*
apartment (*an upscale one*)	manshon	*mahn-shohn*
building	biru	*bee-roo*
condominium	bunjō manshon	*boon-joh mahn-shohn*
elevator	erebētā	*eh-reh-beh-tah*
ground floor	ikkai	*eek-kah-ee*
landlord	yanushi	*yah-noo-shee*
rent	yachin	*yah-cheen*
• **rent**	kariru (*v*)	*kah-ree-roo*
superintendent	kanrinin	*kahn-ree-neen*
tenant	kyojūsha	*kyoh-joo-shah*

24. EATING AND DRINKING

a. MEALS

breakfast	asagohan	*ah-sah-goh-hahn*
	chōshoku	*choh-shoh-koo*
dinner	bangohan	*bahn-goh-hahn*
	yūshoku	*yoo-shoh-koo*
food	tabemono	*tah-beh-moh-noh*
lunch	hirugohan	*hee-roo-goh-hahn*
	chūshoku	*choo-shoh-koo*
meal	shokuji	*shoh-koo-jee*
snack	kanshoku	*kahn-shoh-koo*
	oyatsu	*oh-yah-tsoo*
	sunakku	*soo-nahk-koo*

b. PREPARATION

baked	tenpi de yaita (*adj*)	*tehn-pee deh yah-ee-tah*
boiled	yudeta (*adj*)	*yoo-deh-tah*
broiled	jikabi de yaita (*adj*)	*jee-kah-bee deh yah-ee-tah*
cooking, cuisine	ryōri	*ryoh-ree*
fried	ageta (*adj*)	*ah-geh-tah*
grilled	amiyaki no (*adj*)	*ah-mee-yah-kee noh*
marinated	marine shita (*adj*)	*mah-ree-neh shtah*
medium	midiamu no (*adj*)	*mee-dee-ah-moo noh*
rare	rea no (*adj*)	*reh-ah noh*
roast	rōsuto	*roh-stoh*

| steamed | mushita (*adj*) | *moo-shee-tah* |
| well-done | yoku yaita (*adj*) | *yoh-koo yah-ee-tah* |

c. MEAT AND POULTRY

bacon	bēkon	*beh-kohn*
beef	gyūniku	*gyoo-nee-koo*
	bīfu	*bee-foo*
chicken	toriniku	*toh-ree-nee-koo*
	chikin	*chee-keen*
duck	ahiru	*ah-hee-roo*
	dakku	*dahk-koo*
ham	hamu	*hah-moo*
kidney	jinzō	*jeen-zoh*
lamb	kohitsuji no niku	*koh-hee-tsoo-jee noh nee-koo*
	ramu	*rah-moo*
liver	kanzō	*kahn-zoh*
	rebā	*reh-bah*
meat	niku	*nee-koo*
mutton	yōniku	*yoh-nee-koo*
	maton	*mah-tohn*
oxtail	okkusʋtēru	*ohk-ksoo-teh-roo*
pork	butaniku	*boo-tah-nee-koo*
	pōku	*poh-koo*
salami	sarami sōsēji	*sah-rah-mee SOH-seh-jee*
sausage	sōsēji	*soh-seh-jee*
tongue	tan	*tahn*
turkey	shichimenchō	*shee-chee-mehn-choh*
veal	koushi no niku	*koh-oo-shee noh nee-koo*

d. FISH, SEAFOOD, AND SHELLFISH

abalone	awabi	*ah-wah-bee*
anchovy	anchobi	*ahn-choh-bee*
clam	hamaguri	*hah-mah-goo-ree*
crab	kani	*kah-nee*
cod	tara	*tah-rah*
eel	unagi	*oo-nah-gee*
fish	sakana	*sah-kah-nah*
flounder	hirame	*hee-rah-meh*
halibut	ohyō	*oh-hyoh*
herring	nishin	*nee-sheen*
lobster	robusutā	*roh-boo-stah*
mackerel	saba	*sah-bah*

mussel	mūrugai	*mōo-roo-gah-ee*
octopus	tako	*tah-koh*
oyster	kaki	*KAH-kee*
porgy	tai	*tah-ee*
prawn, shrimp	ebi	*eh-bee*
salmon	sake	*SAH-keh*
sardine	iwashi	*ee-wah-shee*
scallops	kaibashira	*kah-ee-bah-shee-rah*
sea bass	suzuki	*soo-zoo-kee*
smelt	kisu	*kee-soo*
squid	ika	*ee-kah*
sole	shitabirame	*shee-tah-bee-rah-meh*
swordfish	kajiki	*kah-jee-kee*
trout	masu	*mah-soo*
tuna	maguro	*mah-goo-roh*

e. VEGETABLES

artichoke	ātichōku	*ah-tee-chōh-koo*
asparagus	asuparagasu	*ahs-pah-rah-gah-soo*
bamboo shoot	takenoko	*tah-keh-noh-koh*
bean	mame	*mah-meh*
bean sprout	moyashi	*moh-yah-shee*
beet	satōdaikon	*sah-tōh-dah-ee-kohn*
broccoli	burokkori	*boo-rohk-koh-ree*
burdock	gobō	*goh-bōh*
cabbage	kyabetsu	*kyah-beh-tsoo*
carrot	ninjin	*neen-jeen*
cauliflower	karifurawā	*kah-ree-foo-rah-wāh*
celery	serori	*seh-roh-ree*
corn	tōmorokoshi	*tōh-moh-roh-koh-shee*
cucumber	kyūri	*kyōo-ree*
eggplant	nasu	*nah-soo*
garlic	ninniku	*neen-nee-koo*
green pepper	pīman	*pēe-mahn*
leek	naganegi	*nah-gah-neh-gee*
lettuce	retasu	*reh-tahs*
lotus root	renkon	*rehn-kohn*
mushroom	kinoko	*kee-noh-koh*
onion	tamanegi	*tah-mah-neh-gee*
peas	endōmame	*ehn-dōh-mah-meh*
potato	jagaimo	*jah-gah-ee-moh*
pumpkin	kabocha	*kah-boh-chah*
radish (*Japanese*)	daikon	*dah-ee-kohn*
spinach	hōrensō	*hoh-rehn-sōh*
spring onion, scallion	hosonegi	*hoh-soh-neh-gee*

string bean	sayaingen	*sah-yah-een-gehn*
sweet potato	satsumaimo	*sah-tsoo-mah-ee-moh*
taro	satoimo	*sah-toh-ee-moh*
tomato	tomato	*toh-mah-toh*
turnip	kabu	*kah-boo*
vegetables	yasai	*yah-sah-ee*
zucchini	zukkīni	*zook-kēē-nee*

f. FRUITS

apple	ringo	*reen-goh*
apricot	anzu	*ahn-zoo*
banana	banana	*bah-nah-nah*
blueberry	burūberī	*boo-rōō-beh-rēē*
cherry	sakuranbo	*sah-koo-rahn-boh*
chestnut	kuri	*koo-ree*
date	natsume	*nah-tsoo-meh*
fig	ichijiku	*ee-chee-jee-koo*
fruit	kudamono	*koo-dah-moh-noh*
grape	budō	*boo-dōh*
grapefruit	gurēpufurūtsu	*goo-rēh-poo-foo-rōō-tsoo*
lemon	remon	*reh-mohn*
kiwi	kīwī	*kēē-wēē*
mandarin orange	mikan	*mee-kahn*
mango	mangō	*mahn-goh*
melon	meron	*meh-rohn*
nectarine	nekutarin	*nehk-tah-reen*
orange	orenji	*oh-rehn-jee*
papaya	papaiya	*pah-pah-ee-yah*
peach	momo	*moh-moh*
pear (*Japanese*)	nashi	*nah-shee*
pear (*western*)	yōnashi	*yoh-nah-shee*
persimmon	kaki	*kah-kee*
pineapple	painappuru	*pah-ee-nahp-poo-roo*
plum	sumomo	*soo-moh-moh*
pomegranate	zakuro	*zah-koo-roh*
prune	hoshisumomo	*hoh-shee-soo-moh-moh*
raisin	hoshibudō	*hoh-shee-boo-dōh*
raspberry	kiichigo	*kee-ee-chee-goh*
strawberry	ichigo	*ee-chee-goh*
walnut	kurumi	*koo-roo-mee*
watermelon	suika	*soo-ee-kah*

g. MEAL AND MENU COMPONENTS

aperitif	shokuzenshu	*shoh-koo-zehn-shoo*

appetizer	zensai	*zehn-sah-ee*
bread	pan	*pahn*
cheese	chīzu	*chēē-zoo*
course	kōsu	*koh-soo*
dessert	dezāto	*deh-zah-toh*
fruit	kudamono	*koo-dah-moh-noh*
ice cream	aisukurīmu	*ah-ees-koo-rēē-moo*
main course	meinkōsu	*meh-een-koh-soo*
menu	menyū	*meh-nyoo*
pasta	pasuta	*pah-stah*
pie	pai	*pah-ee*
pudding	purin	*poo-reen*
rice	raisu	*rah-ee-soo*
roll	rōrupan	*roh-roo-pahn*
salad	sarada	*sah-rah-dah*
• salad dressing	doresshingu	*doh-rehs-sheen-goo*
sandwich	sandoitchi	*sahn-doh-eet-chee*
sherbet	shābetto	*shah-beht-toh*
soup	sūpu	*soo-poo*
spaghetti	supagetti	*soo-pah-geht-tee*
wine	wain	*wah-een*
• red wine	reddo wain	*rehd-doh wah-een*
• white wine	howaito wain	*hoh-wah-ee-toh wah-een*

h. DAIRY PRODUCTS, EGGS, AND RELATED FOODS

butter	batā	*bah-tah*
cheese	chīzu	*chēē-zoo*
cream	kurīmu	*koo-rēē-moo*
cottage cheese	kotēji chīzu	*koh-TEH-jee chēē-zoo*
dairy product	nyūseihin	*nyoo-seh-heen*
egg	tamago	*tah-mah-goh*
• fried egg	medamayaki	*meh-dah-mah-yah-kee*
• hard-boiled egg	yudetamago	*yoo-deh-tah-mah-goh*
• omelette	omuretsu	*oh-moo-reh-tsoo*
• soft-boiled egg	hanjuku	*hahn-joo-koo*
ice cream	aisukurīmu	*ah-ees-koo-rēē-moo*
milk	gyūnyū	*gyoo-nyoo*
	miruku	*mee-roo-koo*
• skim milk	sukimu miruku	*skee-moo mee-roo-koo*
yogurt	yōguruto	*yoh-goo-roo-toh*

i. GRAINS AND GRAIN PRODUCTS

barley	ōmugi	*oh-moo-gee*

biscuit	bisuketto	*bees-keht-toh*
bread	pan	*pahn*
buckwheat	sobako	*soh-bah-koh*
cereal	shiriaru	*shee-ree-ah-roo*
• cornflakes	kōnfurēku	*kōhn-foo-rēh-koo*
• oatmeal	ōtomīru	*ōh-toh-mēe-roo*
cracker	kurakkā	*koo-rahk-kāh*
cookie	kukkī	*kook-kēe*
corn	tōmorokoshi	*toh-moh-roh-koh-shee*
• corn chip	kōnchippu	*kōhn-cheep-poo*
• popcorn	poppukōn	*pohp-poo-kōhn*
flour	komugiko	*koh-moo-gee-koh*
oat	ōtomugi	*ōh-toh-moo-gee*
pastry	pesutorī	*pehs-toh-rēe*
rice (cooked)	gohan	*goh-hahn*
rice (uncooked)	kome	*koh-meh*
• rice cake (*Japanese*)	mochi	*moh-chee*
• rice cracker (*Japanese*)	senbei	*sehn-bēh*
rye	raimugi	*rah-ee-moo-gee*
wheat	komugi	*koh-moo-gee*

j. CONDIMENTS AND SPICES

butter	batā	*bah-tāh*
cream	kurīmu	*koo-rēe-moo*
horseradish (*Japanese*)	wasabi	*wah-sah-bee*
horseradish (*western*)	hōsuradisshu	*hōh-soo-rah-dees-shoo*
garlic	ninniku	*neen-nee-koo*
grated ginger (*Japanese*)	oroshi shōga	*oh-roh-shee shōh-gah*
grated radish (*Japanese*)	daikon oroshi	*dah-ee-kohn oh-roh-shee*
herb	hābu	*hāh-boo*
honey	hachimitsu	*hah-chee-mee-tsoo*
jam	jamu	*jah-moo*
ketchup	kechappu	*keh-chahp-poo*
lemon	remon	*reh-mohn*
margarine	māgarin	*māh-gah-reen*
marmalade	māmarēdo	*mah-mah-rēh-doh*
mayonnaise	mayonēzu	*mah-yoh-nēh-zoo*
mint	minto	*meen-toh*
mustard	karashi	*kah-rah-shee*
	masutādo	*mahs-tāh-doh*
oil	oiru	*oh-ee-roo*
parsley	paseri	*pah-seh-ree*
paprika	papurika	*pah-poo-ree-kah*

pepper	koshō	*koh-shōh*
rosemary	rōzumarī	*roh-zoo-mah-rēe*
salt	shio	*shee-oh*
soy sauce	shōyu	*shōh-yoo*
spice	yakumi	*yah-koo-mee*
sugar	satō	*sah-tōh*
syrup	shiroppu	*shee-rohp-poo*
Tabasco	tabasuko	*tah-bah-skoh*
vinegar	su	*soo*
Worcestershire sauce	sōsu	*sōh-soo*

k. DRINKS

alcoholic beverage	arukōru inryō	*ah-roo-kōh-roo een-ryōh*
aperitif	shokuzenshu	*shoh-koo-zehn-shoo*
beer	bīru	*bēe-roo*
bourbon whiskey	bābon	*bah-bohn*
brandy	burandē	*boo-rahn-dēh*
club soda	tansan (sui)	*tahn-sahn (soo-ee)*
Coca-Cola	kokakōra	*koh-kah-kōh-rah*
coffee	kōhī	*koh-hēe*
cognac	konyakku	*koh-nyahk-koo*
diet soda	daietto no nomimono	*dah-ee-eht-toh noh noh-mee-moh-noh*
drink	nomimono	*noh-mee-moh-noh*
espresso	esupuresso	*ehs-poo-rehs-soh*
gin	jin	*jeen*
ginger ale	jinjaēru	*jeen-jah-ēh-roo*
juice	jūsu	*jōo-soo*
lemonade	remonēdo	*reh-moh-nēh-doh*
liqueur	rikyūru	*ree-kyōo-roo*
mineral water	mineraru wōtā	*mee-neh-rah-roo wōh-tāh*
Pepsi-Cola	pepushikōra	*peh-poo-shee-kōh-rah*
rice wine (Japanese)	sake	*sah-keh*
rum	ramu	*rah-moo*
scotch whiskey	sukotchi	*skoht-chee*
soft drink	sofuto dorinku	*soh-foo-toh doh-reen-koo*
Sprite	supuraito	*spoo-rah-ee-toh*
tea (*Japanese*)	ocha	*oh-chah*
tea (*western*)	kōcha	*kōh-chah*
vodka	wokka	*wohk-kah*
water	mizu	*mee-zoo*
whiskey	uisukī	*oo-ee-skēe*
wine	wain	*wah-een*

l. AT THE TABLE

bottle	bin	*been*
bowl	bōru	*bōh-roo*
cup	kōhījawan	*koh-hēe-jah-wahn*
cutlery, tableware	shokutakuyō shokkigu	*shohk-tah-koo-yōh shohk-kee-goo*
fork	fōku	*fōh-koo*
glass	koppu	*kohp-poo*
knife	naifu	*nah-ee-foo*
napkin	napukin	*nah-poo-keen*
plate	sara	*sah-rah*
saucer	ukezara	*oo-keh-zah-rah*
spoon	supūn	*soo-pōon*
table	tēburu	*tēh-boo-roo*
tablecloth	tēburukurosu	*tēh-boo-roo-koo-roh-soo*
teaspoon	kosaji	*koh-sah-jee*
toothpick	yōji	*yōh-jee*
tray	obon	*oh-bohn*
wine glass	waingurasu	*wah-een-goo-rah-soo*

Tableware for a Japanese meal may include the following items:

---

chopstick	hashi	*hah-shee*
chopstick rest	hashioki	*hah-shee-oh-kee*
large teapot	dobin	*doh-been*
pickle dish	okozara	*oh-koh-zah-rah*
rice bowl	ochawan	*oh-chah-wahn*
	gohanjawan	*goh-hahn-jah-wahn*
sake cup	sakazuki	*sah-kah-zoo-kee*

FOCUS: *Phrases for Drinking and Eating*

Cheers!	Kanpai.	*kahn-pah-ee*
I hope you like it.	Okuchi ni au to ii no desu ga.	*ohk-chee nee AH-oo toh ēe noh dehs gah.*

The following ritual expressions are used at mealtimes:

Before beginning the meal:	Itadakimasu.	*ee-tah-dah-kee-mahs*
After finishing the meal:	Gochisōsama deshita.	*goh-chee-sōh-sah-mah deh-shtah*

sake jug	tokkuri	*tohk-koo-ree*
small teapot	kyūsu	*kyōo-soo*
soup bowl	owan	*oh-wahn*
soy sauce	shōyu	*shoh-yoo*
soy sauce dish	okozara	*oh-koh-zah-rah*
soy sauce pitcher	shōyusashi	*shoh-yoo-sah-shee*
teacup	yunomijawan	*yoo-noh-mee-jah-wahn*
teacup saucer	chataku	*chah-tah-koo*

m. DINING OUT

bartender	bāten	*bah-tehn*
bill, check	kanjō	*kahn-joh*
cafeteria	kafeteria	*kah-feh-teh-ree-ah*
cover charge	kabā chāji	*kah-bah chah-jee*
fixed price	kimatta nedan	*kee-maht-tah neh-dahn*
price	nedan	*neh-dahn*
reservation	yoyaku	*yoh-yah-koo*
• reserved	yoyakushitearu (*adj*)	*yoh-yah-koo-shteh-ah-roo*
restaurant	resutoran	*reh-stoh-rahn*
• informal restaurant	keishikibaranai resutoran	*keh-shee-kee-bah-rah-nah-ee reh-stoh-rahn*
service	sābisu	*sah-bee-soo*
• self-service	serufu sābisu	*seh-roo-foo sah-bee-soo*
service charge	sābisu ryō	*sah-bee-soo ryoh*
snack bar	sunakku	*soo-nahk-koo*
take out	mochikaeru (*v*)	*moh-chee-kah-eh-roo*
tax	zeikin	*zeh-keen*
tip	chippu	*cheep-poo*
• tip	chippu o ageru (*v*)	*cheep-poo oh ah-geh-roo*
waiter	uēta	*oo-eh-tah*
waitress	uētoresu	*oo-eh-toh-reh-soo*
wine list	wain risuto	*wah-een ree-stoh*

n. BUYING FOOD AND DRINK

bakery	pan ya	*pahn yah*
butcher shop	niku ya	*nee-koo yah*
convenience store	konbini sutoā	*kohn-bee-nee stoh-ah*
dairy	gyūnyū ya	*gyōo-nyōo yah*
delicatessen	derikatessen	*deh-ree-kah-tehs-sehn*
fish store	sakana ya	*sah-kah-nah yah*
fruit store	kudamono ya	*koo-dah-moh-noh yah*
grocery store	shokuryōhin ten	*shoh-koo-ryoh-heen tehn*

ice cream parlor	aisukurīmu ya	*ah-ees-koo-rēe-moo yah*
liquor store	sakaya	*sah-kah-yah*
market	ichiba	*ee-chee-bah*
pastry shop	kēki ya	*kēh-kee yah*
produce market	yasai ichiba	*yah-sah-ee ee-chee-bah*
rice store	okome ya	*oh-koh-meh ya*
supermarket	sūpā	*soo-pāh*
tea store	ocha ya	*oh-chah yah*
vegetable store	yasai ya	*yah-sah-ee yah*

o. FOOD AND DRINK: ACTIVITIES

add up the bill	kanjō ni tsuketasu (v)	*kahn-jōh nee tskeh-tah-soo*
bake	tenpi de yaku (v)	*tehn-pee deh yah-koo*
beat	kakuhansuru (v)	*kah-koo-hahn-soo-roo*
be hungry	onaka ga suite imasu	*oh-nah-kah gah soo-ee-teh ee-mahs*
be thirsty	nodo ga kawaite imasu	*noh-doh gah kah-wah-ee-teh ee-mahs*
boil	yuderu (v)	*yoo-deh-roo*
broil	jikabi de yaku (v)	*jee-kah-bee deh yah-koo*
carve	kiriwakeru (v)	*kee-ree-wah-keh-roo*
chop	kizamu (v)	*kee-zah-moo*
clear the table	atokatazukesuru (v)	*ah-toh-kah-tah-zoo-keh-soo-roo*
cook	ryōrisuru (v)	*ryōh-ree-soo-roo*
cost	kakaru (v)	*kah-kah-roo*
cut	kiru (v)	*KEE-roo*
drink	nomu (v)	*noh-moo*
eat	taberu (v)	*tah-beh-roo*
grate	orosu (v)	*oh-roh-soo*
grill	amiyaki ni suru (v)	*ah-mee-yah-kee nee soo-roo*
have a snack	kanshokusuru (v)	*kahn-shoh-koo-soo-roo*
have breakfast	asagohan o taberu (v)	*ah-sah-goh-hahn oh tah-beh-roo*
have dinner	bangohan o taberu (v)	*bahn-goh-hahn oh tah-beh-roo*
have lunch	hirugohan o taberu (v)	*hee-roo-goh-hahn oh tah-beh-roo*
mix	mazeru (v)	*mah-zeh-roo*
order	chūmonsuru (v)	*chōo-mohn-soo-roo*
peel	kawa o muku (v)	*kah-wah oh moo-koo*
pour	tsugu (v)	*tsoo-goo*
serve (*food or drink*)	dasu (v)	*dah-soo*
set the table	tēburu o totonoeru (v)	*tēh-boo-roo oh toh-toh-noh-eh-roo*

shop for food	shokuryōhin o kau (v)	*shoh-koo-ryōh-heen oh kah-oo*
slice	usugiri ni suru (v)	*oo-soo-gee-ree nee soo-roo*
steam	musu (v)	*moo-soo*
stir	kakimawasu (v)	*kah-kee-mah-wah-soo*
take out (*food to go*)	mochikaeru (v)	*moh-chee-kah-eh-roo*
toast	kongari yaku (v)	*kohn-gah-ree yah-koo*
weigh	mekata o hakaru (v)	*meh-kah-tah oh hah-kah-roo*

p. DESCRIBING FOOD AND DRINK

appetizing	oishisō na (adj)	*oh-ee-shee-sōh nah*
bad	mazui (adj)	*mah-zoo-ee*
bitter	nigai (adj)	*nee-gah-ee*
cheap	yasui (adj)	*yah-soo-ee*
chilled	hiyashita (adj)	*hee-yah-shtah*
cold	tsumetai (adj)	*tsoo-meh-tah-ee*
double	daburu no (adj)	*dah-boo-roo noh*
expensive	takai (adj)	*tah-kah-ee*
good	oishii (adj)	*oh-ee-shēē*
hot (*spice*)	karai (adj)	*kah-rah-ee*
hot (*temperature*)	atsui (adj)	*ah-tsoo-ee*
lukewarm	namanurui (adj)	*nah-mah-noo-roo-ee*
mild	karakunai (adj)	*kah-rah-koo-nah-ee*
salty	shiokarai (adj)	*shee-oh-kah-rah-ee*
single	shinguru no (adj)	*sheen-goo-roo noh*
sour	suppai (adj)	*soop-pah-ee*
spicy	piritto shita (adj)	*pee-reet-toh shtah*
strong	tsuyoi (adj)	*tsoo-yoh-ee*
sweet	amai (adj)	*ah-mah-ee*
tasty	oishii (adj)	*oh-ee-shēē*
weak	yowai (adj)	*yoh-wah-ee*
with ice	kōri o irete (adv)	*kōh-ree oh ee-reh-teh*
without ice	kōri o irenaide (adv)	*kōh-ree oh ee-reh-nah-ee-deh*

Sake (Japanese rice wine) is pronounced *sah-keh*, not *SAH-kee*. There are several ways of serving it.

chilled sake	reishu	*rēh-shou*
hot sake	atsukan	*ahts-kahn*
sake on the rocks	sake no on za rokku	*sah-keh noh ohn zah rokku*
straight sake	hiya	*hee-yah*

25. SHOPPING AND ERRANDS

a. GENERAL VOCABULARY

bag (*shopping*)	kaimonobukuro	*kah-ee-moh-noh-boo-koo-roo*
bill	seikyūsho	*seh-kyōō-shoh*
buy	kau (*v*)	*kah-oo*
cash register	shiharai basho	*shee-hah-rah-ee bah-shoh*
• cashier	shiharaigakari	*shee-hah-rah-ee-gah-kah-ree*
change (*money*)	otsuri	*oh-tsoo-ree*
• change	kuzusu (*v*)	*koo-zoo-soo*
cost	nedan	*neh-dahn*
• cost	kakaru (*v*)	*kah-kah-roo*
• How much does it cost?	Ikura desu ka.	*EE-koo-rah dehs kah*
counter	kauntā	*kah-oon-tāh*
customer	okyaku	*oh-kyah-koo*
department (*of a store*)	uriba	*oo-ree-bah*
entrance	iriguchi	*ee-ree-goo-chee*
exchange	kōkansuru (*v*)	*koh-kahn-soo-roo*
exit	deguchi	*deh-goo-chee*
gift	gifuto	*gee-foo-toh*
look for something	sagasu (*v*)	*sah-gah-soo*
package	tsutsumi	*tsoo-tsoo-mee*
pay	harau (*v*)	*hah-rah-oo*
• with cash	genkin de (*adv*)	*gehn-keen deh*
• with a check	kogitte de (*adv*)	*koh-geet-teh deh*
• with a credit card	kurejittokādo de (*adv*)	*koo-reh- jeet-toh-kāh-doh deh*
price	nedan	*neh-dahn*
• discount	waribiki no (*adj*)	*wah-ree-bee-kee noh*
• expensive	takai (*adj*)	*tah-kah-ee*
• fixed price	teika	*teh-kah*
• inexpensive	yasui (*adj*)	*yah-soo-ee*
• price tag	nedanhyō	*neh-dahn-hyōh*
• reduced price	waribiki nedan	*wah-ree-bee-kee neh-dahn*
purchase	kaimono	*kah-ee-moh-noh*
• purchase	kau (*v*)	*kah-oo*
receipt	reshīto	*reh-shēē-toh*
• Receipt, please!	Reshīto o onegai shimasu.	*reh-SHĒ Ē-toh oh oh-neh-gah-ee shee-mahs*
refund	haraimodoshi	*hah-rah-ee-moh-doh-shee*
• refund	haraimodosu (*v*)	*hah-rah-ee-moh-doh-soo*
sale	hanbai	*hahn-bah-ee*
• for sale	uridashichū	*oo-ree-dah-shee-chōō*

• on sale	sēru	*seh-roo*
• sell	uru (*v*)	*oo-roo*
shop	mise	*mee-seh*
• shop	kaimonosuru (*v*)	*kah-ee-moh-noh-soo-roo*
spend	tsukau (*v*)	*tsoo-kah-oo*
store	mise	*mee-seh*
• closed	heiten	*heh-tehn*
• closing time	heiten jikan	*heh-tehn jee-kahn*
• department store	depāto	*deh-pah-toh*
• open	kaitensuru (*v*)	*kah-ee-tehn-soo-roo*
• opening hours	eigyō jikan	*eh-gyoh jee-kahn*
• store clerk	ten-in	*tehn-een*
• store/shop window	shōwindō	*shoh-ween-doh*
take (*purchase*)	kau (*v*)	*kah-oo*
• take back	kaesu (*v*)	*kah-eh-soo*

b. HARDWARE

battery	denchi	*dehn-chee*
	batterī	*baht-teh-ree*
bolt	boruto	*boh-roo-toh*
cable	hifuku densen	*hee-foo-koo dehn-sehn*
clamp	shimegu	*shee-meh-goo*
drill	doriru	*doh-ree-roo*
electrical	denki (no) (*adj*)	*dehn-kee (noh)*
file	yasuri	*yah-soo-ree*
flashlight	kaichūdentō	*kah-ee-choo-dehn-toh*
fuse	hyūzu	*hyoo-zoo*
glue	setchakuzai	*seht-chah-koo-zah-ee*
hammer	kanazuchi	*kah-nah-zoo-chee*

> a hard-headed person = kanazuchi atama   *kah- nah-zoo-chee*
> (*lit.* a hammer head)   *ah-tah-mah*

hardware store	daikudōgu ten	*dah-ee-koo-doh-goo tehn*
insulation (*wire*)	zetsuen	*zeh-tsoo-ehn*
light (*bulb*)	denkyū	*dehn-kyoo*
• fluorescent light	keikōtō	*keh-koh-toh*
masking tape	masukingu tēpu	*mahs-keen-goo teh-poo*
mechanical	shudō no (*adj*)	*shoo-doh noh*
monkey wrench	jizai supana	*jee-zah-ee spah-nah*
nail	kugi	*koo-gee*
nut	natto	*naht-toh*
outlet	konsento	*kohn-sehn-toh*
plane	kanna	*kahn-nah*
pliers	penchi	*pehn-chee*

plug	puragu	*POO-rah-goo*
plumbing	haikan	*hah-ee-kahn*
punch	panchi	*pahn-chee*
sandpaper	kamiyasuri	*kah-mee-yah-soo-ree*
saw	nokogiri	*noh-koh-gee-ree*
screw	neji	*neh-jee*
screwdriver	nejimawashi	*neh-jee-mah-wah-shee*
shovel	shaberu	*shah-beh-roo*
tool	daikudōgu	*dah-ee-koo-dōh-goo*
transformer	henatsuki	*hehn-ah-tsoo-kee*
vise	manriki	*mahn-ree-kee*
washer	wasshā	*wahs-shah*
wire	harigane	*hah-ree-gah-neh*
wrench	supana	*spah-nah*

c. STATIONERY

adhesive tape	setchaku tēpu	*seht-chah-koo tēh-poo*
ballpoint pen	bōrupen	*bōh-roo-pehn*
eraser	keshigomu	*keh-shee-goh-moo*
envelope	fūtō	*foo-tōh*
felt tip pen	feruto pen	*feh-roo-toh pehn*
fountain pen	mannenhitsu	*mahn-nehn-hee-tsoo*
glue	setchakuzai	*seht-chah-koo-zah-ee*
ink	inku	*een-koo*
notebook	nōto	*noh-toh*
paper	kami	*kah-mee*
paper clip	kurippu	*koo-reep-poo*
pen	pen	*pehn*
pencil	enpitsu	*ehn-pee-tsoo*
pencil sharpener	enpitsu kezuri	*ehn-pee-tsoo keh-zoo-ree*
rubber band	wagomu	*wah-goh-moo*
ruler	jōgi	*jōh-gee*
scissors	hasami	*hah-sah-mee*
staple	hotchikisu no hari	*hoht-chee-kee-soo noh hah-ree*
stapler	hotchikisu	*hoht-chee-kee-soo*
stationery	binsen	*been-sehn*
stationery store	bunbōgu ten	*boon-bōh-goo tehn*
string	himo	*hee-moh*
thumbtack	gabyō	*gah-byōh*
writing pad	hikki yōshi	*heek-kee yōh-shee*

d. PHOTO/CAMERA

camera	kamera	*kah·meh-rah*
• **camcorder**	kamukōdā	*kah-moo-koh-dah*
• **video camera**	bideo kamera	*bee-deh-oh kah-meh-rah*
camera shop	kamera ya	*kah-meh-rah yah*
develop	genzōsuru (v)	*gehn-zoh-soo-roo*
• **development**	genzō	*gehn-zoh*
enlarge	hikinobasu (v)	*hee-kee-noh-bah-soo*
• **enlargement**	hikinobashi	*hee-kee-noh-bah-shee*
extra copy	yakimashi	*yah-kee-mah-shee*
film	fuirumu	*foo-ee-roo-moo*
• **black and white film**	shiro kuro no fuirumu	*shee-roh koo-roh noh foo-ee-roo-moo*
• **color film**	karā fuirumu	*kah-rah foo-ee-roo-moo*
filter	firutā	*fee-roo-tah*
finish	shiagari	*shee-ah-gah-ree*
• **glossy**	kōtaku no aru (adj)	*koh-tah-koo noh ah-roo*
• **matte**	tsuyakeshi no (adj)	*tsoo-yah-keh-shee noh*
flash	furasshu	*foo-rahs-shoo*
lens	renzu	*rehn-zoo*
• **telescopic lens**	bōen renzu	*boh-ehn rehn-zoo*
• **wide angle lens**	kōkaku renzu	*koh-kah-koo rehn-zoo*
• **zoom lens**	zūmu renzu	*zoo-moo rehn-zoo*
photo, picture	shashin	*shah-sheen*
• **clear**	senmei na (adj)	*sehn-meh nah*
• **out of focus**	pinboke no (adj)	*peen-boh-keh noh*
• **color picture**	karā shashin	*kah-rah shah-sheen*
• **focus**	shōten o awaseru (v)	*shoh-tehn oh ah-wah-seh-roo*
• **in black and white**	shiro kuro de	*shee-roh koo-roh deh*
• **take a picture**	sahshin o toru (v)	*shah-sheen oh toh-roo*
• **The picture turned out badly.**	Shashin wa, yoku utsutte imasen deshita.	*shah-sheen wah, YOH-koo oo-tsoot-teh ee-mah-sehn deh-shtah*
• **The picture turned out well.**	Shashin wa, yoku utsutte imashita.	*shah-sheen wah, YOH-koo oo-tsoot-teh ee-mah-shtah*
print	purinto	*poo-reen-toh*
screen	sukurīn	*skoo-reen*
slide	suraido	*soo-rah-ee-doh*
tripod	sankyaku	*sahn-kyah-koo*

e. TOBACCO

cigar	hamaki	*hah-mah-kee*
cigarette	tabako	*tah-bah-koh*
lighter	raitā	*rah-ee-tah*
matches	matchi	*maht-chee*
pipe	paipu	*pah-ee-poo*
tobacco	kizami tabako	*kee-zah-mee tah-bah-koh*
tobacco shop	tabako senmonten	*tah-bah-koh sehn-mohn-tehn*

f. COSMETICS/TOILETRIES

bath oil	basu oiru	*bah-soo oh-ee-roo*
cologne	ōdekoron	*oh-deh-koh-rohn*
comb	kushi	*koo-shee*
cosmetics shop	keshōhin ten	*keh-shoh-heen tehn*
curler	kārā	*kah-rah*
deodorant	deodoranto	*deh-oh-doh-rahn-toh*
electric razor	denki kamisori	*dehn-kee kah-mee-soh-ree*
emery board	tsume yasuri	*tsoo-meh yah-soo-ree*
eyeliner	airainā	*ah-ee-rah-ee-nah*
eye shadow	aishadō	*ah-ee-shah-doh*
face powder	oshiroi	*oh-shee-roh-ee*
hairbrush	heā burashi	*heh-ah boo-rah-shee*
hair conditioner	rinsu	*reen-soo*
hair dryer	heā doraiyā	*heh-ah doh-rah-ee-yah*
hairspray	heā supurē	*heh-ah spoo-reh*
hand lotion	hando rōshon	*hahn-doh roh-shohn*
lipstick	kuchibeni	*koo-chee-beh-nee*
makeup	okeshō	*oh-keh-shoh*
mascara	masukara	*mahs-kah-rah*
mirror	kagami	*kah-gah-mee*
nail clippers	tsume kiri	*tsoo-meh kee-ree*
nail polish	manikyua eki	*mah-nee-kyoo-ah eh-kee*
nail polish remover	jokōeki	*joh-koh-eh-kee*
perfume	kōsui	*koh-soo-ee*
razor	kamisori	*kah-mee-soh-ree*
razor blade	kamisori no ha	*kah-mee-soh-ree noh hah*
shampoo	shanpū	*shahn-poo*
shaving cream	shēbingu kurīmu	*sheh-been-goo koo-ree-moo*
soap	sekken	*sehk-kehn*
talcum powder	shikkarōru	*sheek-kah-roh-roo*
tissues	tisshū	*tees-shoo*
toothbrush	haburashi	*hah-boo-rah-shee*

| toothpaste | nerihamigaki | *neh-ree-hah-mee-gah-kee* |
| tweezers | kenuki | *keh-noo-kee* |

g. LAUNDRY

bleach	hyōhakuzai	*hyoh-hah-koo-zah-ee*
button	botan	*boh-tahn*
clean	kirei na (*adj*)	*kee-reh nah*
clothes	sentakumono	*sehn-tah-koo-moh-noh*
• clothes basket	sentaku kago	*sehn-tah-koo kah-goh*
• clothespin	sentakubasami	*sehn-tah-koo-bah-sah-mee*
dirty	yogoreta (*adj*)	*yoh-goh-reh-tah*
dry cleaner	doraikurīningu ya	*doh-rah-ee-koo-rēe-neen-goo yah*
fabric softener	sofuto shiagezai	*soh-foo-toh shee-ah-geh-zah-ee*
hole	ana	*ah-nah*
iron	airon	*ah-ee-rohn*
• iron	airon o kakeru (*v*)	*ah-ee-rohn oh kah-keh-roo*
laundromat	koin randorī	*koh-een rahn-doh-rēe*
laundry	sentakumono	*sehn-tah-koo-moh-noh*
mend	tsukurou (*v*)	*tsoo-koo-roh-oo*
pocket	poketto	*poh-keht-toh*
sew	nuu (*v*)	*noo-oo*
sleeve	sode	*soh-deh*
soap powder	konasekken	*koh-nah-sehk-kehn*
spot, stain	shimi	*shee-mee*
starch	sentaku nori	*sehn-tah-koo noh-ree*
stitch	hitohari	*hee-toh-hah-ree*
wash	sentakusuru (*v*)	*sehn-tahk-soo-roo*
• washable	araeru (*adj*)	*ah-rah-eh-roo*
zipper	jippā	*jeep-pāh*

h. PHARMACY/DRUGSTORE

antacid	isan	*ee-sahn*
antibiotic	kōseibusshitsu	*koh-seh-boos-shee-tsoo*
antiseptic	shōdokuyaku	*shoh-doh-koo-yah-koo*
aspirin	asupirin	*ahs-pee-reen*
bandage	hōtai	*hoh-tah-ee*
Band-Aid	bandoeido	*bahn-doh-eh-ee-doh*
cortisone	kōchizon	*koh-chee-zohn*
cotton	dasshimen	*dahs-shee-mehn*
cotton swab	menbō	*mehn-boh*
cough syrup	sekidome shiroppu	*seh-kee-doh-meh shee-rohp-poo*

drugstore	doraggusutoā	*doh-rahg-goo-stoh-āh*
eye drops	megusuri	*meh-goo-soo-ree*
gauze	gāze	*gah-zeh*
injection	chūsha	*chōo-shah*
insulin	inshurin	*een-shoo-reen*
laxative	gezai	*geh-zah-ee*
medicine	kusuri	*ksoo-ree*
ointment	nankō	*nahn-koh*
penicillin	penishirin	*peh-nee-shee-reen*
pharmaceutical drug	chōgōyaku	*choh-goh-yah-koo*
pharmacist	yakuzaishi	*yah-koo-zah-ee-shee*
pharmacy	yakkyoku	*yahk-kyoh-koo*
pill	ganyaku	*gahn-yah-koo*
powder	konagusuri	*koh-nah-goo-soo-ree*
prescription	shohōsen	*shoh-hoh-sehn*
sanitary napkin	seiri napukin	*seh-ree nah-poo-keen*
sodium bicarbonate	jūtansannatoriumu	*jōo-tahn-sahn-nah-toh-ree-oo-moo*
sodium citrate	kuensansōda	*koo-ehn-sahn-soh-dah*
syrup	shiroppu	*shee-rohp-poo*
tablet	jōzai	*joh-zah-ee*
tampon	tanpon	*tahn-pohn*
thermometer	taionkei	*tah-ee-ohn-keh*
tincture of iodine	yōdochinki	*yoh-doh-cheen-kee*
vitamin	bitaminzai	*bee-tah-meen-zah-ee*

i. JEWELRY

artificial	jinkō no (*adj*)	*jeen-koh noh*
bracelet	udewa	*oo-deh-wah*
brooch	burōchi	*boo-roh-chee*
carat	karatto .	*kah-raht-toh*
chain	kusari	*ksah-ree*
diamond	daiamondo	*dah-ee-ah-mohn-doh*
earring	iaringu	*ee-ah-reen-goo*
emerald	emerarudo	*eh-meh-rah-roo-doh*
false	imitēshon no (*adj*)	*ee-mee-teh-shohn noh*
fix, repair	shūrisuru (*v*)	*shōo-ree-soo-roo*
gold	kin	*keen*
jewel	hōseki	*hoh-seh-kee*
jeweler	hōshokuten	*hoh-shoh-koo-tehn*
necklace	nekkuresu	*nehk-koo-reh-soo*
opal	opāru	*oh-pah-roo*
pearl	shinju	*sheen-joo*
	pāru	*pah-roo*

| Pearls (cast) before swine. | = Buta ni shinju. | *boo-tah nee sheen-joo* |

platinum	purachina	*poo-rah-chee-nah*
precious stone	kiseki	*kee-seh-kee*
ring	yubiwa	*yoo-bee-wah*
ruby	rubī	*roo-bee*
sapphire	safaia	*sah-fah-ee-ah*
silver	gin	*geen*
topaz	topāzu	*TOH-pah-zoo*
true	honmono no (*adj*)	*hohn-moh-noh noh*
watch, clock	tokei	*toh-keh*
• **watchband**	tokei no bando	*toh-keh noh bahn-doh*
• **wristwatch**	udedokei	*oo-deh-doh-keh*

j. MUSIC

band	bando	*bahn-doh*
	gakudan	*gah-koo-dahn*
cassette	kasetto	*kah-seht-toh*
classical music	kurashikku myūjikku	*koo-rah-sheek-koo myoo-jeek-koo*
compact disc	konpakuto disuku	*kohn-pahk-toh dees-koo*
composer	sakkyoku ka	*sahk-kyoh-koo kah*
conductor	shikisha	*shkee-shah*
dance music	dansu ongaku	*dahn-soo ohn-gah-koo*
group	gurūpu	*goo-roo-poo*
jazz	jazu	*jah-zoo*
music	ongaku	*ohn-gah-koo*
musical	myūjikaru	*myoo-jee-kah-roo*
opera	opera	*oh-peh-rah*
orchestra	ōkesutora	*oh-kehs-toh-rah*
popular music	popyurā myūjikku	*poh-pyoo-rah myoo-jeek-koo*
record	rekōdo	*reh-koh-doh*
singer	kashu	*kah-shoo*
	shingā	*sheen-gah*
song	uta	*oo-tah*
tape	tēpu	*teh-poo*

k. CLOTHING

articles of clothing	irui	*ee-roo-ee*

bathing suit	mizugi	*mee-zoo-gee*
bathrobe	basurōbu	*bah-soo-roh-boo*
blazer	burēzā	*boo-reh-zah*
blue jeans	jīnzu	*jeen-zoo*
belt	beruto	*beh-roo-toh*
blouse	burausu	*boo-rah-oo-soo*
bra	burajā	*boo-rah-jah*
cap	bōshi	*boh-shee*
cardigan	kādigan	*kah-dee-gahn*
clothing store	yōfuku ya	*yoh-foo-koo yah*
coat	kōto	*koh-toh*
dress	doresu	*DOH-reh-soo*
dressing room	shichakushitsu	*shchah-koo-shtsoo*
fashion	fasshon	*fahs-shohn*
fur coat	kegawa no kōto	*keh-gah-wah noh koh-toh*
glove	tebukuro	*teh-boo-koo-roo*
handkerchief	hankachi	*hahn-kah-chee*
hat	bōshi	*boh-shee*
jacket	jaketto	*jah-keht-toh*
men's shop	shinshifuku ten	*sheen-shee-fkoo tehn*
pajamas	pajama	*pah-jah-mah*
panties	pantī	*pahn-tee*
pants	zubon	*zoo-bohn*
pantyhose	pantīsutokkingu	*pahn-tee-stohk-keen-goo*
raincoat	reinkōto	*reh-een-koh-toh*
scarf	sukāfu	*skah-foo*
shirt	shatsu	*shah-tsoo*
shorts	shōtsu	*shoh-tsoo*
	hanzubon	*hahn-zoo-bohn*
size	saizu	*sah-ee-zoo*
skirt	sukāto	*skah-toh*
slacks	surakkusu	*soo-rahk-koo-soo*
slip	surippu	*sco-reep-poo*
suit	sūtsu	*soo-tsoo*
sweater	sētā	*seh-tah*
sweatshirt	torēnā	*toh-reh-nah*
tee-shirt	tīshatsu	*tee-shah-tsoo*
three-piece suit	mitsuzoroi	*mee-tsoo-zoh-roh-ee*
tie	nekutai	*nehk-tah-ee*
tights	taitsu	*tah-ee-tsoo*
trenchcoat	torenchikōto	*toh-rehn-chee-koh-toh*
trousers	zubon	*zoo-bohn*
underwear	shitagi	*shtah-gee*
women's shop	fujinfuku ten	*foo-jeen-fkoo tehn*

l. DESCRIBING CLOTHING

> For colors, see Section 7.

beautiful	utsukushii (*adj*)	*oots-kshēē*
big	ōkii (*adj*)	*oh-kēē*
cotton	momen	*moh-mehn*
elegant	ereganto na (*adj*)	*eh-reh-gahn-toh nah*
fabric	kiji	*kee-jee*
in the latest style/fashion	ima hayatte iru	*ee-mah hah-yaht-teh ee-roo*
leather	kawa	*kah-wah*
linen	asa	*ah-sah*
loose	yuttarishita (*adj*)	*yoot-tah-ree-shtah*
nylon	nairon	*nah-ee-rohn*
polyester	poriesuteru	*poh-ree-ehs-teh-roo*
silk	shiruku	*shee-roo-koo*
small	chiisai (*adj*)	*chēē-sah-ee*
suede	suēdo	*soo-eh-doh*
tight	kitsui (*adj*)	*kee-tsoo-ee*
ugly	minikui (*adj*)	*mee-nee-koo-ee*
wool	ūru	*ōō-roo*

m. CLOTHING: ACTIVITIES

alteration	shitatenaoshi	*shee-tah-teh-nah-oh-shee*
change clothes	kigaeru (*v*)	*kee-gah-eh-roo*
enlarge	ōkikusuru (*v*)	*oh-keek-soo-roo*
fold	tatamu (*v*)	*tah-tah-moo*
get dressed	kiru (*v*)	*kee-roo*
hang	kakeru (*v*)	*kah-keh-roo*
lengthen	nagakusuru (*v*)	*nah-gahk-soo-roo*
loosen	yurumeru (*v*)	*yoo-roo-meh-roo*
put on	kiru (*v*)	*kee-roo*
shorten	mijikakusuru (*v*)	*mee-jee-kahk-soo-roo*
take off	nugu (*v*)	*noo-goo*
tighten	pittarisaseru (*v*)	*peet-tah-ree-sah-seh-roo*
try on	tamesu (*v*)	*tah-meh-soo*
undress	nugu (*v*)	*noo-goo*
wear	kiru (*v*)	*kee-roo*

n. SHOES

boot	būtsu	*bōo-tsoo*
heel	kakato	*kah-kah-toh*
high-heeled shoe	haihīru	*hah-ee-hēe-roo*
pair	issoku	*ees-soh-koo*
sandal	sandaru	*sahn-dah-roo*
shoe	kutsu	*ktsoo*
shoe department	kutsu uriba	*ktsoo oo-ree-bah*
shoe lace	kutsu himo	*ktsoo hee-moh*
shoe polish	kutsuzumi	*ktsoo-zoo-mee*
shoe store	kutsu ya	*ktsoo yah*
size	saizu	*sah-ee-zoo*
slipper	surippa	*soo-reep-pah*
sneaker	sunīka	*soo-nēe-kah*
sole	kutsu zoko	*ktsoo zoh-koh*
sock	sokkusu	*sohk-ksoo*
stocking	sutokkingu	*stohk-keen-goo*

o. BOOKS

book	hon	*hohn*
• best seller	besuto serā	*beh-stoh seh-rāh*
bookstore	hon ya	*hohn yah*
comics	manga	*mahn-gah*
cookbook	ryōri no hon	*ryōh-ree noh hohn*
dictionary	jisho	*jee-shoh*
encyclopedia	hyakkajiten	*hyahk-kah-jee-tehn*
guidebook	gaidobukku	*gah-ee-doh-book-koo*
magazine	zasshi	*zahs-shee*
mystery	misuterī	*mees-teh-rēe*
newspaper	shinbun	*sheen-boon*
novel	shōsetsu	*shōh-seh-tsoo*
poetry	shi	*shee*
reference book	sankōsho	*sahn-kōh-shoh*
romance	renaishōsetsu	*rehn-ah-ee-shōh-seh-tsoo*
science fiction	saiensu fikushon	*sah-ee-ehn-soo feek-shohn*
technical book	senmonsho	*sehn-mohn-shoh*
textbook	kyōkasho	*kyōh-kah-shoh*

26. BANKING AND COMMERCE

For numerical concepts, see Section 1.

account	kōza	*koh-zah*
• close an account	kōza o tojiru	*koh-zah oh toh-jee- roo*
• open an account	kōza o hiraku	*koh-zah oh hee-rah-koo*
bank	ginkō	*geen-koh*
• head office	honten	*hohn-tehn*
• work in a bank	ginkō de hataraku	*geen-koh deh hah-tah-rah-koo*
bank book	ginkō tsūchō	*geen-koh tsoo-choh*
bank rate	kōteibuai	*koh-teh-boo-ah-ee*
• fixed	kotei (no) (*adj*)	*koh-teh (noh)*
• variable	hendo (no) (*adj*)	*hehn-doh (noh)*
bill, bank note	osatsu	*oh-sah-tsoo*
• dollar	doru	*doh-roo*
• large bill	ōkii osatsu	*oh-kee oh-sah-tsoo*
• small bill	chiisai osatsu	*chee-sah-ee oh-sah-tsoo*
• yen	en	*ehn*
bond	saiken	*sah-ee-kehn*
budget	yosan	*yoh-sahn*
cash	genkin	*gehn-keen*
• cash	genkinkasuru (*v*)	*gehn-keen-kah-soo-roo*
cashier, teller	madoguchigakari	*mah-doh-goo-chee-gah-kah-ree*
check	kogitte	*koh-geet-teh*
• checkbook	kogitte chō	*koh-geet-teh choh*
cost of living	seikatsuhi	*seh-kah-tsoo-hee*
credit	shinyō	*sheen-yoh*
• credit card	kurejitto kādo	*koo-reh-jeet-toh kah-doh*
currency	tsūka	*tsoo-kah*
current account	tōza kanjō	*toh-zah kahn-joh*
customer	kokyaku	*koh-kyah-koo*
debit	kashikata	*kah-shee-kah-tah*
debt	fusai	*foo-sah-ee*
deposit	yokin	*yoh-keen*
• deposit	yokinsuru (*v*)	*yoh-keen-soo-roo*
• deposit slip	yokinhyō	*yoh-keen-hyoh*
discount	waribiki	*wah-ree-bee-kee*
draft	tegata furidashi	*teh-gah-tah foo-ree-dah-shee*
employee (*bank*)	ginkōin	*geen-koh-een*
endorse	uragakisuru (*v*)	*oo-rah-gah-kee-soo-roo*
• endorsement	uragaki	*oo-rah-gah-kee*
exchange	kōkan	*koh-kahn*
• exchange	kōkansuru (*v*)	*koh-kahn-soo-roo*
• exchange rates	kōkan ritsu	*koh-kahn ree-tsoo*

expiry date	tegata kaitori saishūbi	*teh-gah-tah kah-ee-toh-ree sah-ee-shoo-bee*
income	shūnyū	*shoo-nyoo*
insurance	hoken	*hoh-kehn*
interest	rishi	*ree-shee*
• interest rate	riritsu	*ree-ree-tsoo*
invest	tōshisuru (v)	*toh-shee-soo-roo*
• investment	tōshi	*toh-shee*
line	retsu	*reh-tsoo*
• line up	narabu (v)	*nah-rah-boo*
loan	rōn	*rohn*
• get a loan	yūshi o ukeru (v)	*yoo-shee oh oo-keh-roo*
loose change	kozeni	*koh-zeh-nee*
manager	manējā	*mah-neh-jah*
money	okane	*oh-kah-neh*
money order	kawase	*kah-wah-seh*
mortgage	jūtaku rōn	*joo-tah-koo rohn*
	teitōken	*teh-toh-kehn*
pay	harau (v)	*hah-rah-oo*
• pay off	zengaku shiharau (v)	*zehn-gah-koo shee-hah-rah-oo*
• payment	shiharai	*shee-hah-rah-ee*
postdate	jigohizuke ni suru (v)	*jee-goh-hee-zoo-keh nee soo-roo*
promissory note	yakusoku tegata	*yahk-soh-koo teh-gah-tah*
receipt	uketorishō	*oo-keh-toh-ree-shoh*
safe	kinko	*keen-koh*
• safe deposit box	kashikinko	*kah-shee-keen-koh*
salary	sararī	*sah-rah-ree*
• save	chokinsuru (v)	*choh-keen-soo-roo*
• savings	chokin	*choh-keen*
sign	shomeisuru (v)	*shoh-meh-soo-roo*
• signature	shomei	*shoh-meh*
stock, share	kabuken	*kah-boo-kehn*
• stock market	kabushikishijō	*kah-boo-shee-kee-shee-joh*
teller's window	madoguchi	*mah-doh-goo-chee*
traveler's check	toraberā chekku	*toh-rah-beh-rah chehk-koo*
withdraw	hikidasu (v)	*hee-kee-dah-soo*
• withdrawal	hikidashi	*hee-kee-dah-shee*
• withdrawal slip	hikidashihyō	*hee-kee-dah-shee-hyoh*

27. GAMES AND SPORTS

a. GAMES, HOBBIES, AND PHYSICAL FITNESS

billiards	tamatsuki	*tah-mah-tskee*
• **billiard ball**	tamatsuki no tama	*tah-mah-tskee noh tah-mah*
• **billiard table**	tamatsuki no tēburu	*tah-mah-tskee noh tēh-boo-roo*
• **cue**	tamatsuki no kyū	*tah-mah-tskee noh kyōo*
• **cushion**	kusshon	*koos-shohn*
• **pocket**	poketto	*poh-keht-toh*
bingo	bingo	*been-goh*
• **bingo card**	bingo no kādo	*been-goh noh kah-doh*
checkers	chekkā	*chehk-kah*
• **checkerboard**	chekkā ban	*chehk-kah bahn*
• **checker piece**	chekkā no koma	*chehk-kah noh koh-mah*
chess	chesu	*cheh-soo*
• **bishop**	bishoppu	*bee-shohp-poo*
• **chessboard**	chesu ban	*cheh-soo bahn*
• **king**	kingu	*keen-goo*
• **knight**	naito	*nah-ee-toh*
• **pawn**	pōn	*pohn*
• **queen**	kuīn	*koo-ēen*
• **rook**	rūku	*rōo-koo*
coin	kōka	*koh-kah*
• **coin collecting**	kōka shūshū	*koh-kah shōo-shōo*
cooking	ryōri	*ryoh-ree*
dice	daisu	*dah-ee-soo*
fishing	tsuri	*tsoo-ree*
game	gēmu	*geh-moo*
gardening	engei	*ehn-geh*
hobby	shumi	*shoo-mee*
hunting	shuryō	*shoo-ryoh*
instrument	gakki	*gahk-kee*
• **play** (*an instrument*)	ensōsuru (*v*)	*ehn-soh-soo-roo*
jog	jogingusuru (*v*)	*joh-geen-goo-soo-roo*
• **jogging**	jogingu	*joh-geen-goo*
painting	kaiga	*kah-ee-gah*
play (*a game*)	suru (*v*)	*soo-roo*
playing cards	toranpu	*toh-rahn-poo*
practice a sport	undōsuru (*v*)	*oon-doh-soo-roo*

reading	dokusho	*dohk-shoh*
sports	supōtsu	*spoh-tsoo*
stamp	kitte	*keet-teh*
• stamp collecting	kitte shūshū	*keet-teh shoo-shoo*

Several games are popular leisure-time activities, especially among men. **Go**, Japan's national board game, is a highly sophisticated territorial version of checkers.

Japanese checkers	go	*goh*
Japanese chess	shōgi	*shoh-gee*
Japanese pinball	pachinko	*pah-cheen-koh*
mah-jongg	mājan	*mah-jahn*

---

b. SPORTS

amateur	amachua	*ah-mah-choo-ah*
athlete	undō no senshu	*oon-doh noh sehn-shoo*
badminton	badominton	*bah-doh-meen-tohn*
ball	bōru	*boh-roo*
• catch	toru (v)	*toh-roo*
• hit	utsu (v)	*oo-tsoo*
• kick	keru (v)	*keh-roo*
• pass	pasusuru (v)	*pahs-soo-roo*
• throw	nageru (v)	*nah-geh-roo*
baseball	yakyū	*yah-kyoo*
• base	bēsu	*beh-soo*
• bat	batto	*baht-toh*
• batter	battā	*baht-tah*
• catcher's mask	kyatchā no masuku	*kyaht-chah noh mahs-koo*
• foul line	fāru rain	*fah-roo rah-een*
• glove	gurōbu	*goo-roh-boo*
• home (base)	hōmu	*hoh-moo*
• pitcher	pitchā	*peet-chah*
basketball	basukettobōru	*bahs-keht-toh-boh-roo*
bicycle racing	jitensha kyōsō	*jee-tehn-shah kyoh-soh*
body building	bodī biru	*boh-dee bee-roo*
• weight lifting	jūryōage	*joo-ryoh-ah-geh*
bowling	bōringu	*boh-reen-goo*
• bowl	tama o korogasu (v)	*tah-mah oh koh-roh-gah-soo*
• bowling alley	bōringujō	*boh-reen-goo-joh*
• bowling ball	bōringu no bōru	*boh-reen-goo noh boh-roo*
• bowling pin	pin	*peen*
boxing	bokushingu	*bohk-sheen-goo*

• boxing gloves	gurabu	*goo-rah-boo*
• boxing ring	ringu	*reen-goo*
coach	kōchi	*koh-chee*
competition	kyōgi	*kyoh-gee*
fencing	fenshingu	*fehn-sheen-goo*
• fencing outfit	fenshingu no yunifōmu	*fehn-sheen-goo noh yoo-nee-foh-moo*
• mask	masuku	*mahs-koo*
field	kyōgijō	*kyoh-gee-joh*
football	futtobōru	*foot-toh-boh-roo*
game, match	shiai	*shee-ah-ee*
goal	gōru	*goh-roo*
golf	gorufu	*goh-roo-foo*
gymnasium	jimu	*jee-moo*
• work out	torēningusuru (v)	*toh-reh-neen-goo-soo-roo*
helmet	herumetto	*heh-roo-meht-toh*
ice hockey	aisu hokkē	*ah-ee-soo hohk-keh*
• hockey rink	hokkējō	*hohk-keh-joh*
• hockey stick	sutikku	*steek-koo*
• puck	pakku	*pahk-koo*
mountain climbing	tozan	*TOH-zahn*
• knapsack	nappuzakku	*nahp-poo-zahk-koo*
• mountain boot	tozangutsu	*toh-zahn-goo-tsoo*
• rope	zairu	*zah-ee-roo*
• snow goggles	gōguru	*goh-goo-roo*
net	netto	*neht-toh*
penalty	penarutī	*peh-nah-roo-tee*
Ping-Pong	pinpon	*peen-pohn*
play	shiaisuru (v)	*shee-ah-ee-soo-roo*
• player	senshu	*sehn-shoo*
• playoff	yūshō kettei shirīzu	*yoo-shoh keht-teh shee-ree-zoo*
point	tokuten	*tohk-tehn*
professional	puro	*poo-roh*
race	rēsu	*reh-soo*
• horse racing	keiba	*keh-bah*
referee	refurī	*reh-foo-ree*
run	hashiru (v)	*hah-shee-roo*
sailing	sēringu	*seh-reen-goo*
score	tokuten	*tohk-tehn*
• draw	hikiwake	*hee-kee-wah-keh*
• draw	hikiwakeru (v)	*hee-kee-wah-keh-roo*
• lose	makeru (v)	*mah-keh-roo*
• loss	haiboku	*hah-ee-boh-koo*
• tie	dōten	*doh-tehn*
• win	katsu (v)	*kah-tsoo*
skate	sukēto de suberu (v)	*skeh-toh deh soo-beh-roo*

• skating	sukēto	*skeh-toh*
• roller-skating	rōra sukēto	*roh-rah skeh-toh*
ski	sukī o suru (v)	*skee oh soo-roo*
• skiing	sukī	*skee*
• water skiing	wōtā sukī	*woh-tah skee*
soccer	sakkā	*sahk-kah*
• corner	kōnā	*koh-nah*
• goalkeeper	gōrukīpā	*goh-roo-kee-pah*
• goal kick	gōru kikku	*goh-roo-keek-koo*
sport	supōtsu	*spoh-tsoo*
• sports fan	supōtsu fan	*spoh-tsoo fahn*
• winter sports	fuyu no supōtsu	*foo-yoo noh spoh- tsoo*
stadium	sutajiamu	*stah-jee-ah-moo*
surfing	sāfin	*sah-feen*
swim	oyogu (v)	*oh-yoh-goo*
• swimming	suiei	*soo-ee-eh*
• swimming pool	pūru	*poo-roo*
team	chīmu	*chee-moo*
tennis	tenisu	*teh-nee-soo*
• racket	raketto	*rah-keht-toh*
ticket	ken	*kehn*
tournament	tōnamento	*toh-nah-mehn-toh*
track	torakku	*toh-rahk-koo*
track and field	rikujōkyōgi	*ree-koo-joh-kyoh-gee*
volleyball	barēbōru	*bah-reh-boh-roo*
water polo	suikyū	*soo-ee-kyoo*
wind surfing	windo sāfin	*ween-doh sah-feen*
wrestling	resuringu	*reh-soo-reen-goo*

FOCUS: *Traditional Japanese Sports*

Sumo is centuries-old Japanese wrestling; Professional **sumo** is Japan's national sport.

sumō	*soo-moh*

The Japanese martial arts are also practiced as sports. The most popular kinds are **judo**, **karate**, and **kendo** (Japanese fencing).

jūdō	*joo-doh*
karate	*kah-rah-teh*
kendō	*kehn-doh*

---

28. THE ARTS

a. CINEMA

actor	danyū	*dahn-yoo*

actress	joyū	*joh-yoo*
aisle	tsūro	*tsoo-roh*
box office	kippu uriba	*keep-poo oo-ree-bah*
charge	ryōkin	*ryoh-keen*
first-run film	fūkiri eiga	*foo-kee-ree eh-gah*
foreign movie	gaikoku eiga	*gah-ee-koh-koo eh-gah*
lobby	robī	*roh-bee*
movie, film	eiga	*eh-gah*
• make a movie	eiga o seisakusuru (v)	*eh-gah oh seh-sahk-soo-roo*
• premiere showing	puremia shō	*poo-reh-mee-ah shoh*
movie director	eiga kantoku	*eh-gah kahn-toh-koo*
movie star	eiga sutā	*eh-gah stah*
movie theater	eiga gekijō	*eh-gah geh-kee-joh*
producer	seisakusha	*seh-sahk-shah*
row	retsu	*reh-tsoo*
screen	sukurīn	*skoo-reen*
seat	seki	*seh-kee*
soundtrack	saundotorakku	*sah-oon-doh-toh-rahk-koo*
subtitle	jimaku	*jee-mah-koo*

b. ART/SCULPTURE/ARCHITECTURE

architect	kenchikuka	*kehn-cheek-kah*
• architecture	kenchiku	*kehn-chee-koo*
• blueprint	aojashin	*ah-oh-jah-sheen*
art	geijutsu	*geh-joo-tsoo*
• art gallery	āto gyararī	*ah-toh gyah-rah-ree*
artist	geijutsuka	*geh-joo-tsoo-kah*
brush	burashi	*boo-rah-shee*
drawing	sobyō	*soh-byoh*
easel, tripod	īzeru	*ee-zeh-roo*
etching	etchingu	*eht-cheen-goo*
exhibition	tenjikai	*tehn-jee-kah-ee*
fresco painting	hekiga	*heh-kee-gah*
masterpiece	meisaku	*meh-sah-koo*
museum	bijutsukan	*bee-joo-tsoo-kahn*
paint	e o kaku (v)	*eh oh kah-koo*
• oil paint	aburaenogu	*ah-boo-rah-eh-noh-goo*
• painter	gaka	*gah-kah*
• painting	kaiga	*kah-ee-gah*
palette	paretto	*pah-reht-toh*
pastel	pasuteru	*pahs-teh-roo*
portrait	pōtorēto	*poh-toh-reh-toh*
sculpt	chōkokusuru (v)	*choh-kohk-soo-roo*
• sculptor	chōkokuka	*choh-koh-koo-kah*

• sculpture	chōkoku	*choh-koh-koo*
show	shō	*shoh*
watercolor	suisaiga	*soo-ee-sah-ee-gah*

c. MUSIC/DANCE

accordion	akōdion	*ah-koh-dee-ohn*
ballet	barē	*bah-reh*
brass instruments	kinkan gakki	*keen-kahn gahk-kee*
• horn	horun	*hoh-roon*
• trombone	toronbōn	*toh-rohn-bohn*
• trumpet	toranpetto	*toh-rahn-peht-toh*
• tuba	chūba	*choo-bah*
classical music	kurashikku myūjikku	*koo-rah-sheek-koo myoo-jeek-koo*
composer	sakkyoku ka	*sahk-kyoh-koo kah*
• composition	sakkyoku	*sahk-kyoh-koo*
concert	konsāto	*kohn-sah-toh*
dance	dansu	*dahn-soo*
• dance	odoru (v)	*oh-doh-roo*
• dancer	dansā	*dahn-sah*
	butō ka	*boo-toh kah*
folk dance	fōku dansu	*foh-koo dahn-soo*
folk music	fōku myūjikku	*foh-koo myoo-jeek-koo*
guitar	gitā	*gee-tah*
• guitarist	gitarisuto	*gee-tah-ree-stoh*
harmony	hāmonī	*hah-moh-nee*
harp	hāpu	*hah-poo*
instrument	gakki	*gahk-kee*
• play an instrument	gakki o ensōsuru (v)	*gahk-kee oh ehn-soh-soo-roo*
jazz	jazu	*jah-zoo*
keyboard instruments	kenban gakki	*kehn-bahn gahk-kee*
• grand piano	gurando piano	*goo-rahn-doh pee-ah-noh*
• harpsichord	hapushikōdo	*hah-pshee-koh-doh*
• keyboard	kenban	*kehn-bahn*
• organ	orugan	*oh-roo-gahn*
• piano	piano	*pee-ah-noh*
• synthesizer	shinsesaizā	*sheen-seh-sah-ee-zah*
• upright piano	tategata piano	*tah-teh-gah-tah pee-ah-noh*
light music	kei ongaku	*keh ohn-gah-koo*
mandolin	mandorin	*mahn-doh-reen*
modern dance	modan dansu	*moh-dahn dahn-soo*
music	ongaku	*ohn-gah-koo*
• musician	ongakuka	*ohn-gahk-kah*

note	onpu	*ohn-poo*
opera	opera	*oh-peh-rah*
orchestra	ōkesutora	*oh-kehs-toh-rah*
orchestra conductor	ōkesutora no shikisha	*oh-kehs-toh-rah noh shee-kee-shah*
percussion instruments	dagakki	*dah-gahk-kee*
• bass drum	ōdaiko	*oh-dah-ee-koh*
• cymbals	shinbaru	*sheen-bah-roo*
• drum	taiko	*tah-ee-koh*
• set of drums	taiko no setto	*tah-ee-koh noh seht-toh*
• tambourine	tanbarin	*tahn-bah-reen*
• timpani	tinpanī	*teen-pah-nee*
pianist	pianisuto	*pee-ah-nee-stoh*
player	ensōka	*ehn-soh-kah*
rhythm	rizumu	*ree-zoo-moo*
score	gakufu	*gahk-foo*
show	shō	*shoh*
song	uta	*oo-tah*
• sing	utau (v)	*oo-tah-oo*
• singer	kashu	*kah-shoo*
stringed instruments	gengakki	*gehn-gahk-kee*
• banjo	banjō	*bahn-joh*
• bow	yumi	*yoo-mee*
• cello	chero	*cheh-roh*
• double bass	kontorabasu	*kohn-toh-rah-bah-soo*
• string	gen	*gehn*
• ukulele	ukurere	*oo-koo-reh-reh*
• viola	biora	*bee-oh-rah*
• violin	baiorin	*bah-ee-oh-reen*
symphony	shinhonī	*sheen-hoh-nee*
violinist	baiorin ensōsha	*bah-ee-oh-reen ehn-soh-shah*
wind instruments	mokkan gakki	*mohk-kahn gahk-kee*
• bagpipes	baggupaipu	*bahg-goo-pah-ee-poo*

FOCUS: *Traditional Japanese Dance, Music, and Musical Instruments*

folk dance	bon odori	*bohn oh-doh-ree*
formal dance	nihon buyō	*nee-hon boo-yoh*
court music	gagaku	*gah-gah-koo*
bamboo clarinet	shakuhachi	*shah-koo-hah-chee*
Japanese harp	koto	*koh-toh*
Japanese mandolin	shamisen	*shah-mee-sehn*

- **bassoon** fagotto *fah-goht-toh*
- **clarinet** kurarinetto *koo-rah-ree-neht-toh*
- **flute** furūto *foo-rōō-toh*
- **oboe** ōboe *ōh-boh-eh*
- **saxophone** sakisofōn *sah-kee-soh-fōhn*

d. LITERATURE

appendix	furoku	*foo-roh-koo*
autobiography	jiden	*jee-dehn*
biography	denki	*dehn-kee*
chapter	shō	*shōh*
character (*novel, play*)	tōjō jinbutsu	*toh-jōh jeen-boo-tsoo*
criticism	hyōron	*hyōh-rohn*
essay	essei	*ehs-sēh*
fable	gūwa	*gōō-wah*
fairy tale	dōwa	*doh-wah*
fiction	fikushon	*feek-shohn*
genre	yōshiki	*yoh-shee-kee*
literature	bungaku	*boon-gah-koo*
myth	shinwa	*sheen-wah*
mythology	shinwa	*sheen-wah*
novel	shōsetsu	*shoh-seh-tsoo*
plot	suji	*soo-jee*
poet	shijin	*shee-jeen*
poetry	shi	*shee*
preface	maeoki	*mah-eh-oh-kee*
prose	sanbun	*sahn-boon*
short story	tanpen shōsetsu	*tahn-pehn shōh-seh-tsoo*
style	buntai	*boon-tah-ee*
theme	tēma	*tēh-mah*
work (*literary*)	chosaku	*choh-sah-koo*
writer	sakka	*sahk-kah*

e. THEATER

act	maku	*mah-koo*
• **act**	enjiru (*v*)	*ehn-jee-roo*
applause	hakushu	*hahk-shoo*
• **applaud**	hakushusuru (*v*)	*hahk-shoo-soo-roo*
audience	kankyaku	*kahn-kyah-koo*
comedian	kigeki yakusha	*kee-geh-kee yahk-shah*
comedy	kigeki	*kee-geh-kee*
curtain	maku	*mah-koo*
drama	dorama	*doh-rah-mah*

hero	shujinkō	*shoo-jeen-kōh*
heroine	onna shujinkō	*ohn-nah shoo-jeen-kōh*
intermission	makuai	*mah-koo-ah-ee*
mime	mugon geki	*moo-gohn geh-kee*
pantomime	monomane	*moh-noh-mah-neh*
play	engeki	*ehn-geh-kee*
playwright	geki sakka	*geh-kee sahk-kah*
plot	suji	*soo-jee*
program	puroguramu	*poo-roh-goo-rah-moo*
scene	bamen	*bah-mehn*
scenery	haikei	*hah-ee-kēh*
stage	butai	*boo-tah-ee*
theater	gekijō	*geh-kee-jōh*
tragedy	higeki	*hee-geh-kee*

FOCUS: *Three Major Forms of Traditional Japanese Theater*

dance-drama	Kabuki	*kah-boo-kee*
masked play	Noh	*nōh*
puppet theater	Bunraku	*boon-rah-koo*

29. HOLIDAYS AND GOING OUT

a. HOLIDAYS/SPECIAL OCCASIONS

anniversary	kinenbi	*kee-nehn-bee*
birthday	tanjōbi	*tahn-jōh-bee*
Christmas	kurisumasu	*koo-ree-soo-mah-soo*
engagement	konyaku	*kohn-yah-koo*
holiday	shukujitsu	*shoo-koo-jee-tsoo*
New Year's Day	shinnen	*sheen-nehn*
New Year's Eve	ōmisoka no ban	*ōh-mee-soh-kah noh bahn*
picnic	pikunikku	*pee-koo-neek-koo*
vacation	bakansu	*BAH-kahn-soo*
wedding	kekkonshiki	*kehk-kohn-shkee*

b. GOING OUT

dance	dansu	*dahn-soo*
• **dance**	odoru (*v*)	*oh-doh-roo*
disco	disuko	*dees-koh*
go out	dekakeru (*v*)	*deh-kah-keh-roo*
have fun	tanoshimu (*v*)	*tah-noh-shee-moo*

party	pātī	*pah-tee*
remain	nokoru (*v*)	*noh-koh-roo*
return	kaeru (*v*)	*kah-eh-roo*
visit	hōmonsuru (*v*)	*hoh-mohn-soo-roo*

c. SPECIAL GREETINGS

Best wishes!	Gokōun o.	*goh-koh-oon oh.*
Congratulations!	Omedetō gozaimasu.	*oh-meh-deh-toh goh-zah-ee-mahs*
Happy Birthday!	Tanjōbi omedetō.	*tahn-joh-bee oh-meh-deh-toh*
Happy New Year!	Shinnen omedetō.	*sheen-nehn oh-meh-deh-toh*
Have a good holiday!	Oyasumi o, otano-shimi kudasai.	*oh-yah-soo-mee oh, oh-TAH-noh-shee-mee koo-dah-sah-ee*
Have fun!	Tanoshinde kite kudasai.	*tah-noh-sheen-deh kee-teh koo-dah-sah-ee*
Merry Christmas!	Kurisumasu omedetō.	*koo-ree-soo-mah-soo oh-meh-deh-toh*

TRAVEL

30. CHOOSING A DESTINATION

For more related vocabulary, see Section 13e.

a. AT THE TRAVEL AGENCY

abroad	kaigai ni (*adv*)	*kah-ee-gah-ee nee*
brochure	panfuretto	*pahn-foo-reht-toh*
charter flight	chāta bin	*chah-tah been*
city	toshi	*toh-shee*
• capital city	shuto	*shoo-toh*
class	kurasu	*koo-rah-soo*
• business class	bijinesu kurasu	*bee-jee-nehs koo-rah-soo*
• economy class	ekonomī kurasu	*eh-koh-noh-mee koo-rah-soo*
• first class (*plane*)	fāsuto kurasu	*fah-stoh koo-rah-soo*
• first class (*train*)	gurīn sha	*goo-reen shah*
connection	konekushon	*koh-nehk-shohn*
continent	tairiku	*tah-ee-ree-koo*
country	kuni	*koo-nee*
discount	waribiki	*wah-ree-bee-kee*
• group discount	dantai waribiki	*dahn-tah-ee wah-ree-bee-kee*
• senior discount	kōreisha waribiki	*koh-reh-shah wah-ree-bee-kee*
• student discount	gakusei waribiki	*gahk-seh wah-ree-bee-kee*
downtown	toshin	*toh-sheen*
excursion	gurūpu tsuā	*goo-roo-poo tsoo-ah*
insurance	hoken	*hoh-kehn*
nation	kokka	*kohk-kah*
outskirts, suburbs	kōgai	*koh-gah-ee*
passport	pasupōto	*pahs-poh-toh*
reservation	yoyaku	*yoh-yah-koo*
• reserve	yoyakusuru (*v*)	*yoh-yahk-soo-roo*
see	miru (*v*)	*mee-roo*
ticket	ken	*kehn*
• advance ticket	maeuri ken	*mah-eh-oo-ree kehn*
• boat ticket	fune no ken	*foo-neh noh kehn*
• buy a ticket	ken o kau (*v*)	*kehn oh kah-oo*

• one-way ticket	katamichi ken	*kah-tah-mee-chee kehn*
• plane ticket	kōkū ken	*koh-koo kehn*
• round-trip ticket	ōfuku ken	*oh-fkoo kehn*
• train ticket	kisha no kippu	*kee-shah noh keep-poo*
tour	kankō ryokō	*kahn-koh ryoh-koh*
tour bus	kankō basu	*kahn-koh bah-soo*
tour guide	kankō gaido	*kahn-koh gah-ee-doh*
tourist	kankō kyaku	*kahn-koh kyah-koo*
travel	ryokō	*ryoh-koh*
• travel	ryokōsuru (*v*)	*ryoh-koh-soo-roo*
• travel agency	ryokō dairiten	*ryoh-koh dah-ee-ree-tehn*
trip, journey	ryokō	*ryoh-koh*
• Have a nice trip!	Ryokō o, otanoshimi kudasai.	*ryoh-koh oh oh-tah-noh-shee-mee koo-dah-sah-ee*
• take a trip	ryokō ni iku	*ryoh-koh nee ee-koo*
visa	biza	*bee-zah*
visit	hōmonsuru (*v*)	*hoh-mohn-soo-roo*
world	sekai	*seh-kah-ee*

b. COUNTRIES AND CONTINENTS

Africa	Afurika	*ah-foo-ree-kah*
America	Amerika	*ah-meh-ree-kah*
• Central America	Chūō Amerika	*choo-oh ah-meh-ree-kah*
• Latin America	Raten Amerika	*rah-tehn ah-meh-ree-kah*
• North America	Kita Amerika	*kee-tah ah-meh-ree-kah*
• South America	Minami Amerika	*mee-nah-mee ah-meh-ree-kah*
Argentina	Aruzenchin	*ah-roo-zehn-cheen*
Asia	Ajia	*ah-jee-ah*
Australia	Ōsutoraria	*oh-stoh-rah-ree-ah*
Austria	Ōsutoria	*oh-stoh-ree-ah*
Belgium	Berugī	*beh-roo-gee*
Bolivia	Boribia	*boh-ree-bee-ah*
Brazil	Burajiru	*boo-rah-jee-roo*
Burma	Biruma	*bee-roo-mah*
Canada	Kanada	*kah-nah-dah*
Chile	Chiri	*chee-ree*
China	Chūgoku	*choo-goh-koo*
Colombia	Koronbia	*koh-rohn-bee-ah*
Czechoslovakia	Chekosurobakia	*cheh-koh-soo-roh-bah-kee-ah*
Denmark	Denmāku	*dehn-mah-koo*
Ecuador	Ekuadoru	*eh-koo-ah-doh-roo*
Egypt	Ejiputo	*eh-jee-poo-toh*

England	Igirisu	*ee-gee-ree-soo*
Europe	Yōroppa	*yoh-rohp-pah*
Finland	Finrando	*feen-rahn-doh*
France	Furansu	*foo-rahn-soo*
Germany	Doitsu	*doh-ee-tsoo*
Greece	Girisha	*gee-ree-shah*
Holland	Oranda	*oh-rahn-dah*
India	Indo	*een-doh*
Indonesia	Indoneshia	*een-doh-neh-shee-ah*
Iran	Iran	*ee-rahn*
Iraq	Iraku	*ee-rah-koo*
Ireland	Airurando	*ah-ee-roo-rahn-doh*
Israel	Isuraeru	*ee-soo-rah-eh-roo*
Italy	Itaria	*ee-tah-ree-ah*
Japan	Nihon/Nippon	*nee-hohn/neep-pohn*
Jordan	Yorudan	*yoh-roo-dahn*
Kenya	Kenia	*keh-nee-ah*
Korea	Kankoku	*kahn-koh-koo*
Kuwait	Kuwēto	*koo-weh-toh*
Lebanon	Rebanon	*reh-bah-nohn*
Malaysia	Marēshia	*mah-reh-shee-ah*
Mexico	Mekishiko	*meh-kee-shee-koh*
Middle and Near East	Chūkintō	*choo-keen-toh*
New Zealand	Nyūj īrando	*nyoo-jee-rahn-doh*
Norway	Noruwē	*noh-roo-weh*
Pakistan	Pakisutan	*pah-kees-tahn*
Peru	Perū	*peh-roo*
Philippines	Firippin	*fee-reep-peen*
Poland	Pōrando	*poh-rahn-doh*
Portugal	Porutogaru	*poh-roo-toh-gah-roo*
Russia	Roshia	*roh-shee-ah*
Saudi Arabia	Saujiarabia	*sah-oo-jee-ah-rah-bee-ah*
Singapore	Shingapōru	*sheen-gah-poh-roo*
South Africa	Minami Afurika	*mee-nah-mee ah-foo-ree-kah*
Soviet Union	Sobieto Yunion	*soh-bee-eh-toh yoo-nee-ohn*
Spain	Supein	*soo-peh-een*
Sweden	Suwēden	*soo-weh-dehn*
Switzerland	Suisu	*SOO-ee-soo*
Thailand	Taikoku	*tah-ee-koh-koo*
Turkey	Toruko	*toh-roo-koh*
United States of America	Amerika	*ah-meh-ree-kah*
Uruguay	Uruguai	*oo-roo-goo-ah-ee*
Venezuela	Benezuera	*beh-neh-zoo-eh-rah*
Yugoslavia	Yūgosurabia	*yoo-goh-soo-rah-bee-ah*

c. A FEW CITIES

Bangkok	Bankokku	*bahn-kohk-koo*
Beijing	Bējin	*beh-jeen*
Berlin	Berurin	*beh-roo-reen*
Chicago	Shikago	*shee-kah-goh*
Frankfurt	Furankufuruto	*foo-rahn-koo-foo-roo-toh*
Hong Kong	Honkon	*hohn-kohn*
Honolulu	Honoruru	*hoh-noh-roo-roo*
Jakarta	Jakaruta	*jah-kah-roo-tah*
Kuala Lumpur	Kuararunpūru	*koo-ah-rah-roon-pōō-roo*
Kyoto	Kyōto	*kyoh-toh*
London	Rondon	*rohn-dohn*
Los Angeles	Rosanjerusu	*roh-sahn-jeh-roo-soo*
Manila	Manira	*mah-nee-rah*
Milan	Mirano	*mee-rah-noh*
Moscow	Mosukuwa	*mohs-koo-wah*
New York	Nyūyōku	*nyōō-yoh-koo*
Osaka	Ōsaka	*oh-sah-kah*
Paris	Pari	*pah-ree*
Rome	Rōma	*roh-mah*
San Francisco	Sanfuranshisuko	*sahn-foo-rahn-shees-koh*
Seoul	Sōru	*soh-roo*
Taipei	Taipei	*tah-ee-peh*
Tokyo	Tōkyō	*toh-kyoh*

d. NATIONALITIES AND LANGUAGES

American	Amerikajin	*ah-meh-ree-kah-jeen*
• **English**	eigo	*eh-goh*
Arab	Arabiajin	*ah-rah-bee-ah-jeen*
• **Arabic**	Arabiago	*ah-rah-bee-ah-goh*
Australian	Ōsutorariajin	*oh-stoh-rah-ree-ah-jeen*
• **English**	eigo	*eh-goh*
Austrian	Ōsutorijin	*oh-stoh-ree-ah-jeen*
• **German**	Doitsugo	*doh-ee-tsoo-goh*
Belgian	Berugijin	*beh-roo-gee-jeen*
• **French**	Furansugo	*foo-rahn-soo-goh*
• **Flemish**	Furandāsugo	*foo-rahn-dāh-soo-goh*
Brazilian	Burajirujin	*boo-rah-jee-roo-jeen*
• **Portuguese**	Porutogarugo	*poh-roo-toh-gah-roo-goh*
Canadian	Kanadajin	*kah-nah-dah-jeen*
• **English**	eigo	*eh-goh*
• **French**	Furansugo	*foo-rahn-soo-goh*
Chinese	Chūgokujin	*chōō-goh-koo-jeen*
• **Chinese**	Chūgokugo	*chōō-goh-koo-goh*

Dane	Denmākujin	*dehn-mah̄-koo-jeen*
• **Danish**	Denmākugo	*dehn-mah̄-koo-goh*
Dutchman	Orandajin	*oh-rahn-dah-jeen*
• **Dutch**	Orandago	*oh-rahn-dah-goh*
Englishman	Igirisujin	*ee-gee-ree-soo-jeen*
• **English**	eigo	*eh̄-goh*
Finn	Finrandojin	*feen-rahn-doh-jeen*
• **Finnish**	Finrandogo	*feen-rahn-doh-goh*
Frenchman	Furansujin	*foo-rahn-soo-jeen*
• **French**	Furansugo	*foo-rahn-soo-goh*
German	Doitsujin	*doh-ee-tsoo-jeen*
• **German**	Doitsugo	*doh-ee-tsoo-goh*
Greek	Girishajin	*gee-ree-shah-jeen*
• **Greek**	Girishago	*gee-ree-shah-goh*
Israeli	Isuraerujin	*ee-soo-rah-eh-roo-jeen*
• **Hebrew**	Heburaigo	*heh-boo-rah-ee-goh*
Italian	Itariajin	*ee-tah-ree-ah-jeen*
• **Italian**	Itariago	*ee-tah-ree-ah-goh*
Japanese	Nihonjin	*nee-hohn-jeen*
• **Japanese**	Nihongo	*nee-hohn-goh*
Korean	Kankokujin	*kahn-koh-koo-jeen*
• **Korean**	Kankokugo	*kahn-koh-koo-goh*
Malaysian	Marējin	*mah-reh̄-jeen*
• **Malay**	Marēgo	*mah-reh̄-goh*
Norwegian	Noruwējin	*noh-roo-weh̄-jeen*
• **Norwegian**	Noruwēgo	*noh-roo-weh̄-goh*
Pole	Pōrandojin	*poh̄-rahn-doh-jeen*
• **Polish**	Pōrandogo	*poh̄-rahn-doh-goh*
Portuguese	Porutogarujin	*poh-roo-toh-gah-roo-jeen*
• **Portuguese**	Porutogarugo	*poh-roo-toh-gah-roo-goh*
Russian	Roshiajin	*roh-shee-ah-jeen*
• **Russian**	Roshiago	*roh-shee-ah-goh*
Spaniard	Supeinjin	*soo-peh-een-jeen*
• **Spanish**	Supeingo	*soo-peh-een-goh*
Swede	Suwēdenjin	*soo-weh̄-dehn-jeen*
• **Swedish**	Suwēdengo	*soo-weh̄-dehn-goh*
Thai	Taijin	*tah-ee-jeen*
• **Thai**	Taigo	*tah-ee-goh*
Turk	Torukojin	*toh-roo-koh-jeen*
• **Turkish**	Torukogo	*toh-roo-koh-goh*

31. PACKING AND GOING THROUGH CUSTOMS

baggage, luggage	nimotsu	*nee-moh-tsoo*
• **hand luggage**	tenimotsu	*teh-nee-moh-tsoo*
border	kokkyō	*kohk-kyoh̄*

carry	hakobu (v)	*hah-koh-boo*
carry-on	kinai mochikomi hin	*kee-nah-ee moh-chee-koh-mee heen*
customs	zeikan	*zeh-kahn*
• customs officer	zeikan no kakariin	*zeh-kahn noh kah-kah-ree-een*
declare	shinkokusuru (v)	*sheen-kohk-soo-roo*
• There's nothing to declare.	Nani mo, shinkokusuru mono ga arimasen.	*nah-nee moh, sheen-kohk-soo-roo moh-noh gah ah-ree-mah-sehn*
• There's something to declare.	Shinkokusuru mono ga arimasu.	*sheen-kohk-soo-roo moh-noh gah ah-ree-mahs*
documents	shorui	*shoh-roo-ee*
duty	kanzei	*kahn-zeh*
• pay customs/duty	kanzei o harau (v)	*kahn-zeh oh hah-rah-oo*
foreign currency	gaikoku tsūka	*gah-ee-koh-koo tsoo-kah*
foreigner	gaikokujin	*gah-ee-koh-koo-jeen*
form (to fill out)	shoshiki	*shoh-shee-kee*
identification (paper)	mibun shōmeisho	*mee-boon shoh-meh-shoh*
import	yunyūsuru (v)	*yoo-nyoo-soo-roo*
knapsack	nappuzakku	*nahp-poo-zahk-koo*
measurement	sunpō	*soon-poh*
pack (one's bags/luggage)	nizukurisuru (v)	*nee-zoo-koo-ree-soo-roo*
passport	pasupōto	*pahs-poh-toh*
passport control	ryoken shinsa	*ryoh-kehn sheen-sah*
suitcase, piece of luggage	sūtsukēsu	*soo-tsoo-keh-soo*
tariff	kanzei	*kahn-zeh*
visa	biza	*bee-zah*
weight	mekata	*meh-kah-tah*
• heavy	omoi (adj)	*oh-moh-ee*
• light	karui (adj)	*kah-roo-ee*
• maximum	saidai no (adj)	*sah-ee-dah-ee noh*

32. TRAVELING BY AIR

a. IN THE TERMINAL

airline	kōkūgaisha	*koh-koo-gah-ee-shah*
airport	kūkō	*koo-koh*
arrival	tōchaku	*toh-chah-koo*
boarding	tōjō	*toh-joh*
• boarding pass	tōjō ken	*toh-joh kehn*
business class	bijinesu kurasu	*bee-jee-neh-soo koo-rah-soo*
check-in	chekkuin	*chehk-koo-een*
connection	konekushon	*koh-neh-koo-shohn*

departure	shuppatsu	*shoop-pah-tsoo*
economy class	ekonomī kurasu	*eh-koh-noh-mee koo-rah-soo*
first class	fāsuto kurasu	*fah-soo-toh koo-rah-soo*
flight	bin	*been*
gate	gēto	*geh-toh*
information desk	annaisho	*ahn-nah-ee-shoh*
lost and found	ishitsubutsugakari	*ee-shee-tsoo-boo-tsoo-gah-kah-ree*
no smoking	kin-en	*keen-ehn*
porter	pōtā	*poh-tah*
reservation	yoyaku	*yoh-yah-koo*
terminal	tāminaru	*tah-mee-nah-roo*
ticket	ken	*kehn*
ticket agent	chikettogakari	*chee-keht-toh-gah-kah-ree*
waiting room	raunji	*rah-oon-jee*

b. FLIGHT INFORMATION

canceled	kyanseru sareta	*kyan-seh-roo sah-reh-tah*
early	hayai (*adj*)	*hah-yah-ee*
	hayaku (*adv*)	*hah-yah-koo*
late	osoi (*adj*)	*oh-soh-ee*
	okurete (*adv*)	*oh-koo-reh-teh*
on time	teikoku ni (*adv*)	*teh-koh-koo nee*

c. ON THE PLANE

airplane	hikōki	*hee-koh-kee*
aisle	tsūro	*tsoo-roh*
captain	kichō	*kee-choh*
co-pilot	fuku sōjūshi	*foo-koo soh-joo-shee*
crew	tōjōin	*toh-joh-een*
flight attendant	kyakushitsu jōmuin	*kyah-koo-shtsoo joh-moo-een*
flight engineer	kōkū kikanshi	*koh-koo kee-kahn-shee*
headphones	heddohōn	*hehd-doh-hohn*
land	chakurikusuru (*v*)	*chah-koo-reek-soo-roo*
landing gear	chakuriku sōchi	*chah-koo-ree-koo soh-chee*
life jacket	kyūmeidōgi	*kyoo-meh-doh-gee*
luggage compartment	tenimotsu dana	*teh-nee-moh-tsoo dah-nah*
passenger	jōkyaku	*joh-kyah-koo*
pilot	sōjūshi	*soh-joo-shee*
runway	kassōro	*kahs-soh-roh*
seat	seki	*seh-kee*

• aisle	tsūrogawa	*tsoo-roh-gah-wah*
• window	madogawa	*mah-doh-gah-wah*
seat belt	shītoberuto	*shee-toh-beh-roo-toh*
• fasten	shimeru (v)	*shee-meh-roo*
sit down	suwaru (v)	*soo-wah-roo*
steward	suchuwādo	*soo-choo-wāh-doh*
stewardess	suchuwādesu	*soo-choo-wāh-deh-soo*
takeoff	ririku	*ree-ree-koo*
• take off	ririkusuru (v)	*ree-ree-koo-soo-roo*
toilet	toire	*toh-ee-reh*
tray	tēburu	*teh-boo-roo*
turbulence	rankiryū	*rahn-kee-ryoo*
wheel	sharin	*shah-reen*
wing	tsubasa	*tsoo-bah-sah*

33. ON THE ROAD

a. VEHICLES

ambulance	kyūkyūsha	*kyoo-kyoo-shah*
automobile	jidōsha	*jee-doh-shah*
bicycle	jitensha	*jee-tehn-shah*
• brake	burēki	*boo-reh-kee*
• chain guard	chēn gādo	*chehn gah-doh*
• handlebar	handoru	*hahn-doh-roo*
• pedal	pedaru	*peh-dah-roo*
• spoke	supōku	*spoh-koo*
• seat	sadoru	*sah-doh-roo*
• tire	taiya	*tah-ee-yah*
bus	basu	*bah-soo*
• streetcar	romendensha	*roh-mehn-dehn-shah*
• trolley	torōrīkā	*toh-roh-ree-kah*
car	jidōsha	*jee-doh-shah*
cement mixer	konkurīto mikisā	*kohn-koo-ree-toh mee-kee-sah*
compact car	konpakutokā	*kohn-pahk-toh-kah*
convertible	konbāchiburu	*kohn-bah-chee-boo-roo*
fire engine	shōbōsha	*shoh-boh-shah*
jeep	jīpu	*jee-poo*
limousine	rimujīn	*ree-moo-jeen*
motorcycle	ōtobai	*oh-toh-bah-ee*
• scooter	sukūtā	*skoo-tah*
passenger car	jōyōsha	*joh-yoh-shah*
rental car	rentakā	*rehn-tah-kah*
sports car	supōtsukā	*spoh-tsoo-kah*
station wagon	wagonsha	*wah-gohn-shah*

taxi	takushi	*tah-koo-shee*
trailer	torērā	*toh-reh-rah*
transporter	jidōsha unpansha	*jee-doh-shah oon-pahn-shah*
truck	torakku	*toh-rahk-koo*
• dump truck	danpukā	*dahn-poo-kah*
• garbage truck	gomi shūshūsha	*goh-mee shoo-shoo-shah*
• tow truck	rekkāsha	*rehk-kah-shah*
van	ban	*bahn*

b. DRIVING: PEOPLE AND DOCUMENTS

driver	untenshu	*oon-tehn-shoo*
• to drive	untensuru (v)	*oon-tehn-soo-roo*
driver's license	unten menkyosho	*oon-tehn mehn-kyoh-shoh*
insurance card	hoken sho	*hoh-kehn-shoh*
ownership papers	shoyū shōsho	*shoh-yoo shoh-shoh*
passenger	dōjōsha	*doh-joh-shah*
pedestrian	hokōsha	*hoh-koh-shah*
police	keisatsu	*keh-sah-tsoo*
• highway police	haiwē patorōru	*hah-ee-weh pah-toh-roh-roo*
• policeman	keikan	*keh-kahn*
• policewoman	fujin keikan	*foo-jeen keh-kahn*
• traffic police	kōtsū junsa	*koh-tsoo joon-sah*
registration papers	tōrokusho	*toh-roh-koo-shoh*
road map	dōro chizu	*doh-roh chee-zoo*

c. DRIVING: ADDITIONAL VOCABULARY

accident	jiko	*jee-koh*
back up	bakkusuru (v)	*bahk-koo-soo-roo*
brake	burēki	*boo-reh-kee*
breakdown	koshō	*koh-shoh*
bridge	hashi	*hah-shee*
corner (street)	kado	*kah-doh*
curve	kābu	*kah-boo*
distance	kyori	*kyoh-ree*
drive	untensuru (v)	*oon-tehn-soo-roo*
fine, ticket	ihan no ken	*ee-hahn noh kehn*
gas station	gasorin sutando	*gah-soh-reen stahn-doh*
• check the oil	oiru o chekkusuru (v)	*oh-ee-roo oh chehk-koo-soo-roo*
• fill up	mantan ni suru (v)	*mahn-tahn nee soo-roo*
• fix	naosu (v)	*nah-oh-soo*

• gas	gasorin	*gah-soh-reen*
• leaded gas	regyurā	*reh-gyoo-rah*
• mechanic	shūriko	*shoo-ree-koh*
• self-service	serufu sābisu	*seh-roo-foo sah-bee-soo*
• tools	dōgu	*doh-goo*
• unleaded gas	muen gasorin	*moo-ehn gah-soh-reen*
gearshift	gia shifuto	*gee-ah shee-foo-toh*
go forward	zenshinsuru (v)	*zehn-sheen-soo-roo*
going through a red light	shingō mushi	*sheen-goh moo-shee*
highway	kōsokudōro	*koh-soh-koo-doh-roh*
intersection	kōsaten	*koh-sah-tehn*
lane (traffic)	shasen	*shah-sehn*
park	chūshasuru (v)	*choo-shah-soo-roo*
• parking	chūsha	*choo-shah*
• public parking	chūshajō	*choo-shah-joh*
pass	oikosu (v)	*oh-ee-koh-soo*
pedestrian crossing	ōdanhodō	*oh-dahn-hoh-doh*
ramp	intāchenji	*een-tah-chehn-jee*
road	michi	*mee-chee*
rush hour	rasshu awā	*rahs-shoo ah-wah*
signal	shigunaru	*shee-goo-nah-roo*
speed	sokudo	*soh-koo-doh*
• slow down	jokōsuru (v)	*joh-koh-soo-roo*
• speed limit	sokudo seigen	*soh-koo-doh seh-gehn*
• speed up	kasokusuru (v)	*kah-sohk-soo-roo*
start (car)	enjin o kakeru (v)	*ehn-jeen oh kah-keh-roo*
toll booth	ryōkinsho	*ryoh-keen-shoh*
toll road	yūryō dōro	*yoo-ryoh doh-roh*
traffic	kōtsū	*koh-tsoo*
• traffic jam	kōtsū jūtai	*koh-tsoo joo-tah-ee*
traffic light	shingō	*sheen-goh*
tunnel	tonneru	*tohn-neh-roo*
turn	magaru (v)	*mah-gah-roo*
• turn to the left	hidari ni magaru (v)	*hee-dah-ree nee mah-gah-roo*
• turn to the right	migi ni magaru (v)	*mee-gee nee mah-gah-roo*

d. ROAD SIGNS

Bicycle Path	jitenshadō	*jee-tehn-shah-doh*
Emergency Lane	kinkyū shasen	*keen-kyoo shah-sehn*
Intersection	kōsaten	*koh-sah-tehn*
Level Crossing	fumikiri	*foo-mee-kee-ree*
Merge	gōryū	*goh-ryoo*
No Entry	shinnyū kinshi	*sheen-nyoo keen-shee*
No Left Turn	sasetsu kinshi	*sah-seh-tsoo keen-shee*

Emergency
Telephone

Caution

Stop

Slow Down

Minimum
Speed

Maximum Parking
60 Minutes
(8AM–8PM)

No Passing

Sound Horn

Parking

No Parking
(8AM–8PM)

No Parking,
No Standing
(8AM–8PM)

Standing
Permitted

Pedestrians
Only

Cars Only

Bicycles Only

Service Area

Detour

Exit

No Entrance

Entrance to Expressway

Road Closed

National Highway

No Right Turn

No U Turn

Traffic Island

Two Way Traffic Dividing Line

One Way

This Lane for Motorcycles and Lightweight Cars

No Parking	chūsha kinshi	*chōō-shah keen-shee*
No Passing	oikoshi kinshi	*oh-ee-koh-shee keen-shee*
No Right Turn	usetsu kinshi	*oo-seh-tsoo keen-shee*
No Stopping	teisha kinshi	*teh-shah keen-shee*
No Thoroughfare	tsūkōdome	*tsōō-koh-doh-meh*
No U-Turn	yūtān kinshi	*yōo-tahn keen-shee*
One Way	ippōtsūkō	*eep-poh-tsōō-koh*
Passing Lane	oikoshisen	*oh-ee-koh-shee-sehn*
Speed Limit	sokudo seigen	*soh-koo-doh seh-gehn*
Stop	teishi	*teh-shee*
Toll	ryōkinsho	*ryoh-keen-shoh*
Tow-Away Zone	ken-in chiiki	*kehn-een chee-ee-kee*
Work in Progress	kōjichū	*koh-jee-choo*
Yield	yūsen	*yōo-sehn*

e. THE CAR

air conditioner	eakon	*eh-ah-kohn*
battery	batterī	*baht-teh-rēē*
brake	burēki	*boo-reh-kee*
bumper	banpā	*bahn-pah*
car body	bodī	*boh-dēē*
car window	windō	*ween-doh*
carburetor	kyaburetā	*kyah-boo-reh-tah*
choke	chōku	*choh-koo*
clutch (*pedal*)	kuratchi	*koo-raht-chee*
dashboard	dasshubōdo	*dahs-shoo-boh-doh*
door	doa	*doh-ah*
fender	fendā	*fehn-dah*
filter	firutā	*fee-roo-tah*
gas pedal	akuseru	*ah-koo-seh-roo*
gas tank	gasorin tanku	*gah-soh-reen tahn-koo*
gearshift	shifuto rebā	*shee-foo-toh reh-bah*
glove compartment	gurōbu bokkusu	*goo-roh-boo bohk-ksoo*
hazard flash	hazādo ranpu	*hah-zah-doh rahn-poo*
heater	hītā	*hēē-tah*
hood	bonnetto	*bohn-neht-toh*
horn	keiteki	*keh-teh-kee*
horsepower	bariki	*bah-ree-kee*
license plate	nanbā purēto	*nahn-bah poo-rēh-toh*
lights	raito	*rah-ee-toh*
motor	enjin	*ehn-jeen*
• fan	fan	*fahn*
• gas pump	ponpu	*pohn-poo*
• generator	jenerētā	*jeh-neh-rēh-tah*
• piston	pisuton	*pees-tohn*

• shaft	shafuto	*shah-foo-toh*
• spark plug	supāku puragu	*soo-pah-koo poo-rah-goo*
• valve	barubu	*bah-roo-boo*
muffler	mafurā	*mah-foo-rah*
oil	oiru	*oh-ee-roo*
oil filter	oiru firutā	*oh-ee-roo fee-roo-tah*
power brake	pawā burēki	*pah-wah boo-reh-kee*
power steering	pawā handoru	*pah-wah hahn-doh-roo*
power window	pawā windō	*pah-wah ween-doh*
rearview mirror	bakkumirā	*bahk-koo mee-rah*
roof	rūfu	*roo-foo*
seat	shīto	*shee-toh*
seat belt	shīto beruto	*shee-toh beh-roo-toh*
side mirror	saido mirā	*sah-ee-doh mee-rah*
speedometer	sokudokei	*soh-koo-doh-keh*
steering wheel	handoru	*hahn-doh-roo*
tire	taiya	*tah-ee-yah*
trunk	toranku	*toh-rahn-koo*
turn signal	hōkō shijiki	*hoh-koh shee-jee-kee*
vent	benchirētā	*behn-chee-reh-tah*
wheel	sharin	*shah-reen*
windshield	furontogarasu	*foo-rohn-toh-gah-rah-soo*
• windshield wiper	waipā	*wah-ee-pah*

34. TRAIN, BUS, AND SUBWAY

bus	basu	*bah-soo*
bus driver	basu no untenshu	*bah-soo noh oon-tehn-shoo*
bus station, depot	basu no hatchakusho	*bah-soo noh haht-chah-koo-shoh*
bus stop	basu no teiryūsho	*bah-soo noh teh-ryoo-shoh*
change	norikaeru (v)	*noh-ree-kah-eh-roo*
coach	futsū	*foo-tsoo*
conductor	shashō	*shah-shoh*
commuter train	densha	*dehn-shah*
compartment	koshitsu	*koh-shtsoo*
• nonsmoking	kin-en no (adj)	*keen-ehn noh*
• smoking	kitsuen no (adj)	*kee-tsoo-ehn noh*
connection	noritsugi	*noh-ree-tsoo-gee*
dining car	shokudōsha	*shoh-koo-doh-shah*
direct train	chokutsū ressha	*chohk-tsoo rehs-shah*
express train	kyūkō	*kyoo-koh*
fare box	ryōkinbako	*ryoh-keen-bah-koh*
leave, depart	hasshasuru (v)	*hahs-shah-soo-roo*
limited express train	tokkyū	*tohk-kyoo*

local train	kakueki teisha (no kisha)	*kah-koo-eh-kee teh-shah (noh kee-shah)*
miss (the train)	norisokonau (v)	*noh-ree-soh-koh-nah-oo*
newsstand	shinbun uriba	*sheen-boon oo-ree-bah*
platform	purattohōmu	*poo-raht-toh-hoh-moo*
porter	akabō	*ah-kah-boh*
railroad	tetsudō	*teh-tsoo-doh*
• station	eki	*eh-kee*
schedule	yoteihyō	*yoh-teh-hyoh*
• early	hayai (adj)	*hah-yah-ee*
• late	osoi (adj)	*oh-soh-ee*
• on time	jikandōri ni (adv)	*jee-kahn-doh-ree nee*
seat	seki	*seh-kee*
• economy seat	futsū seki	*foo-tsoo seh-kee*
• first class	gurīnsha no seki	*goo-reen-shah noh seh-kee*
• reserved seat	shitei seki	*shteh seh-kee*
• unreserved seat	jiyū seki	*jee-yoo seh-kee*
sleeping car	shindaisha	*sheen-dah-ee-shah*
stop	tomaru (v)	*toh-mah-roo*
subway	chikatetsu	*chee-kah-teh-tsoo*
• subway station	chikatetsu no eki	*chee-kah-teh-tsoo noh eh-kee*
take/catch the train, etc.	noru (v)	*noh-roo*
ticket	ken	*kehn*
• buy a ticket	ken o kau (v)	*kehn o kah-oo*
• ticket-canceling machine	jidō kaisatsuki	*jee-doh kah-ee-sah-tsoo-kee*
• ticket counter	kippu uriba	*keep-poo oo-ree-bah*
timetable	jikokuhyō	*jee-koh-koo-hyoh*
track	sen	*sehn*
train	kisha	*kee-shah*
• All aboard!	Gojōsha kudasai.	*goh-JOH-shah koo-dah-sah-ee*
• train station	eki	*eh-kee*
wait for	matsu (v)	*mah-tsoo*

35. HOTELS

a. LODGING

hotel	hoteru	*hoh-teh-roo*
• luxury hotel	kōkyū hoteru	*koh-kyoo hoh-teh-roo*
motel	moteru	*moh-teh-roo*
youth hostel	yūsu hosuteru	*yoo-soo hohs-teh-roo*

FOCUS: *Other Kinds of Lodging in Japan*

Major hotels are similar in quality and service to those in Western cities. Another category is the business hotel, also Western-style, but inexpensive, with small rooms and no-frills service. Business hotels are clean and are conveniently located near train stations or in the business districts.

| **business hotel** | bijinesu hoteru | *bee-jee-neh-soo hoh-teh-roo* |

Japanese inns, or **ryokan**, have traditional Japanese-style accommodations and service. As with Western-style hotels, they range in quality and price from luxurious to simple. Breakfast and dinner are included in the price.

| **Japanese inn** | ryokan | *ryoh-kahn* |

Minshuku are guest houses where travelers can stay. Many are located in resort and vacation areas, and their rates are much lower than at hotels or **ryokan**. Because most are family-run operations, regular hotel services (maid, laundry, etc.) are not provided. Breakfast and dinner are included in the rate, and guests eat with the family.

| **family guest house** | minshuku | *meen-shoo-koo* |

b. STAYING IN HOTELS

bill	kanjō	*kahn-joh*
• ask for the bill	kanjō o tanomu	*kahn-joh oh tah-noh-moo*
• Charge it to my bill.	Watakushi no kanjō ni, tsukete oite kudasai.	*wah-tahk-shee noh kahn-joh nee, tsoo-keh-teh oh-ee-teh koo-dah-sah-ee*
bellhop	bōi	*boh-ee*
breakfast	asa gohan	*ah-sah goh-hahn*
• breakfast included	chōshoku komi	*choh-shoh-koo koh-mee*
complain	kujō o noberu (v)	*koo-joh oh noh-beh-roo*
• complaint	kujō	*koo-joh*
doorman	doaman	*doh-ah-mahn*
elevator	erebētā	*eh-reh-beh-tah*
entrance	iriguchi	*ee-ree-goo-chee*

exit	deguchi	*deh-goo-chee*
floor (level)	kai	*kah-ee*
garage	chūshajō	*chōō-shah-jōh*
hotel clerk	hoteru no kakariin	*hoh-teh-roo noh kah-kah-ree-een*
identification card	mibun shōmeisho	*mee-boon shoh-meh-shoh*
key	kagi	*kah-gee*
• **give back the room key**	kagi o kaesu	*kah-gee oh kah-eh-soo*
lobby	robī	*roh-bēē*
luggage	nimotsu	*nee-moh-tsoo*
maid	mēdo	*mēh-doh*
manager	manējā	*mah-neh-jāh*
message	dengon	*dehn-gohn*
passport	pasupōto	*pahs-pōh-toh*
pay	harau (*v*)	*hah-rah-oo*
• **cash**	genkin	*gehn-keen*
• **credit card**	kurejitto kādo	*koo-reh-jeet-toh kāh-doh*
• **traveler's check**	toraberā chekku	*toh-rah-beh-rāh chehk-koo*
price, rate	ryokin	*ryoh-keen*
• **low season**	isogashikunai toki	*ee-soh-gah-shee-koo-nah-ee toh-kee*
• **peak season**	isogashii toki	*ee-soh-gah-shēē toh-kee*
porter	pōtā	*poh-tāh*
receipt	reshīto	*reh-shēē-toh*
request a taxi	takushī o tanomu	*tahk-shēē oh tah-noh-moo*
reservation	yoyaku	*yoh-yah-koo*
• **reserve**	yoyakusuru (*v*)	*yoh-yah-koo-soo-roo*
room	heya	*heh-yah*
• **Do you have a vacant room?**	Heya ga arimasu ka.	*heh-yah gah ah-ree-mahs kah*
• **double room**	daburu no heya	*dah-boo-roo noh heh-yah*
• **have baggage taken to one's room**	nimotsu o heya e motte itte morau	*nee-moh-tsoo oh heh-yah eh moht-teh eet-teh moh-rah-oo*
• **room with bath**	basu tsuki no heya	*bah-soo tsoo-kee noh heh-yah*
• **room with two beds**	tsuin no heya	*tsoo-een noh heh-yah*
• **single room**	shinguru no heya	*sheen-goo-roo noh heh-yah*
services	sābisu	*sāh-bee-soo*
stairs	kaidan	*kah-ee-dahn*
swimming pool	pūru	*pōō-roo*

view	nagame	*nah-gah-meh*
wake-up call	mōningu kōru	*moh-neen-goo koh-roo*

c. THE HOTEL ROOM

armchair	hijikake isu	*hee-jee-kah-keh ee-soo*
balcony	barukonī	*bah-roo-koh-nee*
• sliding door	hikido	*hee-kee-doh*
bathroom	basurūmu	*bah-soo-roo-moo*
bathtub	yokusō	*yohk-soh*
bed	beddo	*behd-doh*
• double bed	daburu beddo	*dah-boo-roo behd-doh*
bedside table	saido tēburu	*sah-ee-doh teh-boo-roo*
blanket	mōfu	*moh-foo*
chest of drawers	yōdansu	*yoh-dahn-soo*
closet	oshiire	*oh-shee-ee-reh*
clothes hanger	hangā	*hahn-gah*
curtains	kāten	*kah-tehn*
dresser	kyōdai	*kyoh-dah-ee*
faucet	jaguchi	*jah-goo-chee*
lamp	ranpu	*rahn-poo*
lights	akari	*ah-kah-ree*
• current	denryū	*dehn-ryoo*
• switch	suitchi	*soo-eet-chee*
• turn off	kesu (v)	*keh-soo*
• turn on	tsukeru (v)	*tsoo-keh-roo*
mirror	kagami	*kah-gah-mee*
pillow	makura	*mah-koo-rah*
radio	rajio	*rah-jee-oh*
soap	sekken	*sehk-kehn*
shampoo	shanpū	*shahn-poo*
sheets	shītsu	*shee-tsoo*
shower	shawā	*shah-wah*
sink, wash basin	senmendai	*sehn-mehn-dah-ee*
• cold water	mizu	*mee-zoo*
• hot water	oyu	*oh-yoo*
table	tēburu	*teh-boo-roo*
telephone	denwa	*dehn-wah*
television set	terebi	*teh-reh-bee*
thermostat	jidō chōon sōchi	*jee-doh choh-ohn soh-chee*
toilet	toire	*toh-ee-reh*
• toilet paper	toiretto pēpā	*toh-ee-reht-toh peh-pah*
towel	taoru	*tah-oh-roo*

FOCUS: *At a Japanese Inn*

Besides the vocabulary for the hotel room, some special vocabulary
may be needed for staying at a Japanese inn or **ryokan**.

armrest	hijikake	*hee-jee-kah-keh*
backrest	semotare	*seh-moh-tah-reh*
bathroom	furoba	*foo-roh-bah*
floor cushion	zabuton	*zah-boo-tohn*
Japanese bedding	futon	*ftohn*
light cotton kimono	yukata	*yoo-kah-tah*
sash (for kimono)	obi	*oh-bee*
time for taking bath	ofuro no jikan	*oh-foo-roh noh jee-kahn*
time for breakfast	chōshoku no jikan	*choh-shoh-koo noh jee-kahn*
time for dinner	yūshoku no jikan	*yoo-shoh-koo noh jee-kahn*
thermos	mahōbin	*mah-hoh-been*
wooden clogs	geta	*geh-tah*

36. ON VACATION

a. SIGHTSEEING

amphitheater	enkei engijō	*ehn-keh ehn-gee-joh*
art gallery	garō	*gah-roh*
avenue	tōri	*toh-ree*
bell tower	shōrō	*shoh-roh*
bridge	hashi	*hah-shee*
castle	shiro	*shee-roh*
cathedral	daiseidō	*dah-ee-seh-doh*
church	kyōkai	*kyoh-kah-ee*
city	toshi	*toh-shee*
city map	toshi chizu	*toh-shee chee-zoo*
corner	kado	*kah-doh*
downtown	toshin	*toh-sheen*
garbage bin	gomiire	*goh-mee-ee-reh*
garden	niwa	*nee-wah*
guide	gaido	*gah-ee-doh*
interpreter	tsūyaku	*tsoo-yah-koo*

intersection	kōsaten	*kōh-sah-tehn*
kiosk	kiosuku	*kee-oh-skoo*
monument	kinentō	*kee-nehn-tōh*
museum	bijutsukan	*bee-joo-tsoo-kahn*
park	kōen	*kōh-ehn*
park bench	kōen no benchi	*kōh-ehn noh behn-chee*
parking meter	chūsha mētā	*chōo-shah mēh-tah*
pedestrian crosswalk	ōdan hodō	*ōh-dahn hoh-dōh*
public garden	kōkyo no kōen	*kōh-kyoh noh kōh-ehn*
public notices	kōji	*koh-jee*
public phone	kōshū denwa	*kōh-shōo dehn-wah*
public washroom	kōshū benjo	*kōh-shōo behn-joh*
railway crossing	fumikiri	*foo-mee-kee-ree*
shrine	jinja	*jeen-jah*
sidewalk	hodō	*hoh-dōh*
square	hiroba	*hee-roh-bah*
street	michi	*mee-chee*
• **street sign**	dōro hyōshiki	*dōh-roh hyōh-shee-kee*
take an excursion	gurūpu tsuā ni sankasuru (v)	*goo-rōo-poo tsoo-ah nee sahn-kah-soo-roo*
temple	otera	*oh-teh-rah*
tower	tō	*tōh*
traffic light	shingō	*sheen-gōh*
water fountain	funsui	*foon-soo-ee*

b. GETTING OUT OF THE CITY

beach	kaigan	*kah-ee-gahn*
• **at the beach**	kaigan de	*kah-ee-gahn deh*
• **get a suntan**	hiyakesuru (v)	*hee-yah-keh-soo-roo*
• **get some sun**	hi ni ataru (v)	*hee nee ah-tah-roo*
boat	bōto	*bōh-toh*
brook	ogawa	*oh-gah-wah*
camping area	kyanpujō	*kyahn-poo-jōh*
canoe	kanū	*kah-nōo*
cap	bōshi	*bōh-shee*
cruise	kurūzu	*koo-rōo-zoo*
fishing	tsuri	*tsoo-ree*
hiking	haikingu	*hah-ee-keen-goo*
in the country	inaka de	*ee-nah-kah deh*
in the mountains	yama de	*yah-mah deh*
knapsack	nappuzakku	*nahp-poo-zahk-koo*
lake	mizuumi	*mee-zoo-oo-mee*
mountain boots	tozangutsu	*toh-zahn-goo-tsoo*
mountain climbing	tozan	*toh-zahn*
river	kawa	*kah-wah*

rope	zairu	zah-ee-roo
sea	umi	oo-mee
skiing	sukī	soo-kee
ski resort	sukījō	soo-kee-joh
sleeping bag	surīpingubaggu	soo-ree-peen-goo-bahg-goo
tent	tento	tehn-toh
trip	ryokō	ryoh-koh
vacation	bakansu	BAH-kahn-soo

c. ASKING FOR DIRECTIONS

across ...	... o yokogitte	... oh yoh-koh-geet-teh
ahead ...	... no saki ni	... noh sah-kee nee
at the end of ...	... no owari ni	... noh oh-wah-ree nee
back ...	... no ushiro ni	... noh oo-shee-roh nee
behind ...	... no kage ni	... noh kah-geh nee
cross (over) ...	... o yokogiru (v)	... oh yoh-koh-gee-roo
• cross the street	michi o yokogiru (v)	mee-chee oh yoh-koh-gee-roo
down ...	... o kudatta tokoro ni	... oh koo-daht-tah toh-koh-roh nee
enter	hairu (v)	hah-ee-roo
everywhere	doko demo (adv)	doh-koh deh-moh
exit, go out	deru (v)	deh-roo
far (from)	tōi (adj)	toh-ee
follow	tadotte iku (v)	tah-doht-teh ee-koo
go	iku (v)	ee-koo
go down	kudaru (v)	koo-dah-roo
go up	sakanoboru (v)	sah-kah-noh-boh-roo
here	koko ni	koh-koh nee
in front of ...	... no mae ni	... noh mah-eh nee
inside ...	... no naka ni	... noh nah-kah-nee
near ...	... no chikaku ni	... noh chee-kah-koo nee
outside ...	... no soto ni	... noh soh-toh nee
straight ahead	kono mama massugu	koh-noh mah-mah mahs-soo-goo
there	soko ni	soh-koh nee
through ...	... o tootte	... o toh-oht-teh
to the east	higashi ni	hee-gah-shee nee
to the left	hidari ni	hee-dah-ree nee
to the north	kita ni	kee-tah nee
to the right	migi ni	mee-gee nee
to the south	minami ni	mee-nah-mee nee
to the west	nishi ni	nee-shee nee
toward ...	... no hō e	... noh hoh eh

turn	magaru (v)	*mah-gah-roo*
Can you tell me where ...?	... ga doko ni aru ka oshiete kudasai.	*... gah doh-koh nee ah-roo kah oh-shee-eh-teh koo-dah-sah-ee*
How do you get to ...?	... niwa, dō yatte ikimasu ka.	*... nee-wah, DOH-yaht-teh ee-kee-mahs kah*
Where is ...?	... wa, doko desu ka.	*... wah, DOH-koh dehs kah*

SCHOOL AND WORK

37. SCHOOL

a. TYPES OF SCHOOLS AND GRADES

coed school	danjo kyōgaku no gakkō	*dahn-joh kyōh-gah-koo noh gahk-kōh*
conservatory	ongaku gakkō	*ohn-gah-koo gahk-kōh*
day care	takujisho	*tah-koo-jee-shoh*
elementary school	shōgakkō	*shoh-gahk-kōh*
evening school	yagaku	*yah-gah-koo*
grade	gakunen	*gah-koo-nehn*
• grade one	ichinen	*ee-chee-nehn*
• grade two	ninen	*nee-nehn*
high school	kōkō	*kōh-kōh*
junior high school	chūgaku	*chōo-gah-koo*
kindergarten	yōchien	*yoh-chee-ehn*
nursery school	hoikuen	*hoh-ee-koo-ehn*
private school	shiritsu gakkō	*shee-ree-tsoo gahk-kōh*
technical/vocational school	shokugyō gakkō	*shoh-koo-gyōh gahk-kōh*
university	daigaku	*dah-ee-gah-koo*
year (*e.g., at university*)	gakunen	*gah-koo-nehn*
• first year	ichinen	*ee-chee-nehn*
• second year	ninen	*nee-nehn*

b. THE CLASSROOM

assignment	shukudai	*shoo-koo-dah-ee*
assignment book	shukudai chō	*shoo-koo-dah-ee chōh*
atlas	chizu chō	*chee-zoo chōh*
ballpoint pen	bōrupen	*boh-roo-pehn*
blackboard	kokuban	*koh-koo-bahn*
blackboard eraser	kokubankeshi	*koh-koo-bahn-keh-shee*
book	hon	*hohn*
bookcase	hondana	*hohn-dah-nah*
chalk	chōku	*chōh-koo*
compass	konpasu	*kohn-pah-soo*
desk	tsukue	*tskoo-eh*
dictionary	jisho	*jee-shoh*
encyclopedia	hyakkajiten	*hyahk-kah-jee-tehn*
eraser	keshigomu	*keh-shee-goh-moo*

eyeglasses	megane	*meh-gah-neh*
film projector	eishaki	*ēh-shah-kee*
ink	inku	*een-koo*
magazine	zasshi	*zahs-shee*
map	chizu	*chee-zoo*
notebook	chōmen	*choh-mehn*
overhead projector	ōbāheddo purojekutā	*oh-bah-hehd-doh poo-roh-jehk-tah*
paper	kami	*kah-mee*
pen	pen	*pehn*
pencil	enpitsu	*ehn-pee-tsoo*
pencil sharpener	enpitsukezuri	*ehn-pee-tsoo-keh-zoo-ree*
record player	rekōdo purēyā	*reh-koh-doh poo-reh-yah*
ruler	jōgi	*joh-gee*
school bag	tsūgaku kaban	*tsoo-gah-koo kah-bahn*
slide projector	suraido eishaki	*soo-rah-ee-doh ēh-shah-kee*
tape recorder	tēpurekōdā	*teh-poo-reh-koh-dah*
textbook	kyōkasho	*kyoh-kah-shoh*
thumbtack	gabyō	*gah-byoh*

c. AREAS OF A SCHOOL

campus	kōnai	*koh-nah-ee*
classroom	kyōshitsu	*kyoh-shee-tsoo*
gymnasium	taiikukan	*tah-ee-ee-koo-kahn*
hallway	rōka	*roh-kah*
laboratory	jikkenshitsu	*jeek-kehn-shee-tsoo*
language laboratory	gaikokugo rabo	*gah-ee-koh-koo-goh rah-boh*
library	toshokan	*toh-shoh-kahn*
main office	jimushitsu	*jee-moo-shee-tsoo*
professor's office	kenkyūshitsu	*kehn-kyoo-shtsoo*
school yard	kōtei	*koh-teh*
toilet	toire	*toh-ee-reh*

d. SCHOOL: PEOPLE

assistant	joshu	*joh-shoo*
class (of students)	gakkyū	*gahk-kyoo*
classmate	kyūyū	*kyoo-yoo*
dean	gakubuchō	*gah-koo-boo-choh*
janitor	yōmuin	*yoh-moo-een*
librarian	toshokan-in	*toh-shoh-kahn-een*
president of a university	gakuchō	*gahk-choh*

principal	kōchō	koh-choh
professor	kyōju	kyoh-joo
pupil	seito	seh-toh
schoolmate	gakuyū	gah-koo-yoo
secretary	hisho	hee-shoh
student	gakusei	gahk-seh
teacher	kyōshi	kyoh-shee

e. SCHOOL: SUBJECTS

accounting	kaikeigaku	kah-ee-keh-gah-koo
anatomy	kaibōgaku	kah-ee-boh-gah-koo
anthropology	jinruigaku	jeen-roo-ee-gah-koo
archeology	kōkogaku	koh-koh-gah-koo
architecture	kenchikugaku	kehn-chee-koo-gah-koo
art	bijutsu	bee-joo-tsoo
arts	kyōyō kamoku	kyoh-yoh kah-moh-koo
astronomy	tenmongaku	tehn-mohn-gah-koo
biology	seibutsugaku	seh-boo-tsoo-gah-koo
botany	shokubutsugaku	shoh-koo-boo-tsoo-gah-koo
calculus	bisekibungaku	bee-seh-kee-boon-gah-koo
chemistry	kagaku	kah-gah-koo
commerce	shōgyō	shoh-gyoh
economics	keizai	keh-zah-ee
engineering	kōgaku	koh-gah-koo
foreign languages	gaikokugo	gah-ee-koh-koo-goh
fine arts	bijutsu	bee-joo-tsoo
geography	chiri	chee-ree
geometry	kikagaku	kee-kah-gah-koo
history	rekishi	reh-kee-shee
humanities	jinbunkagaku	jeen-boon-kah-gah-koo
law	hōgaku	hoh-gah-koo
linguistics	gengogaku	gehn-goh-gah-koo
literature	bungaku	boon-gah-koo
mathematics	sūgaku	soo-gah-koo
medicine	igaku	ee-gah-koo
music	ongaku	ohn-gah-koo
natural science	shizen kagaku	shee-zehn kah-gah-koo
philosophy	tetsugaku	teh-tsoo-gah-koo
physics	butsurigaku	boo-tsoo-ree-gah-koo
physiology	seirigaku	seh-ree-gah-koo
political science	seijigaku	seh-jee-gah-koo
psychology	shinrigaku	sheen-ree-gah-koo
sciences	kagaku	kah-gah-koo
sociology	shakaigaku	shah-kah-ee-gah-koo
statistics	tōkeigaku	toh-keh-gah-koo

subject	gakka	*gahk-kah*
trigonometry	sankakuhō	*sahn-kahk-hoh*
zoology	dōbutsugaku	*doh-boo-tsoo-gah-koo*

f. ADDITIONAL SCHOOL VOCABULARY

> For concepts of thought, see Section 22.

answer	kotae	*koh-tah-eh*
• answer	kotaeru (v)	*koh-tah-eh-roo*
• brief	kantan na (adj)	*kahn-tahn nah*
• long	nagai (adj)	*nah-gah-ee*
• right	tadashii (adj)	*tah-dah-shee*
• short	mijikai (adj)	*mee-jee-kah-ee*
• wrong	machigatta (adj)	*mah-chee-gaht-tah*
assignments, homework	shukudai	*shoo-koo-dah-ee*
attend school	gakkō ni iku (v)	*gahk-koh nee ee-koo*
audit	chōkōsuru (v)	*choh-koh-soo-roo*
be absent	kesseki (desu)	*kehs-seh-kee (dehs)*
be present	shusseki (desu)	*shoos-seh-kee (dehs)*
be promoted	shinkyūsuru (v)	*sheen-kyoo-soo-roo*
class (of students)	gakkyū	*gahk-kyoo*
• lesson	jugyō	*joo-gyoh*
• skip a class	jugyō o saboru (v)	*joo-gyoh oh sah-boh-roo*
• skip school, play hooky	gakkō o saboru (v)	*gahk-koh oh sah-boh-roo*
• There is no class today.	Kyō wa, gakkō ga arimasen.	*kyoh wah, gahk-koh gah ah-ree-mah-sehn*
composition	sakubun	*sah-koo-boon*
copy	kakikata	*kah-kee-kah-tah*
• good, final copy	seisho	*seh-shoh*
• rough copy, draft	shitagaki	*shee-tah-gah-kee*
course	kamoku	*kah-moh-koo*
• take a course/subject	kamoku o toru (v)	*kah-moh-koo oh toh-roo*
degree (university)	gakui	*gah-koo-ee*
• master	shūshigō	*shoo-shee-goh*
• doctorate	hakasegō	*hah-kah-seh-goh*
• get a degree	gakui o toru (v)	*gah-koo-ee oh toh-roo*
dictation	kakitori	*kah-kee-toh-ree*
diploma	sotsugyō shōsho	*soh-tsoo-gyoh shoh-shoh*
• get a diploma	sotsugyō shōsho o morau (v)	*soh-tsoo-gyoh shoh-shoh oh moh-rah-oo*
• high school diploma	kōkō no sotsugyō shōsho	*koh-koh noh soh-tsoo-gyoh shoh-shoh*

draw	e o kaku (v)	*eh oh kah-koo*
• drawing	e	*eh*
education	kyōiku	*kyoh-ee-koo*
• get an education	kyōiku o ukeru (v)	*kyoh-ee-koo oh oo-keh-roo*
error	machigai	*mah-chee-gah-ee*
essay	essei	*ehs-seh*
exam	shiken	*shee-kehn*
• entrance exam	nyūgaku shiken	*nyoo-gah-koo shee-kehn*
• fail an exam	shiken ni ochiru (v)	*shee-kehn nee oh-chee-roo*
• oral exam	mensetsu shiken	*mehn-seh-tsoo shee-kehn*
• pass an exam	shiken ni ukaru (v)	*shee-kehn nee oo-kah-roo*
• take an exam	shiken o ukeru (v)	*shee-kehn oh oo-keh-roo*
• written exam	hikki shiken	*heek-kee shee-kehn*
exercise	renshū mondai	*rehn-shoo mohn-dah-ee*
explanation	setsumei	*seh-tsoo-meh*
• explain	setsumeisuru (v)	*seh-tsoo-meh-soo-roo*
field of study	kenkyū bunya	*kehn-kyoo boon-yah*
give/hand back	kaesu (v)	*kah-eh-soo*
grade/mark	seiseki	*seh-seh-kee*
graduate	sotsugyōsuru (v)	*soh-tsoo-gyoh-soo-roo*
grammar	bunpō	*boon-poh*
learn	narau (v)	*nah-rah-oo*
• learn by memory	ankisuru (v)	*ahn-kee-soo-roo*
lecture	kōgi	*koh-gee*
• lecture	kōgisuru (v)	*koh-gee-soo-roo*
listen to	kiku (v)	*kee-koo*
memorize	ankisuru (v)	*ahn-kee-soo-roo*
mistake	machigai	*mah-chee-gah-ee*
• make mistakes	machigaeru (v)	*mah-chee-gah-eh-roo*
note	nōto	*noh-toh*
• take notes	nōto o toru (v)	*noh-toh oh toh-roo*
problem	mondai	*mohn-dah-ee*
• solve a problem	mondai o toku (v)	*mohn-dah-ee oh toh-koo*
question	shitsumon	*shee-tsoo-mohn*
• ask a question	shitsumonsuru (v)	*shee-tsoo-mohn-soo-roo*
read	yomu (v)	*yoh-moo*
• reading passage	yomikata	*yoh-mee-kah-tah*
registration	tetsuzuki	*teh-tsoo-zoo-kee*
• registration fee	tetsuzuki ryō	*teh-tsoo-zoo-kee ryoh*
repeat	kurikaesu (v)	*koo-ree-kah-eh-soo*
review	fukushū	*fkoo-shoo*
• review	fukushūsuru (v)	*fkoo-shoo-soo-roo*
school	gakkō	*gahk-koh*
• finish school	gakkō o oeru (v)	*gahk-koh oh oh-eh-roo*
• go to school	gakkō ni iku (v)	*gahk-koh nee ee-koo*
study	benkyōsuru (v)	*behn-kyoh-soo-roo*
submit	teishutsusuru (v)	*teh-shoo-tsoo-soo-roo*

take attendance	shusseki o toru (*v*)	*shoos-seh-kee oh toh-roo*
teach	oshieru (*v*)	*oh-shee-eh-roo*
test	tesuto	*tehs-toh*
thesis	ronbun	*rohn-boon*
type	taipu de utsu (*v*)	*tah-ee-poo deh oo-tsoo*
typewriter	taipuraitā	*tah-ee-poo-rah-ee-tāh*
understand	rikaisuru (*v*)	*ree-kah-ee-soo-roo*
write	kaku (*v*)	*kah-koo*

38. WORK

a. JOBS AND PROFESSIONS

accountant	kaikeishi	*kah-ee-keh-shee*
actor	dan-yū	*dahn-yōo*
actress	joyū	*joh-yōo*
architect	kenchikuka	*kehn-chee-koo-kah*
baker	panyaki no shokunin	*pahn-yah-kee noh shoh-koo-neen*
banker	ginkōka	*geen-kōh-kah*
barber	rihatsushi	*ree-hah-tsoo-shee*
builder	kenchikugyōsha	*kehn-chee-koo-gyōh-shah*
bus driver	basu no untenshu	*bah-soo noh oon-tehn-shoo*
businessman	bijinesuman	*bee-jee-neh-soo-mahn*
businesswoman	bijinesuūman	*bee-jee-neh-soo-ōo-mahn*
butcher	nikuya	*nee-koo-yah*
carpenter	daiku	*dah-ee-koo*
construction worker	kenchikugenba no sagyōin	*kehn-chee-koo-gehn-bah noh sah-gyōh-een*
consultant	konsarutanto	*kohn-sah-roo-tahn-toh*
cook	chōrishi	*chōh-ree-shee*
dentist	haisha	*hah-ee-shah*
doctor	isha	*ee-shah*
editor	henshūsha	*hehn-shōo-shah*
electrician	denkikō	*dehn-kee-kōh*
engineer	gishi	*gee-shee*
eye doctor	meisha	*meh-ee-shah*
factory worker	kōin	*kōh-een*
farmer	nōgyō jūjisha	*noh-gyōh jōo-jee-shah*
fireman	shōbōshi	*shoh-bōh-shee*
florist	hanaya	*hah-nah-yah*
government worker	kōmuin	*kōh-moo-een*
• **national government worker**	kokka kōmuin	*kohk-kah kōh-moo-een*

• **local government worker**	chihō kōmuin	*chee-hoh koh-moo-een*
hairdresser	biyōshi	*bee-yoh-shee*
job	shigoto	*shee-goh-toh*
journalist	jānarisuto	*jah-nah-ree-stoh*
lawyer	bengoshi	*behn-goh-shee*
mechanic	jidōsha shūriko	*jee-doh-shah shoo-ree-koh*
movie director	eiga kantoku	*eh-gah kahn-toh-koo*
musician	ongakuka	*ohn-gahk-kah*
nurse	kangofu	*kahn-goh-foo*
occupation	shokugyō	*shoh-koo-gyoh*
office worker (*male*)	sararīman	*sah-rah-ree-mahn*
office worker (*female*)	ōeru	*oh-eh-roo*
painter (*artist*)	gaka	*gah-kah*
painter (*of buildings, rooms*)	penkiya	*pehn-kee-yah*
pharmacist	yakuzaishi	*yah-koo-zah-ee-shee*
photographer	shashinka	*shah-sheen-kah*
pilot	pairotto	*pah-ee-roht-toh*
plumber	haikankō	*hah-ee-kahn-koh*
policeman	keikan	*keh-kahn*
policewoman	fujinkeikan	*foo-jeen-keh-kahn*
politician	seijika	*seh-jee-kah*
professor	kyōju	*kyoh-joo*
profession	shokugyō	*shoh-koo-gyoh*
professional	puro no (*adj*)	*poo-roh noh*
psychiatrist	seishinkai	*seh-sheen-kuh-ee*
psychologist	shinrigakusha	*sheen-ree-gahk-shah*
real estate agent	fudōsan assennin	*foo-doh-sahn ahs-sehn-neen*
scientist	kagakusha	*kah-gah-koo-shah*
secretary	hisho	*hee-shoh*
singer	kashu	*kah-shoo*
store clerk	ten-in	*tehn-een*
storekeeper	tenshu	*tehn-shoo*
steward	suchuwādo	*soo-choo-wah-doh*
stewardess	suchuwādesu	*soo-choo-wah-dehs*
surgeon	gekai	*geh-kah-ee*
tailor	shitateya	*shee-tah-teh-yah*
taxi driver	takushī no untenshu	*tahk-shee noh oon-tehn-shoo*
teacher	kyōshi	*kyoh-shee*
tour guide	tsuā gaido	*tsoo-ah gah-ee-doh*
truck driver	torakku no untenshu	*toh-rahk-koo noh oon-tehn-shoo*
typist	taipisuto	*tah-ee-pee-stoh*
writer	sakka	*sahk-kah*

b. INTERVIEWING FOR A JOB

See also Section 11f — Basic Personal Information.

Name	namae	*nah-mah-eh*
first name	namae	*nah-mah-eh*
	mei	*meh*
surname, family name	myōji	*myoh-jee*
	sei	*seh*
signature	shomei	*shoh-meh*
Address	jūsho	*joo-shoh*
number	banchi	*bahn-chee*
city	shi	*shee*
prefecture	ken	*kehn*
state	shū	*shoo*
ward	ku	*koo*
zip code	yūbin bangō	*yoo-been bahn-goh*
Telephone number	denwa bangō	*dehn-wah bahn-goh*
area code	shigai kyokuban	*shee-gah-ee kyoh-koo-bahn*
extension	naisen	*nah-ee-sehn*
fax number	fakkusu bangō	*fahk-koo-soo bahn-goh*
Date and place of birth	seinengappi to shusseichi	*seh-nehn-gahp-pee toh shoos-seh-chee*
date	seinengappi	*seh-nehn-gahp-pee*
day	hi	*hee*
month	tsuki	*tsoo-kee*
place	shusseichi	*shoos-seh-chee*
year	toshi	*toh-shee*
Age	nenrei	*nehn-reh*
Sex	seibetsu	*seh-beh-tsoo*
male	otoko	*oh-toh-koh*
female	onna	*ohn-nah*
Marital Status	kekkon shikaku	*kehk-kohn shee-kah-koo*
divorced	rikon	*ree-kohn*
married	kikon	*kee-kohn*
single	dokushin	*doh-koo-sheen*
Nationality	kokuseki	*kohk-seh-kee*

See also Section 30d — Nationalities and Languages.

Education	gakureki	*gah-koo-reh-kee*
elementary school	shōgakkō	*shoh-gahk-koh*
junior high school	chūgaku	*choo-gah-koo*

high school	kōkō	koh-koh
junior college	tandai	tahn-dah-ee
university	daigaku	dah-ee-gah-koo
graduate school	daigakuin	dah-ee-gah-koo-een
Profession	shokureki	shoh-koo-reh-kee
Resume	rirekisho	ree-reh-kee-shoh
Special Skills	tokugi	toh-koo-gee

c. THE OFFICE

See also Sections 20 and 25.

---

adhesive tape	setchaku tēpu	seht-chah-koo teh-poo
appointment book	yotei hyō	yoh-teh hyoh
briefcase	atasshe kēsu	ah-tahs-sheh keh-soo
calendar	karendā	kah-rehn-dah
chair	isu	ee-soo
file	bunsho fairu	boon-shoh fah-ee-roo
filing card	fairu yō kādo	fah-ee-roo yoh kah-doh
intercom	intāfon	een-tah-fohn
pen	pen	pehn
pencil	enpitsu	ehn-pee-tsoo
photocopier	fukushaki	fkoo-shah-kee
ruler	jōgi	joh-gee
scissors	hasami	hah-sah-mee
staple	hotchikisu no hari	hoht-chee-kee-soo noh hah-ree
stapler	hotchikisu	hoht-chee-kee-soo
telephone	denwa	dehn-wah
thumbtack	gabyō	gah-byoh
typewriter	taipuraitā	tah-ee-poo-rah-ee-tah
wastebasket	kuzukago	koo-zoo-kah-goh
word processor	wāpuro	wah-poo-roo

d. ADDITIONAL WORK VOCABULARY

advertising	kōkoku	koh-koh-koo
bankruptcy	hasan	hah-sahn
• go bankrupt	hasansuru (v)	hah-sahn-soo-roo
benefit	onkei	ohn-keh
be transferred	tenkinsuru (v)	tehn-keen-soo-roo
boss (in an office)	jōshi	joh-shee

branch	shiten	shee-tehn
career	keireki	keh-reh-kee
classified ad	kōmokubetsu kōkoku	koh-moh-koo-beh-tsoo koh-koh-koo
colleague	dōryō	doh-ryoh
commerce	shōgyō	shoh-gyoh
company	kaisha	kah-ee-shah
contract	keiyaku	keh-yah-koo
earn	kasegu (v)	kah-seh-goo
employ	yatou (v)	yah-toh-oo
employee	shain	shah-een
	jūgyōin	joo-gyoh-een
employer	koyōsha	koh-yoh-shah
employment agency	shokugyō shōkaisho	shoh-koo-gyoh shoh-kah-ee-shoh
factory	kōjō	koh-joh
fire (dismiss)	kaikosuru (v)	kah-ee-koh-soo-roo
hire	yatou (v)	yah-toh-oo
job description	shokumu naiyō	shoh-koo-moo nah-ee-yoh
labor union	rōdō kumiai	roh-doh koo-mee-ah-ee
layoff	ichiji kaiko	ee-chee-jee kah-ee-koh
lifetime job security	shūshin koyō seido	shoo-sheen koh-yoh seh-doh
manager	manējā	mah-neh-jah
market	shijō	shee-joh
office	ofisu	oh-fee-soo
overtime work	zangyō	zahn-gyoh
• work overtime	zangyōsuru (v)	zahn-gyoh-soo-roo
plant	kōjō	koh-joh
retirement	taishoku	tah-ee-shoh-koo
• retire	taishokusuru (v)	tah-ee-shohk-soo-roo
• retirement money	taishoku kin	tah-ee-shoh-koo keen
salary	kyūryō	kyoo-ryoh
seniority system	nenkōjoretsu sei	nehn-koh-joh-reh-tsoo seh
subordinate	buka	boo-kah
unemployment	shitsugyō	shee-tsoo-gyoh
unemployment compensation	shitsugyō teate	shee-tsoo-gyoh teh-ah-teh
wage	chingin	cheen-geen
work	shigoto	shee-goh-toh
• work	hataraku (v)	hah-tah-rah-koo

EMERGENCIES

39. REPORTING AN EMERGENCY

a. FIRE

ambulance	kyūkyūsha	*kyōō-kyōō-shah*
building	biru	*bee-roo*
burn (*injury*)	yakedo	*yah-keh-doh*
• burn (*on fire*)	moeru (*vi*)	*moh-eh-roo*
call	denwasuru (*v*)	*dehn-wah-soo-roo*
catch fire	hi ga tsuku	*HEE gah tsoo-koo*
danger	kiken	*kee-kehn*
destroy	hakaisuru (*v*)	*hah-kah-ee-soo-roo*
emergency exit	hijōguchi	*hee-joh-goo-chee*
escape, get out	nogareru (*v*)	*noh-gah-reh-roo*
extinguish, put out	kesu (*v*)	*keh-soo*
fire	kaji	*kah-jee*
• be on fire	moete iru	*moh-eh-teh ee-roo*
• Fire!	Kaji da.	*KAH-jee dah*
• fire alarm	kasai hōchiki	*kah-sah-ee hoh-chee-kee*
• fire department	shōbōsho	*shoh-boh-shoh*
• fire engine	shōbōsha	*shoh-boh-shah*
• fire extinguisher	shōkaki	*shoh-kah-kee*
• firefighter	shōbōshi	*shoh-boh-shee*
• fire hose	shōka yō hōsu	*shoh-kah yoh hoh-soo*
• fire hydrant	shōkasen	*shoh-kah-sehn*
fireproof	taikasei no (*adj*)	*tah-ee-kah-seh noh*
first aid	ōkyū teate	*oh-kyōō teh-ah-teh*
flame	honoo	*hoh-noh-oh*
help	tasuke	*tahs-keh*
• help	tasukeru (*v*)	*tahs-keh-roo*
• Help!	Tasukete.	*tahs-KEH-teh*
• give help	tasukete ageru	*tahs-keh-teh ah-geh-roo*
out	soto e (*adv*)	*soh-toh eh*
• Everybody out!	Soto e dete kudasai.	*soh-toh eh DEH-teh koo-dah-sah-ee*
protect	fusegu (*v*)	*foo-seh-goo*
rescue	kyūjo	*kyōō-joh*
shout	sakebi	*sah-keh-bee*
• shout	sakebu (*v*)	*sah-keh-boo*
siren	sairen	*sah-ee-rehn*
smoke	kemuri	*keh-moo-ree*
spark	hinoko	*hee-noh-koh*

victim	giseisha	*gee-seh-shah*

b. ROBBERY AND ASSAULT

argue	iiarasou (*v*)	*ee-ah-rah-soh-oo*
arrest	taiho	*tah-ee-hoh*
• **arrest**	taihosuru (*v*)	*tah-ee-hoh-soo-roo (v)*
assault	osou (*v*)	*oh-soh-oo*
catch	tsukamaeru (*v*)	*tskah-mah-eh-roo*
Come quickly!	Isoide kite.	*ee-SOH-ee-deh kee-teh*
crime	hanzai	*hahn-zah-ee*
• **crime wave**	hanzai no nami	*hahn-zah-ee noh nah-mee*
• **criminal**	hanzaisha	*hahn-zah-ee-shah*
description	ninsōgaki	*neen-soh-gah-kee*
fight	kakutō	*kahk-toh*
firearm	kaki	*KAH-kee*
gun	jū	*joo*
handcuffs	tejō	*teh-joh*
hurry	isogu (*v*)	*ee-soh-goo*
injure, wound	kegasaseru (*vt*)	*keh-gah-sah-seh-roo*
• **injury, wound**	kega	*keh-gah*
kill	korosu (*v*)	*koh-roh-soo*
• **killer**	satsujinsha	*sah-tsoo-jeen-shah*
knife	naifu	*nah-ee-foo*
• **switchblade**	tobidashi naifu	*toh-bee-dah-shee nah-ee-foo*
murder	satsujin	*sah-tsoo-jeen*
• **murder**	korosu (*v*)	*koh-roh-soo*
• **murderer**	satsujinsha	*sah-tsoo-jeen-shah*
pickpocket	suri	*soo-ree*
police	keisatsu	*keh-sah-tsoo*
• **policeman**	keikan	*keh-kahn*
• **policewoman**	fujinkeikan	*foo-jeen-keh-kahn*
• **call the police**	keisatsu o yobu (*v*)	*keh-sah-tsoo oh yoh-boo*
rape	gōkan	*goh-kahn*
• **rape**	gōkansuru (*v*)	*goh-kahn-soo-roo*
rifle	raifuru	*rah-ee-foo-roo*
rob	ubau (*v*)	*oo-bah-oo*
• **robber**	gōtō	*goh-toh*
• **armed robbery**	busō gōtō	*boo-soh-goh-toh*
• **robbery**	gōtō	*goh-toh*
• **Stop thief!**	Dorobō.	*doh-roh-boh*
steal	nusumu (*v*)	*noo-soo-moo*
suspect	yōgisha	*yoh-gee-shah*
thief	dorobō	*doh-roh-boh*
victim	higaisha	*hee-gah-ee-shah*

violence	bōryoku	*boh-ryoh-koo*
weapon	kyōki	*kyoh-kee*
• shoot	utsu (*v*)	*oo-tsoo*

c. TRAFFIC ACCIDENTS

accident	jiko	*jee-koh*
• serious accident	daijiko	*dah-ee-jee-koh*
• traffic accident	kōtsū jiko	*koh-tsoo jee-koh*
ambulance	kyūkyūsha	*kyoo-kyoo-shah*
• call an ambulance	kyūkyūsha o yobu (*v*)	*kyoo-kyoo-shah oh yoh-boo*
be run over	hikareru (*v*)	*hee-kah-reh-roo*
bleed	shukketsusuru (*v*)	*shook-keh-tsoo-soo-roo*
• blood	chi	*chee*
broken bone	kossetsu	*kohs-seh-tsoo*
bump	kobu	*koh-boo*
collision	shōtotsu	*shoh-toh-tsoo*
• collide	shōtotsusuru (*v*)	*shoh-tohts-soo-roo*
crash	shōtotsu	*shoh-toh-tsoo*
• crash	shōtotsusuru (*v*)	*shoh-tohts-soo-roo*
doctor	isha	*ee-shah*
• get a doctor	isha o yobu (*v*)	*ee-shah oh yoh-boo*
first aid	ōkyū teate	*oh-kyoo teh-ah-teh*
• antiseptic	shōdokuyaku	*shoh-doh-koo-yah-koo*
• bandage	hōtai	*hoh-tah-ee*
• gauze	gāze	*gah-zeh*
• scissors	hasami	*hah-sah-mee*
• splint	fukuboku	*fkoo-boh-koo*
• tincture of iodine	yōdochinki	*yoh-doh-cheen-kee*
Help!	Tasukete.	*tahs-KEH-teh*
hospital	byōin	*byoh-een*
• emergency hospital	kyūkyū byōin	*kyoo-kyoo byoh-een*
• X-rays	rentogen	*rehn-toh-gehn*
police	keisatsu	*keh-sah-tsoo*
• call the police	keisatsu o yobu (*v*)	*keh-sah-tsoo oh yoh-boo*
shock	shokku	*shohk-koo*
wound, injury	kega	*keh-gah*

40. MEDICAL CARE

a. THE DOCTOR

> See also Section 12 — The Body.

acne	nikibi	*nee-kee-bee*
allergy	arerugī	*ah-reh-roo-gee*
appendicitis	mōchōen	*moh-choh-ehn*
• appendix	mōchō	*moh-choh*
appointment	yoyaku	*yoh-yah-koo*
artery	dōmyaku	*doh-myah-koo*
arthritis	kansetsuen	*kahn-seh-tsoo-ehn*
aspirin	asupirin	*ahs-pee-reen*
bandage	hōtai	*hoh-tah-ee*
• bandage	hōtai o maku (v)	*hoh-tah-ee oh mah-koo*
blood	ketsueki	*keh-tsoo-eh-kee*
• blood pressure	ketsuatsu	*keh-tsoo-ah-tsoo*
• blood test	ketsueki kensa	*keh-tsoo-eh-kee kehn-sah*
bone	hone	*hoh-neh*
brain	nō	*noh*
bronchitis	kikanshien	*kee-kahn-shee-ehn*
capsule	kapuseru	*kah-poo-seh-roo*
cold	kaze	*kah-zeh*
convalescence	kaifuku	*kah-ee-foo-koo*
cough	seki	*seh-kee*
• cough	seki o suru (v)	*seh-kee oh soo-roo*
cure	ryōhō	*ryoh-hoh*
• cure	naosu (vt)	*nah-oh-soo*
• get cured	yokunaru (v)	*yoh-koo-nah-roo*
dandruff	fuke	*foo-keh*
digestive system	shōka keitō	*shoh-kah keh-toh*
• anus	kōmon	*koh-mohn*
• defecate	haibensuru (v)	*hah-ee-behn-soo-roo*
• intestine	chō	*choh*
• large intestine	daichō	*dah-ee-choh*
• rectum	chokuchō	*chohk-choh*
• small intestine	shōchō	*shoh-choh*
• stomach	i	*ee*
• have a stomachache	i ga itai	*ee gah ee-tah-ee*
doctor	isha	*ee-shah*
doctor's instruments	shinryō kigu	*sheen-ryoh kee-goo*
• electrocardiograph	shindenkei	*sheen-dehn-keh*
• stethoscope	chōshinki	*choh-sheen-kee*
• syringe	chūshaki	*choo-shah-kee*
• thermometer	taionkei	*tah-ee-ohn-keh*
doctor's visit	ōshin	*oh-sheen*
examine (*medically*)	shinsatsusuru (v)	*sheen-sahts-soo-roo*
• get examined	shinsatsu o ukeru (v)	*sheen-sah-tsoo oh oo-keh-roo*
eye doctor	me isha	*meh ee-shah*
• contact lenses	kontakuto renzu	*kohn-tahk-toh rehn-zoo*
• eyeglasses	megane	*meh-gah-neh*

• eyesight	shiryoku	*shee-ryoh-koo*
feel	kanji ga suru	*kahn-jee gah soo-roo*
• feel bad	kibun ga warui	*kee-boon gah wah-roo-ee*
• feel well	kibun ga ii	*kee-boon gah ēē*
• strong	genki na (*adj*)	*gehn-kee nah*
• weak	yowayowashii (*adj*)	*yoh-wah-yoh-wah-shēē*
• How do you feel?	kibun wa, dō desu ka.	*kee-boon wah, DŌH dehs kah*
fever	netsu	*neh-tsoo*
flu	ryūkan	*ryōo-kahn*
headache	zutsū	*zoo-tsōo*
• have a headache	zutsū ga suru	*zoo-tsōo gah soo-roo*
heal	naoru (*v*)	*nah-oh-roo*
health	kenkō	*kehn-koh*
• healthy	kenkō na (*adj*)	*kehn-koh nah*
heart	shinzō	*sheen-zōh*
• heart attack	shinzō mahi	*sheen-zōh mah-hee*
hurt	itamu (*v*)	*ee-tah-moo*
infection	kanō	*kah-nōh*
injection	chūsha	*chōo-shah*
itch	kayumi	*kah-yoo-mee*
lymphatic system	rinpasen	*reen-pah-sehn*
measles	hashika	*hah-shee-kah*
medicine (*one takes*)	kusuri	*koo-soo-ree*
muscle	kinniku	*keen-nee-koo*
nerves	shinkei	*sheen-keh*
• nervous system	shinkei keitō	*sheen-keh-keh-toh*
nurse	kangofu	*kahn-goh-foo*
operation	shujutsu	*shoo-joo-tsoo*
• operating room	shujutsushitsu	*shoo-joo-tsoo-shee-tsoo*
optician	megane ya	*meh-gah-neh yah*
pain	itami	*ee-tah-mee*
• painful	itai (*adj*)	*ee-tah-ee*
• painkiller	chintsūzai	*cheen-tsōo-zah-ee*
patient	kanja	*kahn-jah*
pill	ganyaku	*gahn-yah-koo*
pimple	nikibi	*nee-kee-bee*
pneumonia	haien	*hah-ee-ehn*
pregnant	ninshinchū no (*adj*)	*neen-sheen-chōo noh*
prescription	shohōsen	*shoh-hōh-sehn*
pulse	myaku	*myah-koo*
respiratory system	kokyū keitō	*koh-kyōo kēh-toh*
• breath	kokyū	*koh-kyōo*
• breathe	kokyūsuru (*v*)	*koh-kyōo-soo-roo*
• be out of breath	iki ga kireru	*ee-kee gah kee-reh-roo*
• lung	hai	*hah-ee*
• nostril	bikō	*bee-kōh*

rheumatism	ryūmachi	*ryōo-mah-chee*
secretary	hisho	*hee-shoh*
sedative	chinseizai	*cheen-seh-zah-ee*
sick	byōki no (*adj*)	*byoh-kee noh*
• **get sick**	byōki ni naru (*v*)	*byoh-kee nee nah-roo*
• **sickness, disease**	byōki	*byoh-kee*
sneeze	kushami	*koo-shah-mee*
• **sneeze**	kushami o suru (*v*)	*koo-shah-mee oh soo-roo*
sore back	kata no kori	*kah-tah noh koh-ree*
sore/stiff neck	kubi no kori	*koo-bee noh koh-ree*
specialist	senmonka	*sehn-mohn-kah*
suffer	kurushimu (*v*)	*koo-roo-shee-moo*
suppository	zayaku	*zah-yah-koo*
surgeon	gekai	*geh-kah-ee*
• **surgery**	shujutsu	*shoo-joo-tsoo*
swollen	hareta (*adj*)	*hah-reh-tah*
tablet	jōzai	*joh-zah-ee*
temperature (fever)	netsu	*neh-tsoo*
• **take one's**		
temperature	netsu o hakaru (*v*)	*neh-tsoo oh hah-kah-roo*
throat	nodo	*noh-doh*
• **sore throat**	nodo no itami	*noh-doh noh ee-tah-mee*
• **have a sore throat**	nodo ga itamu	*noh-doh gah ee-tah-moo*
throw up	haku (*v*)	*HAH-koo*
tonsils	hentōsen	*hehn-toh-sehn*
urinary system	hinyō keitō	*hee-nyoh keh-toh*
• **kidney**	jinzō	*jeen-zoh*
• **urinate**	hainyōsuru (*v*)	*hah-ee-nyoh-soo-roo*
vein	jōmyaku	*joh-myah-koo*
vomit	haku (*v*)	*HAH-koo*
wheelchair	kurumaisu	*koo-roo-mah-ee-soo*

b. THE DENTIST

anesthetic	masui	*mah-soo-ee*
appointment	yoyaku	*yoh-yah-koo*
cavity, tooth decay	mushiba	*moo-shee-bah*
clean, brush (*teeth*)	ha o migaku (*v*)	*hah oh mee-gah-koo*
crown	shikan	*shee-kahn*
dentist	haisha	*hah-ee-shah*
• **at the dentist's**	haisha de	*hah-ee-shah deh*
• **dentist's office**	haisha no shinryōsho	*hah-ee-shah noh sheen-ryoh-shoh*
denture, false teeth	ireba	*ee-reh-bah*
drill	doriru	*doh-ree-roo*
examine	shiraberu (*v*)	*shee-rah-beh-roo*

extract, pull	nuku (v)	noo-koo
• extraction	basshi	bahs-shee
filling	tsumemono	tsoo-meh-moh-noh
mouth	kuchi	koo-chee
• gums	haguki	hah-goo-kee
• jaw	ago	ah-goh
• lip	kuchibiru	kchee-bee-roo
• Open your mouth!	Kuchi o, akete kudasai.	koo-chee oh, ah-keh-teh koo-dah-sah-ee
• palate	kōgai	koh-gah-ee
• tongue	shita	shtah
needle	hari	hah-ree
office hours	shinryō jikan	sheen-ryoh jee-kahn
rinse	kuchi o susugu (v)	koo-chee oh soo-soo-goo
tooth	ha	hah
• canine	kenshi	kehn-shee
• incisor	monba	mohn-bah
• molar	kyūshi	kyoo-shee
• root	shikon	shee-kohn
• wisdom tooth	oyashirazu	oh-yah-shee-rah-zoo
toothache	shitsū	shee-tsoo
• have a toothache	ha ga itamu	hah gah ee-tah-moo
• My tooth hurts!	Ha ga, itai desu.	hah gah, ee-tah-ee dehs
• Which tooth hurts?	Dono ha ga, itamimasu ka.	DOH-noh hah gah, ee-tah-mee-mahs kah
toothbrush	haburashi	hah-boo-rah-shee
toothpaste	nerihamigaki	neh-ree-hah-mee-gah-kee
X-rays	rentogen	rehn-toh-gehn

41. LEGAL MATTERS

accusation	kokuhatsu	koh-koo-hah-tsoo
• accuse	kokuhatsusuru (v)	koh-koo-hah-tsoo-soo-roo
• accused person	hikoku	hee-koh-koo
• accuser	kokuhatsunin	koh-koo-hah-tsoo-neen
address oneself to	hanashikakeru (v)	hah-nah-shee-kah-keh-roo
admit	mitomeru (v)	mee-toh-meh-roo
agree	gōisuru (v)	goh-ee-soo-roo
appeal	jōkokusuru (v)	joh-kohk-soo-roo
arbitration	chōtei	choh-teh
brief	tekiyōsho	teh-kee-yoh-shoh
• brief	chinjutsusuru (v)	cheen-joo-tsoo-soo-roo
capital punishment	shikei	shee-keh
chief of police	keisatsu shochō	keh-sah-tsoo shoh-choh
client	irainin	ee-rah-ee-neen
confess	jihakusuru (v)	jee-hahk-soo-roo

• confession	jihaku	*jee-hah-koo*
controversy	rongi	*rohn-gee*
convince	kakushinsaseru (v)	*kahk-sheen-sah-seh-roo*
court	saibansho	*sah-ee-bahn-shoh*
• court of appeal	kōsoin	*koh-soh-een*
• supreme court	saikō saibansho	*sah-ee-koh sah-ee-bahn-shoh*
courtroom	hōtei	*hoh-teh*
debate	tōron	*toh-rohn*
• debate	tōronsuru (v)	*toh-rohn-soo-roo*
decision	hanketsu	*hahn-keh-tsoo*
• final decision	saishū kettei	*sah-ee-shoo keht-teh*
• interim decision	kari kettei	*kah-ree keht-teh*
defend oneself	jikobengosuru (v)	*jee-koh-behn-goh-soo-roo*
disagree	hantaisuru (v)	*hahn-tah-ee-soo-roo*
discuss	sōdansuru (v)	*soh-dahn-soo-roo*
evidence	shōko	*shoh-koh*
guilt	tsumi	*tsoo-mee*
• guilty	yūzai no (adj)	*yoo-zah-ee noh*
innocence	muzai	*moo-zah-ee*
• innocent	muzai no (adj)	*moo-zah-ee noh*
judge	saibankan	*sah-ee-bahn-kahn*
• judge	hanketsu o kudasu (v)	*hahn-keh-tsoo oh koo-dah-soo*
jury	baishin	*bah-ee-sheen*
justice	seigi	*seh-gee*
law	hōritsu	*hoh-ree-tsoo*
• lawful, legal	gōhō no (adj)	*goh-hoh noh*
• unlawful, illegal	ihō no (adj)	*ee-hoh noh*
• civil law	minpō	*meen-poh*
• criminal law	keihō	*keh-hoh*
lawsuit, charge	soshō	*soh-shoh*
• lose a lawsuit	haisosuru (v)	*hah-ee-soh-soo-roo*
• win a lawsuit	shōsosuru (v)	*shoh-soh-soo-roo*
lawyer	bengoshi	*behn-goh-shee*
• trial lawyer	hōtei bengoshi	*hoh-teh behn-goh-shee*
litigate	soshō o okosu (v)	*soh-shoh oh oh-koh-soo*
• litigation	soshō	*soh-shoh*
magistrate	keihanzai no hanji	*keh-hahn-zah-ee noh hahn-jee*
object	igi o tonaeru (v)	*ee-gee oh toh-nah-eh-roo*
• objection	igi	*ee-gee*
persuade	settokusuru (v)	*seht-tohk-soo-roo*
plaintiff	genkoku	*gehn-koh-koo*
plea	tangan	*tahn-gahn*
• plea for mercy	jihi no tangan	*jee-hee noh tahn-gahn*
• plead	tangansuru (v)	*tahn-gahn-soo-roo*

police station	keisatsusho	keh-sah-tsoo-shoh
prison, jail	keimusho	keh-moo-shoh
• **imprison**	togokusuru (v)	toh-gohk-soo-roo
• **life imprisonment**	muki chōeki	moo-kee chōh-eh-kee
public prosecutor	kensatsukan	kehn-sahts-kahn
represent	daihyōsuru (v)	dah-ee-hyōh-soo-roo
right, privilege	kenri	kehn-ree
sentence	hanketsu	hahn-keh-tsoo
• **life sentence**	shūshinkei	shōo-sheen-keh
• **prison sentence**	yūkikei	yōo-kee-keh
• **pass a sentence**	hanketsu o iiwatasu (v)	hahn-keh-tsoo oh ēe-wah-tah-soo
• **serve a sentence**	keiki ni fukusuru (v)	keh-kee nee foo-koo-soo-roo
settlement	wakai	wah-kah-ee
• **out of court settlement**	jidan	jee-dahn
sue	uttaeru (v)	oot-tah-eh-roo
summons	shōkanjō	shoh-kahn-jōh
testify	shōgensuru (v)	shoh-gehn-soo-roo
• **testimony**	shōgen	shoh-gehn
trial	saiban	sah-ee-bahn
• **be on trial**	saiban ni tatsu (v)	sah-ee-bahn nee tah-tsoo
• **put someone on trial**	kokuhatsusuru (v)	kohk-hahts-soo-roo
verdict	hyōketsu	hyōh-keh-tsoo
• **guilty**	yūzai	yōo-zah-ee
	kuro	koo-roh
• **not guilty**	muzai	moo-zah-ee
	shiro	shee-roh
witness	shōnin	shoh-neen
• **eyewitness**	mokugekisha	moh-koo-geh-kee-shah
• **for the defense**	bengogawa no (adj)	behn-goh-gah-wah noh
• **for the prosecution**	kensatsugawa no (adj)	kehn-sah-tsoo-gah-wah noh

THE CONTEMPORARY WORLD

42. SCIENCE AND TECHNOLOGY

a. THE CHANGING WORLD

> For more vocabulary on basic matter, see Section 13.

antenna	antena	*ahn-teh-nah*
• **dish antenna**	parabora antena	*pah-rah-boh-rah AHN-teh-nah*
astronaut	uchū hikōshi	*oo-choo hee-koh-shee*
atom	genshi	*gehn-shee*
• **electron**	denshi	*dehn-shee*
• **molecule**	bunshi	*boon-shee*
• **neutron**	chūseishi	*choo-seh-shee*
• **proton**	yōshi	*yoh-shee*
compact disc	konpakuto disuku	*kohn-pahk-toh dees-koo*
fax machine	fakkusu	*fahk-koo-soo*
laser	rēzā	*reh-zah*
• **laser beam**	rēzā kōsen	*reh-zah koh-sehn*
microwave	chōtanpa	*choh-tahn-pah*
missile	misairu	*mee-sah-ee-roo*
• **launch pad**	hasshadai	*hahs-shah-dah-ee*
monorail vehicle	monorēru	*moh-noh-reh-roo*
nuclear industry	genshiryoku sangyō	*gehn-shee-ryoh-koo sahn-gyoh*
• **fission reactor**	kakubunretsuro	*kah-koo-boon-reh-tsoo-roh*
• **fusion reactor**	kakuyūgōro	*kah-koo-yoo-goh-roh*
• **nuclear energy**	kaku enerugī	*kah-koo eh-neh-roo-gee*
• **nuclear reactor**	genshiro	*gehn-shee-roh*
robot	robotto	*roh-boht-toh*
satellite	jinkōeisei	*jeen-koh-eh-seh*
scientific research	kagaku kenkyū	*kah-gah-koo kehn-kyoo*
spacecraft	uchūsen	*oo-choo-sehn*
• **lunar module**	tsuki chakurikusen	*tskee chah-koo-reek-sehn*
• **space shuttle**	supēsushatoru	*speh-soo-shah-toh-roo*
technology	gijutsu	*gee-joo-tsoo*
• **advanced technology**	sentan gijutsu	*sehn-tahn gee-joo-tsoo*
telecommunications	enkyori tsūshin	*ehn-kyoh-ree tsoo-sheen*
• **teleconferencing**	terekonfarensu	*teh-reh-kohn-fah-rehn-soo*

• telex machine	terekkusu	*teh-rehk-ksoo*
theory of relativity	sōtaisei genri	*soh-tah-ee-seh gehn-ree*
• quantum theory	ryōshiron	*ryoh-shee-rohn*

b. COMPUTERS

artificial intelligence	jinko chinō	*jeen-koh chee-noh*
byte	baito	*bah-ee-toh*
compatible	konpachi (no) (*adj*)	*kohn-pah-chee (noh)*
computer	konpyūta	*kohn-pyoo-tah*
• computer language	konpyūta gengo	*kohn-pyoo-tah gehn-goh*
• computer science	konpyūta saiensu	*kohn-pyoo-tah sah-ee-ehn-soo*
data	dēta	*deh-tah*
• database	dētabēsu	*deh-tah-beh-soo*
• data processing	dēta shori	*deh-tah shoh-ree*
disk	disuku	*dees-koo*
• floppy disk	furoppī (disuku)	*foo-rohp-pee (dees-koo)*
function	kinō	*keen-noh*
hardware	hādowea	*hah-doh-weh-ah*
integrated circuit	shūseki kairo	*shoo-seh-kee kah-ee-roh*
interface	intāfēsu	*een-tah-feh-soo*
keyboard	kībōdo	*kee-boh-doh*
• keyboard operator	kībōdo operēta	*kee-boh-doh oh-peh-reh-tah*
memory	memori	*meh-moh-ree*
• random access memory	randamu akusesu memori	*rahn-dah-moo ahk-seh-soo meh-moh-ree*
menu	menyū	*meh-nyoo*
microcomputer	maikurokonpyūta	*mah-ee-koo-roh-kohn-pyoo-tah*
modem	modemu	*moh-deh-moo*
office automation	ofisu ōtomēshon	*oh-fee-soo oh-toh-meh-shohn*
peripherals	shūhen sōchi	*shoo-hehn soh-chee*
personal computer	pasokon	*pah-soh-kohn*
printer	purintā	*poo-reen-tah*
program	puroguramu	*poo-roh-goo-rah-moo*
• programmer	puroguramā	*poo-roh-goo-rah-mah*
• programming	puroguramingu	*poo-roh-goo-rah-meen-goo*
screen	sukurīn	*skoo-reen*
• software	sofuto wea	*soh-ftoh weh-ah*
terminal	tāminaru	*tah-mee-nah-roo*
user-friendly	yūza furendorī	*yoo-zah foo-rehn-doh-ree*
word processing	wāpuro shori	*wah-poo-roh shoh-ree*

| • word processor | wāpuro | *wah-poo-roh* |

43. POLITICS

> See also Sections 16, 17, 21, and 22.

advanced country	senshinkoku	*sehn-sheen-koh-koo*
arms race	gunbi kyōsō	*goon-bee kyoh-soh*
arms reduction	gunbi sakugen	*goon-bee sah-koo-gehn*
assembly	shūkai	*shoo-kah-ee*
cabinet	naikaku	*nah-ee-kah-koo*
• cabinet member	kakuryō	*kah-koo-ryoh*
communism	kyōsanshugi	*kyoh-sahn-shoo-gee*
• communist	kyōsanshugisha	*kyoh-sahn-shoo-gee-shah*
congress	gikai	*gee-kah-ee*
• congressman	giin	*gee-een*
conservative	hoshuteki na (*adj*)	*hoh-shoo-teh-kee nah*
• conservative party	hoshutō	*hoh-shoo-toh*
council	chihōgikai	*chee-hoh-gee-kah-ee*
democracy	minshushugi	*meen-shoo-shoo-gee*
• democrat	minshushugisha	*meen-shoo-shoo-gee-shah*
• democratic	minshushugi no (*adj*)	*meen-shoo-shoo-gee noh*
demonstration	demo	*deh-moh*
developing country	hatten tojōkoku	*haht-tehn toh-joh-koh-koo*
Diet (*Japanese congress*)	kokkai	*kohk-kah-ee*
• Diet member	kokkai giin	*kohk-kah-ee gee-een*
disarmament	gunbi teppai	*goon-bee tehp-pah-ee*
dissolve	kaisansuru (*v*)	*kah-ee-sahn-soo-roo*
economy	keizai	*keh-zah-ee*
elect	erabu (*v*)	*eh-rah-boo*
• election	senkyo	*sehn-kyoh*
faction	habatsu	*hah-bah-tsoo*
govern	tōjisuru (*v*)	*toh-jee-soo-roo*
• government	seifu	*seh-foo*
ideology	ideorogī	*ee-deh-oh-roh-gee*
inflation	infure	*een-foo-reh*
labor/trade union	rōdōkumiai	*roh-doh-koo-mee-ah-ee*
legislation	rippō	*reep-poh*
liberal	kakushinteki na (*adj*)	*kahk-sheen-teh-kee nah*
• liberal party	kakushintō	*kahk-sheen-toh*
minister	daijin	*dah-ee-jeen*
monarchy	kunshusei	*koon-shoo-seh*
• emperor	tennō	*tehn-noh*
• empress	kōgō	*koh-goh*

• king	kokuō	*koh-koo-oh*
• queen	jō-ō	*joh-oh*
• prince	ōji	*oh-jee*
• princess	ōjo	*oh-joh*
mutual	sōgoteki na (*adj*)	*soh-goh-teh-kee nah*
parliament	gikai	*gee-kah-ee*
• elected politician, representative	giin	*gee-een*
• House of Representatives (*U.S.*)	kain	*kah-een*
• House of Councilors (*Japanese*)	sangiin	*sahn-gee-een*
• House of Representatives (*Japanese*)	shūgiin	*shoo-gee-een*
• Senate (*U.S.*)	jōin	*joh-een*
• senator	jōin giin	*joh-een gee-een*
• universal suffrage/ right to vote	futsū senkyoken	*foo-tsoo sehn-kyoh-kehn*
peace	heiwa	*heh-wah*
policy	seisaku	*seh-sah-koo*
politician	seijika	*seh-jee-kah*
• left wing	sayoku	*sah-yoh-koo*
• right wing	uyoku	*oo-yoh-koo*
politics	seiji	*seh-jee*
• political party	seitō	*seh-toh*
• political power	seijiryoku	*seh-jee-ryoh-koo*
president	daitōryō	*dah-ee-toh-ryoh*
prime minister	shushō	*shoo-shoh*
protest	kōgi	*koh-gee*
• protest	kōgisuru (*v*)	*koh-gee-soo-roo*
reform	kaikaku	*kah-ee-kah-koo*
• reform	kaikakusuru (*v*)	*kah-ee-kahk-soo-roo*
republic	kyōwakoku	*kyoh-wah-koh-koo*
revolt	hanran	*hahn-rahn*
• revolt	hanransuru (*v*)	*hahn-rahn-soo-roo*
• revolution	kakumei	*kah-koo-meh*
riot	bōdō	*boh-doh*
socialism	shakaishugi	*shah-kah-ee-shoo-gee*
• socialist	shakaishugisha	*shah-kah-ee-shoo-gee-shah*
state	kokka	*kohk-kah*
• head of state	genshu	*gehn-shoo*
strike	sutoraiki	*stoh-rah-ee-kee*
• go on strike	sutoraiki ni hairu (*v*)	*stoh-rah-ee-kee nee hah-ee-roo*

Third World	daisansekai	*dah-ee-sahn-seh-kah-ee*
unilateral	ippōteki na (*adj*)	*eep-poh-teh-kee nah*
vote	tōhyō	*toh-hyoh*
• vote	tōhyōsuru (*v*)	*toh-hyoh-soo-roo*
• voter	tōhyōsha	*toh-hyoh-shah*
welfare	shakai fukushi	*shah-kah-ee foo-koo-shee*

44. CONTROVERSIAL ISSUES

a. THE ENVIRONMENT

> For more vocabulary, see Sections 13 and 42.

air pollution	kūki osen	*koo-kee oh-sehn*
conservation	shizen hogo	*shee-zehn hoh-goh*
consumption	shōhi	*shoh-hee*
ecology	seitaigaku	*seh-tah-ee-gah-koo*
ecosystem	seitaikei	*seh-tah-ee-keh*
energy	enerugī	*eh-neh-roo-gee*
• energy crisis	enerugī kiki	*eh-neh-roo-gee kee-kee*
• energy needs	enerugī juyō	*eh-neh-roo-gee joo-yoh*
• energy source	enerugī shigen	*eh-neh-roo-gee shee-gehn*
• energy waste	enerugī rōhi	*eh-neh-roo-gee roh-hee*
environment	kankyō	*kahn-kyoh*
geothermal energy	chinetsu enerugī	*chee-neh-tsoo eh-neh-roo-gee*
natural resources	tennen shigen	*tehn-nehn shee-gehn*
petroleum	sekiyu	*seh-kee-yoo*
pollution	kōgai	*koh-gah-ee*
radiation	hōshasen	*hoh-shah-sehn*
• radioactive waste	hōshasei haikibutsu	*hoh-shah-seh hah-ee-kee-boo-tsoo*
solar cell	taiyō denchi	*tah-ee-yoh dehn-chee*
solar energy	taiyō enerugī	*tah-ee-yoh eh-neh-roo-gee*
thermal energy	netsu enerugī	*neh-tsoo eh-neh-roo-gee*
water pollution	mizu osen	*mee-zoo oh-sehn*
wind energy	fūryoku enerugī	*foo-ryoh-koo eh-neh-roo-gee*

b. SOCIETY

| abortion | datai | *dah-tah-ee* |
| • fetus | taiji | *tah-ee-jee* |

AIDS	eizu	*eh-ee-zoo*
capital punishment	shikei	*shee-keh*
censorship	ken-etsu	*kehn-eh-tsoo*
contraception	hinin	*hee-neen*
discrimination	sabetsu	*sah-beh-tsoo*
drugs	mayaku	*mah-yah-koo*
• drug addiction	mayaku chūdoku	*mah-yah-koo chōo-doh-koo*
• drug pusher	mayaku mitsubainin	*mah-yah-koo mee-tsoo-bah-ee-neen*
• drug trafficking	mayaku baibai	*mah-yah-koo bah-ee-bah-ee*
• take drugs	mayaku o tsukau (v)	*mah-yah-koo oh tsoo-kah-oo*
feminism	feminizumu	*feh-mee-nee-zoo-moo*
• feminist	feminisuto	*feh-mee-nee-stoh*
homosexual	dōseiai no (adj)	*dōh-seh-ah-ee noh*
• homosexuality	dōseiai	*dōh-seh-ah-ee*
morality	dōtoku	*dōh-toh-koo*
nuclear war	kaku sensō	*kah-koo sehn-sōh*
nuclear weapon	kaku heiki	*kah-koo heh-kee*
• antinuclear protest	hankaku demo	*hahn-kah-koo deh-moh*
• atomic bomb	genshi bakudan	*gehn-shee bah-koo-dahn*
• hydrogen bomb	suiso bakudan	*soo-ee-soh bah-koo-dahn*
• chemical weapon	kagaku heiki	*kah-gah-koo heh-kee*
pornography	poruno	*poh-roo-noh*
prostitute	baishunfu	*bah-ee-shoon-foo*
• prostitution	baishun	*bah-ee-shoon*
racism	jinshu sabetsu	*jeen-shoo sah-beh-tsoo*

c. EXPRESSING YOUR OPINION

according to me	watakushi ni yoreba	*wah-tahk-shee nee yoh-reh-bah*
as a matter of fact	jissai	*jees-sah-ee*
by the way	tokorode	*toh-koh-roh deh*
for example	tatoeba	*tah-toh-eh-bah*
from my point of view	watakushi no mikata dewa	*wah-tahk-shee noh mee-kah-tah deh-wah*
I believe that ...	... to omoimasu	*... toh oh-moh-ee-mahs*
I don't know if ...	... ka dō ka shirimasen	*... kah dōh kah shee-ree-mah-sehn*
I doubt that ...	... ka dō ka gimon desu	*... kah dōh kah gee-mohn dehs*
I think that ...	... to omoimasu	*... toh oh-moh-ee-mahs*

I'd like to say …	… to iitai no desu ga	… *toh ēe-tah-ee noh dehs gah*
I'm not sure that …	… ka dō ka tashika dewa arimasen	… *kah dōh kah tah-shkah deh-wah ah-ree-mah-sehn*
I'm sure that …	… wa, tashika desu	… *wah, tah-shkah dehs*
in conclusion	ketsuron to shitewa	*keh-tsoo-rohn toh shteh-wah*
in my opinion	watakushi no iken dewa	*wah-tahk-shee noh ee-kehn deh-wah*
in my view	watakushi no kangae dewa	*wah-tahk-shee noh kahn-gah-eh deh-wah*
It seems that …	… yō desu	… *yoh dehs*
It's clear that …	… wa, akiraka desu	… *wah, ah-kee-rah-kah dehs*
that is to say	sunawachi	*soo-nah-wah-chee*
There's no doubt that …	… wa, utagai no yochi mo arimasen	… *wah, oo-tah-gah-ee noh yoh-chee moh ah-ree-mah-sehn*
therefore	soreyue	*soh-reh-yoo-eh*

ENGLISH–JAPANESE WORDFINDER

This alphabetical listing of all of the English words in *Japanese Vocabulary* will enable you to find the information you need quickly and efficiently. If all you want is the Japanese equivalent of an entry word, you will find it here. If you also want pronunciation and usage aids, or closely associated words and phrases, use the reference number(s) and letter(s) to locate the section(s) in which the entry appears. This is especially important for words that have multiple meanings.

A

abalone awabi 鮑 24d

abbreviation shōryakukei 省略形 19c

abdomen fukubu 腹部 12a

abortion datai 堕胎 44b

above ue no *(adj)* 上の 3d

above ue ni *(adv)* 上に 3d

above zero reido ijō no 零度以上の 6c

abroad gaikoku 外国 19e

abroad kaigai ni *(adv)* 海外に 30a

accent akusento アクセント 8a, 19c

accept ukeireru *(v)* 受け入れる 21b

acceptable ukeirerareru *(adj)* 受け入れられる 21b

accident jiko 事故 33c

according to me watakushi ni yoreba 私によれば 17a

accordion akōdion アコーディオン 28c

account kōza 口座 26

accountant kaikeishi 会計士 38a

accounting kaikeigaku 会計学 37e

accusation hinan 非難 17a

accusation kokuhatsu 告発 41

accuse hinansuru *(v)* 非難する 17a

accuse kokuhatsusuru *(v)* 告発する 41

accused person hikoku 被告 41

accuser kokuhatsunin 告発人 41

acid san 酸 13c

acid rain sanseiu 酸性雨 13c

acne nikibi にきび 40a

acquaintance chijin 知人 10b, 16b

across mukōgawa no *(adj)* 向う側の 3d

across ... ... o yokogitte を横切って 36c

act enjiru *(v)* 演じる 28e

act maku 幕 28e

active nōdōtai no *(adj)* 能動態の 8a

active katsudōteki na *(adj)* 活動的な 11e

active kappatsu na *(adj)* 活発な 21a

activity katsudō 活動 11e

actor danyū 男優 28a

actress joyū 女優 28a

actually ... Jitsu wa, ... 実は 17b

acute-angled eikaku *(adj)* 鋭角 2a

acute angle eikaku 鋭角 2b

adapt tekigōsaseru *(vt)* 適合させる 11e

adaptable tekigōsei ga aru *(adj)* 適合性がある 11e

add kuwaeru/tasu *(v)* 加える／足す 1e

addition tashizan 足し算 1e

address jūsho 住所 11f, 19e, 38b

addressee naatenin 名宛人 19e

address oneself to hanashikakeru *(v)* 話しかける 41

add up the bill kanjō ni tsuketasu *(v)* 勘定につけたす 24o

adhesive tape setchaku tēpu 接着テープ 25c, 38c

adjacent angle rinsetsukaku 隣接角 2b

adjective keiyōshi 形容詞 8a

admit mitomeru *(v)* 認める 41

adolescent shishunki no *(adj)* 思春期の 11b

adult otona 大人 11b

advanced country senshinkoku 先進国 43

advanced technology sentan gijutsu 先端技術 42a

advance ticket maeuri ken 前売券 30a

adventure bōken 冒険 20a

adverb fukushi 副詞 8a

advertising kōkoku 広告 20a, 38d

advice jogen 助言 17a

advise jogensuru *(v)* 助言する 17a

affection aijō 愛情 11e, 21a

affectionate aijō no fukai *(adj)* 愛情の深い 11e, 21a

affectionately kokoro o komete 心を込めて 19b

affirmative kōtei *(adj)* 肯定 8a

Africa Afurika アフリカ 30b

after ato de *(adv)* 後で 4e

afternoon gogo 午後 4a

again mata *(adv)* また 4e

age nenrei/toshi 年齢／年 11b

age toshitoru *(v)* 年取る 11b

age nenrei 年齢 38b

aggressive kōgekiteki na *(adj)* 攻撃的な 11e, 21a

aggressiveness kōgekisei 攻撃性 11e

agnostic fukachiron no *(adj)* 不可知論の 11d

agnosticism fukachiron 不可知論 11d

ago mae ni *(adv)* 前に 4e

agree sanseisuru *(v)* 賛成する 21a

agree gōisuru *(v)* 合意する 41

agreeable kokoroyoi *(adj)* 快い 21a

agriculture nōgyō 農業 14a

ahead, forward mukōgawa ni *(adv)* 向こう側に 3d

ahead, forward saki no *(adj)* 先の 3d

ahead ... ...no saki ni の先に 36c

AIDS eizu エイズ 40b

air kūki 空気 6a, 13b, c

air conditioner eakon エアコン 23e, 33e

air conditioning reibō 冷房 23e

airline kōkūgaisha 航空会社 32a

airmail kōkūbin 航空便 19e

airplane hikōki 飛行機 32c

air pollution kūki osen 空気汚染 44a

airport kūkō 空港 32a

aisle tsūro 通路 28a

aisle tsūrogawa 通路側 32c

alarm clock mezamashi 目覚まし 4d

alcoholic beverage arukōru inryō アルコール飲料 24k

alcove tokonoma 床の間 23b

algebra daisū 代数 1f

algebraic daisū no *(adj)* 代数の 1f

a little sukoshi *(adv)* 少し 3c

all zenbu 全部 8i

all, everything subete *(adv)* 全て 3c

all, everything zenbu 全部 3c

All aboard! Gōjōsha kudasai. ご乗車ください。 34

all day ichinichijū 一日中 4a

allegory tatoebanashi 例え話 17a

allergy arerugī アレルギー 40a

alligator arigēta アリゲーター 15c

allude honomekasu *(v)* ほのめかす 17a

almost, nearly hotondo *(adv)* ほとんど 3c

almost, never hotondo ~ shinai *(adv)* 殆ど～しない 4e

a lot, much takusan 沢山 3c

alphabet arufabetto アルファベット 8a

already sude ni/mō *(adv)* 既に／もう 4e

alteration shitatenaoshi 仕立て直し 25m

altruism aitashugi 愛他主義 11e

altruist aitashugisha 愛他主義者 11e

altruistic aitateki na *(adj)* 愛他的な 11e

always itsumo *(adv)* いつも 4e

amateur amachua アマチュア 27b

ambition taibō 大望 11e

ambitious nozomi ga takai *(adj)* 望みが高い 11e

ambulance kyūkyūsha 救急車 33a

America Amerika アメリカ 30b

American Amerikajin アメリカ人 30d

ammonia anmonia アンモニア 13c

among naka ni 中に 3d

amphibian ryōseirui 両生類 15c

amplifier anpu アンプ 20b

analogy ruihi 類比 17a

anatomy kaibōgaku 解剖学 37e

anchovy anchobi アンチョビ 24d

and (at the beginning of a sentence) soshite そして 8k

and (between nouns) to と 8j

anesthetic masui 麻酔 40b

anger ikari 怒り 11e, 21a

angle kakudo 角度 2b

angry okotta *(adj)* 怒った 11e, 21a

animal dōbutsu 動物 15a

ankle ashikubi 足首 12a

anniversary kekkon kinenbi 結婚記念日 11c

anniversary kinenbi 記念日 29a

announce shiraseru *(v)* 知らせる 17a

announcement happyō 発表 17a

answer kotae 答え 9, 17a, 37f

answer kotaeru *(v)* 答える   9, 17a, 37f

answer denwa ni deru *(v)* 電話にでる 18b

answering machine rusuban denwa 留守番電話 18a

ant ari 蟻 15d

antacid isan 胃散 25h

Antarctic Circle nankyokuken 南極圏 13e

Antarctic Ocean nanpyōyō 南氷洋 13b

antenna antena アンテナ 20b, 42a

anterior saki no *(adj)* 先の 4e

anthropology jinruigaku 人類学 37e

antibiotic kōseibusshitsu 抗生物質 25h

antiseptic shōdokuyaku 消毒薬 25h

anus kōmon 肛門 40a

anxiety fuankan 不安感 11e

anxiety, anxiousness fuan 不安 21a

anxious shinpai na *(adj)* 心配な 11e

anxious fuan na *(adj)* 不安な 21a

apartment (an inexpensive one) apāto アパート 23g

apartment (an upscale one) manshon マンション 23g

aperitif shokuzenshu 食前酒 24g, 24k

A pleasure! Yorokonde. 喜んで。 16b

apostrophe aposutorofi アポストロフィ 19c

appeal jōkokusuru *(v)* 上告する 41

appendicitis mōchōen 盲腸炎 40a

appendix furoku 附録 20a, 28d

appendix mōchō 盲腸 40a

appetizer zensai 前菜 24g

appetizing oishisō na *(adj)* おいしそうな 24p

applaud hakushusuru *(v)* 拍手する 28e

applause hakushu 拍手 28e

apple ringo 林檎 14d

apple tree ringo no ki 林檎の木 14c

appointment yoyaku 予約 40a, b

appointment book yotei hyō 予定表 38c

approval zenin 是認 21b

approve mitomeru *(v)* 認める 21b

approximately ōyoso *(adv)* おおよそ 3c

apricot anzu 杏 14d

April shigatsu 四月 5b

Aquarius mizugameza 水瓶座 5d

Arab Arabiajin アラビア人 30d

Arabic Arabiago アラビア語 30d

Arabic numeral Arabia sūji アラビア数字 1d

arbitration chōtei 調停 41

archbishop daishikyō 大司教 11d

archeology kōkogaku 考古学 37e

archipelago guntō 群島 13b

architect kenchikuka 建築家 28b

architecture kenchiku 建築 28b

architecture kenchikugaku 建築学 37e

Arctic Circle hokkyokuken 北極圏 13e

Arctic Ocean hoppyōyō 北氷洋 13b

area menseki 面積 3a

area code shigaikyokuban 市外局番 18b, 38c

Are you joking? Jōdan desho. 冗談でしょ。 21c

Argentina Aruzenchin アルゼンチン 30b

argue gironsuru *(v)* 議論する 17a

argue iiarasou *(v)* 言い争う 39b

argument giron 議論 17a

Aries ohitsujiza 牡羊座 5d

arithmetical sansū no *(adj)* 算数の 1f

arithmetical operations enzan 演算 1e

arm ude 腕 12a

armchair hijikakeisu 肘掛け椅子 23c, 35c

armed robbery busō gōtō 武装強盗 39b

armrest hijikake 肘掛け 35c

arms race gunbi kyōsō 軍備競争 43

arms reduction gunbi sakugen 軍備削減 43

arrest taiho 逮捕 39b

arrest taihosuru *(v)* 逮捕する 39b

arrival tōchaku 到着 32a

arrive tsuku *(v)* 着く 32a

arrogance gōman 傲慢 11e

arrogant gōman na *(adj)* 傲慢な 11e

art geijutsu 芸術 28b

art gallery āto gyararī アートギャラリー 28b

art gallery garō 画廊 36a

arthritis kansetsuen 関節炎 40a

artichoke ātichōku アーティチョーク 14e

article kanshi 冠詞 8a

article kiji 記事 20a

articulate hakkiri hyōgensuru (v) はっきりと表現する 17a

artificial jinzō no (adj) 人造の 13d

artificial jinkō no (adj) 人工の 25i

artificial intelligence jinkō chinō 人工知能 42b

artist geijutsuka 芸術家 28b

artistic geijutsuteki na (adj) 芸術的な 11e

arts kyōyō kamoku 教養科目 37e

as a matter of fact jissai 実際 44c

As a matter of fact,... Jissai,... 実際 17b

Asia Ajia アジア 30b

ask kiku (v) 聞く 17a

ask a question shitsumonsuru (v) 質問する 37f

ask for tanomu (v) 頼む 9

ask for something nanika o tanomu 何かを頼む 9

ask for the bill kanjō o tanomu 勘定を頼む 35b

ask someone dareka ni kiku 誰かに聞く 9

as much as dake だけ 3c

asparagus asuparagasu アスパラガス 14e

aspirin asupirin アスピリン 25h

assault osou (v) 襲う 39b

assembly shūkai 集会 43

assignment book shukudai chō 宿題帳 37b

assignments, homework shukudai 宿題 37f

assistant joshu 助手 37d

as soon as sugu ni すぐに 4e

assure ukeau (v) 請け合う 21a

asterisk hoshijirushi 星印 19c

astronaut uchū hikōshi 宇宙飛行士 42a

astronomy tenmongaku 天文学 13a, 37e

astute kibin na (adj) 機敏な 11e

astuteness kibinsa 機敏さ 11e

at ni/de に／で 8j

atheism mushinron 無神論 11d

atheist mushinronsha 無神論者 11d

athlete undō no senshu 運動の選手 27b

at home uchi de うちで 23f

Atlantic Ocean taiseiyō 大西洋 13b

atlas chizu chō 地図帳 20a, 37b

at midnight mayonaka ni 真夜中に 4a

atmosphere taiki 大気 6a, 13b

atmospheric taiki no (adj) 大気の 13b

atmospheric conditions kiatsu 気圧 6a

at night yoru ni 夜に 4a

at noon shōgo ni 正午に 4a

atom genshi 原子 13c, 42a

atomic bomb genshi bakudan 原子爆弾 44b

attend school gakkō ni iku (v) 学校に行く 37f

at the beach kaigan de 海岸で 36b

at the bottom soko ni 底に 3d

at the dentist's haisha de 歯医者で 40b

at the end of ... ...no owari ni の終わりに 36c

at the same time dōji ni 同時に 4e

at the top ichiban ue de 一番上で 3d

attic yaneurabeya 屋根裏部屋 23a

attitude taido 態度 21a

attractive miryokuteki na (adj) 魅力的な 11a, 11e

At what time? Nanji ni. 何時に。 4b

audience kankyaku 観客 28e

audio equipment ōdio sōchi オーディオ装置 20b

audit chōkōsuru (v) 聴講する 37f

August hachigatsu 八月 5b

aunt oba 叔母 10a

aunt obasan 叔母さん 10a

Australia Ōsutoraria オーストラリア 30b

Australian Ōsutorariajin オーストラリア人 30d

Austria Ōsutoria オーストリア 30b

Austrian Ōsutoriajin オーストリア人 30d

authentic honmono no (adj) 本物の 13d

author chosha 著者 20a

autobiography jiden 自伝 28b

automobile jidōsha 自動車 33a

autumnal equinox shūbun　秋分　5c

avarice, greed donyoku　貪欲　11e

avaricious, greedy yoku no fukai *(adj)*
　欲の深い　11e

avenue gai　街　11f

average heikin　平均　1f

away hedatatta *(adj)*　隔たった　3d

away hedatatte *(adv)*　隔たって　3d

awful hidoi *(adj)*　ひどい　6a

axis jiku　軸　2b

B

baby akachan　赤ちゃん　11b

bachelor dokushin　独身　11c

back senaka　背中　12a

back, backward ushiro no *(adj)*　後ろの
　3d

back, backward ushiro ni *(adv)*　後ろに
　3d

back ... ... no ushiro ni　の後ろに　36c

backrest semotare　背もたれ　35c

back up bakkusuru *(v)*　バックする　33c

bacon bēkon　ベーコン　24c

bad mazui *(adj)*　まずい　24p

bad warui *(adj)*　悪い　11e

Badly. Anmari yoku arimasen.　あんま
　りよくありません。　16a

badminton badominton　バドミントン
　27b

bad mood warui kibun　悪い気分　21a

bag fukuro　袋　23d

bag (shopping) kaimonobukuro　買物袋
　25a

baggage, luggage nimotsu　荷物　31

bagpipes baggupaipu　バッグパイプ
　28c

bake tenpi de yaku *(v)*　天火で焼く
　24o

baked tenpi de yaita *(adj)*　天火で焼い
　た　24b

baker panyaki no shokunin　パン焼きの
　職人　38a

bakery pan ya　パン屋　24n

balcony barukonī　バルコニー　35c

ball bōru　ボール　27b

ballet barē　バレー　28c

ballpoint pen bōru pen　ボールペン
　19d, 25c, 37b

bamboo clarinet shakuhachi　尺八　28c

bamboo shoot takenoko　筍　14e, 24e

banana banana　バナナ　14d, 24f

band bando　バンド　25j

band gakudan　楽団　25j

Band-Aid bandoeido　バンドエイド
　25h

bandage hōtai　包帯　25h, 39c, 40a

bandage hōtai o maku *(v)*　包帯を巻く
　40a

Bangkok Bankokku　バンコック　30c

banjo banjō　バンジョー　28c

bank ginkō　銀行　26

bank book ginkō tsūchō　銀行通帳　26

banker ginkōka　銀行家　38a

bank rate kōteibuai　公定歩合　26

bankruptcy hasan　破産　38d

baptism senrei　洗礼　11d

barber rihatsushi　理髪師　38a, 12d

barber shop tokoya　床屋　12d

bark hoeru *(v)*　吠える　15a

barley ōmugi　大麦　24i

barn naya　納屋　15a

barometer kiatsukei　気圧計　6c

barometric pressure kiatsu　気圧　6c

barrel taru　樽　23d

bartender bāten　バーテン　24m

base bēsu　ベース　27b

baseball yakyū　野球　27b

basement chikashitsu　地下室　23a

basil bajiru　バジル　14e

basin bonchi　盆地　13b

basket kago　篭　23d

basketball basukettobōru　バスケット
　ボール　27b

bass drum ōdaiko　大太鼓　28c

bassoon fagotto　ファゴット　28c

bat kōmori　こうもり　15a

bat batto　バット　27b

bath ofuro　お風呂　12d

bathing suit mizugi　水着　25k

bath oil basu oiru　バスオイル　25f

bathrobe basurōbu　バスローブ　25k

bathroom (Japanese style) furoba　風呂
　場　23b, 35c

bathroom (western style) basurūmu　バ
　スルーム　23b, 35c

bathtub yokusō　浴槽　23a, 35c

batter battā　バッター　27b

battery denchi　電池　25b

battery batterī　バッテリー　25b, 33e

bay wan　湾　13b

be about to ～kaketeiru　～かけている
　4e

be absent kesseki (desu) 欠席（です） 37f

beach hama 浜 13b

beach kaigan 海岸 36b

be afraid osoreru (v) 恐れる 21a

be against hantaisuru (v) 反対する 21a

beak kuchibashi くちばし 15b

bean mame 豆 14e, 24e

bean sprout moyashi もやし 14e, 24e

bear kuma 熊 15a

beard agohige あごひげ 12a

be ashamed hajiru (v) 恥じる 21a

beast kemono 獣 15a

beat kakuhansuru 攪拌する 24o

beautician biyōshi 美容師 12d

beautiful utsukushii (adj) 美しい 11a, 25l

beautiful subarashii (adj) 素晴らしい 6a

beautiful weather subarashii tenki 素晴らしい天気 6a

beauty bijin 美人 11a

be born umareru (v) 生まれる 11c

be called yobareru (v) 呼ばれる 11f

Be careful! Ki o tsukete. 気をつけて。 21c

because nazenara なぜなら 8k

be cold samui desu 寒いです 12b

become ~ ni naru になる 4e

become angry okoru (v) 怒る 11e

become big ōkiku naru (v) 大きくなる 3g, 11a

become bored taikutsusuru (vi) 退屈する 21a

become engaged konyakusuru (v) 婚約する 11c

become fat futoru (v) 太る 11a

become friends tomodachi ni naru (v) 友達になる 10b

become old toshitoru (v) 年取る 11b

become sick byōki ni naru (v) 病気になる 11a

become small chiisakunaru (v) 小さくなる 3g

become weak yowakunaru (v) 弱くなる 11a

bed beddo ベッド 23c, 35c

bed bug nankinmushi 南京虫 15d

bedding (Japanese mattress for the floor) futon 布団 23c

be down ki ga meitte iru 気が滅入っている 21a

bedroom shinshitsu 寝室 23b

bedside table saidotēburu サイドテーブル 23c, 35c

bedspread beddokabā ベッドカバー 23d

bee hachi 蜂 15d

beech tree buna ぶな 14c

beef gyūniku 牛肉 24c

beef bīfu ビーフ 24c

beer bīru ビール 24k

beet satōdaikon 砂糖大根 14e, 24e

beetle kōchū 甲虫 15d

be fond of, like konomu (v) 好む 21b

before mae ni (adv) 前に 4e

be from... ...kara kimashita から来ました 11f

beg kongansuru (v) 懇願する 17a

begin hajimaru (vi) 始まる 4e

begin hajimeru (vt) 始める 4e

beginning hajimari 始まり 4e

behind... ...no kage ni の陰に 36c

be hot atsui desu 暑いです 12b

be hungry onaka ga suite imasu おなかが空いています 12b, 24o

Beijing Bējin ベージン 30c

be in a bad mood kigen ga warui 機嫌が悪い 11e

be in a good mood kigen ga ii 機嫌がいい 11e

be interested in kyōmi ga aru (v) 興味がある 22b

be late osokunaru おそくなる 4e

Belgian Berugijin ベルギー人 30d

Belgium Berugī ベルギー 30b

belief shinnen 信念 11d

believe shinjiru (v) 信じる 11d, 22b

believe in shinjiru (v) 信じる 11d

believer shinja 信者 11d

bellhop bōi ボーイ 35b

bell tower shōrō 鐘楼 36a

belly onaka おなか 12a

below zero hyōtenka 氷点下 6c

belt beruto ベルト 25k

benefit onkei 恩恵 38d

be on fire moete iru 燃えている 39a

be on the point/verge of ~kaketeiru ~かけている 4e

be on time jikandōri ni 時間通りに 4e

be on trial saiban ni tatsu (v) 裁判に立つ 41

be out of breath iki ga kireru 息が切れる 40a

be pregnant ninshin chū desu 妊娠中です 11c

be present shusseki (desu) 出席（です） 37f

be promoted shinkyūsuru *(v)* 進級する 37f

be right tadashii (desu) 正しい（です） 22b

Berlin Berurin ベルリン 30c

be run over hikareru *(v)* ひかれる 39c

be seated koshikakeru *(v)* 腰掛ける 16b

Be seated, please! Dōzo okake kudasai. どうぞおかけください。 16b

beside, next to tonari no *(adj)* 隣の 3d

beside, next to tonari ni *(adv)* 隣に 3d

be sleepy nemui desu 眠いです 12b

best-seller besutoserā ベストセラー 20a, 25o

Best wishes! Gokōun o. ご幸運を。 16c, 29c

be thirsty nodo ga kawaite imasu 喉が渇いています 12b, 24o

be tired tsukarete imasu 疲れています 12b

be transferred tenkinsuru *(v)* 転勤する 38d

between aida no *(adj)* 間の 3d

between aida ni *(adv)* 間に 3d

between friends tomodachi no aida no ni/de 友達の間の/に/で 10b

be up ki ga takamatte iru 気が高まっている 21a

be windy kaze ga tsuyoi 風が強い 6a

be wrong machigai (desu) 間違い（です） 22b

beyond koeta *(adj)* 越えた 3d

beyond koete *(adv)* 越えて 3d

bicycle jitensha 自転車 33a

Bicycle Path jitenshadō 自転車道 33d

bicycle racing jitensha kyōsō 自転車競争 27b

big ōkii 大きい 11a, 25l

big, large ōkii *(adj)* 大きい 3c

bigness ōkisa 大きさ 11a

bill seikyūsho 請求書 25a

bill kanjō 勘定 35b

bill, bank note osatsu お札 26

bill, check kanjō 勘定 24m

billiard ball tamatsuki no tama 玉突きの玉 27a

billiards tamatsuki 玉突き 27a

billiard table tamatsuki no tēburu 玉突きのテーブル 27a

billionth jūokubanme 十億番目 1b

bingo bingo ビンゴ 27a

bingo card bingo no kādo ビンゴのカード 27a

biography denki 伝記 28d

biology seibutsugaku 生物学 37e

birch shirakaba 白樺 14c

bird tori 鳥 15b

birth tanjō 誕生 11c

birthday tanjōbi 誕生日 11c, 29a

biscuit bisuketto ビスケット 24i

bisector nitōbunsen 二等分線 2b

bishop bishoppu ビショップ 27a

bishop shikyō 司教 11d

bitter nigai *(adj)* 苦い 24p

black kuro 黒 7a

black kuroi *(adj)* 黒い 7a

black kokujin 黒人 11d

black and white film shiro kuro no fuirumu 白黒のフィルム 25d

blackboard kokuban 黒板 37b

blackboard eraser kokubankeshi 黒板消し 37b

blade ha 刃 23d

blame togameru *(v)* 咎める 17a

blanket mōfu 毛布 23d, 35c

blazer burēzā ブレーザー 25k

bleach hyōhakuzai 漂白剤 25g

bleat mēmē naku *(v)* めーめー鳴く 15a

bleed shukketsusuru *(v)* 出血する 39c

blind me no mienai *(adj)* 目の見えない 12c

blindness mōmoku 盲目 12c

blond kinpatsu no *(adj)* 金髪の 11a

blond kinpatsu no hito 金髪の人 11a

blood chi 血 39c

blood ketsueki 血液 40a

blood chi/ketsueki 血/血液 12a

blood pressure ketsuatsu 血圧 40a

blood test ketsueki kensa 血液検査 40a

bloom hana ga saku *(v)* 花が咲く 14a

blossom hana 花 14a

blouse burausu ブラウス 25k

blue ao 青 7a

blue aoi *(adj)* 青い 7a

blueberry burūberī ブルーベリー 14d, 24f

bluejay aokakesu 青かけす 15b

blue jeans jīnzu ジーンズ 25k

blueprint aojashin 青写真 28b

boarding tōjō 搭乗 32a

boarding pass tōjō ken 搭乗券 32a

boat bōto ボート 36b

boat ticket fune no ken 船の券 30a

bodily physique taikaku 体格 11a

body honbun 本文 19c

body karada 体 11a, 12a

body building bodī biru ボディービル 27b

boil yuderu (v) ゆでる 24o

boiled yudeta (adj) ゆでた 24b

boiling point futtōten 沸騰点 6c

bold daitan na (adj) 大胆な 21a

Bolivia Boribia ボリビア 30b

bolt boruto ボルト 25b

bond saiken 債券 26

bone hone 骨 12a, 40a

book hon 本 20a, 25o, 37b

bookcase hondana 本棚 23c, 37b

bookstore hon ya 本屋 25o

boot būtsu ブーツ 25n

border kyōkai 境界 13e

border sakaisuru (v) 堺する 13e

border kokkyō 国境 31

bore unzarisaseru (vt) うんざりさせる 21a

bored taikutsushita (adj) 退屈した 21a

boredom taikutsu 退屈 21a

boss (in an office) jōshi 上司 38d

botanical shokubutsu no (adj) 植物の 14a

botany shokubutsugaku 植物学 14a, 37e

both ryōhō 両方 3c

bottle bin 瓶 23d, 24l

bottom soko 底 3d

bouquet of flowers hanataba 花束 14b

bourbon whiskey bābon バーボン 24k

bow yumi 弓 28c

bowl bōru ボール 24l

bowl tama o korogasu (v) 球を転がす 27b

bowling bōringu ボーリング 27b

bowling alley bōringujō ボーリング場 27b

bowling ball bōringu no bōru ボーリングのボール 27b

bowling pin pin ピン 27b

box hako 箱 23d

boxing bokushingu ボクシング 27b

boxing gloves gurabu グラブ 27b

boxing ring ringu リング 27b

box office kippu uriba 切符売り場 28a

boy otoko no ko 男の子 11a

boyfriend otoko tomodachi/bōi furendo 男友達／ボーイフレンド 10b

bra burajā ブラジャー 25k

bracelet udewa 腕輪 25i

bracket, parenthesis kakko 括弧 19c

brain nō 脳 12a, 40a

brake burēki ブレーキ 33a, 33c, 33e

branch eda 枝 14a

branch shiten 支店 38d

brandy burandē ブランデー 24k

brash sekkachi na (adj) せっかちな 11e

brass instruments kinkan gakki 金管楽器 28c

Brazil Burajiru ブラジル 30b

Brazilian Burajirujin ブラジル人 30d

bread pan パン 24g, 24l

breakdown koshō 故障 33c

breakfast asagohan 朝御飯 24a, 35b

breakfast chōshoku 朝食 24a

breakfast included chōshoku komi 朝食込み 35b

break off a friendship zekkōsuru (v) 絶交する 10b

breast chibusa 乳房 12a

breath kokyū 呼吸 40a

breathe kokyūsuru (v) 呼吸する 40a

breathe ikizuku (v) 息づく 12b

bride hanayome 花嫁 11c

bridge hashi 橋 33c, 36a

brief kantan na (adj) 簡単な 4e, 37f

brief tekiyōsho 摘要書 41

brief chinjutsusuru (v) 陳述する 41

briefcase attasshe kēsu アタッシェケース 38c

briefly kantan ni (adv) 簡単に 4e

Briefly,... Kantan ni nobereba,... 簡単に述べれば 17b

bright hanayaka na (adj) 華やかな 7b

brilliant sainō ni michita (adj) 才能に満ちた 11e

broccoli burokkori ブロッコリ 14e, 24e

brochure panfuretto パンフレット 30a

broil jikabi de yaku (v) 直火で焼く 24o

broiled jikabi de yaita (adj) 直火で焼いた 24b

broken bone kossetsu 骨折 39c

broken line hasen 破線 2b

bronchitis kikanshien 気管支炎 40a

bronze seidō 青銅 13c

brooch burōchi ブローチ 25i

brook ogawa 小川 36b

broom hōki ほうき 23d

brother-in-law (spouse's elder brother, or elder sister's husband) gikei 義兄 10a

brother-in-law (spouse's younger brother, or younger sister's husband) gitei 義弟 10a

brother-in-law (spouse's elder brother, or elder sister's husband) giri no oniisan 義理のお兄さん 10a

brother-in-law (spouse's younger brother, or younger sister's husband) giri no otōtosan 義理の弟さん 10a

brothers kyōdai 兄弟 10a

brothers gokyōdai ご兄弟 10a

brothers and sisters kyōdai to shimai 兄弟と姉妹 10a

brothers and sisters gokyōdai to goshimai ご兄弟とご姉妹 10a

brown chairo 茶色 7a

brown chairoi (adj) 茶色い 7a

brush fude 筆 19d

brush burashi ブラシ 12d, 28b

brush oneself burashi o kakeru (v) ブラシをかける 12d

buckwheat sobako そば粉 24i

bud tsubomi 蕾 14a

bud tsubomi o motsu (v) 蕾を持つ 14a

Buddhism bukkyō 仏教 11d

Buddhist bukkyō no shinja 仏教の信者 11d

Buddhist bukkyō no (adj) 仏教の 11d

Buddhist priest obōsan お坊さん 11d

Buddhist temple otera お寺 11d

budget yosan 予算 26

buffalo baffaro バッファロー 15a

bug mushi 虫 15d

build tateru (v) 建てる 23f

builder kenchikugyōsha 建築業者 38a

building biru ビル 23g, 39a

bulb kyūkon 球根 14a

bull oushi 雄牛 15a

bump kobu こぶ 39c

bumper banpā バンパー 33e

burdock gobō ごぼう 14e, 24e

Burma Biruma ビルマ 30b

burn (injury) yakedo 火傷 39a

burn (on fire) moeru (vi) 燃える 39a

bus basu バス 33a, 34

bus driver basu no untenshu バスの運転手 34, 38a

business class bijinesu kurasu ビジネスクラス 30a, 32a

business hotel bijinesu hoteru ビジネスホテル 35a

business letter bijinesu retā ビジネスレター 19e

businessman bijinesuman ビジネスマン 38a

businesswoman bijinesuūman ビジネスウーマン 38a

bus station, depot basu no hatchakusho バスの発着所 34

bus stop basu no teiryūsho バスの停留所 34

busy (telephone) hanashichū 話し中 18b

but keredomo/shikashi けれども／しかし 8k

butcher nikuya 肉屋 38a

butcher shop niku ya 肉屋 24n

butter batā バター 24h, 24j

butterfly chōchō 蝶蝶 15d

buttock oshiri おしり 12a

button botan ボタン 25g

buy kau (v) 買う 23f, 25a

buy a ticket ken o kau (v) 券を買う 30a, 34

by de で 8j

by means of de で 8j

byte baito バイト 42b

by the way tokorode ところで 44c

By the way... Tokoro de,... ところで, 17b

C

cabbage kyabetsu キャベツ 14e, 24e

cabinet naikaku 内閣 43

cabinet member kakuryō 閣僚 43

cable kēburu ケーブル 18a

cable hifuku densen 被覆電線 25b

cafeteria kafeteria カフェテリア 24m

calculate keisansuru (v) 計算する 1f

calculation keisan 計算 1f

calculus bisekibungaku 微積分学 37f

calendar karendā カレンダー 5b, 38c

call yobu (v) 呼ぶ 17a

call denwasuru (v) 電話する 39a

call an ambulance kyūkyūsha o yobu (v) 救急車を呼ぶ 39c

calling card meishi 名刺 16b

call the police keisatsu o yobu (v) 警察を呼ぶ 39b, 39c

calm odayaka na (adj) 穏やかな 11e

calmness odayakasa 穏やかさ 11e

camcorder kamukōdā カムコーダー 25d

camel rakuda らくだ 15a

camellia tsubaki 椿 14b

camera kamera カメラ 25d

camera shop kamera ya カメラ屋 25d

camping area kyanpujō キャンプ場 36b

campus kōnai 構内 37c

Canada Kanada カナダ 30b

Canadian Kanadajin カナダ人 30d

canary kanaria カナリア 15b

canceled kyanseru sareta キャンセルされた 32b

Cancer kaniza 蟹座 5d

canine kenshi 犬歯 40b

canoe kanū カヌー 36b

Can you tell me...? ...o, oshiete moraemasu ka. を、教えてもらえますか。 9

Can you tell me where...? ...ga doko ni aru ka oshiete kudasai. がどこにあるか教えて下さい。 36c

cap bōshi 帽子 25k, 36b

capacity yōryō/yōseki 容量／容積 3c

capital shuto 首都 13e

capital city shuto 首都 30a

capital letter ōmoji 大文字 19c

capital punishment shikei 死刑 41, 44b

Capricorn yagiza 山羊座 5d

capsule kapuseru カプセル 40a

captain kichō 機長 32c

car jidōsha 自動車 33a

carat karatto カラット 25i

car body bodī ボディー 33e

carbon tanso 炭素 13c

carburetor kyaburetā キャブレター 33e

cardigan kādigan カーディガン 25k

cardinal number kisū 基数 1d

career keireki 経歴 11f, 38d

carnation kāneshon カーネーション 14b

carp koi 鯉 15c

carpenter daiku 大工 38a

carpet, rug jūtan じゅうたん 23c

car radio kārajio カーラジオ 20b

carriage kyarēji キャレージ 19d

carrot ninjin 人参 14e, 24e

carry hakobu (v) 運ぶ 3f

carry-on kinai mochikomi hin 機内持ち込み品 31

car telephone jidōsha denwa 自動車電話 18a

carve kiriwakeru (v) 切り分ける 24o

car window windō ウィンドー 33e

case kaku 格 8a

case kēsu ケース 23d

cash genkin 現金 26, 35b

cash genkinkasuru (v) 現金化する 26

cashier shiharaigakari 支払係 25a

cashier, teller madoguchigakari 窓口係 26

cash register shiharai basho 支払場所 25a

cassette kasetto カセット 25j

cassette deck kasetto dekki カセットデッキ 20b

cassette tape kasetto tēpu カセットテープ 20b

castle shiro 城 36a

cat neko 猫 15a

catch toru (v) 捕る 27b

catch tsukamaeru (v) 捕まえる 39b

catcher's mask kyatchā no masuku キャッチャーのマスク 27b

catch fire hi ga tsuku 火がつく 39a

catechism kōkyōyōri 公教要理 11d

caterpillar kemushi 毛虫 15d

catfish namazu 鯰 15c

cathedral daiseidō 大聖堂 36a

Catholic katorikkukyōto カトリック教徒 11d

Catholic katorikkukyō no (adj) カトリック教の 11d

Catholicism katorikkukyō shinkō カトリック教信仰 11d

cauliflower karifurawā カリフラワー 14e, 24e

cavity, tooth decay mushiba 虫歯 40b

ceiling tenjō 天井 23a

celebrate one's birthday tanjōbi o iwau 誕生日を祝う 11c

celery serori セロリ 14e, 24e

cell saibō 細胞 14a

cello chero チェロ 28c

Celsius sesshi 摂氏 6c

cement mixer konkurīto mikisā コンクリートミキサー 33a

censorship ken-etsu 検閲 44b

center chūshin 中心 2a

centigrade sesshi 摂氏 6c

centimeter senchi センチ 3a

centipede mukade むかで 15d

Central America Chūō Amerika 中央アメリカ 30b

century seiki 世紀 4c

cereal shiriaru シリアル 24i

chain kusari 鎖 25i

chain guard chēn gādo チェーンガード 33a

chair isu 椅子 23c, 38c

chalk chōku チョーク 37b

change kawaru (vi) 変わる 4e

change kaeru (vt) 変える 4e

change kuzusu (v) くずす 25a

change norikaeru (v) 乗り替える 34

change (money) otsuri おつり 25a

change clothes kigaeru (v) 着替える 25m

change subject wadai o kaeru (v) 話題を変える 17a

channel suiro 水路 13b

channel channeru チャンネル 20b

chapter shō 章 28d

character moji 文字 8a

character seikaku 性格 11e

character (in a novel, play) tōjō jinbutsu 登場人物 28d

characteristic dokutoku na (adj) 独特な 11e

characterize seikakuzukeru (v) 性格づける 11e

charge genshikaku no yōdenka 原子核の陽電荷 13c

charge ryōkin 料金 28a

Charge it to my bill. Watakushi no kanjō ni, tsukete oite kudasai. 私の勘定につけておいてください。 35b

charter flight chātā bin チャーター便 30a

chat zatsudansuru (v) 雑談する 17a

cheap yasui (adj) 安い 24p

check kogitte 小切手 26

check-in chekkuin チェックイン 32a

checkbook kogitte chō 小切手帳 26

checkerboard chekkā ban チェッカー盤 27a

checker piece chekkā no koma チェッカーの駒 27a

checkers chekkā チェッカー 27a

check the oil oiru o chekkusuru (v) オイルをチェックする 33c

cheek hoo 頬 12a

cheerful yōki na (adj) 陽気な 21a

Cheers! Kanpai. 乾杯。 16c, 24l

cheese chīzu チーズ 24g, 24h

chemical kagaku no (adj) 化学の 13c

chemical weapon kagaku heiki 化学兵器 44b

chemistry kagaku 化学 13c, 37e

cherry sakuranbo さくらんぼ 14d, 24f

cherry blossom sakura no hana 桜の花 14b

cherry tree sakura 桜 14c

chestnut tree kuri no ki 栗の木 14c

chess chesu チェス 27a

chessboard chesu ban チェス盤 27a

chest mune 胸 12a

chestnut kuri 栗 14d, 24f

chest of drawers (Japanese style) tansu 箪笥 23c

chest of drawers (western style) yōdansu 洋箪笥 23c, 35c

Chicago Shikago シカゴ 30c

chick hina 雛 15b

chicken niwatori 鶏 15b

chicken toriniku 鳥肉 24c

chicken chikin チキン 24c

chief of police keisatsu shochō 警察署長 41

child kodomo 子供 11b

Chile Chiri チリ 30b

chilled hiyashita (adj) 冷やした 24p

chilled sake reishu 冷酒 24p

chimney entotsu 煙突 23a

chimpanzee chinpanjī チンパンジー 15a

chin ago 顎 12a

China Chūgoku 中国 30b

Chinese Chūgokujin 中国人 30d

Chinese Chūgokugo 中国語 30d

Chinese character Kanji 漢字 8a

chlorine enso 塩素 13c

chlorophyll yōryokuso 葉緑素 14a

choke chōku チョーク 33e

chop kizamu (v) 刻む 24o

chopstick hashi 箸 23d, 24l

chopstick rest hashioki 箸置き 23d, 24l

Christian kirisutokyōto キリスト教徒 11d

Christianity kirisutokyō キリスト教 11d

Christmas kurisumasu クリスマス 29a

chrysanthemum kiku 菊 14b

chum nakayoshi 仲良し 10b

church kyōkai 教会 11d, 36a

cicada semi 蝉 15d

cigar hamaki 葉巻 25e

cigarette tabako たばこ 25e

circle en 円 2a

circumference enshū 円周 2a

citric kankitsurui no (adj) 柑橘類の 14d

citrus kankitsurui 柑橘類 14d

city shi 市 11f, 13e, 38b

city toshi 都市 30a

city map toshi chizu 都市地図 36a

civil law minpō 民法 41

clam hamaguri 蛤 15c, 24d

clamp shimegu 締め具 25b

clap of thunder raimei 雷鳴 6a

clarinet kurarinetto クラリネット 28c

class kurasu クラス 30a

class (students) gakkyū 学級 37d, 37f

classical music kurashikku myūjikku クラシックミュージック 25j, 28c

classified ad kōmokubetsu kōkoku 項目別広告 38d

classmate kyūyū 級友 37d

classroom kyōshitsu 教室 37c

clause setsu 節 8a, 19c

clean kirei na/seiketsu na (adj) きれいな／清潔な 11a, 25g

clean seiketsu na (adj) 清潔な 12d

clean sōjisuru (v) 掃除する 23f

clean, brush (teeth) ha o migaku (v) 歯を磨く 40b

clear harewatatta (adj) 晴れ渡った 6a

clear senmei na (adj) 鮮明な 25d

clear the table atokatazukesuru (v) 後片付けする 23f, 24o

clerk kyokuin 局員 19e

clerk's window madoguchi 窓口 19e

clever kenmei na (adj) 賢明な 11e

client (law) irainin 依頼人 41

climate kikō 気候 6a

clip kurippu クリップ 19d

clock okidokei 置き時計 4d

close an account kōza o tojiru 口座を閉じる 26

closed heiten 閉店 25a

closed circuit kurōzudo sākitto クローズドサーキット 20b

close friend shinyū 親友 10b

closet oshiire 押し入れ 23b, 35c

closing musubi no kotoba 結びの言葉 19c

closing time heiten jikan 閉店時間 25a

clothes sentakumono 洗濯物 25g

clothes basket sentaku kago 洗濯篭 25g

clothes hanger hangā ハンガー 23d, 35c

clothespin sentakubasami 洗濯ばさみ 25g

clothing store yōfuku ya 洋服屋 25k

cloud kumo 雲 6a, 13b

cloudy kumotta (adj) 曇った 6a

club soda tansan (sui) 炭酸（水） 24k

clutch (pedal) kuratchi クラッチ 33e

co-pilot fuku sōjūshi 副操縦士 32c

coach (sports, etc.) kōchi コーチ 27b

coach (transportation) futsū 普通 34

coal sekitan 石炭 13c

coal mine tankō 炭坑 13c

coal mining tankō 炭鉱 13c

coast engan 沿岸 13b

coastal engan no (adj) 沿岸の 13b

coat kōto コート 25k

Coca-Cola kokakōra コカコーラ 24k

cockroach gokiburi ごきぶり 15d

cod tara 鱈 15c, 24d

coed school danjo kyōgaku no gakkō 男女共学の学校 37a

coffee kōhī コーヒー 24k

coffee machine kōhīmēkā コーヒーメーカー 23d

coffee pot kōhīpotto コーヒーポット 23d

cognac konyakku コニャック 24k

coin kōka 硬貨 27a

coin collecting kōka shūshū 硬貨収集 27a

cold samui (adj) 寒い 6a, 6b

cold tsumetai *(adj)* 冷たい 24p

cold kaze 風邪 40a

cold water mizu 水 35c

colleague dōryō 同僚 10b, 38d

collect call jushinninbarai no denwa 受信人払いの電話 18b

collide shōtotsusuru *(v)* 衝突する 39c

collision shōtotsu 衝突 39c

cologne ōdekoron オーデコロン 25f

Colombia Koronbia コロンビア 30b

colon koron コロン 19c

color iro 色 7c

color iro o nuru *(v)* 色を塗る 7c

colored iro o nutta *(adj)* 色を塗った 7c

color film karā fuirumu カラーフイルム 25d

coloring saishoku 彩色 7c

color picture karā shashin カラー写真 25d

comb kushi 櫛 12d, 25f

comb kushi de tokasu *(v)* 櫛でとかす 12d

come kuru *(v)* 来る 3e

comedian kigeki yakusha 喜劇役者 28e

comedy kigeki 喜劇 20a, 28e

Come in! Ohairi kudasai. お入りください。 16b

Come quickly! Isoide kite. 急いで来て。 39b

comet suisei 彗星 13a

comics manga 漫画 20a, 25o

comma konma コンマ 19c

commerce shōgyō 商業 37e, 38d

commercial komāsharu コマーシャル 20b

communicate tsutaeru *(v)* 伝える 17a

communication dentatsu 伝達 17a

communism kyōsanshugi 共産主義 43

communist kyōsanshugisha 共産主義者 43

commuter train densha 電車 34

compact car konpakutokā コンパクトカー 33a

compact disc konpakuto disuku/shīdī コンパクトディスク／シーディー 20b, 25j, 42a

compact disc player shīdī purēyā シーディープレーヤー 20b

company kaisha 会社 38d

compare hikakusuru *(v)* 比較する 17a

comparison hikaku 比較 8a, 17a

compartment koshitsu 個室 34

compass konpasu コンパス 2b, 37b

compass rashinban 羅針盤 3d

compatible konpachi (no) *(adj)* コンパチ（の） 42b

competition kyōgi 競技 27b

complain kujō o noberu *(v)* 苦情を述べる 21a, 35b

complaint kujō 苦情 21a, 35b

complementary angle yokaku 余角 2b

complex number fukusosū 複素数 1d

complicated fukuzatsu na *(adj)* 複雑な 22a

composer sakkyoku ka 作曲家 25j, 28c

composition sakubun 作文 37f

composition (music) sakkyoku 作曲 28c

compound kagōbutsu 化合物 13c

computer konpyūta コンピュータ 42b

computer language konpyūta gengo コンピュータ言語 42b

computer science konpyūta saiensu コンピュータサイエンス 42b

concave angle ōkaku 凹角 2b

concept gainen 概念 22a

concert konsāto コンサート 28c

conclude ketsuron o kudasu *(v)* 結論を下す 17a

conclusion ketsuron 結論 17a

conditional mood jōkenhō 条件法 8a

condominium bunjō manshon 分譲マンション 23g

conductor shikisha 指揮者 25j

conductor shashō 車掌 34

cone ensuitai 円錐体 2a

confess jihakusuru *(v)* 自白する 41

confession jihaku 自白 41

confirmation kenshinrei 堅振礼 11d

conformist junnōsha 順応者 11e

Confucian jusha 儒者 11d

Confucianism jukyō 儒教 11d

congratulate iwau *(v)* 祝う 17a

Congratulations! Omedetō gozaimasu. おめでとうございます。 16c, 29c

congress gikai 議会 43

congressman giin 議員 43

conjugation dōshi no katsuyō 動詞の活用 8a

conjunction setsuzokushi 接続詞 8a

connection konekushon コネクション 30a, 32a

connection noritsugi 乗り継ぎ 34

conscience ryōshin 良心 11e, 22a

conscientious ryōshinteki na (adj) 良心 的な 11e, 22a

conservation shizen hogo 自然保護 44a

conservative hoshuteki na (adj) 保守的 な 11e, 43

conservative party hoshutō 保守党 43

conservatory ongaku gakkō 音楽学校 37f

consonant shion 子音 8a

constant teisū 定数 1f

Constitution Day kenpō kinenbi 憲法記 念日 5f

construction worker kenchikugenba no sagyōin 建築現場の作業員 38a

consultant konsarutanto コンサルタン ト 38a

consumption shōhi 消費 44a

contact lenses kontakuto renzu コンタ クトレンズ 40a

continent tairiku 大陸 13b, 13e, 30a

continental tairikusei no (adj) 大陸性の 6a

continental tairiku no (adj) 大陸の 13b, 13e

continually tsuzukete (adv) 続けて 4e

continue tsuzuku (vi) 続く 4e

continue tsuzukeru (vt) 続ける 4e

contraception hinin 避妊 44b

contract keiyaku 契約 38d

controversy rongi 論議 41

convalescence kaifuku 回復 40a

convenience store konbini sutoā コンビ ニストア 24n

conversation kaiwa 会話 17a

convertible konbāchiburu コンバーチ ブル 33a

convex angle tokkaku 凸角 2b

convince nattokusaseru (v) 納得させる 22b

convince kakushinsaseru (v) 確信させ る 41

cook ryōrisuru (v) 料理する 24o

cook chōrishi 調理士 38a

cookbook ryōri no hon 料理の本 25o

cookie kukkī クッキー 24i

cooking ryōri 料理 27a

cooking, cuisine ryōri 料理 24b

cool suzushii (adj) 涼しい 6a

coordinate zahyō 座標 2b

copper dō 銅 13c

copy kakikata 書き方 37f

corn tōmorokoshi とうもろこし 14e, 24e, 24i

corn chip kōnchippu コーンチップ 24i

corner kōnā コーナー 27b

corner kado 角 36a

corner (street) kado 角 33c

cornflakes kōnfurēku コーンフレーク 24i

correspondence tsūshin 通信 19e

corridor rōka 廊下 23a

cortisone kōchizon コーチゾン 25h

cosecant kosekanto コセカント 2b

cosine kosain コサイン 2b

cosmetics shop keshōhin ten 化粧品店 25f

cosmos uchū 宇宙 13a

cost kakaru (v) かかる 24o, 25a

cost nedan 値段 25a

cost of living seikatsuhi 生活費 26

cotangent kotanjento コタンジェント 2b

cottage cheese kotēji chīzu コテージチ ーズ 24h

cotton men 棉 13c

cotton dasshimen 脱脂綿 25h

cotton momen 木綿 25l

cotton swab menbō 綿棒 25h

cough seki 咳 40a

cough seki o suru (v) 咳をする 40a

cough syrup sekidome shiroppu 咳止め シロップ 25h

council chihōgikai 地方議会 43

count kazoeru 数える 1f

countable kazoerareru (adj) 数えられ る 1f

counter mono o kazoeru kotoba ものを 数える言葉 8a

counter kauntā カウンター 25a

country kuni 国 11f, 13e, 30a

courage yūki 勇気 11e

courageous yūki ga aru (adj) 勇気があ る 11e

courier haitatsunin 配達人 19e

course kōsu コース 24g

course kamoku 科目 37f

court saibansho 裁判所 41

courteous reigi tadashii *(adj)* 礼儀正しい 11e

courtesy reigi 礼儀 11e

court music gagaku 雅楽 28c

court of appeal kōsoin 控訴院 41

courtroom hōtei 法廷 41

cousin itoko いとこ 10a

cousin itokosan いとこさん 10a

cover hyōshi 表紙 20a

cover charge kabā chāji カバーチャージ 24m

cow meushi 雌牛 15a

crab kani 蟹 15c, 24d

cracker kurakkā クラッカー 24i

crane tsuru 鶴 15b

crash shōtotsu 衝突 39c

crash shōtotsusuru *(v)* 衝突する 39c

crayon kureyon クレヨン 7c

crazy, mad kichigaijimita *(adj)* 気違いじみた 11e

cream kurīmu クリーム 24h, 24j

creative sōzōteki na *(adj)* 創造的な 11e

credit shinyō 信用 26

credit card kurejitto kādo クレジットカード 26, 35b

crew tōjōin 搭乗員 32c

cricket kōrogi こうろぎ 15d

crime hanzai 犯罪 39b

crime wave hanzai no nami 犯罪の波 39b

criminal hanzaisha 犯罪者 39b

criminal law keihō 刑法 41

critic hyōronka 評論家 20a

critical hihanteki na *(adj)* 批判的な 11e

criticism hihyō 批評 20a

criticism hyōron 評論 28d

crocodile kurokodairu クロコダイル 15c

cross (over)... ...o yokogiru *(v)* を横切る 36c

cross the street michi o yokogiru *(v)* 道を横切る 36c

crow karasu 烏 15b

crown shikan 歯冠 40b

cruel zankoku na *(adj)* 残酷な 21a

cruise kurūzu クルーズ 36b

cry naku *(v)* 泣く 11e, 21a

cube seirokumentai 正六面体 2a

cubed sanjō no 三乗の 1e

cube root rippōkon 立方根 1e

cubic centimeter rippōsenchi 立方センチ 3a

cubic kilometer rippōkiro 立方キロ 3a

cubic meter rippōmētoru 立方メートル 3a

cubic millimeter rippōmiri 立方ミリ 3a

cucumber kyūri きゅうり 14e, 24e

cue tamatsuki no kyū 玉突きのキュー 27a

cultivate saibaisuru *(v)* 栽培する 14a

cultivation saibai 栽培 14a

Culture Day bunka no hi 文化の日 5f

cultured kyōyō no aru *(adj)* 教養のある 11e

cup (coffee) kōhījawan コーヒー茶碗 23d, 24l

cure ryōhō 療法 40a

cure naosu *(vt)* なおす 40a

curiosity kōkishin 好奇心 11e

curious kōkishin no tsuyoi *(adj)* 好奇心の強い 11e

curler kārā カーラー 12d, 25f

curls kāru カール 12d

curly-haired chijirege no *(adj)* ちじれ毛の 11a

currency tsūka 通貨 26

current denryū 電流 35c

current account tōza kanjō 当座勘定 26

curtain maku 幕 28e

curtains kāten カーテン 23c, 35c

curve kābu カーブ 33c

curved line kyokusen 曲線 2b

cushion kusshon クッション 27a

customer okyaku お客 25a

customer kokyaku 顧客 26

customs zeikan 税関 31

customs officer zeikan no kakariin 税関の係員 31

cut kiru *(v)* 切る 24o

cut flower kiribana 切り花 14b

cutlery, tableware shokutakuyō shokkigu 食卓用食器具 24l

cut off kiru *(v)* 切る 18b

cut one's hair kaminoke o kiru *(v)* 髪の毛を切る 12d

cyclamen shikuramen シクラメン 14b

cylinder enchū 円柱 2a

cymbals shinbaru シンバル 28c

cypress tree itosugi 糸杉 14c

Czechoslovakia Chekosurobakia チェコスロバキア 30b

D

daffodil suisen 水仙 14b

dahlia daria ダリア 14b

daily mainichi no *(adj)* 毎日の 4c

daily newspaper nikkanshi 日刊紙 20a

dairy gyūnyū ya 牛乳屋 24n

dairy product nyūseihin 乳製品 24h

daisy dējī デージー 14b

dance dansu ダンス 28c, 29b

dance odoru *(v)* 踊る 28c

dance-drama (Japanese) Kabuki 歌舞伎 28e

dance music dansu ongaku ダンス音楽 25j

dancer dansā ダンサー 28c

dancer butō ka 舞踏家 28c

dandruff fuke ふけ 40a

Dane Denmākujin デンマーク人 30d

danger kiken 危険 39a

Danish Denmākugo デンマーク語 30d

dark kurai *(adj)* 暗い 6a

dark koi *(adj)* 濃い 7b

dark-haired kuroi kami no ke no *(adj)* 黒い髪の毛の 11a

dark blue kon 紺 7a

dashboard dasshubōdo ダッシュボード 33e

data dēta データ 42b

database dētabēsu データベース 42b

data processing dēta shori データ処理 42b

date natsume 棗 14d, 24f

date hizuke 日付 19c

date seinengappi 生年月日 38b

date and place of birth seinengappi to shusseichi 生年月日と出生地 38b

date of birth seinengappi 生年月日 11f

daughter musume 娘 10a

daughter ojōsan お嬢さん 10a

daughter-in-law musuko no yome 息子の嫁 10a

daughter-in-law musukosan no oyomesan 息子さんのお嫁さん 10a

dawn yoake 夜明け 4a

day ichinichi/hi 一日／日 4a, 4c

day hi 日 38b

day after tomorrow asatte あさって 4a

day before yesterday ototoi おととい 4a

day care takujisho 託児所 37a

day of the week yōbi 曜日 5a

dead flower kareta hana 枯れた花 14b

deaf mimi no tōi *(adj)* 耳の遠い 12c

dean gakubuchō 学部長 37d

Dear... ...sama 様 19b

Dear Madam haikei 拝啓 19a

Dear Sir haikei 拝啓 19a

Dearest shinainaru ...sama 親愛なる...様 19b

dear friend shinyū 親友 10b

death shi/shibō 死／死亡 11c

debate tōronsuru *(v)* 討論する 17a, 41

debate tōron 討論 17a, 41

debit kashikata 貸方 26

debt fusai 負債 26

decade jūnenkan 十年間 4c

decagon jukkakukei 十角形 2a

December jūnigatsu 十二月 5b

decimal shōsū 少数 1f

decision hanketsu 判決 41

declarative heijo *(adj)* 平叙 8a

declare sengensuru *(v)* 宣言する 17a

declare shinkokusuru *(v)* 申告する 31

decrease genshō 減少 3c

decrease genshōsuru *(vi)* 減少する 3c

decrease genshōsaseru *(vt)* 減少させる 3c

deer shika 鹿 15a

defecate haibensuru *(v)* 排便する 40a

defend oneself jikobengosuru *(v)* 自己弁護する 41

definite (article) tei *(adj)* 定 8a

definition gogi 語義 20a

degree do 度 2b, 6c

degree (university) gakui 学位 37f

delicate sensai na *(adj)* 繊細な 11e

delicatessen derikatessen デリカテッセン 24n

Delighted! Ureshii desu. 嬉しいです。 16b

democracy minshushugi 民主主義 43

democrat minshushugisha 民主主義者 43

democratic minshushugi no *(adj)* 民主主義の 43

demonstrate hyōmeisuru *(v)* 表明する 22b

demonstration demo デモ 43

demonstrative shiji *(adj)* 指示 8a

Denmark Denmāku デンマーク 30b

dense mitsudo no takai *(adj)* 密度の高い 3b

density mitsudo/nōdo 密度／濃度 3b

dentist haisha 歯医者 38a, 40b

dentist's office haisha no shinryōsho 歯医者の診療所 40b

denture, false teeth ireba 入れ歯 40b

deny hiteisuru *(v)* 否定する 17a

deodorant deodoranto デオドラント 25f

department (of a store) uriba 売り場 25a

department store depāto デパート 25a

departure shuppatsu 出発 32a

deposit yokin 預金 26

deposit yokinsuru *(v)* 預金する 26

deposit slip yokinhyō 預金票 26

depressed yūutsu na *(adj)* 憂鬱な 21a

depression yūutsu 憂鬱 21a

describe noberu *(v)* 述べる 17a

description kijutsu 記述 17a

description ninsōgaki 人相書 39b

descriptive kijutsu *(adj)* 記述 8a

desert sabaku 砂漠 13b

desk tsukue 机 37b

desperate hisshi no *(adj)* 必死の 21a

dessert dezāto デザート 24g

destroy hakaisuru *(v)* 破壊する 39a

detest kirau *(v)* 嫌う 21b

develop genzōsuru *(v)* 現像する 25d

developing country hatten tojōkoku 発展途上国 43

development genzō 現像 25d

dial mojiban 文字盤 4d

dial daiaru ダイアル 18b

dial daiaru o mawasu *(v)* ダイアルを回す 18b

diameter chokkei 直径 2a

diamond daiamondo ダイアモンド 25i

diamond anniversary kekkon nanajūgoshūnen kinenbi 結婚七十五周年記念日 11c

dice daisu ダイス 27a

dictate kōjutsusuru *(v)* 口述する 17a

dictation kakitori 書き取り 37f

dictionary jisho 辞書 20a, 25o, 37b

die shinu *(v)* 死ぬ 11c

die nakunaru *(v,pol)* 亡くなる 11c

Diet (Japanese Congress) kokkai 国会 43

Diet member kokkai giin 国会議員 43

diet soda daietto no nomimono ダイエットの飲み物 24k

difference sa 差 1f

difficult muzukashii *(adj)* 難しい 22a

dig horu *(v)* 掘る 14a

digestive system shōka keitō 消化系統 40a

digit sūji 数字 1d

digress wakimichi ni soreru *(v)* 脇道にそれる 17a

diligence kinben 勤勉 11e

diligent, hardworking kinben na *(adj)* 勤勉な 11e

dimension jigen 次元 3b

dining car shokudōsha 食堂車 34

dining room shokudō 食堂 23b

dinner bangohan 晩御飯 24a

dinner yūshoku 夕食 24a

diploma sotsugyōshōsho 卒業証書 11f, 37f

diplomatic gaikōteki na *(adj)* 外交的な 11e

direct chokusetsu *(adj)* 直接 8a

direct dialing daiaru chokutsu ダイアル直通 18b

direction hōkō 方向 3d

direct train chokutsū ressha 直通列車 34

dirty kitanai *(adj)* 汚い 11a, 12d

dirty yogoreta *(adj)* 汚れた 25g

disagree sansei shinai 賛成しない 21a

disagree hantaisuru *(v)* 反対する 41

disagreement fusansei 不賛成 21a

disappoint shitsubōsaseru *(vt)* 失望させる 21a

disappointed gakkarishita *(adj)* がっかりした 21a

disappointment shitsubō 失望 21a

disarmament gunbi teppai 軍備撤廃 43

disco disuko ディスコ 29b

discount waribiki no *(adj)* 割引の 25a

discount waribiki 割引 26, 30a

discourse wahō 話法 8a

discourteous shitsurei na *(adj)* 失礼な 11e

discrimination sabetsu 差別 44b

discuss rongisuru (v) 論議する 17a

discuss sōdansuru (v) 相談する 41

discussion rongi 論議 17a

disgust mukamukasaseru (v) むかむかさせる 21b

disgusted unzarishita (adj) うんざりした 21b

dish antenna parabora antena パラボラアンテナ 42a

dishonest fushōjiki na (adj) 不正直な 11e

dishonesty fushōjiki 不正直 11e

dishwasher shokkiaraiki 食器洗い機 23d

disk disuku ディスク 42b

dislike kirau (v) 嫌う 21b

dissatisfaction fuman 不満 21a

dissatisfied fuman no aru (adj) 不満のある 21a

dissolve kaisansuru (v) 解散する 43

distance kyori 距離 3d, 33c

divide waru (v) 割る 1e

divided by watta 割った 1e

division warizan 割り算 1e

divorce rikon 離婚 11c

divorce rikonsuru (v) 離婚する 11c

divorced rikonshita (adj) 離婚した 11c

divorced rikon 離婚 38b

doctor igaku hakase 医学博士 16b

doctor isha 医者 38a, 39c, 40a

doctor's instruments shinryō kigu 診療器具 40a

doctor's visit ōshin 往診 40a

doctor (direct address) sensei 先生 16b

doctorate hakasegō 博士号 37f

documentary dokyumentarī ドキュメンタリー 20b

documents shorui 書類 31

dodecahedron jūnimentai 十二面体 2a

does not equal hitoshikunai 等しくない 1f

dog inu 犬 15a

dogwood hanamizuki 花水木 14c

dollar doru ドル 26

dolphin iruka いるか 15c

Don't mention it! Iie, dō itashimashite. いいえ、どう致しまして。 16c

donkey roba ろば 15a

door to 戸 23a

door doa ドア 33e

doorbell yobirin 呼びリン 23a

doorman doaman ドアマン 35b

double nibai no (adj) 二倍の 3c

double daburu no (adj) ダブルの 24p

double bass kontora basu コントラバス 28c

double bed daburu beddo ダブルベッド 35c

double room daburu no heya ダブルの部屋 35b

doubt utagai 疑い 22a

doubt utagau (v) 疑う 22b

dove kijibato きじばと 15b

down shita no (adj) 下の 3d

down... shita ni (adv) 下に 3d

down... ...o kudatta tokoro ni ...を下った所に 36c

downtown toshin 都心 30a, 36a

Do you have a vacant room? Heya ga arimasu ka. 部屋がありますか。 35b

Dr. (Ph.D. degree) hakase 博士 16b

Dr. (Ph.D.) hakase 博士 11f

draft tegata furidashi 手形振出 26

dragonfly tonbo 蜻 15d

drama dorama ドラマ 20a, 28e

draw sen o hiku (v) 線を引く 2b

draw hikiwake 引き分け 27b

draw hikiwakeru (v) 引き分ける 27b

draw e o kaku (v) 絵を書く 37f

drawer hikidashi 引き出し 23c

drawing sobyō 素描 28b

drawing e 絵 37f

drawing instruments seizu kikai 製図器械 2b

dress doresu ドレス 25k

dresser kyōdai 鏡台 35c

dressing room shichakushitsu 試着室 25k

drill (tool) doriru ドリル 25b

drill (dentist) doriru ドリル 40a

drink nomu (v) 飲む 12b, 24o

drink nomimono 飲み物 24k

drive untensuru (v) 運転する 3e, 33b, 33c

driver untenshu 運転手 33b

driver's license unten menkyosho 運転免許書 33b

drug addiction mayaku chūdoku 麻薬中毒 44b

drug pusher mayaku mitsubainin 麻薬密売人 44b

drugs mayaku 麻薬 44b

drugstore doraggusutōā ドラッグストアー 25h

drug trafficking mayaku baibai 麻薬売買 44b

drum taiko 太鼓 28c

dry kansōshita (adj) 乾燥した 6a

dry kawakasu (v) 乾かす 12d

dry cleaner doraikurīningu ya ドライクリーニング屋 25g

dryer kansōki 乾燥機 23d

duck ahiru あひる 15b, 24c

duck dakku ダック 24c

dull nibui/shizunda (adj) 鈍い／沈んだ 7b

dump truck danpukā ダンプカー 33a

dune sakyū 砂丘 13b

during aida ni (adv) 間に 4e

Dutch Orandago オランダ語 30d

Dutchman Orandajin オランダ人 30d

duty kanzei 関税 31

dynamic seiryokuteki na (adj) 精力的な 11e

E

eagle washi 鷲 15b

ear mimi 耳 12a

early hayai (adj) 早い 4e, 32b, 34

early hayaku (adv) 早く 4e, 32b

earn kasegu (v) 稼ぐ 38b

earphone iyahōn イヤホーン 18a, 20b

earring iaringu イアリング 25i

earth chikyū 地球 13a

earthquake jishin 地震 13b

easel, tripod īzeru イーゼル 28b

east higashi 東 3d

eastern higashi no 東の 3d

easy yasashii (adj) 易しい 22a

eat taberu (v) 食べる 12b, 24o

eccentric fūgawari na (adj) 風変わりな 11e

eclipse shoku 食 13a

ecology seitaigaku 生態学 44a

economics keizai 経済 37f

economy keizai 経済 43

economy class ekonomi kurasu エコノミークラス 30a, 32a

economy seat futsū seki 普通席 34

ecosystem seitaikei 生態系 44a

Ecuador Ekuadoru エクアドル 30b

edge hashi はし 3d

editor henshūsha 編集者 20a, 38a

editorial shasetsu 社説 20a

education kyōiku 教育 11f, 37f

education gakureki 学歴 38b

eel unagi 鰻 15c, 24d

egg tamago 卵 15b, 24h

eggplant nasu なす 14e, 24e

egoism rikoshugi 利己主義 11e

egoist rikoshugisha 利己主義者 11e

egoistic rikoteki na (adj) 利己的な 11e

Egypt Ejiputo エジプト 30b

eight hachi 八 1a

eight yattsu 八つ 1a

eighteen jūhachi 十八 1a

eighteen thousand ichimanhassen 一万八千 1a

eighth hachibanme 八番目 1b

eighth daihachi 第八 1b

eighth yattsume 八つ目 1b

eight hundred happyaku 八百 1a

eight thousand hassen 八千 1a

eighty hachijū 八十 1a

eighty thousand hachiman 八万 1a

elastic danryokusei no aru (adj) 弾力性のある 13d

elbow hiji 肘 12a

elder brother ani 兄 10a

elder brother oniisan お兄さん 10a

elderly person nenpai no hito 年配の人 11b

elder sister ane 姉 10a

elder sister onēsan お姉さん 10a

elect erabu (v) 選ぶ 43

elected politician giin 議員 43

election senkyo 選挙 43

electrical denki no (adj) 電気の 13c, 25b

electrician denkikō 電気工 38a

electricity denki 電気 13c, 23e

electric razor denki kamisori 電気カミソリ 12d, 25f

electrocardiograph shindenkei 心電計 40a

electron denshi 電子 13c, 42a

electronic denshi no (adj) 電子の 13c

elegance yūga / jōhin 優雅／上品 11a

elegant yūga na / jōhin na (adj) 優雅な／上品な 11a

elegant ereganto na (adj) エレガントな 25l

element genso 元素 13c

elementary school shōgakkō 小学校 11f, 37a, 38b

elephant zō 象 15a

elevator erebētā エレベーター 23g, 35b

eleven jūichi 十一 1b

eleventh jūichibanme 十一番目 1b

eleventh daijūichi 第十一 1b

eleven thousand ichimansen 一万千 1a

eloquence yūben 雄弁 11e

eloquent yūben na (adj) 雄弁な 11e

emerald emerarudo エメラルド 25i

Emergency Lane kinkyū shasen 緊急車線 33d

emergency exit hijōguchi 非常口 39a

emergency hospital kyūkyū byōin 緊急病院 39c

emery board tsume yasuri 爪やすり 25f

emotion kanjō 感情 21a

emotional kanjōteki na (adj) 感情的な 21a

emperor tennō 天皇 43

Emperor's Birthday tennō tanjōbi 天皇誕生日 43

emphasis kyōchō 強調 17a

emphasize kyōchōsuru (v) 強調する 17a

employ yatou (v) 雇う 38d

employee jūgyōin 従業員 11f, 38d

employee shain 社員 38d

employee (bank) ginkōin 銀行員 26

employer koyōsha 雇用者 11f, 38d

employment koyō 雇用 11f

employment agency shokugyō shōkaisho 職業紹介所 38d

empress kōgō 皇后 43

empty kara no (adj) 空の 3c

empty kara ni suru (v) 空にする 3c

encourage hagemasu (v) 励ます 21a

encouragement gekirei 激励 21a

encyclopedia hyakkajiten 百科辞典 20a, 25o, 37b

end owari 終わり 4e

end, finish owaru (v) 終わる 4e

endorse uragakisuru (v) 裏書きする 26

endorsement uragaki 裏書 26

enemy teki 敵 10b

energetic enerugisshu na (adj) エネルギッシュな 11e

energy enerugī エネルギー 11e, 13c, 44a

energy crisis enerugī kiki エネルギー危機 44a

energy needs enerugī juyō エネルギー需要 44a

energy source enerugī shigen エネルギー資源 44a

energy waste enerugī rōhi エネルギー浪費 44a

engaged konyakushita (adj) 婚約した 11c

engagement konyaku 婚約 11c, 29a

engineer gishi 技師 38a

engineering kōgaku 工学 37e

England Igirisu イギリス 30b

English eigo 英語 30d

Englishman Igirisujin イギリス人 30d

enlarge hikinobasu (v) 引き伸ばす 25d

enlarge ōkikusuru (v) 大きくする 25m

enlargement hikinobashi 引き伸ばし 25d

enough jūbun na (adj) 十分な 3c

enough jūbun ni (adv) 十分に 3c

Enough! (No more!) Mō yoshinasai. もうよしなさい。 21c

enter hairu (v) 入る 3e, 16b, 36c

enthusiastic nesshin na (adj) 熱心な 21a

entire zentai no (adj) 全体の 3c

entrance iriguchi 入口 23a, 25a, 35b

entrance exam nyūgaku shiken 入学試験 37f

entrance hall (Japanese) genkan 玄関 23b

envelope fūtō 封筒 19d, 19e, 25c

envious urayamashii (adj) うらやましい 11e

environment kankyō 環境 13b, 44a

envy urayamu 羨む 11e

equality dōtō 同等 1f

equals hitoshii 等しい 1f

equation hōteishiki 方程式 1f

equator sekidō 赤道 13e

equilateral tōhen (adj) 等辺 2a

equinox bunten 分点 5c

eraser keshigomu 消しゴム 2b, 19d, 25c, 37b

error machigai 間違い 37f

eruption funka 噴火 13b

escape, get out nogareru (v) 逃れる 39a

espresso esupuresso エスプレッソ 24k

essay essei エッセイ 20a, 28d, 37f

etching etchingu エッチング 28b

Europe Yōroppa ヨーロッパ 30b

evening yūgata 夕方 4a

evening paper yūkan 夕刊 20a

evening school yagaku 夜学 37a

even number gūsū 偶数 1d

every, each dono ~ mo どの～も 3c

Everybody out! Soto e dete kudasai. 外へ出てください。 39a

everyone daremo 誰も 3c, 8i

everything nandemo mina 何でもみな 8i

everywhere doko demo (adv) どこでも 36c

evidence shōko 証拠 41

exam shiken 試験 37f

examine shiraberu (v) 調べる 40b

examine (medically) shinsatsusuru (v) 診察する 40a

exchange kōkansuru (v) 交換する 25, 26

exchange kōkan 交換 26

exchange rates kōkan ritsu 交換率 26

exclamation mark kantanfu 感嘆符 19c

excursion gurūpu tsuā グループツアー 30a

excuse iiwake 言い訳 17a

Excuse me! Sumimasen. すみません。 16c

excuse oneself iiwakesuru (v) 言い訳する 17a

exercise renshū mondai 練習問題 37f

exhibition tenjikai 展示会 28b

existence sonzai 存在 22a

exit deguchi 出口 25a, 35b

exit, go out deru (v) 出る 36c

expensive takai (adj) 高い 24p, 25a

expiry date tegata kaitori saishūbi 手形買い取り最終日 26

explain setsumeisuru (v) 説明する 17a, 37f

explanation setsumei 説明 17a, 37f

express noberu (v) 述べる 17a

expression hyōgen 表現 17a

express train kyūkō 急行 34

extension enchō 延長 3b

extension naisen 内線 38b

extinguish, put out kesu (v) 消す 39a

extra copy yakimashi 焼き増し 25d

extract, pull nuku (v) 抜く 40b

extract a root (mathematics) kon o hiraku 根を開く 1e

extraction (dentistry) basshi 抜歯 40b

eye me 目 12a

eyebrow mayuge まゆげ 12a

eye doctor meisha 眼医者 38a, 40a

eye drops megusuri 目薬 25h

eyeglasses megane 眼鏡 37b, 40a

eyelash matsuge まつげ 12a

eyelid mabuta まぶた 12a

eyeliner airainā アイライナー 25f

eye shadow aishadō アイシャドー 25f

eyesight shiryoku 視力 40a

eyewitness mokugekisha 目撃者 41

F

fable gūwa 寓話 28d

fabric kiji 生地 25l

fabric softener sofuto shiagezai ソフト仕上げ剤 25g

face kao 顔 12a

face powder oshiroi おしろい 25f

facial biganjutsu 美顔術 12d

faction habatsu 派閥 43

factor (mathematics) insū 因数 1f

factor insū ni bunkaisuru (v) 因数に分解する 1f

factorization insūbunkai 因数分解 1f

factory kōjō 工場 38d

factory worker kōin 工員 38a

Fahrenheit kashi 華氏 6c

fail an exam shiken ni ochiru (v) 試験に落ちる 37f

fairy tale dōwa 童話 28d

faith shinkō 信仰 11d

faith, trust shinrai 信頼 21a

faithful shinkōshin ga atsui (adj) 信仰心が厚い 11d

faithful chūjitsu na (adj) 忠実な 11e

fake nise no (adj) にせの 13d

falcon hayabusa 隼 15b

fall ochiru (v) 落ちる 3e

fall aki 秋 5c

fall asleep nekomu (v) 寝込む 12b

fall in love sukininaru (v) 好きになる 11c

false imitēshon no (adj) イミテーションの 25i

family kazoku 家族 10a

family gokazoku ご家族 10a

family friend kazoku no tomodachi 家族の友達 10b

family guest house minshuku 民宿 35a

family name myōji 苗字 11f

family relationship kazoku kankei 家族関係 10a

family relationship gokazoku kankei ご家族関係 10a

fan fan ファン 33e

far tōku no *(adj)* 遠くの 3d

far tōku ni *(adv)* 遠くに 3d

far (from) tōi *(adj)* 遠い 36c

fare box ryōkinbako 料金箱 34

Farewell! Gokigenyō. ご機嫌よう。 16a

farm nōjō 農場 15a

farmer nōfu 農夫 15a

farmer nōgyō jūjisha 農業従事者 38a

farmland nōchi 農地 13b

fascinate miwakusuru *(vt)* 魅惑する 11e

fascinating miwakuteki na *(adj)* 魅惑的な 11e

fascination miwaku 魅惑 11e

fashion fasshon ファッション 25k

fast hayai *(adj)* 速い 3d

fast hayaku *(adv)* 速く 3d

fasten shimeru *(v)* 締める 32c

fat futotta *(adj)* 太った 11a

father chichi 父 10a

father otōsan お父さん 10a

father-in-law gifu 義父 10a

father-in-law giri no otōsan 義理のお父さん 10a

faucet jaguchi 蛇口 23a, 35c

fax fakkusu ファックス 18b

fax machine fakkusu ファックス 18a, 42a

fax number fakkusu bangō ファックス番号 11f, 38b

fear osore 恐れ 21a

feather hane 羽 15b

February nigatsu 二月 5b

feel kanjiru *(v)* 感じる 21a

feel kanji ga suru *(v)* 感じがする 40a

feel bad kibun ga warui 気分が悪い 12b, 40a

feeling kanji 感じ 21a

feel well kibun ga ii 気分がいい 12b, 40a

felt pen majikku pen マジックペン 7c

felt-tip pen feruto pen フェルトペン 19d, 25c

female josei 女性 11a

female onna 女 38b

feminine josei 女性 8a

feminine josei no *(adj)* 女性の 11a

feminine (womanly) joseiteki na *(adj)* 女性的な 11a

feminism feminizumu フェミニズム 44b

feminist feminisuto フェミニスト 44b

fence kakoi 囲い 15a

fencing fenshingu フェンシング 27b

fencing outfit fenshingu no yunifōmu フェンシングのユニフォーム 27b

fender fendā フェンダー 33e

fertilize hiryō o yaru *(v)* 肥料をやる 14a

fertilizer hiryō 肥料 14a

fetus taiji 胎児 44b

fever netsu 熱 40a

fiancé konyakusha 婚約者 10b, 11c

fiancée konyakusha 婚約者 10b, 11c

fiber sen-i 繊維 13c

fiction shōsetsu 小説 20a

fiction fikushon フィクション 28d

field kōya 広野 13b

field kyōgijō 競技場 27b

field of study kenkyū bunya 研究分野 37f

fifteen jūgo 十五 1a

fifteen thousand ichimangosen 一万五千 1a

fifth gobanme 五番目 1b

fifth daigo 第五 1b

fifth itsutsume 五つ目 1b

fifty gojū 五十 1a

fifty-one gojūichi 五十一 1a

fifty thousand goman 五万 1a

fig ichijiku いちじく 14d, 24f

fight kakutō 格闘 39b

fig tree ichijiku no ki イチジクの木 14c

figure of speech hiyuteki hyōgen 比喩的表現 17a

file yasuri やすり 25b

file bunsho fairu 文書ファイル 38c

filing card fairu yō kādo ファイル用カード 38c

fill mitasu (v) 満たす 3c

filling tsumemono 詰め物 40b

fill up mantan ni suru (v) マンタンにする 33c

film fuirumu フィルム 25d

film projector eishaki 映写機 37b

filter firutā フィルター 25d, 33e

fin hire 鰭 15c

final decision saishū kettei 最終決定 41

fine ii (adj) いい 6a

fine, ticket ihan no ken 違反の券 33c

Fine! Junchō desu. 順調です。 16a

fine arts bijutsu 美術 37e

finger yubi 指 12a

fingernail tsume 爪 12a

finish shiagari 仕上がり 25d

finish school gakko o oeru (v) 学校を終える 11f, 37f

Finland Finrando フィンランド 30b

Finn Finrandojin フィンランド人 30d

Finnish Finrandogo フィンランド語 30d

fir momi 樅 14c

fire kaji 火事 39a

Fire! Kaji da. 火事だ。 39a

fire (dismiss) kaikosuru (v) 解雇する 38d

fire alarm kasai hōchiki 火災報知器 39a

firearm kaki 火器 39b

fire department shōbōsho 消防署 39a

fire engine shōbōsha 消防車 33a, 39a

fire extinguisher shōkaki 消火器 39a

firefighter shōbōshi 消防士 39a

firefly hotaru 螢 15d

fire hose shōka yō hōsu 消火用ホース 39a

fire hydrant shōkasen 消火栓 39a

fireman shōbōshi 消防士 38a

fireplace danro 暖炉 23a

fireproof taikasei no (adj) 耐火性の 39a

first ichibanme 一番目 1b

first daiichi 第一 1b

first hitotsume 一つ目 1b

first-run film fūkiri eiga 封切り映画 28a

first aid ōkyū teate 応急手当 39a, 39c

first class (train) gurīnsha no seki グリーン車の席 34

first class (plane) fāsuto kurasu ファーストクラス 30a, 32a

first class (train) gurīn sha グリーン車 30a

first name namae 名前 11f, 38b

first name mei 名 38b

first person ichininshō 一人称 8a

first year ichinen 一年 37a

fish sakana 魚 15c, 24d

fish sakana o tsuru (v) 魚を釣る 15c

fisherman ryōshi 漁師 15c

fishing tsuri 釣り 15c, 27a, 36b

fishing rod tsurizao 釣り竿 15c

fish store sakana ya 魚屋 24n

fission reactor kakubunretsuro 核分裂炉 42a

five go 五 1a

five itsutsu 五つ 1a

five hundred gohyaku 五百 1a

five thousand gosen 五千 1a

fix naosu (v) 直す 33c

fix, repair shūrisuru (v) 修理する 25i

fixed kotei (no) (adj) 固定（の） 26

fixed price kimatta nedan 決まった値段 24m

fixed price teika 定価 25a

flame honoo 炎 39a

flamingo furamingo フラミンゴ 15b

flash furasshu フラッシュ 25d

flash / bolt of lightning inazuma no hikari 稲妻の光 6a

flashlight kaichūdentō 懐中電灯 25b

flatter oseji o iu (v) お世辞を言う 21a

flattery oseji お世辞 21a

flavor aji 味 12c

flea nomi 蚤 15d

Flemish Furandāsugo フランダース語 30d

flight bin 便 32a

flight attendant kyakushitsu jōmuin 客室乗務員 32c

flight engineer kōkū kikanshi 航空機関
士 32c

floor yuka 床 23a

floor (level) kai 階 23a, 35b

floor cushion zabuton 座布団 35c

floppy disk furoppī (disuku) フロッピー
（ディスク） 42b

florist hanaya 花屋 38a

flounder hirame 平目 15c, 24d

flour komugiko 小麦粉 24i

flow nagareru (v) 流れる 13b

flower hana 花 14a, 14b

flower arrangement ikebana 生け花
14b

flower bed kadan 花壇 14b

flu ryūkan 流感 40a

fluorescent light keikōtō 蛍光灯 25b

flute furūto フルート 28c

fly hae 蝿 15d

focus shōten o awaseru (v) 焦点を合わ
せる 25d

fog kiri 霧 6a

foggy kiri no (adj) 霧の 6a

fold tatamu (v) 畳む 25m

foliage ha no shigeri 葉の茂り 14a

folk dance fōku dansu フォークダンス
28c

folk dance (Japanese) bon odori 盆踊
り 28c

folk music fōku myūjikku フォーク
ミュージック 28c

follow shitagau (v) 従う 3e

follow tadotte iku (v) たどって行く
36c

food tabemono 食べもの 24a

food coloring shokumotsu no
chakushokuzai 食物の着色剤 7c

fool bakamono 馬鹿者 11e

foolish, silly bakageta (adj) ばかげた
11e

foot ashi 足 12a

football futtobōru フットボール 27b

footnote kyakuchū 脚注 20a

forehead hitai 額 12a

foreign currency gaikoku tsūka 外国通
貨 31

foreigner gaikokujin 外国人 31

foreign languages gaikokugo 外国語
37e

foreign movie gaikoku eiga 外国映画
28a

forest shinrin 森林 13b

for example tatoeba 例えば 44c

forget wasureru (v) 忘れる 22b

fork fōku フォーク 23d, 24l

form (to fill out) shoshiki 書式 31

formal dance (Japanese) nihon buyō 日
本舞踊 28c

for now ima no tokoro 今のところ 4e

for sale uridashichū 売出し中 25a

for the defense bengogawa no (adj) 弁
護側の 41

for the prosecution kensatsugawa no
(adj) 検察側の 41

Fortunately! Un yoku. 運良く。 21c

forty yonjū 四十 1a

forty-one yonjūichi 四十一 1a

forty-two yonjūni 四十二 1a

forty thousand yonman 四万 1a

fossil fuel saikutsunenryō 採掘燃料
13c

foul line fāru rain ファールライン
27b

fountain pen mannenhitsu 万年筆
19d, 25c

four shi / yon 四 1a

four yottsu 四つ 1a

four-ninths kyūbun no yon 九分の四
1c

four-sided figures shihenkei 四辺形
2a

four hundred yonhyaku 四百 1a

fourteen jūshi / jūyon 十四 1a

fourteen thousand ichiman-yonsen 一
万四千 1a

fourth yobanme 四番目 1b

fourth daiyon 第四 1b

fourth yottsume 四つ目 1b

four thousand yonsen 四千 1a

fox kitsune 狐 15a

fraction bunsū 分数 1d

fractional bunsū no (adj) 分数の 1d

France Furansu フランス 30b

Frankfurt Furankufuruto フランクフ
ルト 30c

freeze kōru (vi) 凍る 6a

freezer reitōko 冷凍庫 23d

freezing point hyōten 氷点 6c

French Furansugo フランス語 30d

Frenchman Furansujin フランス人 30d

frequent hinpan na (adj) 頻繁な 4e

frequently shibashiba しばしば 4e

fresco painting hekiga 壁画 28b
Friday kinyōbi 金曜日 5a
fried ageta *(adj)* 揚げた 24b
fried egg medamayaki 目玉焼き 24h
friend tomodachi 友達 10b
friendly shitashige na *(adj)* 親しげな 11e
friendship yūkō 友好 10b
frog kaeru かえる 15c
from kara から 3d, 8j
from my point of view watakushi no mikata dewa 私の見方では 44c
from now on korekara これから 4e
front page ichimen 一面 20a
frozen kootta *(adj)* 凍った 6a
fruit kudamono 果物 14d, 24f, 24g
fruit store kudamono ya 果物屋 24n
fruit tree kaju 果樹 14a
fuel nenryō 燃料 13c
full ippai no *(adj)* いっぱいの 3c
full moon mangetsu 満月 13a
fun, enjoyment tanoshimi 楽しみ 21a
function (mathematics) kansū 関数 1f
function kinō 機能 42b
funny omoshiroi *(adj)* 面白い 11e
fur coat kegawa no kōto 毛皮のコート 25k
furnace danbōro 暖房炉 23e
furniture kagu 家具 23c
furthermore sonoue その上 8k
fuse hyūzu ヒューズ 25b
fusion reactor kakuyūgōro 核融合炉 42a
fussy kourusai *(adj)* 小うるさい 11e
future shōrai / mirai 将来/未来 4e
future mirai *(adj)* 未来 8a

G

galaxy ginga 銀河 13a
game gēmu ゲーム 27a
game, match shiai 試合 27b
garage shako 車庫 23a
garage chūshajō 駐車場 35b
garbage bin gomiire ゴミ入れ 36a
garbage truck gomi shūshūsha ゴミ収集車 33a
garden niwa 庭 14e, 23a, 36a
gardening engei 園芸 27a
garlic ninniku にんにく 14e, 24e, 24j
gas gasu ガス 13c, 23e

gas gasorin ガソリン 33c
gasoline gasorin ガソリン 13c
gas pedal akuseru アクセル 33e
gas pump ponpu ポンプ 33e
gas station gasorin sutando ガソリンスタンド 33c
gas tank gasorin tanku ガソリンタンク 33e
gate mon 門 23a
gate (airport) gēto ゲート 32a
gather, reap shūkakusuru *(v)* 収穫する 14a
gauze gāze ガーゼ 25h, 39c
gearshift gia shifuto ギアシフト 33c
gearshift shifuto rebā シフトレバー 33e
Gemini futagoza 双子座 5d
gender sei 性 8a
generator jenerētā ジェネレーター 33e
generosity kandaisa 寛大さ 11e
generous kandai na *(adj)* 寛大な 11e
genitals gaiinbu 外陰部 12a
genre yōshiki 様式 28d
gentle yasashii *(adj)* 優しい 11e, 21a
gentleman shinshi 紳士 11a
Gentlemen Haikei 拝啓 19a
geographical chirijō no *(adj)* 地理上の 13c
geography chiri 地理 13e, 37e
geometrical kika no *(adj)* 幾何の 2b
geometry kika 幾何 2b
geometry kikagaku 幾何学 37e
geothermal energy chinetsu enerugī 地熱エネルギー 13c
geranium jeranyūmu ジェラニューム 14b
German Doitsugo ドイツ語 30d
German Doitsujin ドイツ人 30d
Germany Doitsu ドイツ 30b
gerund dōmeishi 動名詞 8a
get a degree gakui o toru *(v)* 学位をとる 37f
get a diploma sotsugyō shōsho o morau *(v)* 卒業証書をもらう 37f
get a doctor isha o yobu *(v)* 医者を呼ぶ 39c
get a loan yūshi o ukeru *(v)* 融資を受ける 26
get an education kyōiku o ukeru *(v)* 教育を受ける 37f

get a suntan hiyakesuru *(v)* 日焼けする 36b

get cured yokunaru *(v)* 良くなる 40a

get dressed kiru *(v)* 着る 25m

get examined shinsatsu o ukeru *(v)* 診察を受ける 40a

get married kekkonsuru *(v)* 結婚する 11c

get sick byōki ni naru *(v)* 病気になる 40a

get some sun hi ni ataru *(v)* 日に当たる 36b

get up okiru *(v)* 起きる 12b

get up, rise okiru *(v)* 起きる 3e

get used to nareru *(v)* 慣れる 11c

gift okurimono 贈り物 11c

gift gifuto ギフト 25a

gin jin ジン 24k

ginger ale jinjaēru ジンジャエール 24k

ginko tree ichō 銀杏 14c

giraffe kirin きりん 15a

girl onna no ko 女の子 11a

girlfriend onna tomodachi/gāru furendo 女友達／ガールフレンド 10b

give, hand back kaesu *(v)* 返す 37f

give a gift okurimono o ageru 贈り物を上げる 11c

give back the room key kagi o kaesu 鍵を返す 35b

give birth umu *(v)* 生む 11c

give help tasukete ageru *(v)* 助けてあげる 39a

Give my regards to... ...san ni yoroshiku さんに宜しく 19b

glacier hyōga 氷河 13b

gladiolus gurajiorasu グラジオラス 14b

gland sen 腺 12a

glass (drinking) koppu コップ 23d, 241

globe chikyū 地球 13e

gloomy inki na *(adj)* 陰気な 21a

glossy kōtaku no aru *(adj)* 光沢のある 25d

glove tebukuro 手袋 25k

glove (baseball) gurōbu グローブ 27b

glove compartment gurōbu bokkusu グローブボックス 33e

glue setchakuzai 接着剤 19d, 25b, 25c

go iku *(v)* 行く 3e, 36c

Go ahead! Dōzo. どうぞ。 17b

goal gōru ゴール 27b

goalkeeper gōrukīpā ゴールキーパー 27b

goal kick gōru kikku ゴールキック 27b

goat yagi 山羊 15a

go away saru *(v)* 去る 3e

go bankrupt hasansuru *(v)* 破産する 38d

god kamisama 神様 11d

go down kudaru *(v)* 下る 36c

go down, descend sagaru *(vi)* 下がる 3e

go down, descend kudaru *(vt)* 下る 3e

go forward zenshinsuru *(v)* 前進する 33c

going through a red light shingō mushi 信号無視 33c

gold kin-iro 金色 7a

gold kin 金 13c, 25i

golden anniversary kekkon gojusshūnen kinenbi 結婚五十周年記念日 11c

goldfish kingyo 金魚 15c

golf gorufu ゴルフ 27b

good ii *(adj)* いい 11e

good, delicious oishii *(adj)* おいしい 24p

good, final copy seisho 清書 37f

Good-bye! Sayōnara. さようなら。 16a

Good afternoon! (Hello!) Konnichiwa. 今日は。 16a

good at (something) jōzu na *(adj)* 上手な 11e

Good evening! (Hello!) Konbanwa. 今晩は。 16a

Good heavens! Oh my! Oya. おや。 21c

Good luck! Goseikō o. ご成功を。 16c

good mood ii kibun いい気分 21a

Good morning! (Hello!) Ohayō gozaimasu. お早うございます。 16a

goodness zenryōsa 善良さ 11e

Good night! Oyasuminasai. お休みなさい。 16a

go on foot aruite iku *(v)* 歩いていく 3e

go on strike sutoraiki ni hairu *(v)* ストライキにはいる 43

goose gachō 鵞 15b

go out dekakeru *(v)* 出かける 29b

go out, exit deru *(v)* 出る 3e

gorilla gorira ゴリラ 15a

gossip uwasabanashi 噂話 17a

gossip uwasabanashi o suru (v) 噂話を
する 17a

go to bed neru (v) 寝る 12b

go to school gakkō ni iku (v) 学校に行
く 11c, 11f, 37f

go up sakanoboru (v) 逆上る 36c

go up, climb noboru (vt) 上る 3e

govern tōjisuru (v) 統治する 43

government seifu 政府 43

government worker kōmuin 公務員
38a

graceful yūga na (adj) 優雅な 11e

grade gakunen 学年 37a

grade, mark seiseki 成績 37f

grade one ichinen 一年 37a

grade two ninen 二年 37a

graduate sotsugyōsei (n) 卒業生 11f

graduate sotsugyōsuru (v) 卒業する
11f, 37f

graduate school daigakuin 大学院
11f, 38b

grain kokurui 穀類 14a

gram guramu グラム 3a

grammar bunpō 文法 8a, 37f

grandchildren mago 孫 10a

grandchildren omagosan お孫さん
10a

grandfather sofu 祖父 10a

grandfather ojiisan おじいさん 10a

grandfather clock hakogata ōdokei 箱
型大時計 4d

grandmother sobo 祖母 10a

grandmother obāsan おばあさん
10a

grand piano gurando piano グランドピ
アノ 28c

grapefruit gurēpufurūtsu グレープフル
ーツ 14d, 24f

grapes budō 葡萄 14d, 24f

grass (field) sōgen 草原 13b

grasshopper batta ばった 15d

grate orosu (v) おろす 24o

grated ginger (Japanese) oroshi shōga
おろし姜 24j

grated radish (Japanese) daikon
oroshi 大根おろし 24j

gravitation inryoku 引力 13a

gravity inryoku 引力 13a

gray haiiro/gurē 灰色/グレー 7a

Greece Girisha ギリシャ 30b

Greek Girishajin ギリシャ人 30d

Greek (language) Girishago ギリシャ
語 30d

green midori iro 緑色 7a

greenhouse onshitsu 温室 14a

green pepper pīman ピーマン 14e,
24e

greet aisatsusuru (v) 挨拶する 16a

greeting aisatsu 挨拶 16a

grill amiyaki ni suru (v) 網焼きにする
24o

grilled amiyaki no (adj) 網焼きの 24b

grocery store shokuryōhin ten 食料品
店 24n

groom (bridegroom) hanamuko 花婿
11c

grooming midashinami 身嗜み 12d

ground floor ikkai 一階 23a, 23g

group gurūpu グループ 25j

group discount dantai waribiki 団体割
引 30a

grow fueru (vi) 増える 3c

grow fuyasu (vt) 増やす 3c

growth zōdai 増大 3c

grow up sodatsu (vi) 育つ 11b

guide gaido ガイド 36a

guidebook gaidobukku ガイドブック
25o

guilt tsumi 罪 41

guilty yūzai no (adj) 有罪の 41

guilty (verdict) yūzai/kuro 有罪/黒
41, 41

guitar gitā ギター 28c

guitarist gitarisuto ギタリスト 28c

gulf wan 湾 13b

gums haguki 歯茎 40b

gun jū 銃 39b

gymnasium jimu ジム 27b

gymnasium taiikukan 体育館 37c

H

habit shūkan 習慣 11e

hail arare あられ 6a

hail arare ga furu (vi) あられが降る
6a

hair kaminoke 髪の毛 12a

hairbrush hea burashi ヘアーブラシ
25f

hair conditioner rinsu リンス 25f

hairdresser biyōshi 美容師 12d, 38a

hairdryer hea doraiyā ヘアードライヤ
ー 12d, 25f

hairspray hea supurē ヘアースプレー
12d, 25f

half hanbun no *(adj)* 半分の 3c

halibut ohyō おひょう 24d

hallway rōka 廊下 37c

ham hamu ハム 24c

hammer kanazuchi 金槌 25b

hand te 手 12a

handcuffs tejō 手錠 39b

handkerchief hankachi ハンカチ 25k

handle (knife) totte 取っ手 23d

handlebar handoru ハンドル 33a

hand lotion hando rōshon ハンドローション 25f

hand luggage tenimotsu 手荷物 31

hand of a clock tokei no hari 時計の針 4d

handshake akushu 握手 16a

handsome (for male) hansamu na *(adj)* ハンサムな 11a

hang kakeru *(v)* 掛ける 25m

hang up kiru *(v)* 切る 18b

happen, occur okoru *(v)* 起こる 4e

happiness shiawase 幸せ 11e, 21a

happy shiawase na *(adj)* 幸せな 11e, 21a

Happy Birthday! Tanjōbi omedetō. 誕生日おめでとう。 11c, 16c, 29c

Happy New Year! Shinnen omedetō 新年おめでとう。 16c, 29c

Happy to make your acquaintance! Shiriau koto ga dekite ureshii desu. 知り合うことができて嬉しいです。 16b

hard katai *(adj)* 堅い 13d

hard-boiled egg yudetamago ゆで卵 24h

hardware (computer) hādowea ハードウェア 42b

hardware store daikudōgu ten 大工道具店 25b

hare nousagi 野うさぎ 15a

harmony hāmonī ハーモニー 28c

harp hāpu ハープ 28c

harpsichord hāpushikōdo ハープシコード 28c

hat bōshi 帽子 25k

hate ken-o 嫌悪 11e

hate totemo kirau *(v)* とても嫌う 11e

hate nikumu *(v)* 憎む 11e

hateful iya na *(adj)* いやな 11e

hatred ken-o 嫌悪 21b

have a baby kodomo ga umareru 子供が生まれる 11c

Have a good holiday! Oyasumi o, otanoshimi kudasai. お休みをお楽しみ下さい。 16c, 29c

Have a good time! Tanoshii toki o, osugoshi kudasai. 楽しい時をお過ごし下さい。 16c

Have a good trip! Ryokō o, otanoshimi kudasai. 旅行をお楽しみ下さい。 16c

have a headache zutsū ga suru 頭痛がする 40a

Have a nice trip! Ryokō o, otanoshimi kudasai. 旅行をお楽しみ下さい。 30a

have a snack kanshoku suru *(v)* 間食する 24o

have a sore throat nodo ga itamu 喉が痛む 40a

have a stomachache i ga itai 胃が痛い 40a

have a toothache ha ga itamu 歯が痛む 40b

have baggage taken to one's room nimotsu o heya e motte itte morau 荷物を部屋へもっていってもらう 35b

have breakfast asagohan o taberu *(v)* 朝御飯を食べる 24o

have chills samuke ga suru 寒けがする 6b

have dinner bangohan o taberu *(v)* 晩御飯を食べる 24o

have fun, enjoy oneself tanoshimu *(v)* 楽しむ 21a, 29c

Have fun! Tanoshinde kite kudasai. 楽しんできて下さい。 29c

have lunch hirugohan o taberu *(v)* 昼御飯を食べる 24o

have white hair shiraga ga aru 白髪がある 11a

hawk taka 鷹 15b

hazard flash hazādo ranpu ハザードランプ 33e

he kare ga/wa 彼が/は 8c

head atama 頭 12a

headache zutsū 頭痛 40a

heading midashi 見出し 19c

headline midashi 見出し 20a

head office honten 本店 26

head of state genshu 元首 43

headphones heddohōn ヘッドホーン 20b, 32c

heal naoru *(v)* 直る 40a

health kenkō 健康 11a, 40a

healthy kenkōteki na *(adj)* 健康的な 11a

healthy kenkō na *(adj)* 健康な 40a

hear kiku *(v)* 聞く 12c

hearing chōryoku 聴力 12c

heart shinzō 心臓 12a, 40a

heart attack shinzō mahi 心臓麻痺 40a

heat netsu 熱 13c

heater hītā ヒーター 33e

heating danbō 暖房 23e

heavier screen, made of paper or fabric fusuma 襖 23c

heavy omoi *(adj)* 重い 3b, 11a, 13d, 31

Hebrew (language) Heburaigo ヘブライ語 30d

Hebrew, Jewish Yudayajin no *(adj)* ユダヤ人の 11d

hectare hekutāru ヘクタール 3a

hectogram hekutoguramu ヘクトグラム 3a

hedge ikegaki 生け垣 14a

heel kakato かかと 12a, 25n

height se no takasa 背の高さ 11a

Hello! (telephone) Moshi moshi. もしもし。 18b

helmet herumetto ヘルメット 27b

help tasuke 助け 39a

help tasukeru *(v)* 助ける 39a

Help! Tasukete. 助けて。 39a, 39c

hemisphere hankyū 半球 13e

hemispheric hankyūjō no *(adj)* 半球状の 13e

hen mendori めんどり 15b

heptagon nanakakukei 七角形 2a

her kanojo no 彼女の 8d

her kanojo o 彼女を 8e

herb hābu ハーブ 14e, 24j

here koko ここ 3d

here koko ni ここに 36c

heredity iden 遺伝 11c

hero shujinkō 主人公 28e

heroine onna shujinkō 女主人公 28e

heron sagi 鷺 15b

herring nishin 鰊 15c, 24d

herself kanojo jishin 彼女自身 8g

hesitate tamerau *(v)* ためらう 17a

hesitation tamerai ためらい 17a

hexagon rokkakukei 六角形 2a

Hi! Yā. *(inf)* やあ。 16a

high takai *(adj)* 高い 6c

high-heeled shoe haihīru ハイヒール 25n

high school kōkō 高校 11f, 37a, 38b

high school diploma kōkō no sotsugyō shōsho 高校の卒業証書 37f

high tide manchō 満潮 13b

highway kōsokudōro 高速道路 33c

highway police haiwē patorōru ハイウェーパトロール 33b

hiking haikingu ハイキング 36b

hill oka 丘 13b

him kare o 彼を 8e

himself kare jishin 彼自身 8g

Hindu Hinzūkyōto ヒンズー教徒 11d

hip oshiri おしり 12a

hippopotamus kaba かば 15a

hire yatou *(v)* 雇う 38d

his kare no 彼の 8d

history rekishi 歴史 37e

hit utsu *(v)* 打つ 27b

hobby shumi 趣味 27a

hockey rink hokkējō ホッケー場 27b

hockey stick sutikku スティック 27b

Hold the line! Kiranaide kudasai. 切らないで下さい。 18b

hole ana 穴 25g

holiday kyūjitsu 休日 5a, 29a

Holland Oranda オランダ 30b

home base hōmu ホーム 27b

homosexual dōseiai no *(adj)* 同性愛の 44b

homosexuality dōseiai 同性愛 44b

honest shōjiki na *(adj)* 正直な 11e

honesty shōjikisa 正直さ 11e

honey hachimitsu はちみつ 24j

honeymoon shinkonryokō 新婚旅行 11c

Hong Kong Honkon 香港 30c

Honolulu Honoruru ホノルル 30c

hood bonnetto ボンネット 33e

hook tsuribari 釣り針 15c

hope nozomi 望み 21a

hope nozomu *(v)* 望む 21a

horizon suihei 水平 3d

horizontal suihei no *(adj)* 水平の 3d

horn horun ホルン 28c

horn keiteki 警笛 33e

horoscope hoshiuranai 星占い 5d

horse uma 馬 15a

horsepower bariki 馬力 33e

horse racing keiba 競馬 27b

horseradish (Japanese) wasabi わさび 24j

horseradish (western) hōsuradisshu ホースラディッシュ 24j

horticulture engei 園芸 14a

hospital byōin 病院 39c

hot (weather) atsui *(adj)* 暑い 6b

hot (spice) karai *(adj)* 辛い 24p

hot (temperature) atsui *(adj)* 熱い 24p

hotel hoteru ホテル 35a

hotel clerk hoteru no kakariin ホテルの係員 35b

hot sake atsukan 熱燗 24p

hot water oyu お湯 35c

hour jikan 時間 4c

hourly jikangoto 時間毎の 4c

hourly jikangoto ni *(adv)* 時間毎に 4c

house ie 家 23a

household Buddhist altar butsudan 仏壇 23c

household Shinto shrine kamidana 神棚 23c

House of Councilors (Japanese) sangiin 参議院 43

House of Representatives (Japanese) shūgiin 衆議院 43

House of Representatives (U.S.) kain 下院 43

How? Dō yatte. *(inf)* どうやって。 9

How's it going? Ikaga desu ka. いかがですか。 16a

How's the weather? Donna tenki desu ka. どんな天気ですか。 6a

How come? Naze. *(inf)* なぜ。 9

How do you get to...? ...niwa, dō yatte ikimasu ka. ...には、どうやって行きますか。 36c

How do you say ... in Japanese? ...wa, nihongo de dō iimasu ka. は、日本語でどう言いますか。 17b

How do you say that in Japanese? Nihongo de sore o nan to iimasu ka. 日本語でそれを何と言いますか。

How do you write your name? Onamae wa, dō kakimasu ka. 御名前は、どう書きますか。 11f

however keredomo/shikashi けれども／しかし 8k

How have you been? Ogenki desu ka. 御元気ですか。 16a

howl hoeru *(v)* 吠える 15a

how much dono kurai どのくらい 3c

How much? Dono kurai desu ka. どのくらいですか。 9

how much (money) ikura いくら 3c

How much? (money) Ikura desu ka. いくらですか。 9

How much does it cost? Ikura desu ka. いくらですか。 25a

How much do you weigh? Anata no taijū wa, dono kurai desu ka. あなたの体重はどの位ですか。 11a

How old are you? Toshi wa, ikutsu desu ka. 年はいくつですか。 11b

How tall are you? Anata no se no takasa wa, dono kurai desu ka. あなたの背の高さはどの位ですか。 11a

human ningen no *(adj)* 人間の 11d

human hito no *(adj)* 人の 15a

human being ningen 人間 11d, 15a

humanitarian jindōshugi no *(adj)* 人道主義の 11e

humanities jinbunkagaku 人文科学 37e

humanity ningensei 人間性 11d

humble hikaeme na *(adj)* 控え目な 11e, 21a

humid shikke ga takai *(adj)* 湿気が高い 6a

humidity shikke 湿気 6a

humility kenson 謙遜 11e

humor yūmoa ユーモア 11e

humorous kokkei na *(adj)* 滑稽な 11e

hundredth hyakubanme 百番目 1b

hunger kūfuku 空腹 12b

hunter hantā ハンター 15a

hunting shuryō 狩猟 15a, 27a

hurricane harikēn ハリケーン 6a

hurry isogu *(v)* 急ぐ 39b

hurt itamu *(v)* 痛む 40a

husband otto 夫 10a, 11c

husband goshujin ご主人 10a

hydrangea ajisai 紫陽花 14b

hydrogen suiso 水素 13c

hydrogen bomb suiso bakudan 水素爆弾 44b

hyena haiena ハイエナ 15a

hygiene eisei 衛生 12d

hygienic eiseiteki na *(adj)* 衛生的な 12d

hyphen haifun ハイフン 19c

hypothesis kasetsu 仮説 22a

I

I watakushi ga/wa 私が／は 8c

I'd like to say... ...to iitai no desu ga. と言いたいのですが。 44c

I'm... Watakushi wa,...desu. 私は...です。 16b

I'm not sure that... ...ka dō ka tashika dewa arimasen. ...かどうか確かではありません。 44c

I'm serious! Honki desu yo. 本気ですよ。 21c

I'm sorry! Sumimasen. すみません。 21c

I'm sure that... Tashika ni,...to omoimasu. 確かに...と思います。 17b

I'm sure that... ...wa, tashika desu. は確かです。 44c

I am...tall. Watakushi no se no takasa wa,...desu. 私の背の高さは...です。 11a

I am cold. Samui desu. 寒いです。 6a, 6b

I am hot. Atsui desu. 暑いです。 6b

I believe that... ...to omoimasu. と思います。 44c

I can't stand the cold. Samusa ni yowai desu. 寒さに弱いです。 6b

I can't stand the heat. Atsusa ni yowai desu. 暑さに弱いです。 6b

ice kōri 氷 6a, 13b

ice cream aisukurīmu アイスクリーム 24g, 24h

ice cream parlor aisukurīmu ya アイスクリーム屋 24n

ice hockey aisu hokkē アイスホッケー 27b

icosahedron nijūmentai 二十面体 2a

idea aidia アイディア 22a

idealism risōshugi 理想主義 11e

idealist risōshugisha 理想主義者 11e

idealistic risōshugiteki na 理想主義的な 11e

identification mibunshōmei 身分証明 11f

identification (paper, card) mibun shōmeisho 身分証明書 31, 35b

identify shikibetsusuru (v) 識別する 17a

ideology ideorogī イデオロギー 43

I didn't understand. Wakarimasen deshita. 分かりませんでした。 17b

I don't believe it! Shinjiraremasen. 信じられません。 21c

I don't feel like... ...ki ni naremasen. 気になりません。 21c

I don't know if... ...ka dō ka shirimasen. かどうか知りません。 44c

I don't understand. Wakarimasen. 分かりません。 9, 17b

I doubt that... ...ka dō ka gimon desu. かどうか疑問です。 44c

ignorant muchi no (adj) 無知の 22a

I have chills. Samuke ga shimasu. 寒気がします。 6b

I hope you like it. Okuchi ni au to ii no desu ga. お口に合うといいのですが。 24l

I live... ...ni sunde imasu. に住んでいます。 11f

illustration irasuto イラスト 20a

I love the cold. Samui no ga suki desu. 寒いのが好きです。 6b

I love the heat. Atsui no ga suki desu. 暑いのが好きです。 6b

imaginary number kyosū 虚数 1d

imagination sōzōryoku 想像力 11e, 22a

imaginative sōzōryoku ni tonda (adj) 想像力に富んだ 11e

imagine sōzōsuru (v) 想像する 22b

impatient kimijika na (adj) 気短かな 11e

imperative mood meireihō 命令法 8a

import yunyūsuru (v) 輸入する 31

Impossible! Muri desu yo. 無理ですよ。 21c

imprison tōgokusuru (v) 投獄する 41

impudence atsukamashisa 厚かましさ 11e

impudent atsukamashii (adj) 厚かましい 11e

impulse shōdō 衝動 11e

impulsive shōdōteki na (adj) 衝動的な 11e

in naka no (adj) 中の 3d

in naka ni (adj) 中に 3d

in ni/de に／で 8j

in an hour's time ichijikan nai ni 一時間内に 4e

in black and white shiro kuro de 白黒で 25d

incisor monshi 門歯 40b

income shūnyū 収入 26

in conclusion ketsuron to shitewa 結論としては 44c

increase zōka 増加 3c
increase zōkasuru (vi) 増加する 3c
increase zōkasaseru (vt) 増加させる 3c
indefinite futei (adj) 不定 8a
independent jishuteki na (adj) 自主的な 11e
index sakuin 索引 20a
index finger hitosashiyubi 人差指 12a
India Indo インド 30b
indicate shisasuru (v) 示唆する 17a
indication shisa 示唆 17a
indicative mood chokusetsuhō 直説法 8a
indifference mukanshin 無関心 21a
indifferent mukanshin na (adj) 無関心な 21a
indirect kansetsu (adj) 間接 8a
individualist kojinshugisha 個人主義者 11e
Indonesia Indoneshia インドネシア 30b
industrial kōgyō no (adj) 工業の 13c
industry kōgyō 工業 13c
inexpensive yasui (adj) 安い 25a
infection kanō 化膿 40a
infinitive futeishi 不定詞 8a
inflation infure インフレ 43
inform tsugeru (v) 告げる 17a
informal restaurant keishikibaranai resutoran 形式ばらないレストラン 24m
information jōhō 情報 18b
information desk annaisho 案内所 32a
infrared light sekigaisen 赤外線 13a
in front of mae no 前の 3d
in front of ... ... no mae ni の前に 36c
ingenious dokusōteki na (adj) 独創的な 11e
ingenuity dokusōsei 独創性 11e
inherit (heredity) iden de uketsugu (v) 遺伝で受け継ぐ 11c
injection chūsha 注射 25h, 40a
injure, wound kegasaseru (vt) 怪我させる 39b
injury, wound kega 怪我 39b
ink inku インク 19d, 25c, 37b
ink stick (calligraphy) sumi 墨 19d
inkstone (calligraphy) suzuri 硯 19d
in love renai chū 恋愛中 11c
in my opinion watakushi no iken dewa 私の意見では 22a, 44c

in my view watakushi no kangae dewa 私の考えでは 44c
innocence mujaki 無邪気 11e
innocence muzai 無罪 41
innocent mujaki na (adj) 無邪気な 11e
innocent muzai no (adj) 無罪の 41
inorganic muki no (adj) 無機の 13c
insect konchū 昆虫 15d
insecticide satchūzai 殺虫剤 14a
inside naka ni (adv) 中に 3d
inside ... ... no naka ni の中に 36c
insolence ōhei 横柄 11e
insolent ōhei na (adj) 横柄な 11e
instant shunji 瞬時 4c
instrument gakki 楽器 27a, 28c
insulation (wire) zetsuen 絶縁 25b
insulin inshurin インシュリン 25h
insurance hoken 保険 26, 30a
insurance card hoken sho 保険書 33b
integer seisū 整数 1d
integrated circuit shūseki kairo 集積回路 42b
intellectual chishikijin 知識人 11e
intelligence chisei 知性 11e
intelligent chiseiteki na (adj) 知性的な 11e
intercom tsūwa sōchi 通話装置 18a
intercom intāfon インターフォン 38c
interest rishi 利子 26
interesting omoshiroi (adj) 面白い 22a
interest rate riritsu 利率 26
interface intāfēsu インターフェース 42b
interim decision kari kettei 仮決定 41
intermission makuai 幕間 28e
interpret tsūyakusuru (v) 通訳する 17a
interpretation tsūyaku 通訳 17a
interpreter tsūyaku 通訳 36a
interrogative gimon (adj) 疑問 8a
interrogative gimonshi 疑問詞 8a
interrupt saegiru (v) さえぎる 17a
interruption chūdan 中断 17a
intersection kōsaten 交差点 33c, 33d, 36a
interview intabyū インタビュー 20a, 20b
intestine chō 腸 12a, 40a
in the afternoon gogo ni 午後に 4a
in the country inaka de 田舎で 36b

in the evening yūgata ni 夕方に 4a

in the latest style/fashion ima hayatte iru 今はやっている 25l

in the meanwhile sono kan ni その間に 4e

in the middle of naka no 中の 3d

in the morning gozenchū ni 午前中に 4a

in the mountains yama de 山で 36b

in time maniatte 間に合って 4e

intransitive verb jidōshi 自動詞 8a

introduce shōkaisuru (v) 紹介する 16b

introduction shōkai 紹介 16b

in two minutes' time nifunkan nai ni 二分間内に 4e

invertebrate musekitsui dōbutsu 無脊椎動物 15a, 15d

invest tōshisuru (v) 投資する 26

investment tōshi 投資 26

invite maneku (v) 招く 17a

iodine yōso 沃素 13c

Iran Iran イラン 30b

Iraq Iraku イラク 30b

irascible okorippoi (adj) 怒りっぽい 11e

Ireland Airurando アイルランド 30b

iris ayame あやめ 14b

iron (metal) tetsu 鉄 13c

iron airon アイロン 25g

iron airon o kakeru (v) アイロンをかける 25g

ironical hiniku na (adj) 皮肉な 11e

irony hiniku 皮肉 11e

irrational number murisū 無理数 1d

irregular verb fukisokudōshi 不規則動詞 8a

irritable tanki na (adj) 短気な 11e

Is ... (name of person) in? ... wa, irasshaimasu ka. は、いらっしゃいますか。 18b

is equivalent to sōtōsuru 相当する 1f

is greater than yori ōkii より大きい 1f

Islam (religion) kaikyō 回教 11d

Islamic kaikyō no (adj) 回教の 11d

island shima 島 13b

is less than yori chiisai より小さい 1f

Isn't it so? Sō dewanai desu ka. そうではないですか。 8l

isosceles nitōhen (adj) 二等辺 2a

Israel Isuraeru イスラエル 30b

Israeli Isuraerujin イスラエル人 30d

is similar to ruijishiteiru 類似している 1f

It's 1:00. Ichiji desu. 一時です。 4b

It's 10:00 AM. Gozen jūji desu. 午前十時です。 4b

It's 10:00 PM. Gogo jūji desu. 午後十時です。 4b

It's 1991. Sen kyūhyaku kyūjū ichi nen desu. 千九百九十一年です。 5e

It's 2:00. Niji desu. 二時です。 4b

It's 2:45. Niji yonjūgofun desu. 二時四十五分です。 4b

It's 2:45. Sanji jūgofun mae desu. 三時十五分前です。 4b

It's 3:00. Sanji desu. 三時です。 4b

It's 3:00 on the dot. Sanji kikkari desu. 三時きっかりです。 4b

It's 3:30. Sanji han desu. 三時半です。 4b

It's 5:00 AM. Gozen goji desu. 午前五時です。 4b

It's 5:00 PM. Gogo goji desu. 午後五時です。 4b

It's 5:50. Rokuji juppun mae desu. 六時十分前です。 4b

It's January second. Ichigatsu futsuka desu. 一月二日です。 5e

It's May third. Gogatsu mikka desu. 五月三日です。 5e

It's October first. Jūgatsu tsuitachi desu. 十月一日です。 5e

It's a bit cold. Chotto samui desu. ちょっと寒いです。 6a

It's a bit hot. Chotto atsui desu. ちょっと暑いです。 6a

It's awful. Hidoi tenki desu. ひどい天気です。 6a

It's beautiful. Subarashii tenki desu. 素晴しい天気です。 6a

It's clear that ... ... wa, akiraka desu. は、明らかです。 44c

It's cloudy. Kumori desu. 曇りです。 6a

It's cold. Samui desu. 寒いです。 6a

It's dark already. Mō kurai desu. もう暗いです。 6a

It's exactly 3:00. Chōdo sanji desu. ちょうど三時です。 4b

It's fine. Ii tenki desu. いい天気です。 6a

It's foul. Warui tenki desu. 悪い天気です。 6a

It's hot. Atsui desu. 暑いです。 6a

It's humid. Shikke ga takai desu. 湿気が高いです。 6a

It's mild. Atatakai desu. 暖かいです。 6a

It's muggy. Mushiatsui desu. 蒸し暑いです。 6a

It's necessary that... ... ga, hitsuyō desu. ...が必要です。 17b

It's not true! Sore wa, hontō dewa arimasen. それは本当ではありません。 17b

It's obvious that ... ...koto wa, akiraka desu. ことは、明らかです。 17b

It's pleasant. Kaiteki desu. 快適です。 6a

It's raining. Ame ga futte imasu. 雨が降っています。 6a

It's rainy. Ame ga futte imasu. 雨が降っています。 6a

It's snowing. Yuki ga futte imasu. 雪が降っています。 6a

It's sunny. Hi ga tette imasu. 日が照っています。 6a

It's thundering. Kaminari ga natte imasu. 雷が鳴っています。 6a

It's true! Sore wa, hontō desu. それは、本当です。 17b

It's very cold. Totemo samui desu. とても寒いです。 6a

It's very hot. Totemo atsui desu. とても暑いです。 6a

It's windy. Kaze ga tsuyoi desu. 風が強いです。 6a

Italian Itariajin イタリア人 30d

Italian (language) Itariago イタリア語 30d

italics itarikkutai イタリック体 19c

Italy Itaria イタリア 30b

itch kayumi かゆみ 40a

It doesn't matter! Kamaimasen. 構いません。 17a

I think that ... ... to omoimasu. と思います。 44c

It seems that ... ... mitai desu. みたいです。 17b

It seems that ... ... yō desu. ようです。 44c

I was born in 19... Sen kyūhyaku ...nen ni umaremashita. 千九百...年に生まれました。 5e

I was born on ... Watakushi wa, ... ni umaremashita. 私は、...に生まれました。 11c

I weigh ... Watakushi no taijū wa, ... desu. 私の体重は...です。 11a

I wish! Sō da to iindesu ga. そうだといいんですが。 21c

J

jacket jaketto ジャケット 25k

Jakarta Jakaruta ジャカルタ 30c

jam jamu ジャム 24j

janitor yōmuin 用務員 37d

January ichigatsu 一月 5b

Japan Nihon/Nippon 日本 30b

Japanese Nihonjin 日本人 30d

Japanese (language) Nihongo 日本語 30d

Japanese-style room washitsu 和室 23b

Japanese cedar sugi 杉 14c

Japanese character kana 仮名 8a

Japanese checkers go 碁 27a

Japanese chess shōgi 将棋 27a

Japanese cypress hinoki 桧 14c

Japanese fencing kendō 剣道 27b

Japanese harp koto 琴 28c

Japanese mandolin shamisen 三味線 28c

Japanese pinball pachinko パチンコ 27a

Japanese wrestling sumō 相撲 27b

jaw ago 顎 12a, 40b

jay kakesu かけす 15b

jazz jazu ジャズ 25j, 28c

jealous shittobukai (adj) 嫉妬深い 11e

jealousy shitto 嫉妬 11e

jeep jīpu ジープ 33a

jellyfish kurage くらげ 15c

jest karakau (v) からかう 17a

Jew Yudayajin ユダヤ人 11d

jewel hōseki 宝石 25i

jeweler hōshokuten 宝飾店 25i

Jewish Yudayajin no (adj) ユダヤ人の 11d

job shigoto 仕事 11f, 38a

job desciption shokumu naiyō 職務内容 38d

jog jogingu suru (v) ジョギングする 12b, 27a

jogging jogingu ジョギング 27a

joke jōdan 冗談 17a

Jordan Yorudan ヨルダン 30b

journalist jānarisuto ジャーナリスト 20a, 38a

joy yorokobi 喜び 21a

Judaism Yudayakyō ユダヤ教 11d

judge saibankan 裁判官 41

judge hanketsu o kudasu (v) 判決を下す 41

judgment handan 判断 22a

judo jūdō 柔道 27b

juice jūsu ジュース 24k

July shichigatsu 七月 5b

June rokugatsu 六月 5b

jungle mitsurin 密林 13b

junior college tandai 短大 11f, 38b

junior high school chūgaku 中学 11f, 37a, 38b

Jupiter mokusei 木星 13a

jury baishin 陪審 41

justice seigi 正義 22a, 41

just now tatta ima たった今 4e

K

karate karate 空手 27b

keep quiet kuchi o hikaeru (v) 口を控える 17a

Kenya Kenia ケニア 30b

ketchup kechappu ケチャップ 24j

kettle yakan やかん 23d

key kagi 鍵 23d, 35b

keyboard kībōdo キーボード 19d, 42b

keyboard kenban 鍵盤 28c

keyboard instruments kenban gakki 鍵盤楽器 28c

keyboard operator kībōdo operētā キーボードオペレーター 42b

kick keru (v) 蹴る 27b

kidney jinzō 腎臓 12a, 24c, 40a

kill korosu (v) 殺す 39b

killer satsujinsha 殺人者 39b

kilogram kiroguramu キログラム 3a

kilometer kiro キロ 3a

kind shinsetsu na (adj) 親切な 11e, 21a

kindergarten yōchien 幼稚園 37a

kindness shinsetsu 親切 11e

king kingu キング 27a

king kokuō 国王 43

kingfisher kawasemi かわせみ 15b

kiosk kiosuku キオスク 36a

kiss kisu/seppun キス／接吻 11c, 21b

kiss kisusuru/seppunsuru (v) キスする／接吻する 11c, 21b

kitchen daidokoro 台所 23b

kitchen sink nagashi 流し 23a

kiwi kīwī キーウィー 24f

knapsack nappuzakku ナップザック 27b, 31, 36b

knee hiza 膝 12a

knife hōchō 包丁 23d

knife naifu ナイフ 24l, 39b

knight naito ナイト 27a

know shiru (v) 知る 22b

know (someone) shitteiru (v) 知っている 16b

knowledge chishiki 知識 22a

knowledgeable yoku shitteiru (adj) 良く知っている 22a

knuckles kobushi 拳 12a

Korea Kankoku 韓国 30b

Korean Kankokujin 韓国人 30d

Korean (language) Kankokugo 韓国語 30d

Kuala Lumpur Kuararunpūru クアラルンプール 30c

Kuwait Kuwēto クウェート 30b

Kyoto Kyōto 京都 30c

L

labor/trade union rōdōkumiai 労働組合 43

Labor Thanksgiving Day kinrō kansha no hi 勤労感謝の日 5f

laboratory jikkenshitsu 実験室 13c, 37c

labor union rōdō kumiai 労働組合 38d

ladle hishaku ひしゃく 23d

lady fujin 婦人 11a

ladybug tentōmushi てんとう虫 15d

laity hirashinto 平信徒 11d

lake mizuumi 湖 13b, 36b

lamb kohitsuji 子羊 15a

lamb kohitsuji no niku 子羊の肉 24c

lamb ramu ラム 24c

lamp ranpu ランプ 23c, 35c

land rikuchi 陸地 13b

land chakurikusuru (v) 着陸する 32c

landing gear chakuriku sōchi 着陸装置 32c

landlord yanushi 家主 23g

landscape keshiki 景色 13b

lane (traffic) shasen 車線 33c

language laboratory gaikokugo rabo 外国語ラボ 37c

large ōkii (adj) 大きい 11a

large bill ōkii osatsu 大きいお札 26

large intestine daichō 大腸 40a

large teapot (Japanese) dobin 土瓶 23d, 24l

lark hibari 雲雀 15b

laser rēzā レーザー 42a

laser beam rēzā kōsen レーザー光線 42a

last tsuzuku (vi) 続く 4e

last tsuzukeru (vt) 続ける 4e

last saigo no (adj) 最後の 4e

last mae no (adj) 前の 4e

last a long time nagai aida tsuzuku 長い 間続く 4e

last a short time tankikan tsuzuku 短期 間続く 4e

last month sengetsu 先月 4e

last night yūbe ゆうべ 4a

last year kyonen 去年 4e

late osoi (adj) 遅い 4e, 32b, 34

late osoku (adv) 遅く 4e

late okurete (adv) 遅れて 32b

Latin America Raten Amerika ラテン アメリカ 30b

latitude ido 緯度 13e

laugh warau (v) 笑う 11e, 21a

laughter waraigoe 笑い声 11e

laughter warai 笑い 21a

launch pad hasshadai 発射台 42a

laundromat koin randorī コインランド リー 25g

laundry sentakumono 洗濯物 25g

lava yōgan 溶岩 13b

law hōgaku 法学 37e

law hōritsu 法律 41

lawful, legal gōhō no (adj) 合法の 41

lawsuit, charge soshō 訴訟 41

lawyer bengoshi 弁護士 38a, 41

laxative gezai 下剤 25h

layoff ichiji kaiko 一時解雇 38d

lay person hirashinto 平信徒 11d

laziness bushō 無精 11e

lazy bushō na (adj) 無精な 11e

lead namari 鉛 13c

leaded gas regyurā レギュラー 33c

leaf ha 葉 14a

leap year uruudoshi うるう年 5b

learn narau (v) 習う 22b, 37f

learn by memory ankisuru (v) 暗記す る 37f

leather kawa 皮 13c, 25l

leave, depart shuppatsusuru (v) 出発す る 3e

leave, depart hasshasuru (v) 発車する 34

Lebanon Rebanon レバノン 30b

lecture kōgi 講義 17a, 37f

lecture kōgisuru (v) 講義する 17a, 37f

leek naganegi 長ねぎ 14e, 24e

left hidari 左 3d

left wing sayoku 左翼 43

leg ashi 脚 12a

legislation rippō 立法 43

lemon remon レモン 14d, 24f, 24j

lemonade remonēdo レモネード 24k

length nagasa 長さ 3a, 3b

lengthen nagakusuru (v) 長くする 25m

lens renzu レンズ 25d

lentil renzumame レンズ豆 14e

Leo shishiza 獅子座 5d

leopard hyō 豹 15a

less yori sukunai より少ない 3c

lesson jugyō 授業 37f

Let me introduce you to ... ... san ni shōkai sasete kudasai. さんに紹介させ てください。 16b

letter moji 文字 8a

letter tegami 手紙 19d

letter (of the alphabet) arufabetto no moji アルファベットの文字 19c

letter carrier, mailman yūbin haitatsu 郵便配達 19e

letterhead binsen tōbu no jōhō insatsu 便箋頭部の情報印刷 19d

lettuce retasu レタス 14e, 24e

level heimen 平面 3d

Level Crossing fumikiri 踏切 33d

liar usotsuki 嘘つき 17a

liberal kakushinteki na (adj) 革新的な 11e, 43

liberal kakushinshugisha (n) 革新主義 者 11e

liberal party kakushintō 革新党 43

Libra tenbinza 天秤座 5d

librarian toshokan-in 図書館員 37d

library toshokan 図書館 37c

license plate nanbā purēto ナンバープ レート 33e

lid futa 蓋 23d

lie uso 嘘 17a

lie uso o tsuku (v) 嘘をつく 17a

lie down yokotawaru (v) 横たわる 3e

life jinsei 人生 11c

life imprisonment muki chōeki 無期懲
役 41
life jacket kyūmeidōgi 救命胴着 32c
life sentence shūshinkei 終身刑 41
lifetime job security shūshin koyō
seido 終身雇用制度 38d
lift mochiageru (v) 持ち上げる 3e
light karui (adj) 軽い 3b, 11a, 13d, 31
light akari 明かり 6a
light akari 灯り 23e
light akarui (adj) 明るい 7b
light hikari/kōsen 光/光線 13a
light (bulb) denkyū 電球 25b
light blue akarui ao 明るい青 7a
light cotton kimono yukata 浴衣 35c
lighter raitā ライター 25e
light music kei ongaku 軽音楽 28c
lightning inazuma 稲妻 6a
lights (car) raito ライト 33e
lights akari 明かり 35c
light year kōnen 光年 13a
like konomu (v) 好む 11e, 21b
liking konomi 好み 21b
lily yuri 百合 14b
lima bean rimamame リマ豆 14e
limited express train tokkyū 特急 34
limousine rimujin リムジーン 33a
line sen 線 2b
line gyō 行 19c
line retsu 列 26
linen asa 麻 25l
line up narabu (v) 並ぶ 26
linguistics gengogaku 言語学 37e
lion raion ライオン 15a
lip kuchibiru 唇 12a, 40b
lipstick kuchibeni 口紅 25f
liqueur rikyūru リキュール 24k
liquid ekitai 液体 13c
liquor store sakaya 酒屋 24n
listen ... ... o, kiite kudasai. を、聞いて
下さい。 17b
listen to (intently) kiku (v) 聴く 12c
listen to kiku (v) 聞く 17a, 20b, 37f
liter rittoru リットル 3a
literal mojidōri no (adj) 文字通りの
17a
literature bungaku 文学 28d, 37e
litigate soshō o okosu (v) 訴訟を起こす
41
litigation soshō 訴訟 41
little chiisai (adj) 小さい 3c
little finger koyubi 小指 12a

live sumu (v) 住む 11c, 11f
live in sumikomu (v) 住み込む 23f
lively ikiikishita (adj) 生き生きした
7b, 11e
lively ikiikito (adv) 生き生きと 11e
liver kanzō 肝臓 12a, 24c
liver rebā レバー 24c
living room ima 居間 23b
lizard tokage とかげ 15c
loan rōn ローン 26
lobby robī ロビー 28a, 35b
lobster robusutā ロブスター 15c, 24d
local call shinai denwa 市内電話 18b
local government worker chihō
kōmuin 地方公務員 38a
local train kakueki teisha (no kisha) 各
駅停車(の汽車) 34
locate ichisuru (v) 位置する 13e
location ichi 位置 13e
logarithm taisū 対数 1f
logarithmic taisū no (adj) 対数の 1f
London Rondon ロンドン 30c
long nagai (adj) 長い 3b, 37f
long-distance call chōkyori denwa 長距
離電話 18b
long-term chōkiteki na (adj) 長期的な
4e
longitude keido 経度 13e
look nagameru (v) 眺める 12c
look at, watch miru (v) 見る 20b
look for something sagasu (v) 探す
25a
look forward to kitaisuru (v) 期待する
4e
loose yuttarishita (adj) ゆったりした
25l
loose change kozeni 小銭 26
loosen yurumeru (v) ゆるめる 25m
loquat biwa びわ 14d
Los Angeles Rosanjerusu ロサンジェ
ルス 30c
lose makeru (v) 負ける 27b
lose a lawsuit haisosuru (v) 敗訴する
41
lose weight yaseru (v) 痩せる 11a
loss haiboku 敗北 27b
lost and found ishitsubutsugakari 遺失
物係 32a
lotus root renkon れんこん 14e, 24e
loudspeaker raudosupīkā ラウドスピ
ーカー 20b
louse (lice) shirami 虱 15d

lovable airashii *(adj)* 愛らしい 11e

love ai 愛 11c, 11e, 21b

love aisuru *(v)* 愛する 11c, 11e, 21b

love affair renai 恋愛 10b

lover koibito 恋人 10b

low hikui 低い 6c

low season isogashikunai toki 忙しくないとき 30d

low tide kanchō 干潮 13b

luggage nimotsu 荷物 35b

luggage compartment tenimotsu dana 手荷物棚 32c

lukewarm namanurui *(adj)* 生ぬるい 24p

lunar eclipse gesshoku 月食 13a

lunar module tsuki chakurikusen 月着陸船 42a

lunch hirugohan 昼御飯 24a

lunch chūshoku 昼食 24a

lung hai 肺 12a, 40a

luxury hotel kōkyū hoteru 高級ホテル 35a

lymphatic system rinpasen リンパ腺 40a

M

mackerel saba 鯖 15c, 24d

madness kyōki 狂気 11e

magazine zasshi 雑誌 20a, 25o, 37f

maggot uji 蛆 15d

magistrate keihanzai no hanji 軽犯罪の判事 41

magnolia mokuren もくれん 14c

mahjong mājan 麻雀 27a

maid mēdo メード 35b

mail yūbin 郵便 19e

mail (letters) dasu *(v)* 出す 19e

mail (package) okuru *(v)* 送る 19e

mailbox (street) posuto ポスト 19e

mailbox (home) yūbinuke 郵便受け 23a

mail delivery yūbin haitatsu 郵便配達 19e

main shu *(adj)* 主 8a

main course meinkōsu メインコース 24g

main office jimushitsu 事務室 37c

make a call denwa o kakeru *(v)* 電話をかける 18b

make a movie eiga o seisakusuru *(v)* 映画を制作する 28a

make mistakes machigaeru *(v)* 間違える 37f

make the bed beddo o totonoeru *(v)* ベッドを整える 23f

makeup (o)keshō （お)化粧 12d, 25f

Malay (language) Marēgo マレー語 30d

Malaysia Marēshia マレーシア 30b

Malaysian Marējin マレー人 30d

male dansei 男性 11a

male otoko 男 11a

malicious akui ni michita *(adj)* 悪意に満ちた 11e

malign, speak badly chūshōsuru *(v)* 中傷する 17a

malleable katansei no aru *(adj)* 可鍛性のある 13d

mammal honyurui 哺乳類 15a

man dansei 男性 11a

manager manējā マネージャー 26, 35b, 38d

mandarin orange mikan みかん 14d, 24f

mandarin orange tree mikan no ki みかんの木 14c

mandolin mandorin マンドリン 28c

mango mangō マンゴー 14d, 24f

manicure manikyua マニキュア 12d

Manila Manira マニラ 30c

Many thanks! Kansha shimasu. 感謝します。 16c

map chizu 地図 13e, 37b

maple tree kaede 楓 14c

March sangatsu 三月 5b

margarine māgarin マーガリン 24j

margin yohaku 余白 19c

marinated marine shita *(adj)* マリネした 24b

marine animal kaisei dōbutsu 海生動物 15c

marital status kekkon shikaku 結婚資格 11c, 38b

marker majikku mākā マジックマーカー 19d

market ichiba 市場 24n

market shijō 市場 38d

marlin kajiki かじき 15c

marmalade māmarēdo マーマレード 24j

marriage, matrimony kekkon 結婚 11c

married kikon no *(adj)* 既婚の 11c, 11f

married kikon 既婚 38b

marry (someone) ~ to kekkonsuru *(v)* ～と結婚する 11c

Mars kasei 火星 13a

mascara masukara マスカラ 12d, 25f

masculine dansei 男性 8a

masculine dansei no *(adj)* 男性の 11a

mask masuku マスク 27b

masked play (Japanese) Nō 能 28e

masking tape masukingu tēpu マスキングテープ 25b

mass ryō 量 3b

Mass misa ミサ 11d

massage massāji マッサージ 12d

master shūshigō 修士号 37f

masterpiece meisaku 名作 28b

matches matchi マッチ 25e

material genryō 原料 13c

mathematics sūgaku 数学 37e

matte tsuyakeshi no *(adj)* 艶消しの 25d

matter busshitsu 物質 13c

maximum saidai 最大 3b

maximum saikō (no) *(adj)* 最高(の) 6c

maximum saidai no *(adj)* 最大の 31

May gogatsu 五月 5b

May I come in? Haittemo yoroshii desu ka. 入ってもよろしいですか。 16c

May I help you? Otetsudai shimashō ka. お手伝いしましょうか。 16c

mayonnaise mayonēzu マヨネーズ 24j

me watakushi o 私を 8e

meadow sōgen 草原 13b

meal shokuji 食事 24a

mean imisuru *(v)* 意味する 17a

meaning imi 意味 17a

measles hashika はしか 40a

measure hakaru *(v)* 計る 3b

measurement sunpō 寸法 31

measuring tape tēpumejā テープメジャー 3b

meat niku 肉 24c

mechanic shūriko 修理工 33c

mechanic jidōsha shūriko 自動車修理工 38a

mechanical shudō no *(adj)* 手動の 25b

mechanical pencil shāpu penshiru シャープペンシル 19d

medicine kusuri 薬 25h, 40a

medicine igaku 医学 37e

medium hōhō 方法 3b

medium chūkan no *(adj)* 中間の 3b

medium midiamu no *(adj)* ミディアムの 24b

medium (average) height chūgurai no se no takasa 中ぐらいの背の高さ 11a

meet au *(v)* 会う 16b

melon meron メロン 14d, 24f

melting point yūten 融点 6c

membrane genkeishitsumaku 原形質膜 14a

memorize ankisuru *(v)* 暗記する 37f

memory memori メモリ 42b

men's shop shinshifuku ten 紳士服店 25k

mend tsukurou *(v)* 繕う 25g

mention noberu *(v)* 述べる 17a

menu menyū メニュー 24g, 42b

mercury suigin 水銀 6c, 13c

Mercury suisei 水星 13a

Merge gōryū 合流 33d

meridian shigosen 子午線 13e

Merry Christmas! Kurisumasu omedetō. クリスマスおめでとう。 16c, 29c

message dengon 伝言 18b, 35b

metal kinzoku 金属 13c

metamorphosis hentai 変態 15d

metaphor inyu 隠喩 17a

meteor ryūsei 流星 13a

meter mētoru メートル 3a

methane metan メタン 13c

metropolis to 都 11f

Mexico Mekishiko メキシコ 30b

microbe biseibutsu 微生物 15d

microcomputer maikurokonpyūta マイクロコンピュータ 42b

microphone maikurohon マイクロホン 20b

microscope kenbikyō 顕微鏡 13c

microwave chōtanpa 超短波 42a

microwave oven denshirenji 電子レンジ 23d

Middle and Near East Chūkintō 中近東 30b

middle finger nakayubi 中指 12c

midnight mayonaka 真夜中 4a

Milan Mirano ミラノ 30c

mild atatakai 暖かい 6a

mild karakunai *(adj)* 辛くない 24p

milk gyūnyū 牛乳 24h

milk miruku ミルク 24h

millimeter miri ミリ 3a

millionth hyakumanbanme 百万番目 1b

mime mugon geki 無言劇 28e

mind kokoro 心 22a

mineral kōbutsu 鉱物 13c

mineral water mineraru wōtā ミネラル ウォーター 24k

minimum saishō 最小 3b

minimum saitei (no) *(adj)* 最低の 6c

minister bokushi 牧師 11d

minister daijin 大臣 43

mint minto ミント 14e, 24j

minus mainasu kigō マイナス記号 1e

minus mainasu マイナス 6c

minute fun 分 4c

mirror kagami 鏡 23c, 25f, 35c

mischievous itazurazuki na *(adj)* いたず らずきな 11e

miss norisokonau *(v)* 乗り損なう 34

Miss, Ms. san さん 11f, 16b

missile misairu ミサイル 42a

mistake machigai 間違い 37f

mix mazeru *(v)* 混ぜる 24o

modal johō no *(adj)* 叙法の 8a

modem modemu モデム 42b

modern dance modan dansu モダンダ ンス 28c

molar kyūshi 臼歯 40b

mole mogura もぐら 15a

molecular bunshi no *(adj)* 分子の 13c

molecular formula bunshishiki 分子式 13c

molecular model bunshi kōzō mokei 分 子構造模型 13c

molecular structure bunshi kōzō 分子 構造 13c

molecule bunshi 分子 13c, 42a

moment shunkan 瞬間 4c

monarchy kunshusei 君主制 43

Monday getsuyōbi 月曜日 5a

money okane お金 26

money order (post office) yūbin kawase 郵便為替 19e

money order kawase 為替 26

monk shūdōshi 修道士 11d

monkey saru 猿 15a

monkey wrench jizai supana 自在スパ ナ 25b

monorail vehicle monorēru モノレー ル 42a

month tsuki 月 4c, 5b, 38b

monthly maitsuki no *(adj)* 毎月の 4c, 5b

monthly magazine gekkanshi 月刊誌 20a

month of the year ichinen no tsuki 一 年の月 5b

monument kinentō 記念塔 36a

mood (grammar) dōshi no hō 動詞の 法 8a

mood kigen 機嫌 11e

mood kibun 気分 21a

moon tsuki 月 5c, 6a, 13a

moonbeam, ray gekkō 月光 13a

morality dōtoku 道徳 44b

more motto *(adv)* もっと 3c

morning asa 朝 4a

morning glory asagao 朝顔 14b

mortgage jutaku rōn 住宅ローン 26

mortgage teitōken 抵当権 26

Moscow Mosukuwa モスクワ 30c

mosque mosuku モスク 11d

mosquito ka 蚊 15d

motel moteru モテル 35a

moth ga 蛾 15d

mother haha 母 10a

mother okāsan お母さん 10a

mother-in-law gibo 義母 10a

mother-in-law giri no okāsan 義理のお 母さん 10a

motion ugoki 動き 3e

motor enjin エンジン 33e

motorcycle ōtobai オートバイ 33a

mountain yama 山 13b

mountain boot tozangutsu 登山靴 27b, 36b

mountain chain sanmyaku 山脈 13b

mountain climbing tozan 登山 27b, 36b

mountainous yama no ōi (adj) 山の多 い 13b

mouse nezumi ねずみ 15a

moustache kuchihige くちひげ 12a

mouth kuchi 口 12a, 40b

move ugoku *(vi)* 動く 3e

move ugokasu *(vt)* 動かす 3e

move hikkosu *(v)* 引っ越す 23f

movement undō 運動 3e

movie, film eiga 映画 28a

movie director eiga kantoku 映画監督 28a, 38a

movie star eiga sutā 映画スター 28a

movie theater eiga gekijō 映画劇場 28a

Mr., Mrs., Ms. san さん 11f, 16b

muffler mafurā マフラー 33e

muggy mushiatsui (adj) 蒸し暑い 6a

mule raba らば 15a

multiple baisū no (adj) 倍数の 1f

multiplication kakezan 掛け算 1e

multiplication table kuku no hyō 九々 の表 1e

multiplied by kaketa 掛けた 1e

multiply kakeru (v) 掛ける 1e

mumble bosoboso iu (v) ぼそぼそ言う 17a

murder satsujin 殺人 39b

murder korosu (v) 殺す 39b

murderer satsujinsha 殺人者 39b

murmur tsubuyaku つぶやく 17a

muscle kinniku 筋肉 12a, 40a

museum bijutsukan 美術館 28b, 36a

mushroom kinoko 茸 14e, 24e

music ongaku 音楽 25j, 28c, 37e

musical myūjikaru ミュージカル 25j

musician ongakuka 音楽家 28c, 38a

Muslim (Moslem) kaikyōto 回教徒 11d

mussel mūrugai ムール貝 15c, 24d

mustard karashi からし 24j

mustard masutādo マスタード 24j

mute gengoshōgai no (adj) 言語障害の 12c

mutton yōniku/maton 洋肉/マトン 24c

mutual sōgoteki na (adj) 相互的な 43

my watakushi no 私の 8d

My God! Komatta. (inf) 困った。 21c

My name is ... Watakushi no namae wa, ... desu. 私の名前は...です。 11f, 16b

myself watakushi jishin 私自身 8g

mystery misuterī ミステリー 20a, 25o

myth shinwa 神話 11d, 28d

mythology shinwa 神話 28d

My tooth hurts! Ha ga, itai desu. 歯が、 痛いです。 40b

N

nag (torment, pester) gamigami iu (v) がみがみ言う 17a

nail (hardware) kugi 釘 25b

nail clippers tsume kiri 爪きり 25f

nail polish manikyuaeki マニキュア液 12d, 25f

nail polish remover jokōeki 除光液 25f

name namae 名前 11f, 38b

nap hirune 昼寝 12b

nap hirunesuru (v) 昼寝する 12b

napkin napukin ナプキン 23d, 24l

narrow semai (adj) 狭い 3b

nation kokka 国家 13e, 30a

national kokka no (adj) 国家の 13e

National Foundation Day kenkoku kinenbi 建国記念日 5f

national government worker kokka kōmuin 国家公務員 38a

nationality kokuseki 国籍 11f, 38b

natural shizen no (adj) 自然の 13b

natural gas tennen gasu 天然ガス 13c

natural number shizensū 自然数 1d

natural resources tennenshigen 天然資 源 13c, 44a

natural science shizen kagaku 自然科 学 37e

nature shizen 自然 13b

near chikai (adj) 近い 3d

near chikaku ni (adv) 近くに 3d

near ... ... no chikaku ni の近くに 36c

neat sapparishita (adj) さっぱりした 11e

neck kubi 首 12a

necklace nekkuresu ネックレス 25i

nectarine nekutarin ネクタリン 14d, 24f

need hitsuyō 必要 21a

need iru (v) いる 21a

needle hari 針 40b

negative hitei (adj) 否定 8a

negative hiteiteki na (adj) 否定的な 21a

negative number fusū 負数 1d

neigh inanaku (v) いななく 15a

nephew oi 甥 10a

nephew oigosan おいごさん 10a

Neptune kaiōsei 海王星 13a

nerves shinkei 神経 40a

nervous system shinkei keitō 神経系統 40a

nest su 巣 15b

net netto ネット 27b

network hōsōmō 放送網 20b

neuter chūsei 中性 8a

neutron chūseishi 中性子 13c, 42a

never kesshite ~ shinai *(adv)* 決して~
しない 4e

New Year's Day ganjitsu 元日 5f

New Year's Day shinnen 新年 29a

New Year's Eve ōmisoka no ban 大晦
日の晩 5f, 29a

New York Nyūyōku ニューヨーク
30c

New Zealand Nyūjīrando ニュージー
ランド 30b

newlyweds shinkon fusai 新婚夫妻
11c

new moon shingetsu 新月 13a

news nyūsu ニュース 20a

newscast nyūsu hōsō ニュース放送
20b

newspaper shinbun 新聞 20a, 25o

news report nyūsu bangumi ニュース
番組 20b

newsstand shinbun uriba 新聞売り場
34

nice ii *(adj)* いい 11e

niece mei 姪 10a

niece meigosan めいごさん 10a

night yoru 夜 4a

nightingale naichingēru ナイチンゲー
ル 15b

nine ku/kyū 九 1a

nine kokonotsu 九つ 1a

nine hundred kyūhyaku 九百 1a

nineteen jūku/jūkyū 十九 1a

nineteen thousand ichimankyūsen 一万
九千 1a

nine thousand kyūsen 九千 1a

ninety kyūjū 九十 1a

ninety thousand kyūman 九万 1a

ninth kyūbanme 九番目 1b

ninth daiku 第九 1b

ninth kokonotsume 九つ目 1b

nitrogen chisso 窒素 13c

No. Iie. いいえ。 16c

No! Dame desu. 駄目です。 16c

No Entry shinnyū kinshi 進入禁止 33d

No Left Turn sasetsu kinshi 左折禁止
33d

No Parking chūsha kinshi 駐車禁止
33d

No Passing oikoshi kinshi 追い越し禁
止 33d

No Right Turn usetsu kinshi 右折禁止
33d

No Stopping teisha kinshi 停車禁止
33d

No Thoroughfare tsūkōdome 通行止
33d

No U-Turn yūtān kinshi ユーターン禁
止 33d

nobody daremo ~ nai だれも ~ない 8i

noise sōon 騒音 12c

noisy yakamashii 喧しい 12c

nonconformist hijunnōsha 非順応者
11e

none daremo ~ nai 誰も~ない 8i

nonfiction nonfikushon ノンフィク
ション 20a

nonsmoking kin-en 禁煙 34

noon hiruma 昼間 4a

no one dare mo ~ nai 誰も~ない 3c,
8i

No problem! Mondai arimasen. 問題あ
りません。 22a

north kita 北 3d

North America Kita Amerika 北アメリ
カ 30b

North Pole hokkyoku 北極 13e

northern kita no 北の 3d

Norway Noruwē ノルウェー 30b

Norwegian Noruwējin ノルウェー人
30d

Norwegian (language) Noruwēgo ノル
ウェー語 30d

nose hana 鼻 12a

No smoking kin-en 禁煙 32a

nostril bikō 鼻孔 12a, 40a

Not bad! Waruku arimasen. 悪くあり
ません。 16a

note mijikai tegami 短い手紙 19e

note chūshaku 注釈 20a

note (music) onpu 音符 28c

note nōto ノート 37f

notebook nōto ノート 25c

notebook chōmen 帳面 37b

not guilty muzai 無罪 41

not guilty shiro 白 41

nothing nani mo ~ nai 何も~ない
3c, 8i

not nice, odious iya na *(adj)* 嫌な 11e

noun meishi 名詞 8a

novel shōsetsu 小説 20a, 25o, 28d

November jūichigatsu 十一月 5b

now ima/genzai 今/現在 4e

now ... Ima ... 今 17b

nowadays genzai dewa 現在では 4e

nowhere dokonimo *(adv)* どこにも 3d

n-sided figures enuhenkei エヌ辺形 2a

nth root enu jō kon エヌ乗根 1e

nuclear energy kaku enerugī 核エネルギー 13c, 42a

nuclear industry genshiryoku sangyō 原子力産業 42a

nuclear reactor genshiro 原子炉 42a

nuclear war kaku sensō 核戦争 44b

nuclear weapon kaku heiki 核兵器 44b

nucleus genshikaku 原子核 13c

nucleus kaku 核 14a

number kazu/sūji 数/数字 1d, 8a

number bangō o tsukeru *(v)* 番号を付ける 1d

number (address) banchi 番地 38b

numeral sūji 数字 1d

numerical kazu no *(adj)* 数の 1d

nun nisō 尼僧 11d

nurse kangofu 看護婦 38a, 40a

nursery school hoikuen 保育園 37a

nut natto ナット 25b

nylon nairon ナイロン 25l

O

OK! Ii desu yo. いいですよ。 16c

oak tree kashi 樫 14c

oat ōtomugi オート麦 24i

oatmeal ōtomīru オートミール 24i

obesity himan 肥満 11a

obituary shibōkiji 死亡記事 20a

object (grammar) mokutekigo 目的語 8a

object igi o tonaeru *(v)* 異議を唱える 41

objection igi 異議 41

oboe ōboe オーボエ 28c

obstinate gōjō na *(adj)* 強情な 11e

obtuse-angled donkaku *(adj)* 鈍角 2a

obtuse angle donkaku 鈍角 2b

occasionally tokidoki *(adj)* 時々 4e

Occidental seiōjin 西欧人 11d

occupation shokugyō 職業 38a

ocean taiyō 大洋 13c

octagon hakkakukei 八角形 2a

octahedron hachimentai 八面体 2a

October jūgatsu 十月 5b

octopus tako 蛸 15c, 24d

odd number kisū 奇数 1d

of, ~'s (possessive marker) no の 8j

offend kanjō o kizutsukeru *(v)* 感情を傷付ける 17a

offer mōshideru *(v)* 申し出る 17a

office ofisu オフィス 38d

office automation ofisu ōtomēshon オフィスオートメーション 42b

office hours shinryō jikan 診療時間 40b

office worker (female) ōeru オーエル 38a

office worker (male) sararīman サラリーマン 38a

often yoku *(adv)* よく 4e

oil sekiyu 石油 13c

oil oiru オイル 24j, 33e

oil filter oiru firutā オイルフィルター 33c

oil paint aburaenogu 油絵の具 28b

ointment nankō 軟膏 25h

old toshitotta *(adj)* 年とった 11b

old age rōgo 老後 11b

older toshiue no *(adj)* 年上の 11b

older brother ani 兄 11b

older sister ane 姉 11b

olive orību オリーブ 14d

omelette omuretsu オムレツ 24h

on ue no *(adj)* 上の 3d

on ue ni *(adj)* 上に 3d

on ni/de に/で 8j

on Mondays getsuyōbi ni 月曜日に 5a

on Saturdays doyōbi ni 土曜日に 5a

on Sundays nichiyōbi ni 日曜日に 5a

once katsute *(adv)* かつて 4e

once in a while tokidoki 時々 4e

once upon a time mukashimukashi 昔々 4e

one ichi 一 1a

one hitotsu 一つ 1a

one hito 人 8i

one's self jibun 自分 8g

one (bound object) issatsu 一冊 1a

one (floor) ikkai 一階 1a

one (liquid or dry measure) ippai 一杯 1a

one (long, thin object) ippon 一本 1a

one (person) hitori 一人 1a

one (small object) ikko/hitotsu 一個/一つ 1a

one (thin, flat object) ichimai 一枚 1a

one-fifth gobun no ichi 五分の一 1c

one-fourth yonbun no ichi 四分の一 1c

one-half nibun no ichi 二分の一 1c

one-third sanbun no ichi 三分の一 1c

one-way ticket katamichi ken 片道券 30a

One Way ippōtsūkō 一方通行 33d

one billion jūoku 十億 1a

one hundred hyaku 百 1a

one hundred and one hyakuichi 百一 1a

one hundred and two hyakuni 百二 1a

one hundred billion sen-oku 千億 1a

one hundred million ichioku 一億 1a

one hundred ten hyakujū 百十 1a

one hundred thousand jūman 十万 1a

one hundred twenty hyakunijū 百二十 1a

one million hyakuman 百万 1a

one million and one hyakuman-ichi 百万一 1a

one million and two hyakuman-ni 百万二 1a

one thousand sen 千 1a

one thousand and one sen-ichi 千一 1a

one thousand ten senjū 千十 1a

one trillion itchō 一兆 1a

one turn (360°) ichi kaiten 一回転 2b

onion tamanegi 玉葱 14e, 24e

only dake だけ 4e

on sale sēru セール 25a

on the air hōsōchū 放送中 20b

on time teikoku ni (adv) 定刻に 32b

on time jikandōri ni (adv) 時間通りに 34

opal opāru オパール 25i

opaque futōmei na/kusunda (adj) 不透明な／くすんだ 7b, 13d

open kaitensuru (v) 開店する 25a

open an account kōza o hiraku 口座を開く 26

opening hours eigyō jikan 営業時間 25a

Open your mouth! Kuchi o, akete kudasai. 口を開けてください。 40b

opera opera オペラ 25j, 28c

operating room shujutsushitsu 手術室 40a

operation shujutsu 手術 40a

operator kōkanshu 交換手 18b

opinion iken 意見 22a

oppose hantaisuru (v) 反対する 21a

opposite angle taichōkaku 対頂角 2b

optician megane ya 眼鏡屋 40a

optimism rakutenshugi 楽天主義 11e

optimist rakutenshugisha 楽天主義者 11e

optimistic rakutenteki na (adj) 楽天的な 11e

or matawa 又は 8k

oral kōtō no (adj) 口頭の 17a

oral exam mensetsu shiken 面接試験 37f

orally kōtō de (adv) 口頭で 17a

orange (color) orenji iro オレンジ色 7a

orange orenji オレンジ 14d, 24f

orange tree orenji no ki オレンジの木 14c

orbit kidō 軌道 13a

orbit kidō ni noru (vi) 軌道に乗る 13a

orbit kidō ni noseru (vt) 軌道に乗せる 13a

orchestra ōkesutora オーケストラ 25j, 28c

orchestra conductor ōkesutora no shikisha オーケストラの指揮者 28c

orchid ran 蘭 14b

order meirei 命令 17a

order meireisuru (v) 命令する 17a

order chūmonsuru (v) 注文する 24o

ordinal number josū 序数 1d

organ naizō 内臓 12a

organ (music) orugan オルガン 28c

organic yūki no (adj) 有機の 13c

organism yūkibutsu/yūkitai 有機物/有機体 14a, 15d

Oriental Ajiajin アジア人 11d

original sōsakuteki na (adj) 創作的な 11e

Orthodox Girishaseikyō no (adj) ギリシャ正教の 11d

Osaka Ōsaka 大阪 30c

ostrich dachō だちょう 15b

others hoka no hito 他の人 8i

otter rakko ラッコ 15c

our watakushitachi no 私達の 8d

ourselves watakushitachi jishin 私達自身 8g

out soto e (adv) 外へ 39a

outlet konsento コンセント 25b

out of court settlement jidan 示談 41

out of focus pinboke no *(adj)* ピンボケ の 25d

outside soto no *(adj)* 外の 3d

outside soto ni *(adv)* 外に 3d

outside ... ... no soto ni の外に 36c

outskirts, suburbs kōgai 郊外 30a

outspokenly enryonaku *(adv)* 遠慮なく 17a

overhead projector ōbaheddo purojekutā オーバーヘッドプロジェ クター 37b

over there asoko あそこ 3d

overtime work zangyō 残業 38d

owl fukurō ふくろう 15b

ownership papers shoyū shōsho 所有証 書 33b

ox oushi 雄牛 15a

oxtail okkusutēru オックステール 24c

oxygen sanso 酸素 13c

oyster kaki 蛎 15c, 24d

P

Pacific taiheiyō no *(adj)* 太平洋の 6a

Pacific Ocean taiheiyō 太平洋 13b

pack (one's bags/luggage) nizukurisuru *(v)* 荷造りする 31

package kozutsumi 小包 19e

package tsutsumi 包 25a

pad hagitorishiki hikkiyōshi 剥ぎ取り 式筆記用紙 19d

pagan ikyōto 異教徒 11d

page pēji 頁 19d, 20a

pail teoke 手おけ 23d

pain itami 痛み 40a

painful itai *(adj)* 痛い 40a

painkiller chintsūzai 鎮痛剤 40a

paint (house) penki o nuru *(v)* ペンキを 塗る 23f

paint e o kaku *(v)* 絵を書く 28b

paint (art) egaku *(v)* 描く 7c

paint (houses, rooms) penki o nuru *(v)* ペンキを塗る 7c

painter (artist) gaka 画家 7c, 28b, 38a

painter (houses, rooms) penkiya ペン キ屋 7c, 38a

painting e/kaiga 絵／絵画 23c, 27a

pair kumi/tsui 組／対 3c

pair issoku 一足 25a

pajamas pajama パジャマ 25k

Pakistan Pakisutan パキスタン 30b

palate kōgai 口蓋 40b

pale usui *(adj)* 薄い 7b

palette paretto パレット 28b

palm tree yashi no ki やしの木 14c

pamphlet, brochure panfuretto パンフ レット 20a

pan hiranabe 平鍋 23d

pancreas suizō 膵臓 12a

panda panda パンダ 15a

panties pantī パンティー 25k

pantomime monomane 物まね 28e

pants zubon ズボン 25k

pantyhose pantīsutokkingu パンティー ストッキング 25k

papaya papaiya パパイヤ 14d, 24f

paper kami 紙 19d, 25c, 37b

paper clip kurippu クリップ 25c

paprika papurika パプリカ 24j

paragraph danraku 段落 19c

parakeet sekiseiinko セキセイインコ 15b

parallelepiped heikōrokumentai 平行六 面体 2a

parallel lines heikōsen 平行線 2b

parallelogram heikōshihenkei 平行四 辺形 2a

parent oya 親 10a

parents ryōshin 両親 10a

parents goryōshin ご両親 10a

Paris Pari パリ 30c

park chūshasuru *(v)* 駐車する 33c

park kōen 公園 36a

park bench kōen no benchi 公園のベン チ 36a

parking chūsha 駐車 33c

parking meter chūsha mētā 駐車メー ター 36a

parliament gikai 議会 43

parrot ōmu おうむ 15b

parsley paseri パセリ 14e, 24j

part bubun 部分 3c

participle bunshi 分詞 8a

particle (grammar) joshi 助詞 8a

particle bibunshi 微分子 13c

party pātī パーティー 29b

pass pasusuru *(v)* パスする 27b

pass oikosu *(v)* 追い越す 33c

pass an exam shiken ni ukaru 試験に受 かる 37f

pass a sentence hanketsu o iiwatasu *(v)* 判決を言い渡す 41

pass by tōrisugiru *(v)* 通り過ぎる 3e

passenger jōkyaku 乗客 32c

passenger dōjōsha 同乗者 33b

passenger car jōyōsha 乗用車 33a

Passing Lane oikoshisen 追い越し線 33d

passive ukemi no (adj) 受け身の 8a

passive shōkyokuteki na (adj) 消極的な 21a

passport pasupōto パスポート 30a, 31, 35b

passport control ryoken shinsa 旅券審査 31

past kako 過去 4e

past kako (adj) 過去 8a

pasta pasuta パスタ 24g

pastel pasuteru パステル 28b

past perfect kakokanryōkei 過去完了形 8a

past progressive kakoshinkōkei 過去進行形 8a

pastry pesutorī ペストリー 24i

pastry shop kēki ya ケーキ屋 24n

patience nintai 忍耐 11e, 21a

patient nintaizuyoi (adj) 忍耐強い 11e, 21a

patient kanja 患者 40a

paw ashi 足 15a

pawn pōn ポーン 27a

pay harau 払う 25a, 26, 35b

pay customs/duty kanzei o harau (v) 関税を払う 31

payment shiharai 支払 26

pay off zengaku shiharau (v) 全額支払う 26

pay phone kōshū denwa 公衆電話 18a

pea endōmame えんどう豆 14e

peace heiwa 平和 43

peach momo 桃 14d, 24f

peach tree momo no ki 桃の木 14c

peacock kujaku 孔雀 15b

peak chōjō 頂上 13b

peak season isogashii toki 忙しいとき 35b

pear (Japanese) nashi 梨 14d, 24f

pear (western) yōnashi 洋梨 14d, 24f

pearl shinju 真珠 25i

pearl pāru パール 25i

pear tree nashi no ki 梨の木 14c

peas endōmame えんどう豆 24e

pedal pedaru ペダル 33a

pedestrian hokōsha 歩行者 33b

pedestrian crossing ōdanhodō 横断歩道 33c

pedestrian crosswalk ōdanhodō 横断歩道 36a

peel kawa o muku (v) 皮を剥く 24o

pelican perikan ペリカン 15b

pen pen ペン 2b, 7c, 19d, 25c, 37b, 38c

penalty penarutī ペナルティー 27b

pencil enpitsu 鉛筆 2b, 19d, 25c, 37b, 38c

pencil sharpener enpitsu kezuri 鉛筆削り 25c, 37b

penguin pengin ペンギン 15b

penicillin penishirin ペニシリン 25h

peninsula hantō 半島 13b

penis penisu ペニス 12a

pentagon gokakukei 五角形 2a

pepper koshō 胡椒 24j

Pepsi-Cola pepushikōra ペプシコーラ 24k

perceive chikakusuru (v) 知覚する 12c

percent pāsento パーセント 1f

percentage ritsu 率 1f

perception chikakuryoku 知覚力 12c

percussion instruments dagakki 打楽器 28c

perfection kanzen 完全 11e

perfectionist kanzenshugisha 完全主義者 11e

perfume kōsui 香水 12d, 25f

per hour jisoku 時速 3a

period shūshiten 終止点 19c

peripherals shūhen sōchi 周辺装置 42b

permanent wave pāmanento パーマネント 12d

per minute funsoku 分速 3a

perpendicular line suisen 垂線 2b

per second byōsoku 秒速 3a

persimmon kaki 柿 14d, 24f

person (grammar) ninshō 人称 8a

person-to-person call pāsonaru kōru パーソナルコール 18b

personal ninshō (adj) 人称 8a

personal computer pasokon パソコン 42b

personality seikaku 性格 11e

perspire ase o kaku (v) 汗をかく 6b

persuade settokusuru (v) 説得する 22b, 41

Peru Perū ペルー 30b

pessimism hikanshugi 悲観主義 11e

pessimist hikanshugisha 悲観主義者 11e

pessimistic hikanteki na *(adj)* 悲観的な 11e

pet petto ペット 15a

petal hanabira 花弁 14b

petroleum sekiyu 石油 13c, 44a

petunia pechunia ペチュニア 14b

pharmaceutical drug chōgōyaku 調合薬 25h

pharmacist yakuzaishi 薬剤師 25h, 38a

pharmacy yakkyoku 薬局 25h

pheasant kiji 雉 15b

Philippines Firippin フィリッピン 30b

philosophy tetsugaku 哲学 37e

phone book denwachō 電話帳 18a

phone booth denwa bokkusu 電話ボックス 18a

phone outlet denwa no sashikomiguchi 電話の差し込み口 18a

phonetics onpyōmoji 音標文字 8a

photo, picture shashin 写真 20a, 25d

photocopier fukushaki 複写機 18a

photographer shashinka 写真家 38a

photosynthesis kōgōsei 光合性 14a

phrase ku 句 19c

physical butsuri no *(adj)* 物理の 13c

physics butsuri/butsurigaku 物理／物理学 13c, 37e

physiology seirigaku 生理学 37e

pianist pianisuto ピアニスト 28c

piano piano ピアノ 28c

pick flowers hana o tsumu *(v)* 花を摘む 14b

pickle dish okozara お小皿 24l

pickpocket suri すり 39b

pick up (the phone) juwaki o toriageru *(v)* 受話器を取り上げる 18b

picky kuchiyakamashii *(adj)* 口やかましい 11e

picnic pikunikku ピクニック 29a

pie pai パイ 24g

piece shōhen 小片 3c

pig buta 豚 15a

pigeon hato 鳩 15b

pill ganyaku 丸薬 25h, 40a

pillow makura 枕 23d, 35c

pillowcase makurakabā 枕カバー 23d

pilot sōjūshi/pairotto 操縦士／パイロット 32c, 38a

pimple nikibi にきび 40a

pinch tsumitoru *(v)* 摘み取る 14a

pineapple painappuru パイナップル 14d, 24f

pine tree matsu 松 14c

Ping-Pong pinpon ピンポン 27b

pink momoiro/pinku 桃色／ピンク 7a

pipe paipu パイプ 25e

Pisces uoza 魚座 5d

piston pisuton ピストン 33e

pitcher pitchā ピッチャー 27b

place basho 場所 3d

place shusseichi 出生地 38b

place of birth shusseichi 出生地 11f

place of employment koyōsaki 雇用先 11f

plain heiya 平野 13b

plaintiff genkoku 原告 41

plane (tool) kanna 鉋 25b

plane figures heimen zukei 平面図形 2a

planet wakusei 惑星 13a

plane ticket kōkū ken 航空券 30a

plant shokubutsu 植物 14a

plant ueru *(v)* 植える 14a

plant (factory) kōjō 工場 38d

plastic purasuchikku プラスチック 13c

plate sara 皿 23d, 24l

plateau kōgen 高原 13b

platform purattohōmu プラットホーム 34

platinum purachina プラチナ 13c, 25i

play geki/engeki 劇／演劇 20a, 28a

play (a game) shiaisuru *(v)* 試合する 27a, 27b

play (an instrument) (gakki o) ensōsuru *(v)* （楽器を）演奏する 27a, 28c

play (a record) kakeru *(v)* かける 20b

player (sports) senshu 選手 27b

player (music) ensōka 演奏家 28c

playing cards toranpu トランプ 27a

playoff yūshō kettei shirīzu 優勝決定シリーズ 27b

playwright geki sakka 劇作家 28e

plea tangan 嘆願 41

plead tangansuru *(v)* 嘆願する 41

plea for mercy jihi no tangan 慈悲の嘆願 41

pleasant, likeable tanoshii *(adj)* 楽しい 11e, 21b

Please! (go ahead) Dōzo. どうぞ。 16c

Please! (request) Onegai shimasu. お願いします。 16c

Please give my regards/greetings to...
...san ni yoroshiku otsutae kudasai. さんによろしくお伝えください。 16a

pliers penchi ペンチ 25b

plot suji 筋 20a, 28e, 28d

plug sashikomi 差し込み 18a

plug puragu プラグ 25b

plum sumomo すもも 14d, 24f

plumber haikankō 配管工 38a

plumbing haikan 配管 25b

plural number fukusū 複数 8a

plus purasu kigō プラス記号 1e

plus purasu プラス 6c

Pluto meiōsei 冥王星 13a

pneumonia haien 肺炎 40a

pocket poketto ポケット 25g, 27a

pocket book bunkohon 文庫本 20a

pocket radio poketto rajio ポケットラジオ 20b

poem shi 詩 20a

poet shijin 詩人 28d

poetry shi 詩 20a, 20o, 28d

point ten 点 2b

point tokuten 得点 27b

point out shitekisuru (v) 指摘する 17a

Poland Pōrando ポーランド 30b

Pole Pōrandojin ポーランド人 30d

pole kyoku 極 13e

police keisatsu 警察 33b, 39b, 39c

policeman keikan 警官 33b, 38a, 39b

police station keisatsusho 警察署 41

policewoman fujin keikan 婦人警官 33b, 38a, 39b

policy seisaku 政策 43

Polish (language) Pōrandogo ポーランド語 30d

political party seitō 政党

political power seijiryoku 政治力 43

political science seijigaku 政治学 37e

politician seijika 政治家 38a, 43

politics seiji 政治 43

pollen kafun 花粉 14a

pollution osen 汚染 13c

pollution kōgai 公害 44a

polyester poriesuteru ポリエステル 25l

polyhedron tamentai 多面体 2a

pomegranate zakuro ざくろ 14d, 24f

pomegranate tree zakuro no ki ざくろの木 14c

pony kouma 小馬 15a

poor misuborashii (adj) みすぼらしい 11e

Poor man! Kawaisō ni. かわいそうに。 21c

Poor woman! Kawaisō ni. かわいそうに。 21c

popcorn poppukōn ポップコーン 24i

poplar tree popura ポプラ 14c

poppy keshi けし 14b

popular music popyurā myūjikku ポピュラーミュージック 25j

porch beranda ベランダ 23a

porgy tai 鯛 15c, 24d

pork butaniku 豚肉 24c

pork pōku ポーク 24c

pornography poruno ポルノ 44b

portable phone keitai denwa 携帯電話 18a

portable radio pōtaburu rajio ポータブルラジオ 20b

porter pōtā ポーター 32a, 35b

porter akabō 赤帽 34

portion bubun 部分 3c

portrait pōtorēto ポートレート 28b

Portugal Porutogaru ポルトガル 30b

Portuguese (language) Porutogarugo ポルトガル語 30d

Portuguese Porutogarujin ポルトガル人 30d

position ichi 位置 3d

positive sekkyokuteki na (adj) 積極的な 21a

positive number seisū 正数 1d

possessive (grammar) shoyū (adj) 所有 8a

possessive shoyūyoku ga tsuyoi (adj) 所有欲が強い 11e

postage yūbin ryōkin 郵便料金 19e

postal rate yūbin ryōkin 郵便料金 19e

postcard hagaki 葉書 19e

postdate jigohizuke ni suru (v) 事後日付にする 26

posterior ato no (adj) 後の 4e

post office yūbinkyoku 郵便局 19e

pot fukanabe 深鍋 23d

potato jagaimo じゃがいも 14e, 24e

pour tsugu (v) 注ぐ 24o

powder konagusuri 粉薬 25h

power brake pawā burēki パワーブレーキ 33e

power steering pawā handoru パワーハンドル 33e

power window pawā windō パワー
ウィンドー 33e

practice a sport undōsuru *(v)* 運動する
27a

praise homeru *(v)* 誉める 17a

prawn, shrimp ebi 海老 24d

pray oinorisuru *(v)* お祈りする 11d

pray inoru *(v)* 祈る 17a

prayer oinori お祈り 11d, 17a

praying mantis kamakiri かまきり
15d

preach sekkyōsuru *(v)* 説教する 17a

precious stone kiseki 貴石 25i

predicate jutsubu 述部 8a

preface maeoki 前置き 28d

prefecture ken 県 11d, 38b

prefer konomu *(v)* 好む 21b

preference konomi 好み 21b

pregnancy ninshin 妊娠 11c

pregnant ninshinchū no *(adj)* 妊娠中の
40a

premiere showing puremia shō プレミ
アショー 28a

preposition zenchishi 前置詞 8a

prescription shohōsen 処方箋 25h,
40a

present genzai 現在 4e

present genzai *(adj)* 現在 8a

present perfect genzaikanryōkei 現在
完了形 8a

present progressive genzaishinkokei 現
在進行形 8a

president daitōryō 大統領 43

president of a university gakuchō 学長
37d

presumptuous buenryo na *(adj)* 無遠
慮な 11e

pretentious mie o hatta *(adj)* 見栄を
はった 11e

previous mae no *(adj)* 前の 4e

previously mae ni *(adv)* 前に 4e

price nedan 値段 24n, 25a

price, rate ryōkin 料金 35b

price tag nedanhyō 値段表 25a

priest seishokusha 聖職者 11d

primate reichōrui 霊長類 15a

prime meridian honsho shigosen 本初
子午線 13e

prime minister shushō 首相 43

prime number sosū 素数 1d

prince ōji 王子 43

princess ōjo 王女 43

principal kōchō 校長 37d

print insatsusuru *(v)* 印刷する 20a

print purinto プリント 25d

printed matter insatsubutsu 印刷物 19e

printer purintā プリンター 42b

printing, typography insatsujutsu 印刷
術 20a

print medium insatsu baitai 印刷媒体
20a

Print your name. Onamae o, kaisho de
kaite kudasai. 御名前を楷書で書いて
下さい。 11f

prism kakuchū 角柱 2a

prison, jail keimusho 刑務所 41

prison sentence yūkikei 有期刑 41

private school shiritsu gakkō 私立学校
37a

problem mondai 問題 1f, 22a, 37f

problem to solve kaiketsusuru mondai
解決する問題 1f

produce market yasai ichiba 野菜市場
24n

producer seisakusha 制作者 28a

product (mathematics) seki 積 1f

Prof. kyōju 教授 11f

profession shokugyō 職業 11f, 38a

profession shokureki 職歴 38b

professional senmonteki na *(adj)* 専門
的な 11f

professional puro プロ 27b

professional puro no *(adj)* プロの 38a

professor kyōju 教授 37d, 38a

professor's office kenkyūshitsu 研究室
37c

program puroguramu プログラム
20b, 42b, 28e

programmer puroguramā プログラマ
ー 42b

programming puroguramingu プログ
ラミング 42b

projector eishaki 映写機 20b

promise yakusokusuru *(v)* 約束する
17a

promise yakusoku 約束 17a

promissory note yakusokutegata 約束
手形 26

pronoun daimeishi 代名詞 8a

pronounce hatsuonsuru *(v)* 発音する
17a

pronunciation hatsuon 発音 8a, 17a

propose mōshikomu *(v)* 申し込む 17a

prose sanbun 散文 28d

prostitute baishunfu 売春婦 44b

prostitution baishun 売春 44b

protect fusegu (v) 防ぐ 39a

protest kōgi 抗議 17a, 43

protest kōgisuru (v) 抗議する 17a, 43

Protestant shinkyōto 新教徒 11d

Protestantism shinkyō 新教 11d

proton yōshi 陽子 42a

protractor bundoki 分度器 2b

proud hokori no takai (adj) 誇りの高い 11e

province shō 省 13e

prudent shinchō na (adj) 慎重な 11e

prune senteisuru (v) 剪定する 14a

prune (fruit) hoshisumomo 干しすもも 14d, 24f

pruning sentei 剪定 14a

P.S. tsuishin 追伸 19c

psychiatrist seishinkai 精神科医 38a

psychologist shinrigakusha 心理学者 38a

psychology shinrigaku 心理学 37e

public garden kōkyō no kōen 公共の公園 36a

public notices kōji 公示 36a

public parking chūshajō 駐車場 33c

public phone kōshū denwa 公衆電話 36a

public prosecutor kensatsukan 検察官 41

public washroom kōshū benjo 公衆便所 36a

publish shuppansuru (v) 出版する 20a

publisher shuppansha 出版者 20a

puck pakku パック 27b

pudding purin プリン 24g

pull hipparu (v) 引っ張る 3e

pulse myaku 脈 40a

pumpkin kabocha かぼちゃ 14e, 24e

punch panchi パンチ 25b

punctuation kutōten 句読点 19c

pupil seito 生徒 37d

puppet theater (Japanese) Bunraku 文楽 28e

purchase kaimono 買物 25a

purchase kau (v) 買う 25a

pure majirike no nai (adj) まじりけのない 7b

pure junsui no (adj) 純粋の 13d

purple murasaki iro 紫色 7a

put oku (v) 置く 3e

put a room in order heya o katazukeru (v) 部屋を片付ける 23f

put down oku (v) 置く 3e

put on kiru (v) 着る 25m

put on makeup okeshōsuru (v) お化粧する 12d

put on perfume kōsui o tsukeru (v) 香水をつける 12d

put someone on trial kokuhatsusuru (v) 告発する 41

pyramid (mathematics) kakusui 角錐 2a

Q

quantity ryō 量 3c

quantum theory ryōshiron 量子論 42a

quart kuōto クォート 3a

queen kuīn クィーン 27a

queen jo-ō 女王 43

question shitsumon 質問 37f

queston mark gimonfu 疑問符 19c

quickly hayaku (adv) 速く 3e

Quiet! Shizuka ni. (inf) 静かに。 21c

Quite well! Umaku itte imasu. うまくいっています。 16a

quotation mark inyōfu 引用符 19c

quotient shō 商 1f

R

rabbi Yudayakyō no rippōhakase ユダヤ教の律法博士 11d

rabbit usagi 兎 15a

raccoon araiguma あらいぐま 15a

race minzoku 民族 11d

race (sports) rēsu レース 27b

racism jinshu sabetsu 人種差別 44b

racket raketto ラケット 27b

radiation hōshasen 放射線 44a

radio rajio ラジオ 20b, 23d, 35c

radio-cassette player rajikase ラジカセ 20b

radioactive waste hōshasei haikibutsu 放射性廃棄物 13c, 44a

radish (Japanese) daikon 大根 14e, 24e

radius hankei 半径 2a

railroad tetsudō 鉄道 34

Railway Crossing fumikiri 踏切 36a

rain ame 雨 6a

rain ame ga furu (v) 雨が降る 6a

raincoat reinkōto レインコート 25k

rain forest urin 雨林 13b

raise (someone) sodateru (v) 育てる 11c

raise to a power ruijōsuru *(v)* 累乗する 1e

raisin hoshibudō 干し葡萄 14d, 24f

ramp intāchenji インターチェンジ 33c

random access memory randamu akusesu memori ランダムアクセスメモリ 42b

rape gōkan 強姦 39b

rape gōkansuru *(v)* 強姦する 39b

rare mare na *(adj)* まれな 4e

rare (steak) rea no *(adj)* レアの 24b

rarely mare ni *(adv)* まれに 4e

raspberry kiichigo 木苺 14d, 24f

rat nezumi ねずみ 15a

ratio hirei 比例 1e

rational number yūrisū 有理数 1d

razor kamisori 剃刀 12d, 25f

razor blade kamisori no ha 剃刀の刃 12d, 25f

read yomu *(v)* 読む 20a, 37f

reader dokusha 読者 20a

reading dokusho 読書 27a

reading (passage) yomikata 読み方 37f

real estate agent fudōsan assennin 不動産幹旋人 38a

Really? Hontō. *(inf)* 本当。 21c

real number jissū 実数 1d

rearview mirror bakkumirā バックミラー 33e

reason riyū 理由 1e

reason ronshōsuru *(v)* 論証する 22b

rebellious hankōteki na *(adj)* 反抗的な 11e

receipt reshīto レシート 25a, 35b

receipt uketorishō 受取証 26

Receipt please! Reshīto o onegai shimasu. レシートをお願いします。 25a

receive uketoru *(v)* 受け取る 19e

receiver (telephone) juwaki 受話器 18a

receiver (audio) reshībā レシーバー 20b

recent saikin no *(adj)* 最近の 4e

reception (wedding) hirōen 披露宴 11c

reciprocal number gyakusū 逆数 1d

recommend suisensuru *(v)* 推薦する 17a

record rekōdo レコード 20b, 25j

record rokuonsuru *(v)* 録音する 20b

record player rekōdo pureyā レコードプレーヤー 20b, 37b

rectangle chōhōkei 長方形 2a

rectum chokuchō 直腸 40a

red aka 赤 7a

red akai *(adj)* 赤い 7a

red-haired akai kaminoke no *(adj)* 赤い髪の毛の 11a

reduced price waribiki nedan 割引値段 25a

red wine reddo wain レッドワイン 24g

referee refurī レフリー 27b

reference book sankōsho 参考書 20a, 25o

refined jōhin na *(adj)* 上品な 11e

reflect shiansuru *(v)* 思案する 22b

reflexive saiki *(adj)* 再帰 8a

reflexive verb saikidōshi 再帰動詞 8a

reform kaikaku 改革 43

reform kaikakusuru *(v)* 改革する 43

refrigerator reizōko 冷蔵庫 23d

refund haraimodoshi 払戻 25a

refund haraimodosu *(v)* 払い戻す 25a

region chihō 地方 13e

registered letter kakitome yūbin 書留郵便 19e

registration tetsuzuki 手続き 37f

registration fee tetsuzuki ryō 手続き料 37f

registration papers tōrokusho 登録書 33b

regular kisokuteki na *(adj)* 規則的な 4e

regularly kisokuteki ni *(adv)* 規則的に 4e

regular verb kisokudōshi 規則動詞 8a

reject kyozetsusuru *(v)* 拒絶する 21b

rejection kyozetsu 拒絶 21b

relate kanrenzukeru *(v)* 関連づける 17a

relative (grammar) kankei *(adj)* 関係 8a

relatives shinseki 親戚 10a

relatives goshinseki ご親戚 10a

relax kutsurogu *(v)* くつろぐ 12b

relief anshin 安心 21a

religion shūkyō 宗教 11d

religious shinkōbukai 信仰深い 11d

remain nokoru *(v)* 残る 29b

remember omoidasu (v) 思い出す 22b

remote control rimokon リモコン 20b

rent yachin 家賃 23g

rent kariru (v) 借りる 23g

rental car rentakā レンタカー 33a

repeat kurikaesu (v) 繰り返す 17a, 37f

repetition kurikaeshi 繰返し 17a

reply henji 返事 19e

reply henji o dasu (v) 返事を出す 19e

report hōkoku 報告 17a

report hōkokusuru (v) 報告する 17a

reporter repōtā レポーター 20a

represent daihyōsuru (v) 代表する 41

representative giin 議員 43

reproach shikaru (v) 叱る 17a

reproduce saiseisuru (v) 再生する 14a

reproduction saisei 再生 14a

reptile hachūrui 爬虫類 15c

republic kyōwakoku 共和国 43

request tanomi 頼み 17a

request tanomu (v) 頼む 17a

request a taxi takushī o tanomu (v) タクシーを頼む 35b

rescue kyūjo 救助 39a

reservation yoyaku 予約 24m, 30a, 32a, 35b

reserve yoyakusuru (v) 予約する 30a, 35b

reserved (character) uchiki na (adj) 内気な 11e

reserved yoyakushitearu (adj) 予約してある 24m

reserved seat shitei seki 指定席 34

residence jūsho 住所 11f

resistant teikōsei no aru (adj) 抵抗性のある 13d

respiratory system kokyū keitō 呼吸系統 40a

rest yasumu (v) 休む 12b

restaurant resutoran レストラン 24m

restless ochitsukanai (adj) 落ち着かない 11e

restore shūfukusuru (v) 修復する 23f

resume rirekisho 履歴書 38b

retire taishokusuru (v) 退職する 38d

retirement taishoku 退職 38d

retirement money taishoku kin 退職金 38d

return kaeru (vi) 帰る 3e, 29b

return kaesu (vt) 返す 3e

return address sashidashinin jūsho 差出人住所 19e

review hyōron 評論 20a

review fukushū 復習 37f

review fukushūsuru (v) 復習する 37f

revolt hanran 反乱 43

revolt hanransuru (v) 反乱する 43

revolution kakumei 革命 43

rhetoric shūji 修辞 17a

rhetorical shūjiteki na (adj) 修辞的な 17a

rhetorical question hango 反語 17a

rheumatism ryūmachi リューマチ 40a

rhinoceros sai 犀 15a

rhombus hishigata 菱形 2a

rhythm rizumu リズム 28c

ribbon ribon リボン 19d

rice (on a plate) raisu ライス 24g

rice (cooked) gohan 御飯 24i

rice (uncooked) kome 米 24i

rice bowl ochawan お茶碗 24l

rice bowl (Japanese) gohanjawan 御飯茶碗 23d, 24l

rice cake (Japanese) mochi 餅 24i

rice cracker (Japanese) senbei せんべい 24i

rice store okome ya お米屋 24n

rice wine (Japanese) sake 酒 24k

rich yūfuku na (adj) 裕福な 11e

rifle raifuru ライフル 39b

right migi 右 3d

right tadashii (adj) 正しい 37f

right, privilege kenri 権利 41

right-angled chokkaku na (adj) 直角な 2a

right angle chokkaku 直角 2b

right away sugu ni (adv) すぐに 4e

right prism chokkakuchū 直角柱 2a

right to vote futsū senkyoken 普通選挙権 43

right wing uyoku 右翼 43

ring yubiwa 指輪 25i

ring (phone) naru (vi) 鳴る 18b

ring finger kusuriyubi 薬指 12a

rinse kuchi o susugu (v) 口をすすぐ 40b

riot bōdō 暴動 43

ripe jukushita (adj) 熟した 14a

ripen jukusu (v) 熟す 14a

ritual gishiki 儀式 11d

river kawa 川 13b, 36b
road michi 道 33c
road map dōro chizu 道路地図 33b
roar hoeru (v) 吠える 15a
roast rōsuto ロースト 24b
rob ubau (v) 奪う 39b
robber gōtō 強盗 39b
robbery gōtō 強盗 39b
robin komadori 駒鳥 15b
robot robotto ロボット 42a
robust ganjō na (adj) 頑丈な 13d
rock iwa 岩 13b
roll rōrupan ロールパン 24g
roller-skating rōra sukēto ローラース
ケート 27b
romance renai 恋愛 20a
romance (novel) renaishōsetsu 恋愛小
説 25o
Roman numerals Rōma sūji ローマ数
字 1d
romantic romanchikku na (adj) ロマン
チックな 11e
Rome Rōma ローマ 30c
roof yane 屋根 23a
roof (car) rūfu ルーフ 33e
rook rūku ルーク 27a
room heya 部屋 23b, 35b
room with bath basu tsuki no heya バ
ス付きの部屋 35b
room with two beds tsuin no heya ツイ
ンの部屋 35b
rooster ondori おんどり 15b
root ne 根 14a
root (dentistry) shikon 歯根 40b
rope (mountain climbing) zairu ザイル
27b, 36b
rose bara 薔薇 14b
rosemary rōzumarī ローズマリー
14e, 24j
rotten kusatta (adj) 腐った 14a
rough soya na (adj) 粗野な 11e
rough copy, draft shitagaki 下書き
37f
round-trip ticket ōfuku ken 往復券
30a
row retsu 列 28a
rubber band wagomu 輪ゴム 25c
ruby rubī ルビー 25i
rude burei na (adj) 無礼な 11e
ruler jōgi 定規 2b, 19d, 25c, 37b,
38c
rum ramu ラム 24k
rumor uwasa うわさ 17a

run hashiru (v) 走る 3e, 12b, 27b
run into (someone) deau (v) 出会う
16b
runway kassōro 滑走路 32c
rush hour rasshu awā ラッシュアワー
33c
Russia Roshia ロシア 30b
Russian Roshiajin ロシア人 30d
Russian (language) Roshiago ロシア語
30d
rye raimugi ライ麦 24i

S

sad kanashige na (adj) 悲しげな 11e
sad kanashii (adj) 悲しい 21a
sadness kanashimi 悲しみ 11e, 21a
safe kinko 金庫 26
safe deposit box kashikinko 貸し金庫
26
Sagittarius iteza 射手座 5d
sailing sēringu セーリング 27b
sake cup sakazuki 盃 24l
sake jug tokkuri 徳利 24l
sake on the rocks sake no on za rokku
酒のオンザロック 24p
salad sarada サラダ 24g
salad dressing doresshingu ドレッシン
グ 24g
salamander sanshōuo 山椒魚 15c
salami sarami sōsēji サラミソーセージ
24c
salary sararī/kyūryō サラリー／給料
26, 38d
sale hanbai 販売 25a
salmon sake 鮭 24d
salt shio 塩 13c, 24j
salty shiokarai (adj) 塩辛い 24p
salutation aisatsu no kotoba 挨拶の言
葉 19c
San Francisco Sanfuranshisuko サンフ
ランシスコ 30c
sand suna 砂 13b
sandal sandaru サンダル 25n
sandpaper kamiyasuri 紙やすり
25b
sandwich sandoitchi サンドイッチ
24g
sanitary napkin seiri napukin 生理ナプ
キン 25h
sapphire safaia サファイア 25i
sarcasm hiniku 皮肉 11e
sarcastic hiniku na (adj) 皮肉な 11e
sardine iwashi 鰯 15c, 24d

sash (for kimono) obi 帯 35c

satellite eisei 衛星 13a

satellite jinkōeisei 人工衛星 42a

satisfaction manzoku 満足 21a

satisfied manzokushita (adj) 満足した 21a

Saturday doyōbi 土曜日 5a

Saturn dosei 土星 13a

saucer ukezara 受け皿 23d, 24l

Saudi Arabia Saujiarabia サウジアラビア 30b

sausage sōsēji ソーセージ 24c

save chokinsuru (v) 貯金する 26

savings chokin 貯金 26

saw nokogiri 鋸 25b

saxophone sakisofōn サキソフォーン 28c

say, tell iu (v) 言う 17a

scalene futōhen/sha (adj) 不等辺／斜 2a

scallop kaibashira 貝柱 15c, 24d

scarf sukāfu スカーフ 25k

scene bamen 場面 28e

scenery haikei 背景 28e

schedule yoteihyō 予定表 34

school gakkō 学校 37f

school bag tsūgaku kaban 通学カバン 37f

schoolmate gakuyū 学友 37d

school yard kōtei 校庭 37f

school year gakunen 学年 5b

science fiction saiensu fikushon サイエンスフィクション 20a, 25o

sciences kagaku 科学 37e

scientific research kagaku kenkyū 科学研究 42a

scientist kagakusha 科学者 38a

scissors hasami はさみ 12d, 19d, 25c, 38c, 39c

scooter sukūtā スクーター 33a

score tokuten 得点 27b

score (music) gakufu 楽譜 28c

Scorpio sasoriza 蠍座 5d

scorpion sasori 蝎 15d

Scotch whiskey sukotchi スコッチ 24k

screen sukurīn スクリーン 25d, 28a, 42b

screen with paper and wooden grid shōji 障子 23c

screw neji ねじ 25b

screwdriver nejimawashi ねじ回し 25b

sculpt chōkokusuru (v) 彫刻する 28b

sculptor chōkokuka 彫刻家 28b

sculpture chōkoku 彫刻 28b

sea umi 海 6a, 13b, 36b

sea bass suzuki 鱸 15c, 24d

seagull kamome 鴎 15b

seal azarashi あざらし 15c

season kisetsu 季節 5c

seat seki 席 28a, 34, 32c

seat (bicycle) sadoru サドル 33a

seat (car) shīto シート 33e

seat belt shītoberuto シートベルト 32c, 33e

sea urchin uni うに 15c

secant sekanto セカント 2b

second nibanme 二番目 1b

second daini 第二 1b

second futatsume 二つ目 1b

second byō 秒 4c

second person (grammar) nininshō 二人称 8a

second year ninen 二年 37a

secretary hisho 秘書 37d, 38a, 40a

sedative chinseizai 鎮静剤 40a

seduction yūwaku 誘惑 11e

seductive miwakuteki na (adj) 魅惑的な 11e

see miru (v) 見る 12c, 30a

seed tane 種 14a

seed tane o maku (v) 種を撒く 14a

See you! Soredewa, mata. それでは、また。 16a

See you Sunday! Soredewa, nichiyōbi ni. それでは、日曜日に。 16a

See you later! Soredewa, nochihodo. それでは、のちほど。 16a

See you soon! Soredewa, chikaiuchi ni. それでは、近いうちに。 16a

segment line senbun 線分 2b

self-service serufu sābisu セルフサービス 24m, 33c

self-sufficient jiritsu shiteiru (adj) 自立している 11e

sell uru (v) 売る 25a

semicolon semikoron セミコロン 19c

senate jōin 上院 43

senator jōin giin 上院議員 43

send okuru (v) 送る 3e, 19e

sender sashidashinin 差出人 19e

senior discount kōreisha waribiki 高齢者割引 30a

seniority system nenkōjoretsu sei 年功序列制 38d

sense kankaku 感覚 12c

sense, feel kanjiru (v) 感じる 12c

sense of humor yūmoa no kankaku ユーモアの感覚 11e

sensitive binkan na (adj) 敏感な 11e

sentence bun 文 8a, 19c

sentence (court) hanketsu 判決 41

sentimental kanshōteki na (adj) 感傷的な 11e

Seoul Sōru ソウル 30c

separate bekkyosuru (v) 別居する 11c

separated bekkyoshita (adj) 別居した 11c

separation bekkyo 別居 11c

September kugatsu 九月 5b

series renzoku bangumi 連続番組 20b

serious majime na (adj) 真面目な 11e

serious accident daijiko 大事故 39c

sermon sekkyō 説教 17a

serve (food or drink) dasu (v) 出す 24o

serve a sentence keiki ni fukusuru (v) 刑期に服する 41

service sābisu サービス 24m

service charge sābisu ryō サービス料 24m

services sābisu サービス 35b

set shūgō 集合 1f

set of drums taiko no setto 太鼓のセット 28c

set the table tēburu o totonoeru (v) テーブルを整える 23f, 24o

settlement wakai 和解 41

seven shichi/nana 七 1a

seven natsu 七つ 1a

seven hundred nanahyaku 七百 1a

seventeen jūshichi/jūnana 十七 1a

seventeen thousand ichimannanasen 一万七千 1a

seventh nanabanme 七番目 1b

seventh dainana 第七 1b

seventh nanatsume 七つ目 1b

seven thousand nanasen 七千 1a

seventy nanajū 七十 1a

seventy thousand nanaman 七万 1a

several ikutsuka no (adj) いくつかの 3c

sew nuu (v) 縫う 25g

sewing machine mishin ミシン 23d

sex sei 性 11a

sex seibetsu 性別 38b

shadow/shade kage/kage 影/陰 6a

shaft shafuto シャフト 33c

shake hands akushusuru (v) 握手する 16a

shame haji 恥 21a

shampoo shanpū シャンプー 12d, 25f, 35c

shark same 鮫 15c

shave hige o soru (v) ひげをそる 12d

shaving cream shēbingu kurīmu シェービングクリーム 25f

she kanojo ga/wa 彼女が／は 8c

sheep hitsuji 羊 15a

sheet (bed) shītsu シーツ 23d, 35c

shelf tana 棚 23a

sherbet shābetto シャーベット 24g

Shintoism shinto 神道 11d

Shintoist shinto no shinja 神道の信者 11d

Shinto priest kannushi 神主 11d

Shinto shrine jinja 神社 11d

shirt shatsu シャツ 25k

shock shokku ショック 39c

shoe kutsu 靴 25n

shoe department kutsu uriba 靴売り場 25n

shoe lace kutsu himo 靴ひも 25n

shoe polish kutsuzumi 靴墨 25n

shoe store kutsu ya 靴屋 25n

shoot utsu (v) 撃つ 39b

shop mise 店 25a

shop kaimonosuru (v) 買い物する 25a

shop for food shokuryōhin o kau (v) 食料品を買う 24o

shopping bag kaimonobukuro 買物袋 23d

short mijikai (adj) 短い 3b, 37f

short se ga hikui 背が低い 11a

short-term tanki no (adj) 短期の 4e

shorten mijikakusuru (v) 短くする 25m

shorts shōtsu ショーツ 25k

shorts hanzubon 半ズボン 25k

short story tanpen shōsetsu 短編小説 20a, 28d

shoulder kata 肩 12a

shout sakebi 叫び 39a

shout, yell sakebu 叫ぶ 17a, 39a

shovel shaberu シャベル 25b

show shō bangumi ショー番組 20b

show shō ショー 28b

shower shawā シャワー 12d, 23a, 35c

shower shawā o abiru (v) シャワーを浴びる 12d

shrewd nukemenonai (adj) 抜け目のない 11e

shrewdness nukemenasa 抜け目なさ 11e

shrimp ebi 海老 15c

shrine jinja 神社 36a

shut up damaru (vi) 黙る 17a

Shut up! Damare. (inf) 黙れ。 17a, 21c

shy uchiki na (adj) 内気な 11e

sick byōki no (adj) 病気の 11a, 40a

sickness, disease byōki 病気 11a, 40a

side hen 辺 2b

side mirror saido mirā サイドミラー 33e

sidewalk hodō 歩道 36a

sigh of relief ando no tameiki 安堵の溜め息 21a

sight shikaku 視覚 12c

sign shomeisuru (v) 署名する 11f, 19c, 26

signal shigunaru シグナル 33c

signature shomei 署名 11f, 19c, 26, 38b

signs of the zodiac jūnikyūzu no sain 十二宮図のサイン 5d

silence chinmoku 沈黙 17a

silent (person) mukuchi na (adj) 無口な 17a

silk kinu 絹 13c

silk shiruku シルク 25l

silkworm kaiko 蚕 15d

silver (color) gin-iro 銀色 7a

silver gin 銀 13c, 25i

silver anniversary kekkon nijūgoshūnen kinenbi 結婚二十五周年記念日 11c

simple tanjun na (adj) 単純な 11e, 22a

simultaneous dōji no (adj) 同時の 4e

simultaneously dōji ni (adv) 同時に 4e

since kara から 4e

since Monday getsuyōbi kara 月曜日から 4e

sincere seijitsu na (adj) 誠実な 11e

sincerity seijitsusa 誠実さ 11e

since yesterday kinō kara 昨日から 4e

sine sain サイン 2b

sing utau (v) 歌う 28c

Singapore Shingapōru シンガポール 30b

singer kashu 歌手 25j, 28c, 38a

singer shingā シンガー 25j

single mikon no (adj) 未婚の 11f

single shinguru no (adj) シングルの 24p

single dokushin 独身 38b

single room shinguru no heya シングルの部屋 35b

singular number tansū 単数 8a

sink, wash basin senmendai 洗面台 23a, 35c

siren sairen サイレン 39a

sister-in-law giri no ane 義理の姉 10a

sister-in-law giri no imōto 義理の妹 10a

sister-in-law giri no onēsan 義理のお姉さん 10a

sister-in-law giri no imōtosan 義理の妹さん 10a

sisters shimai 姉妹 10a

sisters goshimai ご姉妹 10a

sit down suwaru (v) 座る 3e, 32c

six roku 六 1a

six muttsu 六つ 1a

six hundred roppyaku 六百 1a

sixteen jūroku 十六 1a

sixteen thousand ichimanrokusen 一万六千 1a

sixth rokubanme 六番目 1b

sixth dairoku 第六 1b

sixth muttsume 六つ目 1b

six thousand rokusen 六千 1a

sixty rokujū 六十 1a

sixty thousand rokuman 六万 1a

size saizu サイズ 3b, 25k, 25n

skate sukēto de suberu (v) スケートで滑る 27b

skating sukēto スケート 27b

ski sukī o suru (v) スキーをする 27b

skiing sukī スキー 27b, 36b

skim milk sukimu miruku スキムミルク 24h

skin hifu 皮膚 12a

skinny, thin yaseta (adj) 痩せた 11a

skip a class jugyō o saboru (v) 授業をさぼる 37f

skip school, play hooky gakkō o saboru
(v) 学校をさぼる 37f
ski resort sukijō スキー場 36b
skirt sukāto スカート 25k
skunk sukanku スカンク 15a
sky sora 空 6a, 13b
slacks surakkusu スラックス 25k
sleep nemuru (v) 眠る 12b
sleeping bag surīpingubaggu スリーピ
ングバッグ 36b
sleeping car shindaisha 寝台車 34
sleeve sode 袖 25g
slice usugiri ni suru (v) 薄切りにする
24o
slide suraido スライド 25d
slide projector suraido purojekutā スラ
イドプロジェクター 20b
slide projector suraido eishaki スライ
ド映写機 37b
sliding door hikido 引き戸 35c
slim, slender hossorishita (adj) ほっそ
りした 11a
slip surippu スリップ 25k
slipper surippa スリッパ 25n
sloppy, disorganized darashinai (adj)
だらしない 11e
slow osoi (adj) 遅い 3e, 4e
slow down jokōsuru (v) 徐行する 33c
slowly osoku (adv) 遅く 3e, 4e
slug namekuji なめくじ 15d
small chiisai (adj) 小さい 3c, 25l
small, little chiisai (adj) 小さい 11a
small bill chiisai osatsu 小さいお札
26
small intestine shōchō 小腸 40a
small letter komoji 小文字 19c
small teapot (Japanese) kyūsu きゅう
す 23d, 241
smart rikō na (adj) 利口な 11e
smell nioi 匂い 12c
smell niou (v) 匂う 12c
smelt kisu 鱚 24d
smile hohoemi 微笑み 11e, 21a
smile hohoemu (v) 微笑む 11e, 21a
smoke kemuri 煙 13c, 39a
smoking kitsuen 喫煙 34
smooth namraka na (adj) 滑らかな
13d
snack kanshoku/oyatsu 間食/おやつ
24a
snack sunakku スナック 24a
snack bar sunakku スナック 24m
snail katatsumuri 蝸 15d

snake hebi 蛇 15c
sneaker sunīkā スニーカー 25n
sneeze kushami くしゃみ 40a
sneeze kushami o suru (v) くしゃみを
する 40a
snobbish kidotta (adj) 気取った 11e
snow yuki 雪 6a
snow yuki ga furu (v) 雪が降る 6a
snow goggles gōguru ゴーグル 27b
So, so! Māmā desu. まあまあです。
16a
so, therefore sorede それで 8k
So? Sorede. それで。 9
soap sekken 石鹸 12d, 25f, 35c
soap powder konasekken 粉石鹸 25g
soccer sakkā サッカー 27b
socialism shakaishugi 社会主義 43
socialist shakaishugisha 社会主義者
43
sociology shakaigaku 社会学 37e
sock sokkusu ソックス 25n
sodium natoriumu ナトリウム 13c
sodium bicarbonate jūtansannatoriumu
重炭酸ナトリウム 25h
sodium citrate kuensansōda クエン酸
ソーダ 25h
sofa sofā ソファー 23c
soft yawarakai (adj) 柔らかい 13d
soft-boiled egg hanjuku 半熟 24h
soft drink sofuto dorinku ソフトドリ
ンク 24k
software sofuto wea ソフトウェア
42b
soil dojō 土壌 13b
solar cell taiyō denchi 太陽電池 44a
solar eclipse nisshoku 日食 13a
solar energy taiyō enerugī 太陽
エネルギー 13a, 44a
solar system taiyōkei 太陽系 13a
sole shitabirame したびらめ 15c, 24d
sole (shoe) kutsu zoko 靴底 25n
solid kotai no (adj) 固体の 13c
solid figures rittai 立体 2a
solstice shiten 至点 5c
soluble yōkaisei no aru (adj) 溶解性の
ある 13d
solution kaiketsuhō 解決法 1f
solve kaiketsusuru (v) 解決する 1f
solve a problem mondai o toku (v) 問題
を解く 37f
some ikuraka no (adj) いくらかの 3c
some (people) aru hito ある人 8i
someone dareka 誰か 8i

something nanika 何か 8i

somewhere dokoka どこか 3d

son musuko 息子 10a

son musukosan 息子さん 10a

son-in-law musume no otto 娘の夫 10a

son-in-law ojōsan no goshujin お嬢さんのご主人 10a

song uta 歌 25j, 28c

soon mōsugu (adv) もうすぐ 4e

sooner or later sonouchi そのうち 4e

sore/stiff neck kubi no kori 首の凝り 40a

sore back kata no kori 肩の凝り 40a

sore throat nodo no itami 喉の痛み 40a

sorrow kanashimi 悲しみ 21a

soul tamashii 魂 11d

sound oto 音 12c

soundtrack saundotorakku サウンドトラック 28a

soup sūpu スープ 24g

soup bowl (Japanese) owan お椀 23d, 24l

sour suppai (adj) すっぱい 24p

south minami 南 3d

South Africa Minami Afurika 南アフリカ 30b

South America Minami Amerika 南アメリカ 30b

South Pole nankyoku 南極 13e

southern minami no (adj) 南の 3d

Soviet Union Sobieto Yunion ソビエトユニオン 30b

soy sauce shōyu 醤油 24j, 24l

soy sauce dish okozara お小皿 24l

soy sauce pitcher shōyusashi 醤油差し 24l

space kūkan 空間 2b, 13a

space bar supēsubā スペースバー 19d

spacecraft uchūsen 宇宙船 42a

space shuttle supēsushatoru スペースシャトル 42a

spaghetti supagetti スパゲッティ 24g

Spain Supein スペイン 30b

Spaniard Supeinjin スペイン人 30d

Spanish Supeingo スペイン語 30d

spark hinoko 火の粉 39a

spark plug supāku puragu スパークプラグ 33e

sparrow suzume 雀 15b

speak, talk hanasu (v) 話す 17a

speaker supīkā スピーカー 20b

special delivery sokutatsu 速達 19e

specialist senmonka 専門家 40a

special skills tokugi 特技 38b

species hinshu 品種 14a

speech, talk hanashi 話 17a

speed sokudo 速度 3a, 33c

Speed Limit sokudo seigen 速度制限 33c, 33d

speedometer sokudokei 速度計 33c

speed up kasokusuru (v) 加速する 33c

spelling tsuzuri 綴り 19c

spend tsukau (v) 使う 25a

spend (money) tsukau (v) つかう 4e

spend (time) sugosu (v) 過ごす 4e

sphere kyūkei 球形 2a

spice yakumi 薬味 24j

spicy piritto shita (adj) ピリッとした 24p

spider kumo 蜘蛛 15d

spinach hōrensō ほうれん草 14e, 24e

spine, backbone sebone 背骨 12a

spirit seishin 精神 11d

spiritual seishinteki (adj) 精神的 11d

splint fukuboku 副木 39c

spoke supōku スポーク 33a

spoon supūn スプーン 23d, 24l

sporadic tokiori no (adj) 時折の 4e

sporadically tokiori (adv) 時折 4e

sports supōtsu スポーツ 27a, 27b

sports car supōtsukā スポーツカー 33a

sports fan supōtsu fan スポーツファン 27b

spot, stain shimi しみ 25g

spouse haigūsha 配偶者 11c

spring haru 春 5c

spring onion, scallion hosonegi 細ねぎ 14e, 24e

Sprite Supuraito スプライト 24k

square seihōkei 正方形 2a

square hiroba 広場 11f, 36a

square bracket kaku kakko 角括弧 19c

square centimeter heihōsenchi 平方センチ 3a

squared nijō no 二乗の 1e

square kilometer heihōkiro 平方キロ 3a

square meter heihōmētoru 平方メートル 3a

square millimeter heihōmiri 平方ミリ 3a

square root heihōkon 平方根 1e

squid ika いか 15c, 24d

squirrel risu りす 15a

stable anteishita *(adj)* 安定した 13d

stadium sutajiamu スタジアム 27b

stage butai 舞台 28e

stainless steel sutenresu suchīru ステンレススチール 13c

stairs kaidan 階段 23a, 35b

stamp kitte 切手 19e, 27a

stamp collecting kitte shūshū 切手収集 27a

staple hotchikisu no hari ホッチキスの針 19d, 25c, 38c

stapler hotchikisu ホッチキス 19d, 25c, 38c

star hoshi 星 6a

star kōsei 恒星 13a

starch sentaku nori 洗濯糊 25g

start (car) enjin o kakeru *(v)* エンジンをかける 33c

state shū 州 11f, 13e

state kokka 国家 43, 38b

state noberu *(v)* 述べる 17a

statement seimei 声明 17a

station (broadcasting) hōsōkyoku 放送局 20b

station eki 駅 34

stationery binsen 便箋 25c

stationery store bunbōgu ten 文房具店 25c

station wagon wagonsha ワゴン車 33a

statistical tōkei no *(adj)* 統計の 1f

statistics tōkei/tōkeigaku 統計/統計学 1f, 37e

steal nusumu *(v)* 盗む 39b

steam musu *(v)* 蒸す 24o

steamed mushita *(adj)* 蒸した 24b

steel tekkō 鉄鋼 13c

steering wheel handoru ハンドル 33e

stem kuki 茎 14a

stereo sutereo ステレオ 20b

stethoscope chōshinki 聴診器 40a

steward suchuwādo スチュワード 32c, 38a

stewardess suchuwādesu スチュワーデス 32c, 38a

still mada *(adv)* まだ 4e

stingy kechi na *(adj)* ケチな 11e

stir kakimawasu *(v)* かきまわす 24o

stitch hitohari ひと針 25g

stock, share kabuken 株券 26

stocking sutokkingu ストッキング 25n

stock market kabushikishijō 株式市場 26

stomach i 胃 12a, 40a

stone ishi 石 13b

stop tomaru *(vi)* 止る, 停まる 3e, 34

stop tomeru *(vt)* 止める 3e

Stop teishi 停止 33d

Stop thief! Dorobō. 泥棒。 39b

store mise 店 25a

store/shop window shōwindō ショーウィンドー 25a

store clerk ten-in 店員 25a, 38a

storekeeper tenshu 店主 38a

stork kōnotori こうのとり 15b

storm bōfūu 暴風雨 6a

story monogatari 物語 17a

stove renji レンジ 23d

straight ahead kono mama massugu このままmassugu 36c

straight angle heikaku 平角 2b

straight line chokusen 直線 2b

straight sake (Japanese) hiya 冷や 24p

strawberry ichigo 苺 14d, 24f

street tōri 通り 11f

street michi 道 36a

streetcar romendensha 路面電車 33a

street sign dōro hyōshiki 道路標識 36a

strength chikara/tsuyosa 力/強さ 11a

strike sutoraiki ストライキ 43

string himo 紐 19d, 25c

string (music) gen 弦 28c

string bean sayaingen 莢隠元 14d, 24e

stringed instruments gengakki 弦楽器 28c

strong tsuyoi *(adj)* 強い 11a, 13d, 24j

strong takumashii *(adj)* たくましい 11e

strong genki na *(adj)* 元気な 40a

stubborn ganko na *(adj)* 頑固な 11e

student gakusei 学生 37d

student discount gakusei waribiki 学生割引 30a

study manabu *(v)* 学ぶ 22b

study benkyōsuru *(v)* 勉強する 37f

stuff shizai 資材 13c

stupid oroka na *(adj)* 愚かな 11e

style buntai 文体 28d

subject (grammar) shugo 主語 8a

subject gakka 学科 37e

subjunctive mood kateihō 仮定法 8a

submit teishutsusuru (v) 提出する 37f

subordinate jūzoku (adj) 従属 8a

subordinate buka 部下 38d

substance busshitsu 物質 13c

subtitle jimaku 字幕 28a

subtract hiku (v) 引く 1e

subtraction hikizan 引き算 1e

subway chikatetsu 地下鉄 34

subway station chikatetsu no eki 地下鉄の駅 34

sue uttaeru (v) 訴える 41

suede suēdo スエード 25l

suffer kurushimu (v) 苦しむ 40a

sufficient jūbun na (adj) 十分な 3c

sugar satō 砂糖 24j

suggest teiansuru (v) 提案する 17a

suit sūtsu スーツ 25k

suitcase, piece of luggage sūtsukēsu スーツケース 31

sulphur iō 硫黄 13c

sulphuric acid ryūsan 硫酸 13c

sum gōkei 合計 1f

summarize yōyakusuru (v) 要約する 17a

summary yōyaku 要約 17a

summer natsu 夏 5c

summer solstice geshi 夏至 5c

summons shōkanjō 召喚状 41

sum up gōkeisuru (v) 合計する 1f

sun taiyō 太陽 5c, 6a, 13a

Sunday nichiyōbi 日曜日 5a

sunflower himawari ひまわり 14b

sunlight nikkō 日光 13a

sunray taiyō kōsen 太陽光線 13a

sunrise hinode 日の出 4a

sunset hinoiri 日の入り 4a

superintendent kanrinin 管理人 23a

supermarket sūpā スーパー 24n

superstitious meishinbukai (adj) 迷信深い 11e

supplementary angle hokaku 補角 2b

suppository zayaku 坐薬 40a

supreme court saikō saibansho 最高裁判所 41

surface mail funabin 船便 19e

surfing sāfin サーフィン 27b

surgeon gekai 外科医 38a, 40a

surgery shujutsu 手術 40a

surname, family name myōji 苗字 11f, 38b

surname, family name sei 姓 38b

surprise odoroki 驚き 21a

surprise odorokasu (vt) 驚かす 21a

suspect yōgisha 容疑者 39b

swallow tsubame 燕 15b

swamp shitchi 湿地 13b

swan hakuchō 白鳥 15b

swear (in court) chikau (v) 誓う 17a

swear (profanity) kitanai kotobazukai o suru (v) 汚い言葉使いをする 17a

sweater sētā セーター 25k

sweatshirt torēnā トレーナー 25k

Swede Suwēdenjin スウェーデン人 30d

Sweden Suwēden スウェーデン 30b

Swedish (language) Suwēdengo スウェーデン語 30d

sweet (character) yasashii (adj) 優しい 11e

sweet amai (adj) 甘い 24p

sweet potato satsumaimo 薩摩芋 14e, 24e

swim oyogu (v) 泳ぐ 27b

swimming suiei 水泳 27b

swimming pool pūru プール 27b, 35b

switch suitchi スイッチ 23a, 35c

switchblade tobidashi naifu 飛び出しナイフ 39b

switchboard kōkandai 交換台 18b

Switzerland Suisu スイス 30b

swollen hareta (adj) 腫れた 40a

swordfish kajiki かじき 15c, 24d

symbol (mathematics) kigō 記号 1f

symbol shōchō 象徴 17a

sympathetic dōjōteki na (adj) 同情的な 21a

sympathy dōjō 同情 21a

symphony shinhonī シンフォニー 28c

synagogue Yudayakyō jiin ユダヤ教寺院 11d

synthesizer shinsesaizā シンセサイザー 28c

synthetic gōsei no (adj) 合成の 13d

syringe chūshaki 注射器 40a

syrup shiroppu シロップ 24j, 25h

T

tab tabu タブ 19d

Tabasco tabasuko タバスコ 24j

table tēburu テーブル 23c, 24l, 35c

tablecloth tēburukurosu テーブルクロス 23d, 24l

tablet jōzai 錠剤 25h, 40a

tableware shokutakuyō shokkigu 食卓
用食器具 23d

tail shippo しっぽ 15a

tailor shitateya 仕立て屋 38a

Taipei Taipei 台北 30c

take/catch the train, etc. noru (v) 乗る
34

take (purchase) kau (v) 買う 25a

take a bath ofuro ni hairu (v) お風呂に
はいる 12d

take a course/subject kamoku o toru
(v) 科目をとる 37f

take an exam shiken o ukeru (v) 試験
を受ける 37f

take an excursion gurūpu tsuā ni
sankasuru (v) グループツアーに参加
する 36a

take a picture shashin o toru (v) 写真
を撮る 25a

take a trip ryokō ni iku 旅行に行く
30a

take attendance shusseki o toru (v) 出
席をとる 37f

take a walk sanpo ni iku (v) 散歩に行
く 3e

take back kaesu (v) 返す 25a

take drugs mayaku o tsukau (v) 麻薬を
使う 44b

take notes nōto o toru (v) ノートを取
る 37f

take off (clothing) nugu (v) 脱ぐ
25m

takeoff (plane) ririku 離陸 32c

take off (plane) ririkusuru (v) 離陸す
る 32c

take one's temperature netsu o hakaru
(v) 熱を計る 40a

take out (food to go) mochikaeru (v) 持
ち帰る 24m, 24o

take place okoru (vi) 起こる 4e

talcum powder shikkarōru シッカロー
ル 25f

tall takai (adj) 高い 3b

tall se ga takai 背が高い 11a

tambourine tanbarin タンバリン
28c

tampon tanpon タンポン 25h

tangent sessen 接線 2a

tangent tanjento タンジェント 2b

tape tēpu テープ 25j

tape recorder tēpu rekōdā テープレコ
ーダー 20b, 37b

tariff kanzei 関税 31

taro satoimo 里芋 14e, 24e

taste ajiwau (v) 味わう 12c

tasty oishii (adj) おいしい 24p

Taurus oushiza 牡牛座 5d

tax zeikin 税金 24m

taxi takushī タクシー 33a

taxi driver takushī no untenshu タクシ
ーの運転手 38a

tea (Japanese) ocha お茶 24k

tea (western) kōcha 紅茶 24k

teach oshieru (v) 教える 37f

teacher sensei 先生 11f

teacher kyōshi 教師 37d, 38a

tea cup (Japanese) yunomijawan 湯飲
み茶碗 23d

teacup saucer chataku 茶托 24l

team chīmu チーム 27b

teapot tīpotto ティーポット 23d

teaspoon kosaji 小さじ 23d, 24l

tea store ocha ya お茶屋 24n

technical/vocational school shokugyō
gakkō 職業学校 37a

technical book senmonsho 専門書
25o

technology gijutsu 技術 42a

tee-shirt tīshatsu ティーシャツ 25k

teenager tīnējā ティーンエージャー
11b

telecommunication enkyori tsūshin 遠
距離通信 18a, 42a

telecommunications satellite tsūshin
eisei 通信衛星 18a

teleconferencing terekonfarensu テレコ
ンファレンス 42a

telephone denwa 電話 18a, 18b, 23e,
35c, 38c

telephone bill denwa ryōkin no
seikyūsho 電話料金の請求書 18b

telephone call denwa 電話 18b

telephone credit card terefon kādo テ
レフォンカード 18a

telephone line kaisen 回線 18b

telephone number denwabangō 電話番
号 11f, 18b, 38b

telescopic lens bōen renzu 望遠レンズ
25d

television terebi テレビ 20b

television set terebi テレビ 20b, 23d,
35c

telex machine terekkusu テレックス
18a, 42a

tell a joke jōdan o iu (v) 冗談を言う 17a

tell a story itsuwa o hanasu (v) 逸話を話す 17a

teller's window madoguchi 窓口 26

temperature kion 気温 6c

temperature (fever) netsu 熱 40a

template tenpurēto テンプレート 2b

temple jiin 寺院 11d

temple otera お寺 36a

temporarily ichijiteki ni (adv) 一時的に 4e

temporary ichijiteki na (adj) 一時的な 4e

ten jū 十 1a

ten tō 十 1a

tenant kyojūsha 居住者 23g

ten billion hyakuoku 百億 1a

ten million senman 千万 1a

tennis tenisu テニス 27b

tense (grammar) jisei 時制 8a

tense kinchōshita (adj) 緊張した 21a

tent tento テント 36b

tenth jūbanme 十番目 1b

tenth daijū 第十 1b

tenth jūbanme/daijū 十番目／第十 1b

ten million senman 千万 1a

ten thousand ichiman 一万 1a

ten thousand and one ichiman-ichi 一万一 1a

ten thousand ten ichiman-jū 一万十 1a

ten thousandth ichimanbanme 一万番目 1b

ten thousand two hundred ichiman-nihyaku 一万二百 1a

terminal (transportation) tāminaru ターミナル 32a

terminal (computer) tāminaru ターミナル 42b

termite shiroari 白蟻 15d

terrace terasu テラス 23a

territory ryōdo 領土 13e

test tesuto テスト 37f

testify shōgensuru (v) 証言する 41

testimony shōgen 証言 41

tetrahedron shimentai 四面体 2a

text honbun 本文 19c, 20a

textbook kyōkasho 教科書 25o, 37b

textile orimono 織物 13c

Thai Taijin タイ人 30d

Thai (language) Taigo タイ語 30d

Thailand Taikoku タイ国 30b

thank kanshasuru (v) 感謝する 17a, 21a

thankful kansha no (adj) 感謝の 21a

thankfulness kansha 感謝 21a

Thank goodness! Arigatai. (inf) ありがたい。 21c

Thank you! Arigatō gozaimasu. 有難うございます。 16c

that sono その 8b

that (over there) ano あの 8b

that is to say sunawachi 即ち 44c

the New Year shinnen 新年 5f

theater gekijō 劇場 28e

their (all female) kanojotachi no 彼女たちの 8d

their (all male, or male and female) karera no 彼等の 8d

them (all female) kanojotachi o 彼女たちを 8e

them (all male, or male and female) karera o 彼等を 8e

theme tēma テーマ 28d

themselves (all females) kanojotachi jishin 彼女たち自身 8g

themselves (all male, or male and female) karera jishin 彼等自身 8g

then sorekara (conj) それから 4e, 8k

then sono toki その時 4e

theory of relativity sōtaisei genri 相対性原理 42a

The pleasure is mine! Kochirakoso. こちらこそ。 16b

there soko そこ 3d

there soko ni そこに 36c

There's lightning. Inazuma ga hikatte imasu. 稲妻が光っています。 6a

There's no doubt that ... ...wa, utagai no yochi mo arimasen. は疑いの余地もありません。 44c

There's nothing to declare. Nani mo, shinkokusuru mono ga arimasen. 何も申告するものがありません。 31

There's something to declare. Shinkokusuru mono ga arimasu. 申告するものがあります。 31

therefore soreyue それゆえ 44c

There is no class today. Kyō wa, gakkō ga arimasen. 今日は、学校がありません。 37f

thermal energy netsu enerugī 熱エネルギー 44a

thermometer ondokei 温度計 6c, 25h, 40a

thermostat jidō chōon sōchi 自動調温
装置 6c, 35c

these korera no これらの 8b

thesis ronbun 論文 37f

The sky is clear. Kaisei desu. 快晴で
す。 6a

The watch is fast. Tokei ga, susumigachi
desu. 時計が進みがちです。 4d

The watch is slow. Tokei ga, okuregachi
desu. 時計が遅れがちです。 4d

The weather is beautiful. Subarashii
tenki desu. 素晴らしい天気です。
6a

they (all female) kanojotachi ga/wa
彼女たちが／は 8c

they (all male, or male and female)
karera ga/wa 彼等が／は 8c

thick atsui *(adj)* 厚い 3b

thief dorobō 泥棒 39b

thigh futomomo ふともも 12a

thin usui *(adj)* 薄い 3b

think kangaeru *(v)* 考える 22b

third sanbanme 三番目 1b

third daisan 第三 1b

third mittsume 三つ目 1b

third person sanninshō 三人称 8a

Third World daisansekai 第三世界
43

thirteen jūsan 十三 1a

thirteenth jūsanbanme 十三番目 1b

thirteen thousand ichimansanzen 一万
三千 1a

thirty sanjū 三十 1a

thirty-one sanjūichi 三十一 1a

thirty-two sanjūni 三十二 1a

thirty thousand sanman 三万 1a

this kono この 8b

this afternoon kyō no gogo 今日の午後
4a

this evening kyō no yūgata 今日の夕方
4a

This is ... Watakushi wa, ...desu ga.
私は...ですが。 16a

This line is busy. Hanashichū desu. 話
し中です。 18b

this morning kesa 今朝 4a

this night konban 今晩 4a

thorn toge 刺 14b

those sorera no それらの 8b

those (over there) arera no あれらの
8b

thought kangae 考え 22a

thousandth senbanme 千番目 1b

threat odokashi おどかし 17a

threaten odokasu *(v)* おどかす 17a

three san 三 1a

three mittsu 三つ 1a

three (bound objects) sansatsu 三冊
1a

three (floors) sangai 三階 1a

three (liquid or dry measure) sanbai 三
杯 1a

three (long, thin objects) sanbon 三本
1a

three (persons) sannin 三人 1a

three (small objects) sanko/mittsu 三
個/三つ 1a

three (thin, flat objects) sanmai 三枚
1a

three-dimentional space sanjigenteki
kūkan 三次元的空間 13a

three-fourths yonbun no san 四分の三
1c

three-piece suit mitsuzoroi 三揃 25k

three hundred sanbyaku 三百 1a

three million sanbyakuman 三百万 1a

three thousand sanzen 三千 1a

throat nodo 喉 12a, 40a

through tōshite *(adv)* 通して 3d

through... ... o tootte を通って 36c

throw nageru *(v)* 投げる 27b

throw up haku *(v)* 吐く 40a

thumb oyayubi 親指 12a

thumbtack gabyō 画びょう 25c, 37b,
38c

thunder kaminari 雷 6a

thunder kaminari ga naru *(v)* 雷が鳴る
6a

Thursday mokuyōbi 木曜日 5a

tick dani だに 15d

ticket ken 券 27b, 30a, 32a, 34

ticket agent chikettogakari チケット係
32a

ticket canceling machine jidō
kaisatsuki 自動改札機 34

ticket counter kippu uriba 切符売り場
34

tide chōryū 潮流 13b

tie nekutai ネクタイ 25k

tie (score) dōten 同点 27b

tiger tora 虎 15a

tight kitsui *(adj)* きつい 25l

tighten pittarisaseru *(v)* ぴったりさせ
る 25m

tights taitsu タイツ 25k

time (as in every time) toki とき 4a

time (hour) ji 時 4a
time (in general) jikan 時間 4a
time for breakfast chōshoku no jikan 朝食の時間 35c
time for dinner yūshoku no jikan 夕食の時間 35c
time for taking a bath ofuro no jikan お風呂の時間 35c
timetable jikokuhyō 時刻表 34
timetable, schedule yoteihyō 予定表 4e
timid okubyō na (adj) 憶病な 21a
timpani tinpanī ティンパニー 28c
tincture of iodine yōdochinki ヨードチンキ 25h, 39c
tint iroai 色合い 7c
tint iroai o tsukeru (v) 色合いを付ける 7c
tip chippu チップ 24m
tip chippu o ageru (v) チップを上げる 24m
tire taiya タイヤ 33a, 33e
tissues tisshū ティッシュー 25f
title shōgō 称号 11f, 16b
title (books, movies, etc.) daimei 題名 20a
to e/ni/made へ/に/まで 8j
to, at ni/de に/で 3d
toad hikigaeru ひきがえる 15c
toast kanpai 乾杯 17a
toast kanpaisuru (v) 乾杯する 17a
toast kongari yaku (v) こんがり焼く 24o
toaster tōsutā トースター 23d
tobacco kizami tabako 刻みたばこ 25e
tobacco shop tabako senmonten たばこ専門店 25e
today kyō 今日 4a
toe ashiyubi 足指 12a
to her kanojo ni 彼女に 8f
to him kare ni 彼に 8f
toilet otearai 御手洗い 23a, 23b
toilet toire トイレ 32c, 35c, 37c
toilet paper toiretto pēpā トイレットペーパー 35c
Tokyo Tōkyō 東京 30c
tolerance kanyō 寛容 21a
tolerant kanyō na (adj) 寛容な 21a

Toll (road sign) ryōkinsho 料金所 33d
toll booth ryōkinsho 料金所 33c
toll road yūryō dōro 有料道路 33c
tomato tomato トマト 14e, 24e
to me watakushi ni 私に 8f
tomorrow ashita 明日 4a
tomorrow afternoon ashita no gogo 明日の午後 4a
tomorrow evening ashita no yūgata 明日の夕方 4a
tomorrow morning ashita no asa 明日の朝 4a
tomorrow night ashita no ban 明日の晩 4a
tongue shita 舌 12a, 40b
tongue tan タン 24c
tonsils hentōsen 扁桃腺 40a
Too bad! Zannen. 残念。 21c
tool daikudōgu 大工道具 23b, 25b
tool dōgu 道具 33c
too much ōsugi 多過ぎ 3c
tooth ha 歯 12a, 40b
toothache shitsū 歯痛 40b
toothbrush haburashi 歯ブラシ 12d, 25f, 40b
toothpaste nerihamigaki 練り歯みがき 12d, 25f, 40b
toothpick yōji 楊子 24l
top ichiban ue 一番上 3d
topaz topāzu トパーズ 25i
tornado tatsumaki 竜巻 6a
to sum up ... ... o yōyakusureba. を要約すれば。 17b
to the east higashi e (ni) 東へ(に) 3d, 36c
to the fourth power yonjō 四乗 1e
to the left hidari ni 左に 3d, 36c
to them (all female) kanojotachi ni 彼女たちに 8f
to them (all male or male and female) karera ni 彼等に 8f
to the north kita ni 北に 3d, 36c
to the nth power enujō エヌ乗 1e
to the power of ruijō 累乗 1e
to the right migi ni 右に 3d, 36c
to the south minami ni 南に 3d, 36c
to the west nishi ni 西に 3d, 36c
to this day konnichi made 今日まで 4e
touch shokkan 触感 12c

touch fureru *(v)* 触れる 12c

tour kankō ryokō 観光旅行 30a

tour bus kankō basu 観光バス 30a

tour guide kankō gaido 観光ガイド 30a

tour guide tsuā gaido ツアーガイド 38e

tourist kankō kyaku 観光客 30a

tournament tōnamento トーナメント 27b

to us watakushitachi ni 私達に 8f

Tow-Away Zone ken-in chiiki 牽引地域 33d

toward ni taishite に対して 3d

toward ... ...no hō e の方へ 36c

towel taoru タオル 12d, 35c

tower tō 塔 36a

to whom dare ni 誰に 8h

To Whom it May Concern kankeisha kakui dono 関係者各位殿 19a

town machi 町 11f

tow truck rekkāsha レッカー車 33a

to you anata ni あなたに 8f

to you (plural) anatatachi ni あなたたちに 8f

track (sports) torakku トラック 27b

track (railroad) sen 線 34

track and field rikujōkyōgi 陸上競技 27b

traditional dentōteki na *(adj)* 伝統的な 11e

traffic kōtsū 交通 33c

traffic accident kōtsū jikō 交通事故 39c

traffic jam kōtsū jūtai 交通渋滞 33c

traffic light shingō 信号 33c, 36a

traffic police kōtsū junsa 交通巡査 33b

tragedy higeki 悲劇 20a, 28e

trailer torērā トレーラー 33a

train kisha 汽車 34

train station eki 駅 34

train ticket kisha no kippu 汽車の切符 30a

transformer henatsuki 変圧器 25b

transitive verb tadōshi 他動詞 8a

translate honyakusuru 翻訳する 17a

translation honyaku 翻訳 17a

transmission sōshin 送信 20b

transparent tōmei na *(adj)* 透明な 7b, 13d

transplant ishoku 移植 14a

transplant ishokusuru *(v)* 移植する 14a

transporter jidōsha unpansha 自動車運搬車 33a

trapezium daikei 台形 2a

travel ryokō 旅行 30a

travel ryokōsuru *(v)* 旅行する 38

travel agency ryokō dairiten 旅行代理店 30a

traveler's check toraberā chekku トラベラーチェック 26, 35b

tray obon お盆 23d, 24l

tray (plane) tēburu テーブル 32c

tree ki 木 14c

trenchcoat torenchikōto トレンチコート 25k

trial saiban 裁判 41

trial lawyer hotei bengoshi 法廷弁護士 41

triangle sankakukei 三角形 2a

tricky zurugashikoi *(adj)* ずるがしこい 11e

trigonometric sankakuhō no *(adj)* 三角法の 2b

trigonometry sankakuhō 三角法 2b, 37e

trim (plants) karikomu *(v)* 刈り込む 14a

trip, journey ryokō 旅行 30a, 36b

triple sanbai no *(adj)* 三倍の 3c

tripod sankyaku 三脚 25k

trolley torōrīkā トローリーカー 33a

trombone toronbōn トロンボーン 28c

tropic kaikisen 回帰線 13e

tropical nettaisei no *(adj)* 熱帯性の 6a

tropical nettai no *(adj)* 熱帯の 13b

tropical zone nettaichitai 熱帯地帯 13e

Tropic of Cancer kitakaikisen 北回帰線 13e

Tropic of Capricorn minamikaikisen 南回帰線 13e

troublemaker monchaku o okosu hito 悶着を起こす人 11e

trousers zubon ズボン 25k

trout masu 鱒 15c, 24d

truck torakku トラック 33a

truck driver torakku no untenshu トラックの運転手 38a

true honmono no *(adj)* 本物の 25i

trumpet toranpetto *(adj)* トランペット 28c

trunk (tree) miki 幹 14a

trunk (car) toranku トランク 33e

trust shinraisuru *(v)* 信頼する 21a

try on tamesu *(v)* 試す 25m

tuba chūba チューバ 28c

Tuesday kayōbi 火曜日 5a

tulip chūrippu チューリップ 14b

tuna maguro 鮪 15c, 24d

tuner chūnā チューナー 20b

tunnel tonneru トンネル 33c

turbulence rankiryū 乱気流 32c

Turk Torukojin トルコ人 30d

turkey shichimenchō 七面鳥 15b, 24c

Turkey Toruko トルコ 30b

Turkish (language) Torukogo トルコ語 30d

turn magaru *(v)* 曲がる 3e, 33c, 36c

turnip kabu 蕪 14e, 24e

turn off kesu *(v)* 消す 20b, 35c

turn on tsukeru *(v)* つける 20b, 35c

turn pages, leaf through pēji o mekuru *(v)* 頁をめくる 20a

turn signal hōko shijiki 方向指示器 33c

turntable tāntēburu ターンテーブル 20b

turn to the left hidari ni magaru *(v)* 左に曲がる 33c

turn to the right migi ni magaru *(v)* 右に曲がる 33c

turtle kame 亀 15c

tweezers kenuki 毛抜き 25f

twelfth jūnibanme 十二番目 1b

twelfth daijūni 第十二 1b

twelve jūni 十二 1a

twelve thousand ichimannisen 一万二千 1a

twenty nijū 二十 1a

twenty-eight nijūhachi 二十八 1a

twenty-five nijūgo 二十五 1a

twenty-four nijūshi/nijūyon 二十四 1a

twenty-nine nijūku/nijūkyū 二十九 1a

twenty-one nijūichi 二十一 1a

twenty-seven nijūshichi/nijūnana 二十七 1a

twenty-six nijūroku 二十六 1a

twenty-third nijūsanbanme 二十三番目 1b

twenty-three nijūsan 二十三 1a

twenty-two nijūni 二十二 1a

twenty thousand niman 二万 1a

twin futago 双子 10a

two ni 二 1a

two futatsu 二つ 1a

two (bound objects) nisatsu 二冊 1a

two (floors) nikai 二階 1a

two (liquid or dry measure) nihai 二杯 1a

two (long, thin objects) nihon 二本 1a

two (persons) futari 二人 1a

two (small objects) niko/futatsu 二個/二つ 1a

two (thin, flat objects) nimai 二枚 1a

two -thirds sanbun no ni 三分の二 1c

two billion nijūoku 二十億 1a

two hundred nihyaku 二百 1a

two hundred and one nihyakuichi 二百一 1a

two hundred ten nihyakujū 二百十 1a

two hundred thousand nijūman 二十万 1a

two million nihyakuman 二百万 1a

two thousand nisen 二千 1a

two thousand and one nisen-ichi 二千一 1a

two trillion nichō 二兆 1a

type taipusuru *(v)* タイプする 19d

type taipu de utsu *(v)* タイプで打つ 37d

typewriter taipuraitā タイプライター 19d, 37f, 38c

typhoon taifū 台風 6a

typist taipisuto タイピスト 38a

U

ugly minikui *(adj)* 醜い 25l

ukulele ukurere ウクレレ 28c

ultraviolet light shigaisen 紫外線 13c

unacceptable ukeiregatai *(adj)* 受け入れ難い 21b

Unbelievable! Shinjirarenai. *(inf)* 信じられない。 21c

uncle oji 叔父 10a

uncle ojisan おじさん 10a

under shita no *(adj)* 下の 3d

under shita ni *(adv)* 下に 3d

underlining andārain アンダーライン 19c

understand rikaisuru *(v)* 理解する 22b, 37f

underwear shitagi 下着 25k

undress nugu *(v)* 脱ぐ 25m

unemployment shitsugyō 失業 38d

unemployment compensation shitsugyō teate 失業手当 38d

Unfortunately! Un waruku. 運悪く。 21c

unilateral ippōteki na *(adj)* 一方的な 43

United States of America Amerika アメリカ 30b

universal suffrage futsū senkyoken 普通選挙権 43

universe uchū 宇宙 13a

university daigaku 大学 11f, 37a, 38b

university degree gakushigō 学士号 11f

unlawful, illegal ihō no *(adj)* 違法の 41

unleaded gas muen gasorin 無鉛ガソリン 33c

unmarried mikon no 未婚の 11c

unpleasant fuyukai na *(adj)* 不愉快な 21b

unreserved seat jiyū seki 自由席 34

until made *(adv)* まで 4e, 8j

up ue no *(adj)* 上の 3d

up ue ni *(adv)* 上に 3d

upright piano tategata piano 立て型ピアノ 28c

Uranus tennōsei 天王星 13a

urinary system hinyō keitō 泌尿系統 40a

urinate hainyōsuru *(v)* 排尿する 40a

Uruguay Uruguai ウルグアイ 30b

us watakushitachi o 私達を 8e

user-friendly yūzā furendorī ユーザーフレンドリー 42b

usually itsumo wa *(adv)* いつもは 4e

utter tsubuyaku *(v)* つぶやく 17a

V

vacation bakansu バカンス 29a, 36b

vacuum cleaner sōjiki 掃除機 23d

vagina chitsu 膣 12a

vain mieppari no *(adj)* みえっぱりの 11e

valley tani 谷 13b

valve (car) barubu バルブ 33e

van ban バン 33a

vapor kitai 気体 13c

variable (mathematics) hensū 変数 1f

variable hendō (no) *(adj)* 変動(の) 26

VCR bideo ビデオ 20b

veal koushi no niku 子牛の肉 24c

vector dōkei 動径 2b

vegetable yasai 野菜 14e, 24e

vegetable garden saien 菜園 14e

vegetable store yasai ya 野菜屋 24n

vegetation kusaki 草木 13b

vein jōmyaku 静脈 40a

Venezuela Benezuera ベネズエラ 30b

vent (car) benchirētā ベンチレーター 33e

Venus kinsei 金星 13a

verb dōshi 動詞 8a

verdict hyōketsu 評決 41

vernal equinox shunbun 春分 5c

versatile tagei na *(adj)* 多芸な 11e

vertebrate sekitsui dōbutsu 脊椎動物 15a

vertex chōten 頂点 2b

vertical suichoku no *(adj)* 垂直の 3d

Very well! Umaku itte imasu. うまくいっています。 16a

victim giseisha 犠牲者 39a

victim higaisha 被害者 39b

video camera bideo kamera ビデオカメラ 20b

video cassette bideo kasetto ビデオカセット 20b

video game bideo gēmu ビデオゲーム 20b

videorock bideo rokku ビデオロック 20b

videotape bideo kasetto ビデオカセット 20b

view nagame 眺め 35b

vinegar su 酢 24j

viola biora ビオラ 28c

violence bōryoku 暴力 39b

violet sumire 菫 14b

violin baiorin バイオリン 28c

violinist baiorin ensōsha バイオリン演奏者 28c

Virgo otomeza 乙女座 5d

virile danseiteki na *(adj)* 男性的な 11a

visa biza ビザ 30a, 31

vise manriki 万力 25b

visit hōmonsuru *(v)* 訪問する 29b, 30a

vitamin bitaminzai ビタミン剤 25h

vivid azayaka na *(adj)* 鮮やかな 7b

vocabulary goi 語彙 17a

vodka wokka ウォッカ 24k

volcano kazan 火山 13b

volleyball barēbōru バレーボール 27b

volume taiseki/yōseki 体積／容積 3a

vomit haku *(v)* 吐く 40a

vote tōhyō 投票 43

vote tōhyōsuru *(v)* 投票する 43

voter tōhyōsha 投票者 43

vowel boin 母音 8a

vulnerable kizutsukiyasui *(adj)* 傷つきやすい 11e

W

wage chingin 賃金 38d

waist koshi 腰 12a

wait matsu *(v)* 待つ 4e

waiter uētā ウエーター 24m

wait for matsu *(v)* 待つ 19e, 34

waiting room raunji ラウンジ 32a

waitress uētoresu ウエートレス 24m

wake-up call mōningu kōru モーニングコール 35b

wake up me o samasu *(v)* 目を覚ます 12b

walk aruku *(v)* 歩く 3e, 12b

walk sanpo 散歩 3e

walkie-talkie toranshībā トランシーバー 20b

wall kabe 壁 23a

walnut kurumi くるみ 14d, 24f

walnut tree kurumi no ki くるみの木 14c

walrus seiuchi せいうち 15c

ward ku 区 11f, 38b

warm up atatakakunaru *(v)* 暖かくなる 6b

warn keikokusuru *(v)* 警告する 17a

warning keikoku 警告 17a

wash arau *(v)* 洗う 12d, 23f

wash (laundry) sentakusuru *(v)* 洗濯する 25g

washable araeru *(adj)* 洗える 25g

washer wasshā ワッシャー 25b

washing machine sentakuki 洗濯機 23d

wash the clothes sentakusuru *(v)* 洗濯する 23f

wash the dishes sara o arau *(v)* 皿を洗う 23f

wasp suzumebachi 雀蜂 15d

wastebasket kuzukago くずかご 38c

watch, clock tokei 時計 4d, 25i

watchband tokei no bando 時計のバンド 4d, 25i

watch battery tokei no denchi 時計の電池 4d

water mizu 水 13b, 13c, 14a, 24k

water (service) suidō 水道 23e

water color suisaiga 水彩画 28b

water fountain funsui 噴水 36a

watermelon suika 西瓜 14d, 24f

water pollution mizu osen 水汚染 44a

water polo suikyū 水球 27b

water skiing wōtā sukī ウォータースキー 27b

wave nami 波 13b

we watakushitachi ga/wa 私達が/は 8c

weak yowayowashii *(adj)* 弱々しい 11a, 11e, 40a

weak yowai *(adj)* 弱い 13d, 24p

weakness yowayowashisa 弱々しさ 11a

weapon kyōki 凶器 39b

wear kiru *(v)* 着る 25m

weather tenki 天気 6a

weather forecast tenki yohō 天気予報 6c

weatherman tenki yohō gakari 天気予報係 6c

wedding kekkonshiki 結婚式 11c, 29a

wedding invitation kekkonshiki e no shōtai 結婚式への招待 11c

wedding ring kekkon yubiwa 結婚指輪 11c

Wednesday suiyōbi 水曜日 5a

week shū 週 4c

weekend shūmatsu 週末 5a

weekly maishū no *(adj)* 毎週の 4c

weekly magazine shūkanshi 週刊誌 20a

weekly periodical shūkanshi 週間紙 20a

weep naku *(v)* 泣く 21a

weigh mekata o hakaru *(v)* 目方を量る 3b, 24o

weigh oneself jibun no taijū o hakaru *(v)* 自分の体重を量る 11a

weight jūryō 重量 3a

weight omosa 重さ 11a

weight mekata 目方 31

weight lifting jūryōage 重量挙げ 27b

welfare shakai fukushi 社会福祉 43

well-done (steak) yoku yaita *(adj)* よく
焼いた 24b
well-mannered reigitadashii *(adj)* 礼儀
正しい 11e
west nishi 西 3d
western nishi no *(adj)* 西の 3d
western seiō no *(adj)* 西欧の 11d
western-style room yōma 洋間 23b
whale kujira 鯨 15c
what nani ga/no/ni 何が/の/に 8h
What? Nani. *(inf)* 何。 9
What's today's date? Kyō wa nannichi
desu ka. 今日は何日ですか。 5e
What's your name? Onamae wa, nan
desu ka. 御名前は、何ですか。
11f, 16b
What color is it? Nani iro desu ka. 何
色ですか。 7a
What day is it? Kyō wa nani yōbi desu
ka. 今日は何曜日ですか。 5a
What does it mean? Sore wa, donna imi
desu ka. それは、どんな意味です
か。 9
What month is it? Nangatsu desu ka.
何月ですか。 5b
What time is it? Nanji desu ka. 何時で
すか。 4b
What was I talking about? Watakushi
wa, nani o hanashiteimashita ka. 私
は、何を話していましたか。 17b
What year is it? Kotoshi wa nannen desu
ka. 今年は何年ですか。 5e
wheat komugi 小麦 24i
wheel sharin 車輪 32c, 33e
wheelchair kurumaisu 車椅子 40a
when itsu *(adv)* いつ 4e
When? Itsu. *(inf)* いつ。 9
When were you born? Itsu umaremashita ka. いつ生まれましたか。
5e
where doko ni *(adv)* どこに 3d
Where? Doko. *(inf)* どこ。 9
Where do you live? Doko ni osumai desu
ka. どこにお住まいですか。 11f
Where is ...? ... wa, doko desu ka. は、
どこですか。 36c
which dore ga/dono/dore o どれが/ど
の/どれを 8h
Which (one)? Dore. *(inf)* どれ。 9
Which tooth hurts? Dono ha ga,
itamimasu ka. どの歯が、痛みます
か。 40b
while ~no aida ni ～の間に 4e

whiskey uisukī ウイスキー 24k
whisper sasayaku *(v)* 囁く 17a
white shiro 白 7a
white shiroi *(adj)* 白い 7a
white wine howaito wain ホワイトワイ
ン 24g
who dare ga 誰が 8h
Who? Dare. *(inf)* 誰。 9
Who's speaking? (telephone) Donata
sama desu ka. どなた様ですか。
18b
Who knows? Dare mo, shirimasen yo.
誰も、知りませんよ。 17b
whom dare o 誰を 8h
whose dare no 誰の 8h
Why? Naze. *(inf)* なぜ。 9
wide hiroi *(adj)* 広い 3b
wide angle lens kōkakurenzu 広角レン
ズ 25d
widow mibōjin 未亡人 11c
widower yamome やもめ 11c
width hirosa 広さ 3b
wife tsuma 妻 10a, 11c
wife okusan 奥さん 10a
wild animal yajū 野獣 15a
wildflower nobana 野花 14b
willingly kokoroyoku *(adv)* 快く 11e
willow yanagi 柳 14c
wilted flower shioreta hana 萎れた花
14b
win katsu *(v)* 勝つ 27b
win a lawsuit shōsosuru *(v)* 勝訴する
41
wind neji o maku *(v)* ネジを巻く
4d
wind kaze 風 6a
wind energy fūryoku enerugī 風力エネ
ルギー 44a
wind instruments mokkan gakki 木管
楽器 28c
window mado 窓 23a
window (plane) madogawa 窓側
32c
window sill madowaku 窓枠 23a
windshield furontogarasu フロントガ
ラス 33e
windshield wiper waipā ワイパー
33e
wind surfing windo sāfin ウィンドサ
ーフィン 27b
wine wain ワイン 24g, 24k
wine glass wainigurasu ワイングラス
24l

wine list wain risuto ワインリスト 24m

wing tsubasa 翼 15b, 32c

winter fuyu 冬 5c

winter solstice tōji 冬至 5c

winter sports fuyu no supōtsu 冬のスポーツ 27b

wire harigane 針金 25b

wisdom kenmei 賢明 11e

wisdom chie 智恵 22a

wisdom tooth oyashirazu 親知らず 40b

wise kenmei na (adj) 賢明な 11e

with to/de と／で 8j

with a check kogitte de (adv) 小切手で 25a

with a credit card kurejittokādo de (adv) クレジットカードで 25a

with cash genkin de (adv) 現金で 25a

withdraw (banking) hikidasu (v) 引き出す 26

withdrawal (banking) hikidashi 引き出し 26

withdrawal slip (banking) hikidashihyō 引き出し票 26

with ice kōri o irete (adv) 氷を入れて 24p

within inai ni 以内に 4e

without ice kōri o irenaide (adv) 氷を入れないで 24p

witness shōnin 証人 41

wolf ōkami 狼 15a

woman josei 女性 11a

women's shop fujinfuku ten 婦人服店 25k

wonderful subarashii (adj) 素晴らしい 21a

wooden clogs (Japanese) geta 下駄 35c

woodpecker kitsutsuki きつつき 15b

woods mori 森 13b

wool ūru ウール 13c, 25l

Worcestershire sauce sōsu ソース 24j

word kotoba 言葉 17a, 19c

word processing wāpuro shori ワープロ処理 42b

word processor wāpuro ワープロ 19d, 38c, 42b

work shigoto 仕事 11f, 38d

work hataraku (v) 働く 11f, 38d

work (literary) chosaku 著作 28d

workday heijitsu 平日 5a

Work in Progress kōjichū 工事中 33d

work in a bank ginkō de hataraku 銀行で働く 26

work out torēningusuru (v) トレーニングする 27b

work overtime zangyōsuru (v) 残業する 38d

world sekai 世界 13a, 30a

worm mushi 虫 15d

wound, injury kega 怪我 39c

woven reed mat floor (Japanese) tatami 畳 23b

wrench supana スパナ 25b

wrestling resuringu レスリング 27b

wrist tekubi 手頸 12a

wristwatch udedokei 腕時計 4d, 25i

write kaku (v) 書く 19e, 20a, 37f

writer sakka 作家 28d, 38a

writing desk desuku デスク 23c

writing pad hikki yōshi 筆記用紙 25c

written exam hikki shiken 筆記試験 37f

wrong machigatta (adj) 間違った 37f

Wrong number! Machigai denwa desu. 間違い電話です。 18b

X

X-rays rentogen レントゲン 39c, 40b

Y

yawn akubi あくび 17a

yawn akubisuru (v) あくびする 17a

year toshi 年 4c, 38b

year (e.g., at university) gakunen 学年 37a

yearly, annually maitoshi no (adj) 毎年の 4c

yellow kiiro 黄色 7a

yellow kiiroi (adj) 黄色い 7a

yellow pages shokugyōbetsu denwa chō 職業別電話帳 18a

yen en 円 26

Yes! Hai. はい。 16c

yesterday kinō 昨日 4a

yesterday afternoon kinō no gogo 昨日の午後 4a

yesterday morning kinō no asa 昨日の朝 4a

yet mada (adv) まだ 4e

Yield yūsen 優先 33d

yogurt yōguruto　ヨーグルト　24h
you anata ga/wa　あなたが／は　8c
you (plural) anatatachi ga/wa　あなたたちが／は　8c
you anata o　あなたを　8e
you (plural) anatatachi o　あなたたちを　8e
You're welcome! Iie, dō itashimashite.　いいえ、どう致しまして。　16c
young wakai *(adj)*　若い　11b
younger toshishita no *(adj)*　年下の　11b
younger brother otōto　弟　10a, 11b
younger brother otōtosan　弟さん　10a
younger sister imōto　妹　10a, 11b
younger sister imōtosan　妹さん　10a
young man wakamono　若者　11a
your anata no　あなたの　8d
your (plural) anatatachi no　あなたたちの　8d
yourself anata jishin　あなた自身　8g
yourselves anatatachi jishin　あなたたち自身　8g
Yours sincerely keigu　敬具　19a
Yours truly keigu　敬具　19a

youth seinen jidai　青年時代　11b
youthful wakawakashii *(adj)*　若々しい　11a
youth hostel yūsu hosuteru　ユースホステル　35a
Yugoslavia Yūgosurabia　ユーゴスラビア　30b

Z

zebra shimauma　縞馬　15a
Zen Buddhism zenshū　禅宗　11d
zero zero/rei　ゼロ／零　1a
zero (temperature) reido/hyōten　零度／氷点　6c
zinnia hyakunichisō　百日草　14b
zip code yūbin bangō　郵便番号　19e, 38b
zipper jippā　ジッパー　25g
zodiac jūnikyūzu　十二宮図　5d
zoo dōbutsuen　動物園　15a
zoological dōbutsugaku no *(adj)*　動物学の　15a
zoology dōbutsugaku　動物学　15a, 37e
zoom lens zūmu renzu　ズームレンズ　25d
zucchini zukkīni　ズッキーニ　14e, 24e